Lift in Ac

Lift in Action

THE SIMPLY FUNCTIONAL
WEB FRAMEWORK FOR SCALA

TIMOTHY PERRETT

MANNING
SHELTER ISLAND

To my Dad
for teaching me that hard work and dedication
can triumph over any problem

Manning Publications Co.   Development editors: Katharine Osborne
20 Baldwin Road   Copyeditor: Andy Carroll
PO Box 261   Typesetter: Dennis Dalinnik
Shelter Island, NY 11964   Cover designer: Marija Tudor

ISBN: 9781935182801
Printed in the United States of America
1 2 3 4 5 6 7 8 9 10 – MAL – 17 16 15 14 13 12 11

brief contents

contents

preface

The web has completely revolutionized the way we live our lives—the average person in the UK now does an average of six Google searches a day. Within the lifetime of one generation, our entire society has changed, and it continues to be catalyzed by technology in a very fundamental way. For me, this is the most fascinating thing to observe and an even more interesting thing to be a part of.

The web development industry has seen sweeping change over the past five or six years as it has attempted to cope with these new social habitats and behaviors. Probably one of the most notable changes was the way in which Ruby on Rails altered developers' outlook toward building applications and the manner in which they approached problems. Massive enterprise architecture was out the window and small, iterative, agile processes became all the rage. At the beginning of 2006, I had been coding Ruby on Rails for quite some time and had built several large systems with the Ruby stack. Although I was blown away by the productivity gains that Rails supplied, taking code to production was a comparative nightmare. I specifically recall Zed Shaw's "Rails is a Ghetto" rant and how that was very similar to my own views at the time. It was then that I started to look for something else, something new.

Before long, I came across Lift, which felt "right" from the very beginning. Scala and Lift's elegant fusion of the functional and object-oriented paradigms was a breath of fresh air when compared to other languages and frameworks. It was great to have all the security features baked right into a framework, and not have to worry about many things that typically cause a lot of headaches for developers. These kinds of choices make a great developer-oriented framework: focusing on removing work from the developer in a pragmatic and logical way while using as little runtime magic as possible.

Having been involved with Lift from an early stage, seeing it grow and evolve in an organic fashion has been very rewarding. Even with an intimate understanding of Lift, writing this book has been far more difficult than I could have ever anticipated. As a framework, Lift is growing at an exponential rate, and I've tried to cover as much of it as possible and keep it up-to-date with the latest advancements, all while providing you with a base from which to understand the *Lift way* of solving problems.

acknowledgments

Many people contributed to this book, both in the tangible sense of giving reviews and feedback, and also in a more intangible regard by giving me the encouragement and positive words to continue with the project, even when there was seemingly no end in sight.

Throughout the course of writing, I was fortunate enough to receive feedback from a wide range of sources, but there are several people that I specifically need to single out and thank. First, I would like to thank Jon-Anders Teigen and Ross Mellgren for being such amazing sounding boards for ideas, and for often providing a much-needed sanity check late at night. In addition, I would like to thank the following people from the Scala community who have had an influence on me during the writing of this book; your blogs, screencasts, and personal discussions have been a source of inspiration and always remind me there is so much more to learn: Martin Odersky, Debasish Ghosh, Tony Morris, Rúnar Bjarnason, Mark Harrah, Jeppe Nejsum Madsen, Jeppe Cramon, Vassil Dichev, Marius Danicu, Derek Chen-Becker, Jorge Ortiz, and Josh Suereth.

I would also like to thank the companies that use Scala commercially and who have constructively given their feedback; particular thanks go to Harry Heymann and all the Foursquare engineers, Daniel Spiewak and David LaPalomento at Novel, Steve Jenson and Robey Pointer at Twitter, and Jonas Bonér and Viktor Klang at Typesafe.

Writing *Lift in Action* has without doubt been one of the most difficult things I've ever done, and it's been a huge personal challenge. During the writing of this book, I've circumnavigated the globe nearly twice, severely broken my hand, learned Italian, and still found time for a day job. None of those things would have been achievable without the support of my family and three best friends: Robert Dodge, Paul Dredge, and Michael Edwards. I simply couldn't wish for closer friends or a more supportive family. You guys are awesome.

I'd also like to say thank you to all the amazing people who have contributed to Lift over the years, and also to David Pollak for founding the project in the first place. Working on Lift and being a part of the community has truly been one of the highlights of my career to date.

The team at Manning has also been a huge, huge help. Working with such a professional group of people has been a joy end-to-end. I would specifically like to thank Michael Stephens for bringing me on board to write this book: his words from our first call together, "…writing a book is completely survivable," are something I have thought about often. Additionally, Katharine Osbourne has been a legendary development editor; without her support and consultation, this book would likely have never made it to completion. Thanks also to the production team of Andy Carroll, Melody Dolab, Dennis Dalinnik, and Mary Piergies; and to Jon Anders Teigen, Graham Tackley, and Phil Wells for their careful technical proofread of the manuscript, shortly before it went to press.

Finally, my thanks to the reviewers who read the manuscript numerous times during development and who provided invaluable feedback: Andy Dingley, Paul Stusiak, Guillaume Belrose, John Tyler, Ted Neward, Andrew Rhine, Jonas Bandi, Tom Jensen, Ross Mellgren, Richard Williams, Viktor Klang, and Dick Wall.

about this book

Lift is an advanced, next-generation framework for building highly interactive and intuitive web applications. Lift aims to give you a toolkit that scales with both your needs as a developer and the needs of your applications. Lift includes a range of features right out of the box that set it apart from other frameworks in the marketplace: namely security, statefulness, and performance.

Lift also includes a range of high-level abstractions that make day-to-day development easy and powerful. In fact, one of the main driving forces during Lift's evolution has been to include only features that have an actual production use. You, as the developer, can be sure that the features you find in Lift are distilled from real production code.

Lift in Action is a step-by-step exploration of the Lift web framework, and it's split into two main parts: chapters 1 through 5 introduce Lift and walk you through building a small, sample application, and then chapters 6 through 15 take a deep dive into the various parts of Lift, providing you with a deep technical reference to help you get the best out of Lift.

Roadmap

Chapter 1 introduces Lift and sets the scene with regard to how it came into existence. It also covers the various modules of the framework to give you an appreciation for the bigger picture.

Chapter 2 shows you how to get up and running with the Scala build tool SBT and start making your first web application with Lift. This chapter focuses on small, incremental steps covering the concepts of development that you'll need in the rest of the book.

Chapter 3, 4, and 5 walk you through the construction of a real-time auction application to cover as many different parts of Lift as possible. This includes creating templates, connecting to a database, and implementing basic AJAX and Comet.

Chapter 6 takes a dive into the practical aspects of Lift WebKit, showing you how to work with the sophisticated templating system, snippets, and form building through `LiftScreen` and `Wizard`. Additionally, this chapter introduces Lift's own abstraction for handling application state in the form of `RequestVar` and `SessionVar`. This chapter concludes with an overview of some useful extension modules, known as widgets, that ship with the Lift distribution.

Chapters 7 focuses on Lift's SiteMap feature, which allows you to control access and security for particular resources.

Chapter 8 covers the internal working of Lift's HTTP pipeline, detailing the various hooks that are available and demonstrating several techniques for implementing HTTP services.

Chapter 9 explores Lift's sophisticated AJAX and Comet support, demonstrating these technologies in practice by assembling a *rock-paper-scissors* game. This chapter also covers Lift's AJAX abstraction called *wiring*, which allows you to build chains of AJAX interaction with ease.

Chapters 10 and 11 cover Lift's persistence systems, Mapper and Record. Mapper is an active-record style object-relational mapper (ORM) for interacting with SQL data stores, whereas Record is store-agnostic and can be used with any backend system from MySQL to modern NoSQL stores such as MongoDB.

Chapter 12 demonstrates Lift's localization toolkit for building applications that can work seamlessly in any language. This includes the various ways in which you can hook in your `ResourceBundles` to store localized content.

Chapter 13 is all about the enterprise aspects often associated with web application development. Technologies such as JPA are prevalent within the enterprise space, and companies often want to reuse them, so this chapter shows you how to implement JPA with Lift. Additionally, this chapter covers messaging using the Akka framework.

Chapter 14 covers testing with Lift and shows you some different strategies for testing snippets. More broadly, it demonstrates how to design code that has a higher degree of decoupling, so your general coding lends itself to testing.

Finally, chapter 15 consolidates all that you've read in the book and shows you how to take your application into production. This includes an overview of various servlet containers, a demonstration of implementing distributed state handling, and a guide to monitoring with Twitter Ostrich.

Who should read this book?

Primarily, this book is intended to demonstrate how to get things done using Lift. With this in mind, the book is largely slanted toward users who are new to Lift, but who have experience with other web development frameworks. Lift has its own unique way of doing things, so some of the concepts may seem foreign, but I make conceptual comparisons to things you may be familiar with from other popular frameworks or libraries to smooth the transition.

If you're coming to Lift with little or no knowledge of Scala, you should know that Lift makes use of many Scala language features. This book includes a Scala rough guide to get you up and running within the context of Lift as quickly as possible.

The book largely assumes that you have familiarity with XML and HTML. Lift's templating mechanism is 100 percent based on XML, and although it's straightforward to use, it's useful to have an understanding of structured XML that makes use of namespaces.

Finally, because Lift is primarily a web framework designed for browser-based experiences, JavaScript is inevitably part of the application toolchain. Lift includes a high-level Scala abstraction for building JavaScript expressions, but having an understanding of JavaScript and client-side scripting can greatly improve your understanding of the client-server interactions supplied by Lift.

Code conventions and examples

This book includes a wide range of examples and code illustrations from Scala code and HTML templates, to plain text configurations for third-party products. Source code in the listings and in the text is presented in a `fixed width font` to separate it from ordinary text. Additionally, Scala types, methods, keywords, and XML-based markup elements in text are also presented using `fixed width font`. Where applicable, the code examples explicitly include import statements to clarify which types and members originate from which packages. In addition, functions and methods have explicitly annotated types where the result type is not clear.

Although Scala code is typically quite concise, there are some listings that needed to be reformatted to fit in the available page space in the book. You are encouraged to download the source code from the online repository, in order to see the sample code in its original form (https://github.com/timperrett/lift-in-action). In addition to some reformatting, all the comments have been removed for brevity. You can also download the code for the examples in the book from the publisher's website at www.manning.com/LiftinAction.

Code annotations accompany many of the source code listings, highlighting important concepts. In some cases, numbered bullets link to explanations in the subsequent text.

Lift itself is released under the Apache Software License, version 2.0, and all the source code is available online at the official Github repository (https://github.com/lift/framework/). Reading Lift's source code can greatly speed your efforts at becoming productive in using Lift for your own applications.

Author Online

Purchase of *Lift in Action* includes free access to a private web forum run by Manning Publications where you can make comments about the book, ask technical questions, and receive help from the author and from other users. To access the forum and subscribe to it, point your web browser to www.manning.com/Liftin Action or www.manning.com/perrett. This page provides information on how to get on the forum once you're registered, what kind of help is available, and the rules of conduct on the forum.

Manning's commitment to our readers is to provide a venue where a meaningful dialog between individual readers and between readers and the author can take place. It's not a commitment to any specific amount of participation on the part of the author, whose contribution to the AO remains voluntary (and unpaid). We suggest you try asking the author some challenging questions lest his interest stray!

The Author Online forum and the archives of previous discussions will be accessible from the publisher's website as long as the book is in print.

about the author

Timothy Perrett is a technical specialist at a business unit of Xerox Corporation and has been a member of the Lift core team since early 2008. He has a wealth of experience programming in different languages and platforms but has now settled on Scala as his language (and community) of choice for nearly all production activities. Timothy is a specialist in enterprise integration and automation systems for manufacturing and marketing workflows.

When not speaking at conferences or blogging about Scala and Lift, Timothy lives by the river in the beautiful city of Bath, England, where he enjoys socializing with friends and drinking the local ale.

about the cover illustration

The figure on the cover of *Lift in Action* is captioned "A Water Carrier." The illustration is taken from a 19th-century edition of Sylvain Maréchal's four-volume compendium of regional dress customs published in France. Each illustration is finely drawn and colored by hand. The rich variety of Maréchal's collection reminds us vividly of how culturally apart the world's towns and regions were just 200 years ago. Isolated from each other, people spoke different dialects and languages. In the streets or in the countryside, it was easy to identify where they lived and what their trade or station in life was just by their dress.

Dress codes have changed since then and the diversity by region, so rich at the time, has faded away. It is now hard to tell apart the inhabitants of different continents, let alone different towns or regions. Perhaps we have traded cultural diversity for a more varied personal life—certainly for a more varied and fast-paced technological life.

At a time when it is hard to tell one computer book from another, Manning celebrates the inventiveness and initiative of the computer business with book covers based on the rich diversity of regional life of two centuries ago, brought back to life by Maréchal's pictures.

Part 1

Getting started

The first two chapters of this book introduce the Lift framework and demonstrate how you can get everything set up and ready for your first development.

Chapter 1 starts by introducing both Scala and Lift concepts, complete with high-level explanations and samples. The aim is to give you grounding in what is a fundamentally different way of thinking. In chapter 2, you'll be building upon the basis laid down in chapter 1 by constructing your very first Hello World application, which will involve the most basic Lift steps. In these chapters, you'll see first-hand how Lift leverages a *view-first architecture* and how easy it is to get up and running with the Lift web framework.

Introducing Lift

This chapter covers

- An overview of Scala and Lift
- Lift's history and design rationale
- An overview of Lift's structure

Lift is an exciting new way of building web applications that feature rich, highly interactive user experiences. Lift is built atop the powerful functional programming language Scala, which lends itself to writing exceedingly concise but powerful code. By leveraging Scala, Lift aims to be expressive and elegant while stressing the importance of maintainability, scalability, and performance.

The first section of this chapter will introduce Scala and functional programming, including some examples of how the language compares and contrasts to the more familiar style of imperative programming. The second section introduces Lift and discusses how it differs from other web programming tools available today. Lift is largely a conceptual departure from many of the traditional approaches to building web frameworks; specifically, Lift doesn't have a controller-dispatched view system and opts for an idea called *view first*. This chapter discusses these core design goals and introduces these new ideas at a high level. Throughout the course of the book, the concepts outlined here will be expanded

3

on in much greater detail, and you'll see concrete examples to assist you in getting up to speed.

If you're reading this book but are new to Scala programming, you can find a rough guide in appendix A that will show you the ropes and give you a foundation for making use of Lift. If you want to get serious with Scala, I highly recommend looking at the other Scala titles published by Manning: *Scala in Action* by NilanjanRaychaudhuri, and then the more advanced *Scala in Depth* by Joshua Suereth.

1.1   *What is Scala?*

Scala (http://www.scala-lang.org/) is a powerful, hybrid programming language that incorporates many different concepts into an elegant fusion of language features and core libraries. Before delving any deeper, let's just consider how functional programming differs from imperative programming with languages such as Java and Ruby, and what a functional programming language actually is.

As the name implies, functional programming languages have a single basic idea at their root: functions. Small units of code are self-contained *functions* that take type A as an argument and return type B as a result; this is expressed more directly in Scala notation: A => B. How this result is achieved is an implementation detail for the most part; as long as the function yields a value of type B, all is well.

> **NOTE** Functional programming languages often derive from a mathematical concept called lambda calculus. You can read more about it on Wikipedia: http://en.wikipedia.org/wiki/Lambda_calculus.

With this single concept in mind, it's possible to boil down complex problems into these much smaller functions, which can then be *composed* to tackle the larger problem at hand; the result of function one is fed into function two and so on, ad infinitum. The upshot of such a language design is that once you wrap your head around this base level of abstraction, many of the language features can be thought of as higher levels built upon this foundation of basic functions.

Immutability is another trait that marks out functional languages against their imperative cousins. Specifically, within functional languages the majority of data structures are *immutable*. That is to say, once they're created there is no changing that instance; rather, you make a copy of that instance and alter your copy, leaving the original unaltered.

Martin Odersky, however, wanted to fuse object orientation and functional programming together in one unified language that could compile and run on the Java Virtual Machine (JVM). From here, Scala was born, and consequently Scala compiles down to Java bytecode, which means that it can run seamlessly on the JVM and interoperate with all your existing Java code, completely toll free. In practical terms, this means that your existing investment in Java isn't lost; simply call that code directly from your Scala functions and vice versa.

With this fusion of programming styles, Scala gives you the ability to write code that's typically two or three times more concise than the comparative Java code. At the same time, the Scala code is generally less error-prone due to the heavy use of immutable data constructs, and it's also more type-safe than Java, thanks to Scala's very sophisticated type system.

These are the general concepts that make up functional programming, and upon which Scala is built. To further exemplify these differences, table 1.1 presents some examples that illustrate the differences in Scala's approach compared to imperative code. If you don't know Java, don't worry: the examples here are pretty easy to follow, and the syntax should be fairly readable for anyone familiar with Ruby, PHP, or similar languages.

Table 1.1 Comparing Java and Scala styles of coding

Java	Scala
When building class definitions, it's common to have to build so-called getter and setter methods in order to set the values of that instance. This typically creates a lot of noise in the implementation (as seen in the Java example that follows). Scala combats this by using the `case` modifier to automatically provision standard functionality into the class definition. Given an instance of the `Person` case class, calling `person.name` would return the `name` value.	

```java
public class Person {
  private int _age;
  private String _name;
  public Person(String n, int a){
    _age = a;
    _name = n;
  }
  String name(){ return _name; }
  int age(){ return _age; }
}
```
```scala
case class Person(
  name: String, age: Int)
```

Most applications at some point have to deal with collections. The examples that follow create an initial list and then produce a new list instance that has the same animal names, but in lowercase. The Java example on the left creates a list of strings, then creates a second empty list, which then has its contents mutated by looping through the first list and calling `toLowerCase()` on each element. The Scala version achieves the exact same result by defining a function that should be executed on each element of the list. The Scala version is a lot more concise and does the exact same thing without the code noise.

```java
List<String> in = Arrays.asList(
  "Dog", "Cat", "Fish");

List<String> out =
  new ArrayList<String>();

for(String i : in){
  out.add(i.toLowerCase());
}
```
```scala
List("Dog","Cat","Fish")
  .map(_.toLowerCase)
```

These are just some of the ways in which Scala is a powerful and concise language. With this broad introduction to Scala and functional programming out of the way, let's learn about Lift.

1.2   *What is Lift?*

First and foremost, Lift (http://liftweb.net/) is a sophisticated web framework for building rich, vibrant applications. Secondly, Lift is a set of well-maintained Scala libraries that are used by many other projects within the broader Scala ecosystem. For example, the Dispatch HTTP project (http://dispatch.databinder.net/Dispatch.html) uses Lift's JSON-handling library extensively for parsing JSON within the context of standalone HTTP clients. This book, however, really focuses on Lift as a web framework, and it's here that our story begins.

User behavior online in recent years has changed; people now spend more time than ever online, and this means they want the way they interact with online services to be more intuitive and natural. But building such rich applications has proven to be tough for many developers, and this often results in interfaces and infrastructures that aren't really up to the job or user expectations. Lift aims to make building real-time, highly interactive, and massively scalable applications easier than it has ever been by supporting advanced features like Comet, which allow you to push data to the browser when it's needed, without the user having to make any kind of request for it.

In fact, Lift has been designed from the ground up to support these kinds of systems better than anything else. Building interactive applications should be fun, accessible, and simple for developers. Lift removes a lot of the burdens that other frameworks place on developers by mixing together the best ideas in the marketplace today and adding some unique features to give it a component set and resume that are unlike any other framework you have likely come across before. Lift brings a lot of new ideas to the web framework space, and to quote one of the Lift community members, "it is not merely an incremental improvement over the status quo; it redefines the state of the art" (Michael Galpin, Developer, eBay). This departure from traditional thinking shouldn't worry you too much, though, because Lift does adopt tried and tested, well-known concepts, such as convention over configuration, to provide sensible defaults for all aspects of your application while still giving you a very granular mechanism for altering that behavior as your project dictates.

One of the areas in which Lift is radically different is in how it dispatches content for a given request. Unlike other frameworks, such as Rails, Django, Struts, and others, Lift doesn't use the traditional implementation of Model-View-Controller (MVC), where view dispatching is decided by the controller. Rather, Lift uses an approach called *view first*. This is one of the key working concepts within Lift, and it affects nearly everything most developers are used to when working with a framework. Specifically, it forces you to separate the concerns of content generation from content rendering markup.

In the early days of web development, it was commonplace to intermingle the code that did business computations with the code that generated the HTML markup for the user interface. This can be an exceedingly painful long-term strategy, as it makes maintaining the code problematic and tends to lead to a lot of duplication within any given project. Conceptually, this is where the MVC pattern should shine, but most implementations still give the developer the ability to write real code within the presentation layer to generate dynamic markup; this can add accidental complexity to a project when the developer unwittingly adds an element of business or process logic to the presentation layer. It takes programmers who are very disciplined to ensure that none of the business or application logic seeps into the view. Lift takes the standpoint that being able to write interpreted code within markup files can lead to all manner of issues, so it's outlawed completely; this ensures that your templates contain nothing but markup.

The view-first idea in Lift really inherits from the broader design goals upon which Lift was conceived. The following sections will cover these design goals, provide some details about Lift's architecture, and give you an overview of the Lift project structure and community.

1.2.1   *Lift design goals*

The design goals upon which Lift was based have remained fairly constant features of the project. For example, the belief that complex problems, such as security, should be the responsibility of a framework, and not of the developer, have remained central ideals. In short, Lift's design goals are security, conciseness, and performance. Let's just take a look at these in closer detail and consider how they impact you when using Lift as a general-purpose web development framework.

SECURITY

The web can be a dangerous place for developers who don't fully appreciate the potential attacks their applications could come under. There are whole rafts of malicious techniques, including cross-site request forgery (CSRF), cross-site scripting (XSS), SQL injection, and lots, lots more. Many developers can't keep up with the constantly changing world of security threats, let alone fully understand how to effectively and securely protect their applications.

To this end, Lift provides protection against common malicious attacks without the need for the developer to do any additional work or configuration; Lift just does the right thing. Whenever you make an AJAX call, use Comet, or even build a simple form, Lift is right there in the background securing the relevant processing from attack. Lift typically does this by replacing input names and URLs with opaque GUIDs that reference specific functions on the server; this essentially completely eliminates tampering, because there is no way for an attacker to know what the right GUID might be. This comprehensive security is covered in more detail in chapters 6 and 9.

A nice illustration of Lift's security credentials is the popular social media site Foursquare.com, which runs on Lift. Even RasmusLerdorf, the inventor of PHP and infamous security pundit, was impressed by not being able to find a single security flaw![1]

CONCISENESS

If you have spent any time coding in a moderately verbose imperative programming language like Java, you'll be more than familiar with the value of conciseness. Moreover, studies have shown that fewer lines of code mean statistically fewer errors, and overall it's easier for the brain to comprehend the intended meaning of the code.[2]

Fortunately, Scala assists Lift in many aspects with the goal of conciseness; Scala has properties, multiple inheritance via *traits*, and as was touched on earlier, it has a complex type system that can infer types without explicit type annotations, which gives an overall saving in character tokens per line of code that you write. These are just some of the ways in which Scala provides a concise API for Lift, and these savings are coupled with the design of the Lift infrastructure, which aims to be short and snappy where possible, meaning less typing and more doing.

PERFORMANCE

No matter what type of application you're building for use on the web, no developer wants his or her work to be slow. Performance is something that Lift takes very seriously, and as such, Lift can be very, very quick. As an example, when using the basic Lift project, you can expect upward of 300 requests per second on a machine with only 1 GB of RAM and a middle-of-the-road processor. In comparison, you should see upwards of 2,000 requests per second on a powerful 64-bit machine with lots of RAM. Whatever your hardware, Lift will give you really great throughput and blistering performance.

1.2.2   *View-first design*

Lift takes a different approach to dispatching views; rather than going via a controller and action, which then select the view template to use based upon the action itself, Lift's view-first approach essentially does the complete opposite. It first chooses the view and then determines what dynamic content needs to be included on that page. For most people new to Lift, trying not to think in terms of controllers and actions can be one of the most difficult parts of the transition. During the early phases of Lift development, there was a conscious choice taken to *not* implement MVC-style controller-dispatched views.

In a system where views are dispatched via a controller, you're essentially tied to having one primary call to action on that page, but with modern applications, this is generally not the case. One page may have many items of page furniture that are equally important.

---

[1] Tweet on Rasmus Lerdorf's Twitter stream: http://twitter.com/rasmus/status/5929904263

[2] For more information, see Gilles Dubochet's paper, "Computer Code as a Medium for Human Communication: Are Programming Languages Improving?" (ÉcolePolytechniqueFédérale de Lausanne, 2009). http://infoscience.epfl.ch/record/138586/files/dubochet2009coco.pdf?version=2

Consider a typical shopping-cart application: the cart itself might feature on multiple pages in a side panel, and a given page could contain a catalog listing with the mini shopping cart on the left. Both are important, and both need to be rendered within the same request. It's at this very point that the MVC model becomes somewhat muddy, because you're essentially forced to decide which is the primary bit of page content. Although there are solutions for such a situation, the concept of having a primary controller action for that request immediately becomes less pure.

In an effort to counter this problem, Lift opts for the view-first approach. Although it's not a pattern you may have heard about before, the three component parts are view, snippet, and model—VSM for short. This configuration is illustrated in figure 1.1.

Figure 1.1 shows that the view is the initial calling component within this architecture, and this is where the view-first name comes from. Let's now take a moment to review each element within the view-first setup.

VIEW
Within the context of view-first, the view refers primarily to the HTML content served for a page request. Within any given Lift application, you can have two types of view:

- Template views that bind dynamic content into a predefined markup template
- Generated views in which dynamic content is created, typically with Scala XML literals

Template views are the most commonly used method of generating view content, and they require that you have a well-formed XHTML or HTML5 template. It's important to note that Lift doesn't allow you to use view code that's invalid; this means that when you're working with a design team, if their templates are W3C-validate, you know they'll work with Lift because the snippet invocations are also part of the markup. This ensures that designers don't inadvertently introduce problems by

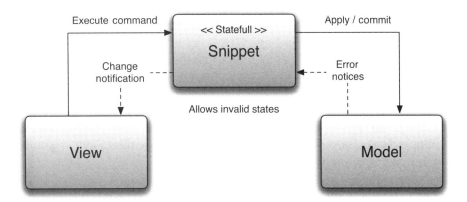

Figure 1.1 A representation of the view-first design. The view invokes the snippets, which in turn call any other component of the application business logic.

altering framework-specific code within the template, which is a common problem with other frameworks.

Generated views are far less common, but sometimes they're used for quick prototyping by using Scala XML literals.

Whichever route you choose to take, the view is the calling component in the architecture, and as such you can invoke as many different (and completely separate) snippets as you like from within any given view. This is a core idea within Lift: views can have more than a single concrete purpose. This helps to minimize the amount of code duplication within an application and lends itself nicely to a pure model of component encapsulation.

SNIPPET

Snippets are rendering functions that take XML input from within a given page template and then transform that input based upon the logic within the snippet function. For example, when rendering a list of items, the template could contain the markup for a single item, and then the snippet function would generate the markup for an entire list of items, perhaps by querying the database and then iterating over the result set to produce the desired list of items.

There's a very tight and deliberate coupling between the snippet and the XML output. The snippet isn't intended to be a controller, such as those found in the MVC design pattern, nor is it meant to take on any control-flow responsibilities. The snippet's sole purpose within Lift is to generate dynamic content and mediate changes in the model back to the view.

MODEL

In this context, the model is an abstract notion that could represent a number of different things. But for most applications, it will represent a model of persistence or data (irrespective of the actual process it undertakes to get that data). You ask the model for value *x*, and it returns it.

In terms of Lift's view-first architecture, the snippet will usually call the model for some values. For example, the snippet might request a list of all the current products in an ecommerce application or ask the model to add an item to the user's shopping cart. Whatever the operation, when the model is asked to do something, it applies whatever business logic it needs to and then responds appropriately to the snippet. The response could include validation errors that the snippet then renders to the view.

The actual mechanism for updating the view isn't important for this discussion (full page load, AJAX, or some other method). Rather, the model responds and the response is passed to the view via the snippet.

1.2.3   *Community and team*

Since the very beginning, the Lift team has always been very diverse; right from the early days, the team grew in a very organic fashion and has continued to do so over recent years. Today the Lift core team consists of professional and highly talented individuals not only from all over the world but in a bewildering array of different market sectors. This gives Lift its vibrancy and overall well-rounded approach.

If you're new to the Lift community, welcome. It's a very stimulating place, and you'll find that the majority of our team members on the mailing list or hanging out in IRC will assist you if you get stuck with something. Although I hope that this book will cover most of the things you might want to know about Lift, there will inevitably be things you wonder about as you continue to use Lift in your own projects. To that end, take a look at the resources listed in table 1.2.

Table 1.2 Helpful Lift resources that can be found online

Resource	Description
Main Lift site	http://liftweb.net
	First and foremost is the main Lift homepage. Here you'll find the latest news about Lift, regularly updated as time goes by. This page also has links to the source code, the issue tracker, and the wiki.
Assembla	https://www.assembla.com/wiki/show/liftweb
	Lift moved to the Assembla platform for its wiki and bug-tracking requirements some time ago, and since then it has accumulated a fair amount of community-created articles.
Mailing list	http://groups.google.com/group/liftweb
	The Google group is the official support channel for Lift. If you have a question, you can come to the mailing list and find a friendly, responsive community that will be more than happy to answer your questions.
IRC channel	#lift on freenode.net
	IRC isn't as popular as it once was, but you'll still find some of the Lift team hanging out in IRC from time to time.

Now that you've had a brief overview of the Lift framework and its evolution, let's get into some technical details as to what it can actually do and how it can help you be more productive and produce higher quality applications.

1.3 Lift features

During the past three years, the Lift codebase has exploded in size and now features all manner of functionality, from powerful HTTP request-response control, right through to enterprise extensions like a monadic transaction API and Actor-based wrappers around AMQP and XMPP.

Lift is broken down into three top-level subprojects: Lift Core and Lift Web, Lift Persistence, and Lift Modules. We'll now take a closer look at each module to give you an overview of its structure and functionality.

1.3.1   *Lift Core and Lift Web*

There are two modules that make up the central framework: *Core* and *Web*. The Core consists of four projects that build to separate libraries that you can use both with and without Lift's Web module. The Web module itself builds upon the Core and supplies Lift's sophisticated components for building secure and scalable web applications. The Web module itself is made up of three projects: the base web systems and two additional projects that provide specialized helpers. Figures 1.2 and 1.3 depict the various modules and their layering.

Let's spend some time going through each module in figure 1.2, working from the bottom up, and discuss their key features and functionality.

LIFT COMMON

The Lift Common module contains a few base classes that are common to everything else within Lift. Probably most important of all, Lift Common can be used in projects that aren't even web applications. Utilities like Box, Full, and Empty (discussed more in appendix C) can be exceedingly useful paradigms for application development, even if the application isn't using any other part of Lift. Lift Common also includes some base abstractions that make working with the logging facade SLF4J (http://www.slf4j.org/) much simpler.

LIFT ACTOR

Actors are a model for concurrent programming whereby asynchronous messaging is used in place of directly working with threads and locks. There are several actor implementations within the Scala ecosystem, and Lift has its own for the specific domain of web development. To that end, Lift Actor provides concrete implementations of the base actor traits that are found within Lift Common (more information on traits can be found in appendix A).

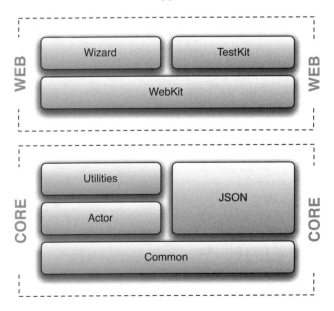

Figure 1.2   An illustration of the module dependencies within the Lift Core and Web subprojects

LIFT UTILITIES

During the development of web applications, there are invariably things that can be reused because there are common idioms in both your and other peoples' work. Lift Utilities is a collection of classes, traits, and objects that are designed to save you time or provide convenience mechanisms for dealing with common paradigms.

A good example is the handling of a time span. Consider the following code, which defines a pair of `TimeSpan` instances by way of *implicitly converting* a regular integer value into a `TimeSpanBuilder`:

```
10 seconds
1 hour
```

Simplistic helpers provide an easy-to-use dialect for handling even complex subjects like time and duration. This example shows both hour and second helpers, where both lines result in `net.liftweb.util.Helpers.TimeSpan` instances.

Here's another example from the `SecurityHelpers` trait. It hashes the string "hello world" with an MD5 algorithm:

```
md5("hello world")
```

Once again, Lift Utilities provides simple-to-use helper methods for common use cases found within web development—everything from handling time to hashing and encrypting values and much more.

LIFT JSON

Probably one of the most popular additions to the Lift Core grouping, Lift JSON provides an almost standalone package for handling JSON in a highly performant way. Needless to say, JSON is becoming one of the standards within the emerging online space, so having great support for it is quite critical for any web framework. The parser included within Lift JSON is approximately 350 times faster than the JSON parser that's included in the Scala standard library—this gives Lift blisteringly fast performance when serializing back and forth to JSON.

You might be wondering if Lift can only parse JSON quickly, or if it also provides a means to construct JSON structures. Well, Lift JSON provides a slick domain-specific language (DSL) for constructing JSON objects.

Let's take a quick look at a basic example:

```
val example = ("name" -> "joe") ~ ("age" -> 35)

compact(JsonAST.render(example))
```

This example defines a value in the first line, which represents a JSON structure with Scala tuples. This structure is then *rendered* to JSON by using the compact and render methods from the `JsonAST` object in the second line. Here's the output:

```
{"name":"joe","age":35}
```

As you can see, this is a straightforward `String` and `Int` construction from the DSL, but we'll cover more in-depth details of Lift-JSON in chapter 9. All you need to know for now is that Lift's JSON provisioning is fast and very versatile.

LIFT WEBKIT

Finally we get to the central part of Lift's web toolkit. The WebKit module is where Lift holds its entire pipeline, from request processing right down to localization and template rendering. For all intents and purposes, it's the main and most important part of Lift.

Rather than covering the various parts of WebKit in detail here, table 1.3 gives an extremely brief overview of each of the core components and notes the chapter that addresses it in more detail.

Table 1.3   Features of Lift WebKit

Feature	Description	Chapter
Snippet processing	Snippets are the core of Lift's rendering and page-display mechanism.	6
SiteMap	SiteMap provides a declarative model for defining security and access control to page resources.	7
HTTP abstraction	Although Lift typically operates within a Java servlet container, it's totally decoupled from the underlying implementation and can run anywhere.	8
Request-response pipeline processing	The whole request and response pipeline is contained within WebKit, as are the associated configuration hooks.	8
REST components	REST features allow you to hook into the request-response pipeline early on and deliver stateless or stateful web services.	8
Secure AJAX	All the AJAX processing and function mapping infrastructure lives in WebKit.	9
Rich Comet support	The Comet support Lift provides is one of the main features WebKit offers.	9

Although you aren't familiar with Lift syntax or classes just yet, the following listing shows an example of a real-time Comet clock to give you a flavor of the kinds of things contained within the WebKit project.

Listing 1.1   `CometActor clock`

```
import scala.xml.Text
import net.liftweb._,
  util.Schedule, util.Helpers._,
  http.CometActor, http.js.JsCmds.SetHtml

class Clock extends CometActor {
  Schedule.schedule(this, Tick, 5 seconds)        ← Schedule redraw
  def render = "#clock_time *" replaceWithtimeNow.toString
  override def lowPriority = {
    case Tick =>
```

```
        partialUpdate(SetHtml("clock_time", Text(timeNow.toString)))
        Schedule.schedule(this, Tick, 5 seconds)
  }
}
```

With only a few lines of code, you get a clock that pushes the updated time to the browser, so it will appear as if there's a *live* clock in the user's browser. All the complexities associated with Comet, like connection handling, long polling, and general plumbing are handled by Lift right out of the box!

1.3.2 *Lift Persistence*

The vast majority of applications will at some point want to save their data for later use. This typically requires some kind of backend storage, and this is where Lift Persistence comes into play. Lift provides you with a number of options for saving your data, whether it's a relational database management system (RDBMS) or one of the new NoSQL solutions.

There are three foundations for persistence, as depicted in figure 1.3; the following subsections take a look at these base components.

LIFT DB AND MAPPER

The vast majority of applications you'll write will no doubt want to communicate with an RDBMS of some description, be it MySQL, SQL Server, or one of the other popular storage systems. When you're working with Lift, Mapper provides you with a unified route for persistence.

At a high level, Mapper takes a design direction that's similar, but not completely faithful to the Active Record pattern. Mapper provides you with an object-relational mapping (ORM) implementation that handles all the usual relationship tasks, such as one-to-one, one-to-many, and many-to-many, so that you don't have to write SQL join queries manually. But when you want to write that raw SQL, perhaps for performance reasons or by preference, you can easily pull back the covers and write SQL directly.

Mapper is unified into many parts of Lift and thus has several advantages out of the box over other solutions that are available within the Scala ecosystem. Consider this very basic example of the Mapper API and how it can be used:

```
User.find(By(User.email, "foo@bar.com"))

User.find(By(User.birthday, new Date("Jan 4, 1975")))
```

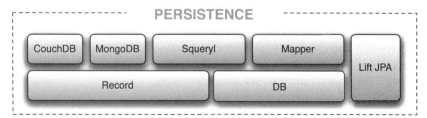

Figure 1.3   Dependency structure of persistence within Lift

Notice that this code is quite readable, even without a prior familiarity with the Mapper API. For example, in the first line, you want to find a user by their email address. In the second line, you're finding a user by their birthday.

LIFT JPA

The Java Persistence API is well known in the wider Java space, and, being Java, it can work right out of the box from the Scala runtime, which shares the common JVM platform. Unfortunately, because JPA is Java, its idiomatic implementation gives it a lot of mutable data structures and other things that are typically not found within Scala code—so much so that you might well choose to avoid writing Java-like code when you're working with Scala.

To that end, a module was added to Lift's persistence options to wrap the JPA API and give it a more idiomatic Scala feel. This module significantly reduces the Java-style code that you need to write when working with JPA and the associated infrastructure. This is covered in more detail in chapter 13.

LIFT RECORD

This is one of the most interesting aspects of Lift Persistence. Record was designed with the idea that persistence has common idioms no matter what the actual backend implementation was doing to interact with the data. Record is a layer that gives users create, read, update, and delete (CRUD) semantics and a set of helpers for displaying form fields, operating validation, and so forth. All this without actually providing the connection to a concrete persistence implementation.

Currently, Record has three backend implementation modules as part of the framework: one for working with the NoSQL document-orientated storage system CouchDB (http://couchdb.apache.org/), a second for the NoSQL data store MongoDB (http://www.mongodb.org/), and finally a layer on top of Squeryl (http://squeryl.org/), the highly sophisticated functional persistence library. These implementations could not be more different in their underlying mechanics, but they share this common grounding through Record because of the abstract semantics the Record infrastructure provides.

At the time of writing, Record is still fairly new. As time goes by, more and more backend implementations will come online, and perhaps eventually the Mapper RDBMS code will also be merged with Record.

Here is a sample from the CouchDB implementation that queries a CouchDB `people_by_age` JavaScript view:

```
Person.queryView("test", "people_by_age", _.key(JInt(30)))
```

It's important to note that third-party backend implementations for Record are starting to appear in the Scala ecosystem, and although they aren't a bona fide part of Lift, they're available on github.com and similar services.

UNDERSTANDING YOUR USE CASE

As you've probably grasped from the framework overview, Lift has many different components, some of which overlap in their intended usage. This isn't a legacy growing pain, quite the opposite: it's deliberate. With Lift there's often more than one way to reach an acceptable solution, and the factors that dictate which route you take are largely application-specific and depend on the particular problem domain you're working with.

Throughout the course of this book, you'll see a range of different approaches to solving problems with Lift. Often the different methods are equally as good, and which you choose is a matter of preference or style. For example, in chapter 14 you'll learn about three different approaches to dependency injection with Scala. These approaches ultimately achieve very similar results, but depending upon your team, environment, or application, one may be a better fit than the others. That's something you must experiment with for yourself to get a feel for which is going to work best for you.

The next section discusses some plugins, or modules of ancillary code that are also available as part of the Lift project. They may help you in building your applications and getting up to speed with less plumbing.

1.3.3 Lift Modules

Lift Modules is where the project houses all the extensions to the core framework. Unlike the other groups of subprojects within Lift, the modules are more organic and have little or no relation to one another. Each module is generally self-contained regarding the functionality it provides.

Rather than go through each module in detail here, table 1.4 lists the modules available at the time of writing.

Table 1.4 Available add-on modules supplied as part of Lift

Module	Description
Advanced Message Queue Protocol (AMQP)	Actor-based wrapper system on AMQP messaging
Facebook integration	API integration module for the popular social networking site
Imaging	Selection of helper methods for manipulating images
Java Transaction API (JTA) integration	Functional style wrapper around the Java Transaction API
Lift state machine	State machine tightly integrated with WebKit and Mapper
OAuth	Building blocks for creating the server component of OAuth

Table 1.4   Available add-on modules supplied as part of Lift *(continued)*

Module	Description
OAuth Mapper	Extension to the OAuth module to use Mapper as a backend
Open ID	Integration module for using OpenID federated providers
OSGi	For those who want to run their Lift app within an OSGI container
PayPal	Integration module for PayPal PDT and IPN services
Test kit	Helpers for writing tests concerning the HTTP operations in Lift
Textile	Scala implementation of a Textile markup parser
Widgets	Selection of helpful widgets (such as calendaring, Gravatar, and JavaScript autocomplete)
XMPP	Actor-based wrappers around XMPP message exchange

At the time of writing, the available modules are located within a separate Git repository (https://github.com/lift/modules), and the community is discussing making the addition of new modules available to non–core team committers.

If you want to create your own modules, it's just a case of depending upon the parts of Lift that you wish to extend. Typically this means creating a small library of your own that depends upon WebKit and extends or implements the relevant types. To use this custom module within another application, you only have to provide some kind of initialization point that will wire the relevant materials into that Lift application during startup. That's all there is to it.

1.4   *Summary*

In this chapter, we've taken a look at both Scala and Lift and outlined their major conceptual differences from more traditional web frameworks. Lift provides developers with a very capable toolkit for building interactive, scalable, and highly performant real-time web applications. These themes really underpin the core design goals of Lift: security, conciseness, and performance.

As the author of a Lift application, you don't need to worry about the bulk of security issues prevalent in other systems: Lift does that for you. The framework is always there securing element names and URIs without you having to intervene. In addition to security, idiomatic Lift application code tends to be brief and make use of powerful Scala language features to create an API that's readable, maintainable, and performant.

Lift also differs quite wildly from other frameworks available today in that it doesn't implement controller-dispatched views as many MVC frameworks do. Instead,

Lift implements its own view-first architecture that gives you a far purer model for creating components and modularity within your code. Your rendering logic takes the form of neat, maintainable functions rather than monolithic stacks of special classes.

Finally, the majority of the code contained within the Lift framework is either running in production, or is a distillation from live production code. To that end, you can have absolute confidence in Lift when building your enterprise applications.

Without further ado, let's move on to setting up your environment and getting your very first Lift-powered application up and running.

Hello Lift

2

This chapter covers

- An introduction to the SBT build tool
- Creating your first Lift-powered application
- Snippet and templating overview

In this chapter, you'll be creating your first Lift application, but before getting to that, you need to set up your environment so you can compile and run your application code. In order to run on the JVM, Scala code must be compiled before it can be executed. Although it's possible to compile Scala source code manually, it's a good idea to have an automated *build tool* that does this for you.

If you're coming from a dynamic language such as Ruby or PHP, you may never have needed a build tool. Essentially, build tools automate parts of your development and deployment processes. Typical tasks include compiling and packaging code into deployable binaries, generating code documentation, and lots of other things.

In this chapter, you'll be setting up the Simple Build Tool (SBT) that you'll use throughout this book. You'll also see how you can get SBT to speed up your development by generating starting points for projects, classes, and markup templates.

Once you have your environment configured, you can get to work making your first Lift application. Section 2.2 walks you through creating this first project and explains the various component parts, their purposes, and how you can add to them.

The final section builds upon this introduction and explains how you can put together your own snippets and templates.

First, though, let's get you set up and working with SBT.

2.1 Getting started with SBT

SBT is primarily a command-line tool and is shipped as an executable JAR file. This section will show you how to configure that executable as a command-line system tool, but it's also possible to leverage it from within your IDE if that's how you prefer to work. For more information on setting up an IDE to work with Scala, see appendix B.

> **NOTE** Scala is fully interoperable with Java, which means that Scala is also very conversant with the range of Java build tools, such as Maven (http://maven.apache.org) and Ant (http://ant.apache.org). These tools have fair support, and you can use them within your IDE of choice if you prefer.

Even though there are a variety of tools available to build your Scala code, SBT is the most prevalent in the community, and it's what you'll find the majority of projects using (including Lift). Broadly speaking, SBT is relatively fast at compiling code, it has a simple command interface, and it's easy to extend with simple Scala plugins, which is likely why it has proven so popular.

In order to set up SBT, you need to take a moment to make sure you have several things in place. As discussed in chapter 1, Scala runs inside the Java runtime, so you'll need to have Java Runtime Edition (JRE) 1.5 or greater installed to work with Lift. At the time of writing, Lift will work equally well with either Java 1.5 or 1.6, but in future versions Java 1.5 will likely be dropped in order to tighten up the Lift API. You can verify your Java version by opening a console window and running the following command;

```
java -version
```

If you have Java installed, this will output something like: `java version "1.6.0_17"`. If you don't have Java, head over to the main download site (http://www.java.com/en/download/index.jsp) and follow the instructions to install it.

Provided Java is on your system, the first thing to do is download the SBT launcher JAR and place it somewhere on the environment path (`$PATH` on Unix and `%PATH%` on Windows). SBT is provided as an executable JAR file, which essentially means that the JAR file is like a mini application; it's a compiled archive that has the ability to be run as a program or process. Invoking it from the command line will load Java and then load the SBT shell.

To get SBT, head over to the SBT downloads page and grab the latest release (http://code.google.com/p/simple-build-tool/downloads/list). At the time of writing 0.7.7, was the latest stable build of the 0.7.x series of SBT, but the instructions that follow should make sense with subsequent versions of SBT.

> **NOTE**   As this book was being finished, the SBT project was starting to release early versions of a completely redesigned version of SBT under the 0.10+ branches. Currently this series is so radically different that the configuration and setup will differ from what is described here. The 0.7 series will continue to be supported for the foreseeable future, so using it is fine, and, when the time comes, migrating to the official 1.0 version of SBT shouldn't be too difficult.

SBT is a command-line application and has no out-of-the-box graphical user interface (GUI) to speak of, so it must be executed from a console window and interacted with from the SBT shell. In order to make executing SBT easy, it's best to wrap it in a small shell script (or .cmd file on Windows) that will let you execute the JAR with the simple command sbt. This small extra step will pay dividends in your development cycle, so let's take a moment to set up the wrapper script, as shown in table 2.1.

Table 2.1   Setting up SBT on your development machine

Configuring SBT		
Step	**Action**	**Result**
1	Download SBT, place it in a well-known location, and name it sbt-launch-VERION.jar. Unix. We recommend putting the file in /usr/local/bin Windows: We recommend putting the file in C:\scala\sbt	The downloaded SBT launcher should have executable permissions and be in a well-known file location.
2	Create a file in the same directory called "sbt" and give it executable permissions. Note: Windows users will need to call their file "sbt.bat" or "sbt.cmd".	📦 sbt 📄 sbt-launch–0.7.5.jar
3	Populate that file with the correct execution command for your operating system.	
	Unix	```java -XX:+CMSClassUnloadingEnabled -XX:MaxPermSize=1024m -Xmx2048M -Xss4M -jar `dirname $0`/sbt-launch.jar "$@"```
	Windows	```set SCRIPT_DIR=%~dp0 java -XX:+CMSClassUnloadingEnabled -XX:MaxPermSize=1024m -Xmx2048M -Xss4M -jar "%SCRIPT_DIR%sbt-launch.jar" %*```

With your SBT script set up and available on your environment path, it should be possible to open a console window, type sbt, and see the following:

```
$ sbt
Project does not exist, create new project? (y/N/s)
```

If you're prompted to create a new project, SBT has successfully been installed! For the moment you can simply enter n as the answer to quit the shell; you'll be creating an application in the next section. But if you don't see a prompt similar to the preceding snippet of terminal output, please refer to the SBT installation documentation (http://code.google.com/p/simple-build-tool/wiki/Setup).

Providing your install went well, from here on you'll only work with SBT from its interactive console to execute tasks and actions. Without further ado, let's get on with creating your first Lift application with your fresh install of SBT!

2.2 *Your first Lift application*

Throughout the course of the next few chapters, you'll be building an auction-style application. The next chapter discusses in detail the application's functionality, so for the moment we'll focus on the fundamental building blocks that form the basis of any Lift project. This will involve creating an empty SBT project and then populating that with the configuration required to run a Lift application. This will give you a fully functioning (albeit very basic) Lift application that you can take forward to subsequent chapters. You'll also be able to use it as a guide for building your own applications, both in terms of the steps used to create the project and in terms of the interaction within the SBT shell.

The next section will walk you through the commands and options involved in creating a new SBT project and also introduce a Lift community tool called Lifty (http://lifty.github.com/Lifty/), which you can use to speed the setup of new projects. With the project structure in place, the subsequent two sections will discuss the various components of the default Lift application and then demonstrate how to boot the built-in web server so you can interact with the application on your local computer.

2.2.1 *Creating the project*

To get started, open a console window switch, with cd, into a new working directory of your choosing. Here you should invoke the sbt command. After doing so, SBT will check to see if a project is already in place, and if not, it will then prompt you to create a new SBT project. SBT determines whether a project already exists by checking for a project directory containing a build.properties file.

When creating a new SBT project, you'll be prompted to answer several questions about the new project configuration. SBT displays the defaults in square brackets next to the question. For each line, just enter the value you would like to use, and press the Enter key. Table 2.2 lists the things SBT will ask for and describes them, providing some suggested values.

Table 2.2 **SBT prompts and suggested values**

Prompt	Description
Name	This value defines the name of your project. It's also used as the artifact identifier for the published binary. For example, having a name of "Sample" will result in a binary named Sample.jar.
Organization	This is typically the group identifier of the output application binary. For example, Lift's WebKit module has organization set as net.liftweb.
Version [1.0]	This is the version number you want to start your project with.
Scala version [2.8.1]	At the time of writing, 2.8.1 was the latest release of Scala that Lift officially supported, and this is what all the code samples in this book are compiled against. The 2.7.x series of Scala is now deprecated.
sbt version [0.7.7]	If you want to specify a newer version of SBT, you can enter it here, and SBT will automatically find the correct JAR online from its repository and use that for this project.

After answering the SBT prompts, the terminal should drop into a shell with a single prompt on the left side—the > prompt that your console window is now displaying. This is the interactive SBT shell, and this is where you must issue commands to control your project and execute tasks. Figure 2.1 shows the full interaction with SBT involved in creating a new project.

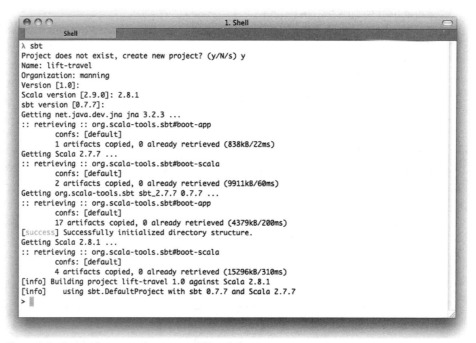

Figure 2.1 **Output from creating a new SBT project**

You may have noticed that SBT has generated a folder structure consisting of several elements that manage the SBT build, providing you with a starting point for any Scala-based application. Right now, this project can only compile standalone Scala code and lacks the required files and configuration to support a web application.

All SBT projects have a project definition class, or project file (typically called Project .scala). By default, SBT doesn't generate this because it isn't mandatory for the most basic Scala console applications, but in order to build a Lift web app, you'll need to create a project file to define dependencies and generally control the build process. To avoid creating this manually, you can use an SBT feature called *processors*, which allow SBT to pull executables from the internet to augment the default commands that SBT ships with.

To get started creating the project structure, you'll use a processor to generate the structure and default files you'll need to start working on the application. From the interactive shell, run this command:

```
> *lift is org.lifty lifty 1.6.1
```

This command instructs SBT to define a processor called `lift`; the asterisk in the command is important, so make sure you include it.

Now, whenever `lift` is entered into the shell, it should use the processor actions defined in the org.lifty.lifty JAR file that's located on the scala-tools.org repository. Because both SBT and Lift are hosted on the same online repository, SBT already knows where to find the Lifty binaries. The first time you define the `lift` processor, there may be a slight pause after pressing Enter, because SBT has to fetch the JAR from the online repository. Don't worry, though; the downloading should only take a few moments.

> **It's Lifty, not Lift**
>
> Lifty is a community project developed by Mads Hartmann Jensen during the 2010 Google Summer of Code, and although it isn't an official part of the Lift project, it has strong links with the Lift community and team. More information about Lifty is available from the project home page (http://lifty.github.com/Lifty/).
>
> Note that you could define the SBT processor as being called "lifty" if you wanted. It won't have any practical impact, so call it whatever you like. For the purposes of this book, though, it will be called `lift`.

Now that the `lift` processor is defined in your SBT setup, you can invoke any of the *actions* that are defined in it. For example, `create` is an action that takes a set of arguments and can create files in your SBT project, whether it's a single snippet or a whole project. If you want more information about the actions available, just type `lift help`. You can also get more specific information on the arguments that a specific template requires by typing `lift <name_of_template>`. For example, `lift create` will tell you specifically what arguments it needs and what the options are.

In order to start creating your application, you need to add the components required for a Lift web project. Fortunately, the `lift` processor already knows how to add these things, so you only need to execute the following command to populate a blank SBT project with Lift web goodness!

```
> lift create project-blank
```

Invoking this command will prompt you for a *mainpack*. This is the main package that you would like the code to be generated in. An example value could be com.mycompany, but by default it will be the value you supplied as the organization when you created the project. Next, it will prompt you for a Lift version; use 2.3 because all of the code samples in this book are compiled and tested against that version of Lift. When you press Enter, Lifty will generate a set of files for your Lift application, including the SBT project definition and all the associated elements (which we'll discuss shortly).

Now you need to tell SBT about the new definition. To do this, type the following commands:

```
> reload
> update
```

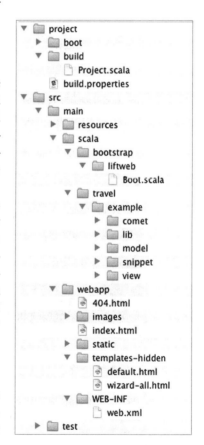

These are important commands that you'll use pretty frequently with SBT. The `reload` command tells SBT to recompile the project definition and refresh the classpath, whereas the `update` command gets SBT to download the necessary dependencies from the repositories defined in the project definition.

All Lift applications depend on a set of libraries that contain the Lift code, and SBT automatically downloads these for you and enables them within the project. The required JAR files will be downloaded into the lib_managed directory that SBT creates. For more information on SBT and how it handles dependencies and Scala versions, head over to the online wiki: http://code.google.com/p/simple-build-tool/wiki/LibraryManagement.

2.2.2   *Inspecting the project*

Now that you have a fresh project created, let's take a moment to inspect the files that were created. The generated source tree should be quite similar to figure 2.2.

For readers familiar with Java web development, you'll notice several familiar elements in the project

Figure 2.2   A new project tree detailing the files you'll see after creating a new project with SBT

structure. In particular, the web.xml file and WEB-INF directory are standard Java web application items. One of the great benefits of Lift is that it utilizes standard Java deployment packages such as Web Application Archives (WAR) and Enterprise Archives (EAR), so it can be easily deployed in your standard Java servlet containers with no changes to code or reinvestment in business infrastructure. It just works.

If you're not familiar with Java web application structure, don't worry too much; these files are essentially default configurations that indicate to the Java web server how it should handle the application when it's deployed.

Let's take a look at generated project structure and the functions of the main components of the source tree.

PROJECT DIRECTORY

Working from the root folder through the project tree, you should see the project directory. This is where SBT holds the information about the application, dependencies, and repositories. You configure the build environment with Scala code, which is fully type-safe, and SBT won't let you proceed if your Project.scala won't compile. The basic project file for the example application should look something like the next listing.

Listing 2.1 The project definition

```
import sbt._

class LiftProject(info: ProjectInfo)                          ❶ Extends
    ➥ extends DefaultWebProject(info) {                          DefaultWebProject
  val liftVersion = "2.3"

  val webkit = "net.liftweb" %% "lift-webkit" %
    liftVersion % "compile->default"
  val logback = "ch.qos.logback" % "logback-classic" %
    "0.9.26" % "compile->default"
  val servlet = "javax.servlet" % "servlet-api" %      ❷ Defines
    "2.5" % "provided->default"                             dependencies
  val jetty6 = "org.mortbay.jetty" % "jetty" %
    "6.1.22" % "test->default"
  val junit  = "junit" % "junit" %
    "4.5" % "test->default"
  val specs  = "org.scala-tools.testing" %% "specs" %
    "1.6.6" % "test->default"

  lazy val scalatoolsSnapshots = ScalaToolsSnapshots
}
```

All SBT project definitions must extend one of the bundled project types, and for web applications that's `DefaultWebProject` ❶. This trait supplies actions for executing a local Jetty server for development and some other web-specific infrastructure that you'll need when developing a web application.

Dependencies within your project are defined by using the percent character as a delimiter between group identifier, artifact identifier, version, and finally the scope that you require from that dependency ❷. You'll also sometimes see artifacts that are delimited by a double percent symbol (%%), and in this case SBT will automatically append the Scala version to the artifact identifier when attempting to resolve the dependency. For example, the main WebKit JAR that this project depends upon uses the %% notation; SBT will automatically append the Scala version, so the dependency is resolved as lift-webkit_2.8.1.jar. This feature was added to SBT because there are distinct binary incompatibilities between different versions of Scala; this neat solution hides having to detail the Scala version for every Scala-based dependency.

If you're new to dependency management, all you need to know is that you have the scopes defined in table 2.3.

Table 2.3   Available SBT dependency scopes

Scope	Description
Compile	Dependencies directly required to compile parts of your code
Provided	Dependencies required to compile your code but that will be provided at deployment time, usually by the servlet container or deployment runtime
Runtime	Dependencies that are required only at runtime, and not for compilation
Test	Dependencies that aren't required for normal operation of the application, but only for testing purposes

There are some additional scopes available, but these are the most common ones you'll use in conjunction with SBT.

SRC DIRECTORY

As the name implies, the src directory is where all the source code for your application lives. In its main directory there are three important directories that you'll need to utilize during your Lift development; table 2.4 describes the purpose of each section. The src directory contains everything that directly contributes to the application's functionality.

Table 2.4   Directories created in the SBT project

Directory	Description
src/main/resources	The resources directory is where you can place configuration and related files that you want to be packaged up with your application deployment WAR. The things you place here will be on the root class-path of the output package, so it's usually a good place to hold things like logging configuration or other resources that you need access to at runtime. Lift's configuration files (ending with .props) typically live in the resources/props folder.
src/main/scala	This is where all the Scala and Lift code you write will be placed and managed from. By default, Lift will look for a Boot class in the bootstrap.liftweb package within your application. In the package name that you supplied earlier on the command line, several sub-packages have been created with a sample HelloWorld.scala file for illustrative purposes.

Table 2.4   Directories created in the SBT project *(continued)*

Directory	Description
src/main/webapp	This directory holds all your XHTML markup files and any associated static resources you might want to use as part of your Lift application. The main difference between this setup and usual Java web applications is the templates-hidden directory. Lift has a very sophisticated templating system, and any markup files that are present in templates-hidden can only be used for templating and not for complete pages. More on this in chapter 6.

There is also the test folder, but as the name implies, it only contains testing materials. Testing is discussed in more detail in chapter 14.

The next section will show you how to take your stub application and run it and start playing with Lift itself.

2.2.3   *Booting the application*

Now that you're fully oriented with your first Lift application, let's get on with getting it running! Fortunately, SBT comes with a built-in Jetty web server (http://jetty.codehaus.org/jetty/) that you can use to run your application while you're developing it, so there's no need to go through the process of building a WAR and deploying to a standalone servlet container as you would do when your application goes to production.

Boot up your application with the following command at the SBT interactive shell:

```
> jetty
```

This will compile all your code before starting up a local Jetty server in the root of your project; you can then visit http://localhost:8080 in your browser to see the application running. Your application is fully functional and will operate exactly the same in this embedded Jetty server as it will in production, which is an invaluable development aid.

> **NOTE**   By default, SBT will attempt to start Jetty on port 8080, but in the event that you already have something running on that port, you can easily swap to an alternative port by overriding the jettyPort method in your SBT configuration: override def jettyPort = 9090.

With Jetty now running, you should be able to open a browser window and see something similar to figure 2.3.

In order to stop the Jetty server, press the Enter key to return to the SBT shell and stop Jetty outputting to the console. Then type this command:

```
> jetty-stop
```

Jetty will then stop what it's doing and shut down.

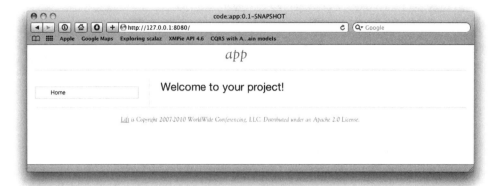

Figure 2.3   A screenshot of the browser window after you start the local development server running the basic Lift application

There are often times when you'll want to work on your project with the compiler running and giving you feedback on the code you're writing at that moment. There's a convenient command for this:

```
> ~compile
```

This will force the compiler into a mode called *continuous compilation*. With continuous compilation running, any files you save will automatically be recompiled. The ~ symbol can be prefixed to any SBT action, and the action will then attempt to do that task continuously.

Now let's look at the basics of snippets and get an overview of Lift's sophisticated templating mechanism.

> **Avoid restarting with JRebel**
>
> During your development cycle, it can be annoying to need to restart the Jetty server when you want to check the effect of some new changes, but, by default, this is the only way to test out the impact of your changes. That's where tools such as JRebel (http://www.zeroturnaround.com/jrebel/current/) can be extremely useful when used in conjunction with continuous compilation. JRebel lets you dynamically reload your altered classes, removing the need to restart Jetty yourself after each change.
>
> JRebel is a commercial tool, but they do kindly offer a free license for pure Scala development—all you need to do is apply online (http://sales.zeroturnaround.com/). After you do so, they'll send you a license that you can use when you're developing your Lift (or any other Scala-based) applications. Awesome!

2.3 *Snippets and templating overview*

Now you've seen the overall structure of a Lift application based upon the generated project, but you haven't yet looked at any Lift code, so you may be wondering exactly how this all hangs together and what the code looks like. Well, several different file groups were generated, but the two we'll look at here form the crux of any Lift application: snippets and templates.

2.3.1 *Snippets*

In chapter 1, we touched on the concept of snippets and mentioned how one of the key principals of the view-first pattern is having small, reusable pieces of rendering logic. Snippets are just functions that take template markup as their input and then transform it by executing the logic defined in that function to produce the desired markup.

Because snippets are just functions, they typically have an encapsulating class to contain them. The default project you generated doesn't have any snippet classes yet, but you can create a new one by giving SBT the following command:

```
>lift create snippet
```

This command will then prompt you to enter a name for the snippet class and ask you which package you would like it to be placed in. Answer these two prompts, and then Lifty will generate a new snippet class.

If you called the snippet class `HelloWorld`, the newly created file would have the definition displayed in the following listing.

Listing 2.2 Default `HelloWorld` snippet

```
package example.travel.snippet

import scala.xml.NodeSeq                               Import implicit
import net.liftweb.util.Helpers._              ◁┘      helpers

class HelloWorld {
  def render = "*" #> <strong>hello world!</strong>    ◁┐   Begin snippet
}                                                      ❶  definition
```

This is a simple Scala class featuring a single snippet method that defines what is known as a CSS transformer ❶. These CSS transformers are essentially functions of `NodeSeq => NodeSeq` and are supplied by importing the `Helpers._` object, which contains the right implicit conversions.

Scala referrers to XML as a `NodeSeq`; that is, a sequence of XML nodes. You can think of snippet methods as things that take in XML, transform it, and then yield an XML output. In listing 2.2, the `render` method will replace the snippet call site with the words *hello world* in bold. CSS transformers are discussed in depth in chapter 6, but just be aware that it's possible to use them to replace or transform the nodes you select with the computed dynamic values that feature in your snippet.

> ### Implicit conversions
>
> The `Helpers` object from Lift Utilities contains a whole set of functions that are somewhat special to the Scala compiler. The functions are known as *implicit conversions*, and what that essentially means is that given a function that knows how to turn type *A* into type *B*, the compiler will automatically apply that function at the right time. This allows you to build APIs that call seemingly nonexistent functions on particular types.
>
> In listing 2.2, `String` doesn't have a definition of `#>` but the compiler knows how to take a `String` and wrap it in such a way so that it's the right type to satisfy the call to `#>`.

Let's take this example a little further and illustrate exactly what the snippet method is doing. Consider the following markup:

```
<p lift="HelloWorld.render">Replace me</p>
```

This markup calls the `render` snippet on the `HelloWorld` class, so assuming this XML is passed into the `render` method from listing 2.2, the resulting markup would be as follows:

```
<strong>hello world!</strong>
```

The entire `<p />` node has been replaced with the `<strong />` node. Although this is a simple example, it's a very powerful concept, and it means that absolutely zero code makes it into your markup templates—they always remain fully valid XHTML files.

You may already be wondering how it is that these templates trigger the right snippet transformations. Well, Lift has several methods for resolving snippets to actual Scala code, but the one that we'll be focusing on for the moment is reflection-based lookup.

Lift can be very clever about the snippet markup so that it remains idiomatic no matter how you like to work or what your conventions are. Given the snippet in listing 2.2, any one of the following would be a valid snippet call in your template.

```
<div lift="HelloWorld.render">...</div>
<div class="l:HelloWorld.render">...</div>
<div class="lift:HelloWorld.render">...</div>
<lift:hello_world.render><p>Replace me</p></lift:hello_world.render>
<lift:HelloWorld.render><p>Replace me</p></lift:HelloWorld.render>
<lift:helloWorld.render><p>Replace me</p></lift:helloWorld.render>
<lift:snippet type="HelloWorld:render"><p>Replace me</p></lift:snippet>
```

Lift uses reflection and some basic name translation rules to look for the correct class, and then uses that to transform the input markup to the desired output markup, which is then piped back into the rendered output to the browser.

Although this fundamental concept of transforming XML is a simple one, it can be very powerful when you're building web applications, and Lift uses the same snippet mechanism for implementing many parts of its default infrastructure. A primary example of that would be Lift's templating support, which is built upon the very same snippet mechanism.

2.3.2 Templating overview

Templates in Lift are *always* fully valid XHTML or HTML5 markup. Lift doesn't let you write invalid markup. Even though templates are just XML without any executable code, templates have a lot more functionality than just being a place to invoke your own application snippets.

In the same way that Lift helps keep your server code cleanly separated, Lift offers some convenient helpers for your templates via some built-in snippets. These snippets let you modularize your template code and promote reuse of both markup and Scala code.

More often than not, your application will use either a single or small collection of top-level templates that contain the majority of the markup. Each page has a much smaller template that contains the static content and calls to whichever snippets are needed to provide the various dynamic items for the page. These smaller page fragments are wrapped with what is referred to as a *surround*, in order for them to *inherit* the full-page template. Surrounds can wrap other pieces of template markup to construct a hierarchical structure within the template so each page has only the minimum markup required to render the page.

The following listing is an example of a template that could have page content inserted by individual pages at the bind point called "content."

Listing 2.3 Example of a template surround

```
<html xmlns=http://www.w3.org/1999/xhtml
      xmlns:lift="http://liftweb.net/">
  <head>
    <title>demo:demo:1.0-SNAPSHOT</title>
  </head>
  <body>
    <lift:bind name="content" />          ❶ Binding point referenced
  </body>                                    by "content"
</html>
```

Listing 2.3 defines a binding point ❶ for specific page content to be injected into, and the handle with which you can reference it with later is content. That is to say, pages can declare surrounds that bind to content, and their markup will be replaced at that location. It's important to note that you can have as many binding points as you like in any given template, and not all the points have to be used in a given page rendering.

From the page-level perspective, each template (for example, index.html) can specify the surrounding template that it will be wrapped with. Importantly though, each child template can only have a single root element, because otherwise it would be an invalid XML document.

An example of using a surround in a page can be seen in the following markup:

```
<lift:surround with="default" at="content">
  <h2>Your content goes here</h2>
</lift:surround>
```

The purpose here is to wrap the <h2>...</h2> code (the particular page content) with the broader page template defined in templates-hidden/default.html. Together they make a full page, inclusive of content.

The surround snippet takes two parameters. The first is with, which defines the template to wrap the content with. In this case, "default" refers to the template located at src/main/webapp/templates-hidden/default.html. By default, your surround, or parent, templates need to be located in templates-hidden in order for Lift to actually find them. The second parameter is at, which defines the reference name of the binding point in the parent template. Essentially, you're telling Lift to take this content and insert it into the parent at a given location based on the <lift:bind /> element discussed in listing 2.3.

In addition to the functionality provided by surrounds, you might find you need to insert markup from another template while building your application, to avoid duplication of markup. For example, a form for adding a product to a system would be much like a form for editing that product in a different section of the system. Lift has this covered; here's an example of using template embedding:

```
<lift:embed what="/foo/_bar"/>
```

This call to <lift:embed> allows you to arbitrarily embed templates into one another so you don't have to worry about duplicating your presentation code. The what attribute parameter takes a path from the root of the webapp directory; in this case, it would include the content from the template in the src/main/webapp/foo/_bar.html file. This can be an extremely effective technique and can really assist you in not repeating yourself in the application markup.

Whether you're embedding or surrounding content, another common idiom that most applications require is to have page-specific items such as JavaScript and CSS elements in the <head> of a page. Lift has some nifty tooling for this. All you need to do is define the <head> element inside of a surround element, and Lift will automatically merge that content with the top <head> element. Consider this example:

```
<lift:surround with="default" at="content">
  <head>
    <script type="text/javascript"
            src="thing.js"></script>        ◁──┐  Demo JS
  </head>                                      ❶  file
  <h2>Whatever Page</h2>
  ...
</lift:surround>
```

In this code block, notice how the sample JavaScript file detailed at ❶ is enclosed in the <head /> element. When Lift runs this template, it will realize that the head element is present and merge its child nodes with the top-level head element so that all your page-specific resources sit where they should.

Alternatively, if you prefer to speed the page loading and place a file before the closing `<body>` tag, as is the current fashion, Lift also supports this via the `<lift:tail />` snippet. The functionality is the same as the head merge, but it instead places content just before the closing `</body>` tag.

These are a few of the out-of-the-box tools Lift supplies for working with dynamic content and page markup. There are a whole set of additional tools that are covered in chapter 6.

2.4 Summary

In this chapter, you built a basic, but fully functioning, Lift application with SBT. In addition, you've had a high-level overview of some of Lift's templating and snippet functionality. You should now have a good idea of how a Lift application is assembled and be aware of some of the high-level components that can be used to get it off the ground. These include the powerful concept of snippets that transform input XML to dynamically rendered output, and the way Lift assists you in keeping your template code concise and empowers you to not repeat yourself.

Importantly, though, you put in place the building blocks for the main application that you'll be building during the course of the book. In the next chapter, you'll enhance the application and start to design and implement some of the core functionality. This will take us deeper into Lift's snippet system, and you'll learn about database connectivity with Mapper.

Part 2

Application tutorial

Now that you're up to speed with the basics of working with Lift, we can pick up the pace and really delve into the framework, demonstrating some of the awesome features it has. In order to do that effectively, we're going to build on your new skills by creating a full-blown application for purchasing last-minute vacations.

In chapter 3, we'll outline the functionality of the tutorial application and we'll build the first stage of the administration site. This will include an introduction to Mapper, Lift's ORM implementation, so you can insert information into the database. We shall also be touching on CRUDify, Lift's super-slick scaffolding functionality.

Chapters 4 and 5 will show you how to implement Lift's highly integrated Comet and AJAX support to create a real-time bidding system and shopping cart, which will let users bid for last minute holiday deals and pay through PayPal.

The auction application

This chapter covers
- Auction application requirements
- Segmenting XHTML templates
- Defining data models and validation with Mapper
- Scaffolding with `CRUDify`

In order to firmly root your understanding of Lift in the real world, we'll create a full-blown auction application. This part of the book will walk you through the first part of building this application, which, among other things, includes a basic AJAX shopping cart, several real-time components, and a checkout via PayPal. As we go through each chapter, adding new elements of functionality, you'll learn about many of Lift's features.

The first two sections in this chapter present an overview of the application you'll be constructing. This includes a breakdown of the application's pages and their functionality, along with how you could integrate content supplied by a frontend design team into your Lift templates.

The last three sections deal with defining and constructing the data model using Lift's object-relational mapping (ORM) tool: Mapper. These sections also show how you can leverage some of the traits within Mapper to get up and running quickly via the Mapper scaffolding, including making a user-registration facility without writing too much boilerplate code. Finally, the last section touches on validation and demonstrates how you can add custom rules to your Mapper models.

3.1   Application requirements

Before starting to code any application, it's important to sketch out your requirements and have an idea of how you would like the page flow to operate in the completed product. Sure, things are bound to change during your development cycle, but it's likely that the overall aim won't have changed much. The auction application is no different in this respect, so let's take a moment to outline our aims and get a feel for what the finished product will be able to do.

The auction application aims to provide its users with auctions on travel. The suppliers will post travel offers into the system that users can then bid for in real time, which means they can see other users' bids as they happen. Upon winning a round of bidding, the trip is then entered into the user's shopping cart, and they can either continue to bid on other auctions or check out through PayPal. This is a fairly typical format for a lot of ecommerce applications.

3.1.1   Frontend

Let's walk through an outline of the application's page flow, as shown in figure 3.1. This will help us visualize the functionality and user experience before we start defining data models and so forth.

GLOBAL ELEMENTS

As visitors navigate through the site, we need to provide them with some common elements in order to keep the interface intuitive and easy to use.

The first common element will be the shopping basket. Each customer using the application will have an associated order that consists of auctions they successfully bid on; it's the usual shopping cart setup that most users will be familiar with. As users might already be in a bidding war but not actually be on the site when the auction is over, use of Lift's state machine to ensure that any auctions the users wins while the site isn't loaded in their browser will be properly attributed to them.

Every page will also include a dynamically generated navigation menu powered by Lift's SiteMap functionality. This might not sound like a particularly important thing to list at this stage, but all will become clear as you move through the book and delve deeper into the operation of SiteMap.

HOME PAGE

As with all good applications, the home page will give a flavor of what's happening on the site and give a short list of the most recent auctions posted by suppliers. Visitors can either click through to a specific auction or just move on to the main auction listing.

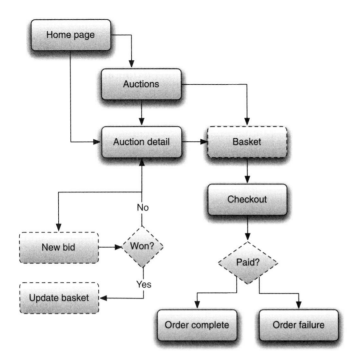

Figure 3.1 The application page flow. The items with dotted borders are asynchronous.

AUCTION DETAIL AND BIDDING

We finally reach the most substantive part of the application. The detail page is where item information is displayed, and it's where users can make bids on auctions.

The auction will have several components, but most importantly it will count down until its closing time in real time. Moreover, any bids that are submitted by other users while the current page is loaded will automatically be reflected in the open page, informing the user that they have been out-bid.

CHECKOUT

When a user has at least one successful auction in their shopping basket, they can check out to render payment to the travel company and complete the transaction. For the purposes of this example application, you'll be using the online payment provider PayPal to collect payment. Assuming the user successfully pays for their items, PayPal will call back to your application and use the out-of-the-box Lift integration for PayPal. You can wire up your own handlers to collect information about that transaction and detail the specifics of the purchases.

3.1.2 Administration

Any good application needs a content-management system from which the administrators can manage the day-to-day running of the site. We'll be building a small admin area that allows administrators to do the following:

- Log into the admin area using HTTP authentication.
- Add new suppliers to the system, including information about their services.
- Specify new auctions for a particular supplier. This is really the core of the system, and the administrator must supply information about the closing date of the offer, a detailed description of the auction, and potentially a picture that might entice users to bid on the auction.

Figure 3.2 outlines the administration structure as a tree.

Generally speaking, the administration side of this application will essentially be a create, read, update, delete (CRUD)-style data entry system. The only real exception to this is the order management, which will be customized rather than using Lift's CRUDify scaffold mechanism.

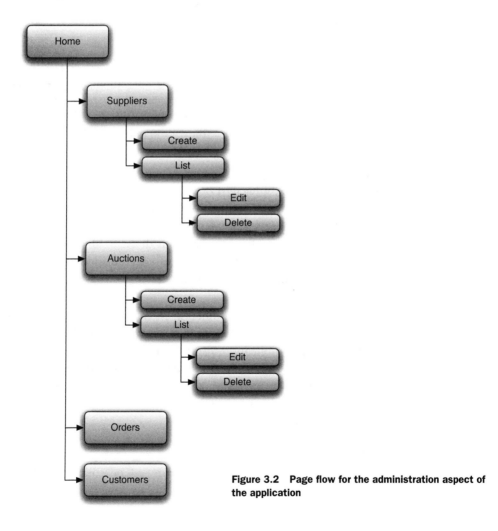

Figure 3.2   Page flow for the administration aspect of the application

Now that we've covered the broad-stroke requirements, we can begin to assemble the application. It's highly likely that real-world requirements will change during each iteration of development, but this outline should provide enough contextual information to get started with the first cycle. Lift aims to let you be as flexible as your business requirements need you to be.

3.2 Template structure

Most applications you build in the real world will require some creative input from a designer or user experience guru, and more often than not, the designers will come up with layouts that can be tricky for developers to implement. Lift can help you, by making it easy to not repeat yourself in markup code and to create complex template hierarchies.

3.2.1 Design workflow

Lift has a great set of features for dealing with the design workflow and letting you create highly modular code. We'll apply a design to the auction application and demonstrate how to use Lift's templating features in a real scenario.

Figure 3.3 displays the implemented design of this auction application. The design is relatively complex and very design-led, with several elements that will be common across multiple pages, such as the shopping basket and stylized frame that surrounds the page content.

Traditionally, designers have worked in an isolated workflow and have usually supplied everything to the developers. The developers then have to make any frontend changes themselves, or face the prospect of sending their templates back to the designers, complete with server-side code; more often than not, the designers unwittingly break critical application functionality while making design alterations.

Lift's templating is based on HTML, and no executable code can slip into the view at all. Instead, Lift developers have some new ways of interacting with designers. When working with Lift, you are always working with fully valid HTML templates, so when designers check their pages for validity, both the designers and developers can have confidence that nothing has inadvertently been broken. This approach can also lead to a more iterative creative process, compared to the "throw it over the wall" approach that's currently practiced by most dev shops.

3.2.2 Template setup

Upon receiving the design from the creative team, you can divide up the design into its component pieces so that the presentation code required for implementing each page is as minimal as possible. Figure 3.4 shows how the nesting and embedding relationships between the surrounding templates and the markup fragments work.

The top level surround is base.html, which carries all the top-level content that makes up a normal web page, such as the <head> element and other wrappers that don't change for each page.

Figure 3.3 The design of the index page for the auction application, as supplied by the designers

On the next level of nesting, we have three templates to choose from in our pages, depending on the content that needs to be displayed:

- default.html has the left sidebar and main body content column.
- wide.html has no left-hand sidebar, and the main content column spans the whole width.
- splash.html is used for pages that need space for a halo banner and two column layout.

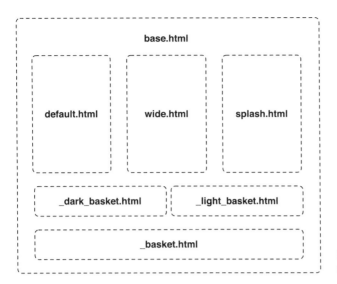

Figure 3.4 Template nesting relationships

In this application, spash.html is only used on the homepage, but it's completely feasible that in a full application you might need to reuse this layout elsewhere, so it deserves its own surround template.

Below the surround templates are the markup fragments that can be embedded in any page that requires them. The basket functionality is going to be the same no matter which wrapper it needs, so we have _basket.html containing the actual basket functionality that lists the won auctions, and then we have _dark_basket.html and _light_basket.html, which are slightly different designs around the same actions.

Before finishing with templating, it's important to note one of the key "gotchas" that most new Lift users encounter: new page templates resulting in 404 errors in the browser. Lift has a component called *SiteMap* that we briefly discussed in chapter 1, and which is fully explored in chapter 7. It's a very powerful feature for managing page access, and unless a page (something you want to be accessible by users) is defined in the SiteMap definition, Lift will yield a 404 Not Found error. Ergo, make sure you add *any* pages you define to your SiteMap, as shown in the next listing.

Listing 3.1 Example `SiteMap` entries

```
import net.liftweb.sitemap.{SiteMap,Menu}

val sitemap = List(
  Menu("Home") / "index",
  Menu("Auctions") / "auctions"
)
LiftRules.setSiteMap(SiteMap(sitemap:_*))
```

This code should be placed in the `Boot.boot` method in order to initialize and configure the SiteMap. Note that each page is given a title and then expresses the full the URL that resource uses. Do be aware that once you set up a SiteMap, you need to add all pages to it if you want them to be accessible. We'll discuss this further in chapter 7.

We've now covered the overall structure of the application and you've had a glimpse of the template setup and workflow. In the next section, we'll add the foundation for the data model with Mapper, which will eventually power all the rich components you'll be adding to this application.

3.3   *Data models*

In order for the application to actually do anything worthwhile, it needs to be able to persist and retrieve data. To that end, let's add some code to the project to connect to the database and build the tables that will power the auctions. We'll start by defining the models and generating the schema, and ultimately connect with the database to make queries and retrieve useful data.

Before getting into writing any Mapper code, be sure to add the dependency to your SBT project definition as shown:

```
val mapper = "net.liftweb" %% "lift-mapper" % liftVersion
```

Don't forget to run `reload` and `update` from the SBT shell in order to refresh the project dependencies.

3.3.1   *Schema definition*

For this auction application, we'll be implementing an Active Record pattern using the Mapper ORM that's included as part of Lift. Figure 3.5 shows an entity-relationship diagram (ERD) detailing the models you'll be building. You'll need to add more fields than are in this diagram as we continue, but this is a good starting point.

> **NOTE**   For more information on the Active Record architectural pattern, see the Wikipedia entry: http://en.wikipedia.org/wiki/Active_record_pattern.

This type of ERD should be familiar to most developers: it communicates the relationships the tables will have to each other. For instance, one auction has many bids. When working with Mapper, you define your model classes and let a special object called `Schemifier` know about the new model. Lift will then automatically create the tables in the database for you.

> **NOTE**   When working with the sample code, the first time you boot the application, it will automatically generate an appropriate data set for you to play around with. You don't have to worry about initial data entry.

The first thing you need to do is define the `Supplier` class and add it to the `Schemifier`. In chapter 2 you used the Lifty SBT helper to create a whole project structure from scratch, and this same helper can generate the Supplier model for you. Simply run the following command in the SBT shell:

```
> lift create mapper Supplier
```

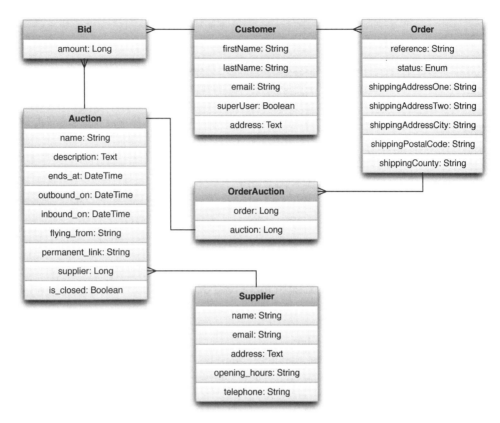

Figure 3.5 An entity-relationship diagram detailing the data flow you'll implement using Mapper

This one line of code will generate the Supplier.scala file. You can then add the fields as in the following completed `Supplier` model.

Listing 3.2 Supplier model definition

```
object Supplier extends Supplier with LongKeyedMetaMapper[Supplier]{
  override def dbTableName = "suppliers"
}

class Supplier extends LongKeyedMapper[Supplier]
    with IdPK
    with CreatedUpdated
    with OneToMany[Long, Supplier] {
  def getSingleton = Supplier
  object name extends MappedString(this, 150)
  object telephone extends MappedString(this, 30)
  object email extends MappedEmail(this, 200)
  object address extends MappedText(this)
  object openingHours extends MappedString(this, 255)
  object auctions extends MappedOneToMany(Auction, Auction.supplier,
    OrderBy(Auction.close_date, Descending))
```

```
    with Owned[Auction]
    with Cascade[Auction]
}
```

Mapper uses a *class and companion object* idiom so that all model objects have the ability to call static methods and instance methods. For example, you could call `Supplier.findAll` to get a list of all the suppliers in the database. This chapter only covers some of the things you need to get going with Mapper, and saves the detailed explanations for later on.

The definition in the following listing is somewhat daunting the first time you see it, but don't worry, it can be easily explained.

Listing 3.3   Class definition type composition

```
class Supplier extends LongKeyedMapper[Supplier]
  with IdPK
  with CreatedUpdated
  with OneToMany[Long, Supplier]
```

`LongKeyedMapper` is a special Mapper type that forms the basis of your model; it has an RDBMS underneath, and it will work with a table that has a `Long` as the primary key. Most applications use tables that have some kind of auto-incrementing primary key, so this should be fairly familiar.

Next, `IdPK` is a trait that tells Mapper to create a primary key column called id. This is a convenience trait for yet another common idiom when defining Mapper entities.

The `CreatedUpdated` trait automatically adds and manages two fields called `createdAt` and `updatedAt` to whichever Mapper classes it's composed with. This is a helpful idiom in most situations as it allows you to keep track of the insert and modification dates of any given table row.

Finally, the `OneToMany[Long,Supplier]` trait indicates that this model is related to another model type—in this case, the `Auction` type. Specifically, the `OneToMany` trait allows you to add a `MappedOneToMany` field to the model definition, which you'll hear about shortly. With the exception of defining relationships, all Mapper fields are defined something like this:

```
object name extends MappedString(this, 150)
```

This field definition represents the underlying Name column in the database. It extends `MappedString`, which is another Mapper type that knows how to operate with different text fields for different databases, such as `nvarchar` in SQL Server and `varchar` in MySQL. All the other field definitions extend some kind of `MappedField` type, which keeps your model definitions database agnostic.

In order to make this `Supplier` class fit into the ERD in figure 3.5, you need to relate it to the `Auction` class. This relationship is mapped to the usual foreign key setup under the hood and is implemented using `MappedOneToMany`. `MappedOneToMany` is a class in Mapper that takes the companion object you wish to connect to and the field you wish to be the foreign key on the target—in this case `Auction.supplier`. As you can also see from the following code snippet, we pass a `QueryParam` called `OrderBy`. It's obvious what this modifier does, but the interesting thing here is that you are also able to compose the `Owned` and `Cascade` traits into the `MappedOneToMany` for additional functionality.

This is the relationship definition to relate the `Supplier` class to the `Auction` class:

```
object auctions extends MappedOneToMany(Auction, Auction.supplier,
    OrderBy(Auction.ends_at, Descending))
      with Owned[Auction]
      with Cascade[Auction]
```

With the `Auction` class defined, we now need to let Lift know about it so that it can automatically create the table in the database when the application is booted up for the first time (when the tables don't already exist). This is done by invoking a special Mapper object known as `Schemifier`, which is done with the following line of code in the `Boot` class:

```
Schemifier.schemify(true, Schemifier.infoF _, Auction, Bid, Customer,
    Order, OrderAuction, Supplier)
```

Notice that the argument list includes some models that we haven't explicitly covered. Rather than cluttering these pages with lots of code definitions that are largely similar to the `Supplier` model, you can find the code for the other models in the online repository on github.com (http://github.com/timperrett/lift-in-action).

3.3.2 Connecting to the database

You may have noticed that we currently have code that compiles but won't actually do anything, because no database connection has been defined. Because Lift runs in any servlet container, you have several options for getting a database connection, just as you would in a traditional Java application. In this section, we'll only deal with a direct application connection to the database, but the other options are covered in full in chapter 10.

In order to make a direct application connection to the database you need to add three declarations to your application's `Boot` class and call some of the helpful Lift connection wrappers. The next listing shows an example of the code you'll need to implement to create the connection.

Listing 3.4 Boot configuration to connect to the database

```
import net.liftweb.mapper.{DB,DefaultConnectionIdentifier}
import net.liftweb.http.{LiftRules,S}

DB.defineConnectionManager(DefaultConnectionIdentifier, DBVendor)

LiftRules.unloadHooks.append(
  () => DBVendor.closeAllConnections_!())

S.addAround(DB.buildLoanWrapper)
```

For completeness, we have included the import statements so that it's clear where the various types are held. First, the call to `DB.defineConnectionManagger` creates the wiring between the application-specific `DBVendor` (defined in the next code snippet) and Lift's connection manager. The next two lines detail what Lift should do during the shutdown process in order to cleanly close any database connections. Finally, configure Lift's specialized loan wrapper so that database operations conducted on the `DefaultConnectionIdentifier` are transactional for the whole HTTP request cycle.

> **NOTE**   Lift's specialized loan wrapper makes use of the Scala Loan pattern. For an introduction to the loan pattern please see: http://jimplush.com/ blog/article/185/Loan-Shark—Using-the-Loan-Pattern-in-Scala

To complete the picture, consider the definition of `DBVendor`, which was specified as an argument to `DB.defineConnectionManager` in listing 3.4:

```
object DBVendor extends StandardDBVendor(
  Props.get("db.class").openOr("org.h2.Driver"),
  Props.get("db.url").openOr("jdbc:h2:database/chapter_3"),
  Props.get("db.user"),
  Props.get("db.pass"))
```

This object definition extends the `StandardDBVendor` trait from Lift's Mapper. `StandardDBVendor` provides the default behavior desired for database connections, such as connection pooling and connection reaping. This is a convenience setup so that pretty much everything is taken care of for you. This `DBVendor` pulls its connection string and credentials from a properties file unless the file and key pair don't exist, in which case it will failover to using the file-based H2 database.

3.4   *Scaffolding*

During the development cycle, having some form of scaffolding that can get you up and running can be extremely helpful. Your client will see quicker results, and you can spend time focusing on business logic rather than common idioms like user registration. There are two forms of scaffolding in Lift:

- Prototype traits for inheriting common functionality into your implementation
- `CRUDify` for generating CRUD-style interfaces for common use cases

These two options differ quite significantly, so we'll cover them separately.

3.4.1   *Prototype traits*

This type of scaffolding usually confuses newcomers to Lift. Rather than there being just one type of trait, the Prototype traits are a common idiom throughout the whole Lift framework, from `ProtoUser`, which handles user registration complete with signup forms and validation emails, right through to `ProtoStateMachine`, which gives you scaffolding for building complex state machines!

In our auction application, we want customers to register for our auction site so we know who's bidding on the deals offered by suppliers. That means we'll need to create customers, so let's take a look at `ProtoUser` and see how we can implement it in our `Customer` class.

If you remember earlier in this chapter, listing 3.2 defined the whole `Supplier` class and its companion (or meta) object. It was important to define the desired fields in the underlying table, but the `Customer` class we're going to implement with `ProtoUser` already knows about a selection of fields that are commonly implemented in user-orientated workflows. The following listing shows the `Customer` class implementing `ProtoUser`.

Listing 3.5   Full customer class

```
object Customer extends Customer
  with KeyedMetaMapper[Long, Customer]
  with MetaMegaProtoUser[Customer]{

  override def dbTableName = "customers"          ❶ Base location URI
  override val basePath = "account" :: Nil     ◁┘
  override def skipEmailValidation = true    ◁┐  Skip email
}                                            ❷  validation
class Customer extends ProtoUser[Customer] {
  def getSingleton = Customer
}
```

The basePath definition sets the URI at which the user actions will be available ❶. In this case, it will let users sign up at /account/sign_up. The method override for skip-EmailValidation tells `ProtoUser` that it doesn't need to validate the registered email address ❷. Listing 3.5 demonstrates that you don't need to define any additional fields in the `Customer` model because things like first name, last name, email, and so forth are all included as part of `ProtoUser`. Very handy!

The usefulness of `ProtoUser` doesn't stop there because `ProtoUser` subtypes can also wire themselves up to the application SiteMap, as shown in the next listing.

Listing 3.6   Wiring up `ProtoUser` types to SiteMap

```
val sitemap = List(
  Menu("Home") / "index",
  Menu("Search") / "search",
  Menu("History") / "history"
) ::: Customer.menus
```

This code takes the existing SiteMap and appends the menus defined by `Proto-User`. This will provide you with a nice Sign Up link on the navigation bar and allow access to the Sign Up, Login, and Logout pages you'll need for user control. `Proto-User` has a range of configuration options for its integrated SiteMap locations, and we encourage you to check the documentation and customize `ProtoUser` to meet your needs.

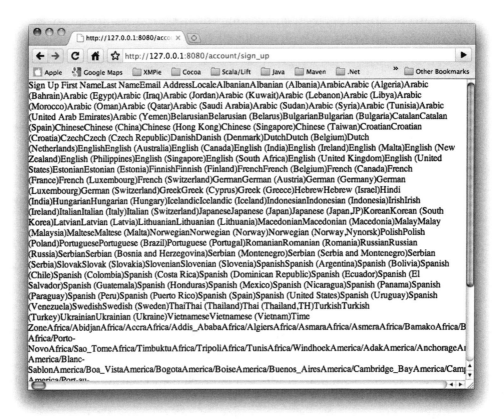

Figure 3.6   The `ProtoUser` configured with no template is unsightly. This is easily fixed by specifying your own template surround.

With `ProtoUser`, you get a fair amount of functionality with little coding, but this isn't quite the end of the story. If you were to boot up the application right now and click on the Sign Up link, you'd see a rather unsightly mess, similar to figure 3.6.

To make `ProtoUser` useable, you need to specify some rendering particulars so that the output of `ProtoUser` is skinned properly and fits in with your design. In the auction application, we have to override the `screenWrap` method in the `Customer` class. The following listing shows the overridden method you need to add to the `Customer` definition.

Listing 3.7   `ScreenWrap` addition to the `Customer` class

```
override def screenWrap: Box[Node] = Full(
  <lift:surround with="default" at="content">
    <div id="box1" class="topbg">
      <lift:msgs showAll="true" />
      <lift:bind />
    </div>
```

❶ **Boxed XML content**

```
      <lift:with-param name="sidebar">
        <lift:embed what="_light_basket" />
      </lift:with-param>
    </lift:surround>
)
```

Here we override the `screenWrap` method and define a boxed `scala.xml.Node`. `Box` types are covered in appendix C, so don't worry about what the call to `Full` is doing right now ❶. Just understand that it's essentially telling Lift that a template is present that it should use. In addition, this code is beginning to use some of the templating techniques discussed at the start of this chapter, but the only real difference is that here the templating is defined inline in the model rather than in a separate HTML template, which would be more typical in production Lift applications.

Template code in models? Are you crazy?

Template code in a model is something that newcomers find difficult to accept. Yes, that's indeed putting view code inside the model class in server code, not in a template. But it's critical that you understand that this isn't the primary pattern in Lift. Binding through snippets keeps a clean separation between view and logic, and we're putting this markup inline with our code for one reason: productivity.

The Proto-series traits are a starting point, not an ending solution. In many ways, they're similar to Rails' scaffolding: they boost productivity in the short term, but in the long term you'll outgrow them and gradually factor them out of your application, either by replacing with your own code or perhaps with code from some plugin or library.

Don't be scared when you see this approach—embrace it for what it is and continue with your application build at full steam.

With the `screenWrap` method in place, running `jetty-run` at the SBT prompt should now give you a very nice-looking form, similar to the one displayed in figure 3.7. It's fully functional and ready to accept new user registrations.

The signup form is now fully operational; once you register, Lift will log you in and redirect you to the home page of the application. The Sign Up link will also disappear from the SiteMap-powered menu at the top of the page.

3.4.2 CRUD generation

The second type of scaffolding in Lift is somewhat different from the Proto traits that we looked at previously. It's called `CRUDify` and it works by a simple composition on any Mapper class. As the name implies, it provides an interface that allows you to create, read, update, and delete records. In many ways, it's an extension to `ProtoUser`; it just provides more complete functionality.

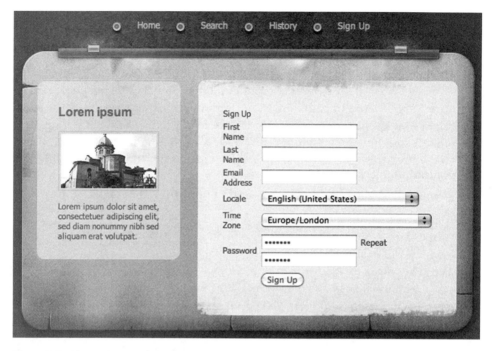

Figure 3.7   Sign-up form complete with surround

In our auction application, we want to have an administration part of the site where administrators can add suppliers, new auctions, and so forth. It needn't be fancy—we just want a quick and easy way to achieve this. Here, CRUDify is a perfect fit.

The original Supplier class defined back in listing 3.2 only needs a few modifications to its companion object in order to implement the CRUDify functionality. The next listing shows the modified Supplier class.

Listing 3.8   Supplier class including CRUDify

```
object Supplier extends Supplier
    with LongKeyedMetaMapper[Supplier]         ❶ Implement
    with CRUDify[Long,Supplier]{                  CRUDify

  override def dbTableName = "suppliers"
  override def pageWrapper(body: NodeSeq) =
    <lift:surround with="admin" at="content">{body}</lift:surround>
  override def calcPrefix =
    List("admin",_dbTableNameLC)
  override def displayName = "Supplier"          ❷ Configure
  override def showAllMenuLocParams =               CRUDify
    LocGroup("admin") :: Nil
  override def createMenuLocParams =
    LocGroup("admin") :: Nil
}
```

Implementing `CRUDify` is quite easy given an existing Mapper model. In this example, ❶ defines the composition of the `CRUDify[Key,Model]` trait by mixing it into the meta object using the `with` keyword. In order to have the `Supplier` class render `CRUDify` pages with the same theme, you need to instruct it on how to wrap the page content, as defined by the `pageWrapper` method, which will give the page the administration template rather than use the default frontend template.

Because you also want this CRUD feature to be accessible as part of the admin backend of the site, overriding `calcPrefix` lets you specify a context from which to generate the subordinate pages. Finally, when the `CRUDify` locations are hooked into the application SiteMap and rendered with the backend interface (which has a menu snippet that only loads items from the admin location group), it's important to let the `CRUDify` trait composed into `Supplier` know that these menu items will also be part of that group ❷.

With all this being said, the code in listing 3.8 currently doesn't *do* anything, because there's no way of accessing this great new functionality. In order to rectify this situation, you need to add some items to the SiteMap definition so that the `CRUDify` options appear in the administration menus. Moreover, it's important to differentiate between the public menu system and the administration menus, so you need to utilize a special `LocParam` class called `LocGroup`.

The new SiteMap definition is shown in the next listing.

Listing 3.9 SiteMap modifications for administration

```
val sitemap = List(
  Menu("Home") / "index" >> LocGroup("public"),
  Menu("Admin") / "admin" / "index" >> LocGroup("admin"),
  Menu("Suppliers") / "admin" / "suppliers" >> LocGroup("admin")
    submenus(Supplier.menus : _*),
) ::: Customer.menus
```

Note that the primary change to the SiteMap has been the addition of a special location parameter, or `LocParam`, to the menu items that identifies each page location as being part of a logical group. For example, the Home location is part of the public group, whereas the administration pages are part of the admin group. These `LocGroups` allow you to select groups of menus in different areas of the application from the individual pages as needed.

Finally, much like you previously added the `Customer` menus from `ProtoUser`, `CRUDify` can also wire itself into SiteMap. Because the `Supplier` menus need to be subordinate to the top-level supplier menu structure, you can simply call the `submenus` method and pass the list of menus from the built-in `CRUDify` trait composed into `Supplier`.

Figure 3.8 shows a screenshot of the admin interface. It includes some very simple CSS so it isn't quite as visually plain, but nothing fundamental has been changed other than the styling. You can see the `CRUDify` menus featured in the top navigation bar. Also note that only `admin` locations are displayed.

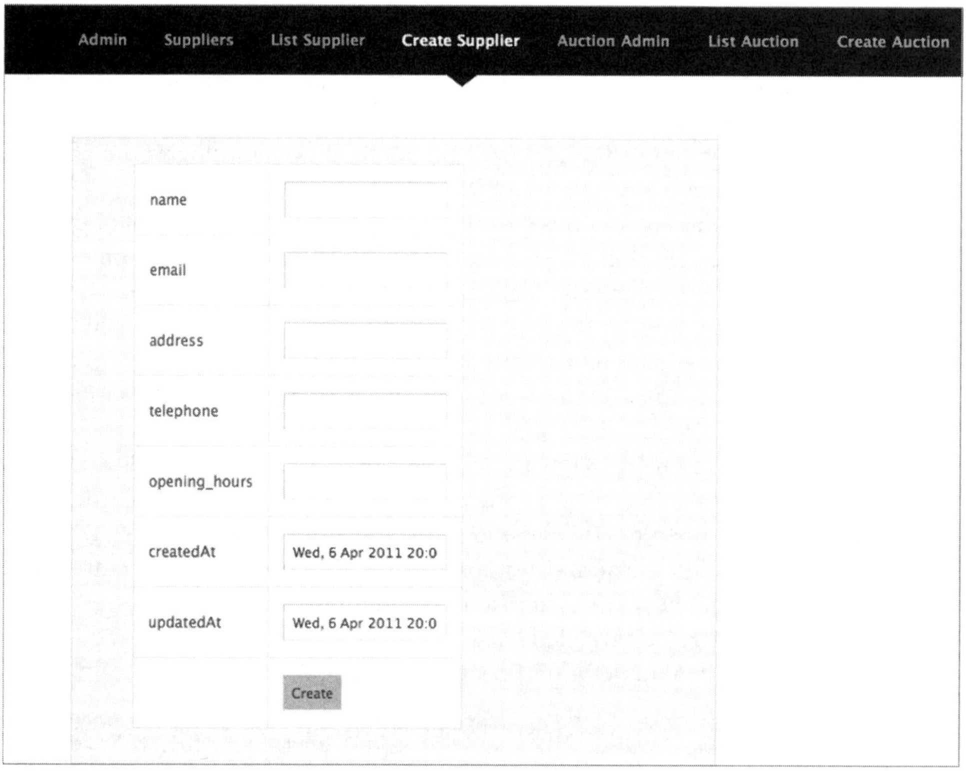

Figure 3.8   Screenshot of the administration interface with the additional CSS styling. Clean but funotional.

These special menu groups are invoked from within the template using the built-in Menu snippet. The following example shows the administration implementation, which only shows items that are part of the admin location group.

```
<lift:menu.builder group="admin" linkToSelf="true" li_item:id="current" />
```

The other options available are discussed in detail in chapter 7.

The implementations for the other aspects of our system are exactly the same: compose the CRUDify trait into your Mapper class (ensuring you have the correct overrides in place on the meta object), and then just add those menus to the SiteMap.

RELATIONSHIP INTERFACES

CRUDify can create a pretty full-featured interface right out of the box, but there are situations where it makes sense to customize forms and relationships so that you can make CRUDify construct inputs for one-to-many and other relationships. For example, in this application, an Auction belongs to a Supplier, so you might want to provide a way for administrators to select which Supplier is hosting this auction.

In order to create a drop-down list, you need to override a special method on the relationship field in the Auction class. The following listing shows the Auction class complete with Supplier relationship modification.

Listing 3.10 Providing a drop-down menu for the auction/supplier relationship

```
class Auction extends LongKeyedMapper[Auction]
    with IdPK with CreatedUpdated {
  def getSingleton = Auction
  object name extends MappedString(this, 150)
  object description extends MappedText(this)
  object endsAt extends MappedDateTime(this)
  object outboundOn extends MappedDateTime(this)
  object inboundOn extends MappedDateTime(this)
  object flyingFrom extends MappedString(this, 100)
  object isClosed extends MappedBoolean(this)
  object startingAmount extends MappedDouble(this)
  object supplier extends LongMappedMapper(this, Supplier){
  override def dbColumnName = "supplier_id"
  override def validSelectValues = Full(Supplier.findMap(          ❶ Override
    OrderBy(Supplier.name, Ascending)){                               method
      case s: Supplier => Full(s.id.is ->s.name.is)
    })
  }
}
}
```

By overriding the validSelectValues method ❶ on the foreign key in the Auction class, the CRUDify trait can determine which values you want the user to be able to select from when it generates the admin interface.

You'll learn more about making queries with Mapper classes in chapter 10, so for now just know that the query returns a list of Supplier objects and maps them onto key/value pairs to display in a HTML select dropdown. So now when you go to create a new Auction in the admin interface, you can just select from the suppliers you have defined in your database. The primary purpose of such a control is so that the user can choose a sensible value for the supplier and doesn't need to guess at a number or enter something invalid.

This brings us nicely to the topic of validation. The next section discusses how you can implement validation in Mapper.

3.5   *Validation*

Validation is something that all applications need in one form or another, and this auction application is no different. You need suppliers to have names and descriptions, and auctions need to have starting bids greater than 0. These are just a couple of things you'd want to validate in the application logic. Fortunately, Lift has a heap of helpers for such common scenarios, and we're going to apply a few of them to the existing model classes before continuing to build out other sections of functionality.

The following sections cover the definition of validation rules, including how you can create your own custom rules and how validation messages are displayed back to the user.

3.5.1   *Definitions*

Validations in Mapper are defined at field level; that is, they're defined on things like `MappedString` and `MappedBoolean`, which were covered in section 3.1. Out of the box, Mapper supports common validation requirements, such as text length, matching regular expressions, and checking for uniqueness.

In the `Auction` class, it's important to make sure that the `permanentLink` field isn't blank. Here's an example of this validator in action:

```
object permanent_link extends MappedString(this, 150){
 override def validations =
  valMinLen(3, "Link URL must be at least 5 characters") _ ::
  super.validations
}
```

Field validations are essentially a list of partial functions that take a particular field type and return a list of errors. If there are no errors, the list will be `Nil`. The cons operator (`::`) is used here to create the list of validations, so if you wanted to add another validation, you could do so very simply by adding another line to the list of validation rules:

```
object permanent_link extends MappedString(this, 150){
 override def validations =
  valMinLen(3, "Link URL must be at least 5 characters") _ ::
  valUnique("That link URL has already been taken") _ ::
  super.validations
}
```

The idiom of validation is pretty much the same for all the `MappedField` derivatives, no matter what the type. There are some specializations worth mentioning, such as `MappedEmail`, which includes automatic validation of email addresses, and `Mapped-PostalCode`, which can perform automatic checks on the format of addresses for popular countries, such as the UK, USA, and a selection of other nations.

3.5.2   *Displaying field errors*

Validations really wouldn't be that useful if we didn't have any way to display them, right? Fortunately, Lift provides a nice API for this purpose that Mapper hooks into, and Lift has built-in snippets to display these errors in your template markup; namely the `Msgs` snippet, which can be used like this:

```
<lift:msgs showAll="true" />
```

Using the `Msgs` snippet couldn't be easier—any notices that are posted from Mapper will be displayed in your markup with the messages you specified in your model.

For the moment, just add this line of markup to the admin.html template in the src/main/webapp/templates-hidden directory so that any errors are displayed in a table wherever you elect to put this line of markup. Lift also supports the display of notices with a specific ID so that you can refine how and where specific messages are displayed to a user. That's covered in chapter 6.

3.6 *Summary*

The application is starting to take shape. In this chapter, we've covered what it takes to create an application that has a basic but functional administration interface and a rather fetching frontend. OK, so the frontend is a little light on functionality right now, but we've covered some of the core working practices of Lift development, including the options available to you when working with designers, how to separate your templates into reusable sections, and Lift's scaffolding mechanisms for boosting development productivity. We also covered Mapper, the default ORM system in Lift, and showed you how to define your models, create database tables, and establish inter-model relationships.

In the next chapter, you'll be adding the bulk of the functionality to the frontend of the auction application: listing available auctions, building the bidding interface, and setting up push notifications. You'll also be learning about Lift's awesome Comet support, which you'll use to implement some of these features, as well as its unified and secure AJAX support.

Customers, auctions, and bidding

This chapter covers

- Binding queries from snippets
- Implementing Comet
- Bidding via AJAX

Now that you have the base of the application in place, the next thing to do is construct the frontend so that visiting customers can browse through the auction catalog and access details on any particular auction. By its very nature, an auction is a highly spontaneous affair, so it's critical to get real-time feedback when other customers bid on the same auction as you, particularly if they placed a higher bid!

These updates will be delivered via Lift's sophisticated Comet mechanism, so if a competing customer places a higher bid, all the other users viewing that auction will receive a notification telling them about this new bid and inviting them to place another bid. The bidding itself will be passed to the server using Lift's built-in AJAX support, so you'll be able to see the interplay between snippets, AJAX, and Comet, all in a single user interface.

We'll be building on chapter 3's CRUD interface assembled with the CRUDify traits and adding custom snippets, and we'll also be covering a range of new topics, including automatic list pagination.

4.1   Building an auction catalog

So far, you've added a very basic CRUD interface in the administration area so administrators can add auctions to the system, but there is currently no way for users to see those auctions and interact with them. This is problematic because without some kind of display, no one will be able to bid on the auctions! To address this, you'll build a catalog of auctions with a new snippet and the existing Mapper models from chapter 3.

4.1.1   Listing auctions

In order to list the auctions that still have time remaining, you need to assemble a query using the Mapper models and then render that list of items using a snippet. For this example, we called our snippet `Listings`, but you may call yours whatever you prefer.

If you remember from figure 3.3 in the previous chapter, space was left on the homepage to display the latest three auctions and provide a link to see the full list of auctions on the system. This functionality will be powered by another snippet that demonstrates how to use the `Auction` model to get a list of all the auctions. This is the code to get the top three rows:

```
Auction.findAll(MaxRows(3), OrderBy(Auction.id, Descending))
```

This should be fairly self-explanatory given the Mapper API naming convention, but to be clear, this code returns a `List[Auction]` that can then be used in the snippet to iterate through and create the corresponding markup. As discussed in part 1 of this book, snippets are essentially just `NodeSeq => NodeSeq` functions, so imagine the function input here to be the markup from the HTML template that defines the display for each auction item on the homepage. The logic in the snippet then iterates through the resulting list of auctions from the database and binds the dynamic content to the respective element from the template.

The next listing shows what the `Listings` snippet should look like.

Listing 4.1   First version of the `Listings` snippet definition

```
import net.liftweb.util.Helpers._
import net.liftweb.mapper._
import net.liftweb.textile.TextileParser

class Listings {
  def top = {
    val auctions = Auction.findAll(By(           ❶ DB query
      Auction.isClosed, false),
      MaxRows(3), OrderBy(Auction.id, Descending))
    ".auction_row *" #> auctions.map { auction =>
      ".name *" #> auction.name &             ❷ CSS-style
      ".desc" #> TextileParser.toHtml(             transformers
        auction.description) &
      "a [href]" #> "/auction/%s".format(
        auction.id.toString)
    }
  }
}
```

You can see that this snippet takes the list of auctions received by the query ❶, and by calling map on the resulting List[Auction] iterates through, binding the various fields of the Auction instance to HTML nodes within the template. In addition, notice that the enclosing selector is marked as ".auction_row *", which tells Lift that it needs to replace the subordinate elements with nested transformation statements ❷. Specifically, these bindings, or transformation statements, attach a bit of dynamic content to an element in the HTML template by choosing it with these CSS-style selectors. The auction name and description are both bound to elements by their class attribute, whereas the link to the auction details page is bound to an anchor element's href attribute. Finally, the description is processed as Textile markup using Lift's Textile support, so this gives the administrator a good level of control over how the content is rendered while still being safe and secure.

If you're struggling to visualize how this pairs with the template, consider the markup being used to call this snippet:

```
<div class="auction_row" lift="listings.top">
  <img src="images/homepage09.jpg" alt="" class="left" />
  <p>
    <strong class="name">NAME</strong> (<a href="#">learn more...</a>)
    <br /><span class="desc">Description</span>
  </p>
</div>
```

Notice how the markup is just plain HTML, and the only Lift-specific part is the Lift attribute placed on the opening <div> tag. If you compare this markup with the snippet definition, you should be able to see how the input => output transformation takes place. CSS selectors are pretty powerful tools for selecting and binding dynamic content to your templates; if you want a more in-depth introduction, there's a full explanation in chapter 6 (section 6.1.2).

Although the code in listing 4.1 is valid and will work just fine, you find yourself about to add another method to list all the auctions in the system and bind that to a similar-looking list. Being a good developer, you don't want to duplicate things at all, so you can refactor the code into a helpful method that will allow you to reuse the binding for rendering single auctions. The following listing shows the refactored snippet class with the additional method.

Listing 4.2 The Listings snippet definition with refactored display methods

```
import net.liftweb.util.Helpers._
import net.liftweb.mapper._
import net.liftweb.textile.TextileParser

class Listings {

  def top =
    ".auction_row *" #> many(Auction.findAll(
      By(Auction.isClosed, false),
      MaxRows(3),
      OrderBy(Auction.id, Descending)))
```

```
    private def many(auctions: List[Auction]) =
      auctions.map(a => single(a))

    private def single(auction: Auction) =
      ".name *" #> auction.name &
      ".desc" #> TextileParser.toHtml(
        auction.description) &
      "#winning_customer *" #> winningCustomer(auction) &
      "#travel_dates" #> auction.travelDates &
      "a [href]" #> "/auction/%s".format(
        auction.id.toString)
}
```

① **Bind auction list**

② **Bind single auction**

In this listing, the binding function has been placed into a private utility method called `many`, which handles the element binding for a list of auctions. By doing this, each snippet method only has to worry about the individual auction list it's going to generate, and the standard binding will automatically be taken care of by passing that list of auctions to the `many` binding method.

Moreover, this listing also abstracts the rendering of default things that other methods might want to bind into a method called `single`. This method can be reused elsewhere or can be composed together with other functions that need to bind elements other than those defined in the `single` method. This is achieved by calling the special `&` operator after calling `single`; this essentially composes the additional bindings with those specified in `single` and keeps the code as clutter free as possible.

> **NOTE** The approach taken here is a baby step in reusing code. Our purpose is to illustrate that you can quite simply externalize common pieces of functionality. In a production system, the binding would more likely be an implicit type class applied by the compiler,[1] but we've taken this approach so that the examples appear less like magic and are more understandable for Scala newcomers.

In addition to the list of top auctions on the homepage, you'll also need a mechanism for displaying all the auctions available, but as this could be a fairly long list, having a way to paginate the results is quite important. To achieve this, you can implement Lift's `MapperPaginatorSnippet` class, which will automatically manage the creation of page links and querying with the right row offset. The following listing shows the modifications you need to make to the `Listings` snippet to use the pagination functionality.

Listing 4.3 Listings snippet definition with pagination

```
import net.liftweb._,
  util.Helpers._,
  http.DispatchSnippet,
  mapper.{MaxRows,By,OrderBy,Descending,StartAt},
```

---

[1] For more about binding with type classes, see the "Using Type Classes for Lift Snippet Binding" entry in my blog, *The Loop*: http://blog.getintheloop.eu/2011/04/11/using-type-classes-for-lift-snippet-binding/

```
   mapper.view.MapperPaginatorSnippet
import example.travel.model.Auction
import example.travel.lib.AuctionHelpers

class Listings extends DispatchSnippet                    ❶ Extend
    with AuctionHelpers {                                     DispatchSnippet trait
  override def dispatch = {
    case "all" => all                                     ❷ Delegate dispatch
    case "top" => top                                        methods
    case "paginate" => paginator.paginate _
  }

  private val paginator =
      new MapperPaginatorSnippet(Auction){               ❸ Display 5
    override def itemsPerPage = 5                             records per page
  }

  def all = "li *" #> many(paginator.page)               ◁┐ Bind list of
                                                         ❹  auctions
  def top = ...
}

trait AuctionHelpers {                                    ◁┐ Move common
  protected def many(auctions: List[Auction]) = ...      ❺  methods into trait
  protected def single(auction: Auction) = ...
}
```

The first thing to note in this code is the addition of a supertype called `Dispatch-Snippet`, which allows you to be very specific about snippet method dispatching ❶. By overriding the `dispatch` method, you can define which method name in the template maps to the appropriate snippet function ❷. This can be particularly helpful if you only want to expose certain methods to the designers but still need them to be public in your application classes. Also notice that the common rendering methods have been factored out into a Scala trait called `AuctionHelpers` ❺ so that they can be reused in other parts of the application where auction information needs to be displayed, such as in the bidding interface you'll create shortly.

The primary change in this listing is the addition of a specialized version of Lift's `Paginator` that knows how to deal with Mapper instances: `MapperPaginator-Snippet` ❸. This class takes two arguments to determine the types of Mapper classes it needs to query. Using this built-in pagination functionality can save a lot of boilerplate in your application, because all you need to do is grab the current page's items from the paginator ❹ and add the relevant controls in the template markup to enable pagination links.

The following listing demonstrates this markup. Of particular interest should be the page control nodes toward the end of the listing.

Listing 4.4   Markup for auction listing including pagination

```
<lift:surround with="wide" at="content">
  <h1>Actions</h1>                                        ❶ Invoke Listings
  <ol class="auctions" lift="listings.all">              ◁┘   snippet
    <li class="top">
```

```
    ...
    </li>
  </ol>

  <div lift="listings.paginate">
    <p><nav:records/></p>
      <nav:first /> |
      <nav:prev/> |
      <nav:allpages> | </nav:allpages> |
      <nav:next/> |
      <nav:last />
  </div>
</lift:surround>
```

| Start pagination controls

| Separate pagination links with pipe

When this page is called, the page content will be displayed with a list of auctions supplied by the call to the listings.all snippet function ❶, followed by a list of pages at the bottom of the screen. Figure 4.1 illustrates the output of this snippet markup.

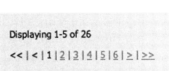

Figure 4.1   Example output of the pagination support

It's important to note that even though the Paginator is a built-in snippet, you could quite easily move the view around without impacting the snippet at all.

4.1.2   Adding to SiteMap

Remember that as you add pages and functionality to your application, you also need to update SiteMap where applicable. Entries need to be added for both the full auction list and the auction details.

The SiteMap definition should now look like the next listing.

Listing 4.5   Complete SiteMap definition

```
val sitemap = List(
  Menu("Home") / "index" >> LocGroup("public"),
  Menu("Auctions") / "auctions" >> LocGroup("public"),
  Menu("Auction Detail") / "auction"
    >> LocGroup("public") >> Hidden,
  Menu("Admin") / "admin" / "index" >> LocGroup("admin"),
  Menu("Suppliers") / "admin" / "suppliers"
    >> LocGroup("admin") submenus(Supplier.menus : _*),
  Menu("Auction Admin") / "admin" / "auctions"
    >> LocGroup("admin") submenus(Auction.menus : _*)
) ::: Customer.menus
```

❶ Exclude from main menu

The interesting part here is the use of a special LocParam called Hidden ❶. The name is fairly self-explanatory and is needed so that the page intended to display a specific auction's detailed information isn't listed in its own right on the main menu, as we only ever want people to visit that page using the fully qualified (rewritten) URL that we'll be defining in the next section.

4.2   *Displaying auctions*

Now we're coming to the really interesting part of the application: displaying auctions and allowing customers to bid on them. In order to display auctions, we'll be touching on several Lift features:

- The rewriting mechanism for providing friendly URLs
- Built-in AJAX support
- JavaScript abstraction
- Comet support

You might have noticed that when you click the link in the auction lists, you see the 404 page. This is because Lift doesn't know what to do with the /auction/1234 URL. Unsurprisingly, no template exists for each of the auctions, so to map this URL pattern to a known template, you need to implement Lift's rewriting mechanism. Rewriting is helpful for a variety of tasks, but it comes in particularly useful when prettifying dynamic URLs.

4.2.1   *Auction detail URLs*

In the booking application, each auction will have a URL based on the ID defined for that row in the database. The URL could be anything you want, but in this case we'll just use the ID column to ensure that the URL is unique. This will give you URLs that look like this:

/auction/12345

To implement this, you need to add the following code to your Boot.scala file as you would do for any other aspect of application configuration:

```
LiftRules.statelessRewrite.append {
  case RewriteRequest(ParsePath("auction" :: key :: Nil,"",true,_),_,_) =>
      RewriteResponse("auction" :: Nil, Map("id" -> key))
}
```

There's quite a lot going on in this short snippet of code, and it might look pretty daunting the first time you see it. Not to worry, though—it's really not that difficult. Let's take a moment to break out some component parts, starting with the RewriteRequest.

The RewriteRequest object is looking for three parameters:

- A matching URI, as determined by the special ParsePath Lift class. This gives you very tight control over the URL, from high-level things like the path, right down to whether or not it has a trailing slash.
- The type of incoming request to match on. You can be specific as to what types of requests should be rewritten: GET, POST, or any other method the HTTP protocol provides.
- The HTTPRequest instance that represents the incoming request. This can be used when you want to extract information from the request that the default matchers don't allow for.

You've probably noticed that this code snippet uses a lot of underscores in place of defining actual parameters. This is a somewhat confusing Scala syntax for newcomers, but in this context it essentially means "any value is fine." You'll see this kind of usage throughout Lift's API and more broadly in idiomatic Scala code.

With this rewrite rule in place, you have the ability to pass a specific auction ID wherever you please, so let's create a snippet that renders the detail view for an `Auction`. This implementation will use another snippet specialization trait in Lift called `StatefulSnippet`. The reason you might want to use a stateful snippet in this scenario is because there will be several things going on in this page view, from Comet through to AJAX, and they all need to interact with the same instance of `Auction`. Without using a `StatefulSnippet`, you would otherwise need to pass around an ID and keep loading the `Auction` from the database, which would have fairly severe performance ramifications and add a degree of accidental complexity and overhead that you can quite easily avoid. By using `StatefulSnippets`, you can keep a single instance of `Auction` around longer than the initial request, allowing access to it from wherever it's needed. `StatefulSnippet` functionality is covered in full in chapter 6 (section 6.1.2), but the key thing to understand here is that `StatefulSnippet` instances are kept around in memory longer than the lifetime of a single request but they're otherwise the same as regular snippets in terms of usage. That is to say that you don't need to do anything very different when it comes to invoking the snippet—the only change is a minor one in the definition itself.

In order to implement the `StatefulSnippet` trait, create another snippet that will present the individual auction. We named this new snippet `Details` and provisioned a couple of methods in the `dispatch` method. Here's a stub implementation with some placeholder method bodies:

```
import net.liftweb.util.Helpers._
import net.liftweb.http.StatefulSnippet

class Details extends StatefulSnippet with AuctionHelpers {
  override def dispatch = {
    case "show" => show
    case "bid" => bid
  }
  def show = "*" #> Text("Not implemented")
  def bid = "*" #> Text("Not implemented")
}
```

Right now there's nothing here that really requires a stateful lifecycle versus regular stateless snippets, but you'll only want to keep a single `Auction` instance around and access that from several snippet locations. This means its necessary to retain the `Auction` instance.

To retain the `Auction` instance after the initial loading it's simply a matter of adding a `val` property to the class that grabs the specific auction from the database based on the key in the URL. The `StatefulSnippet` then takes care of retaining that value for later use; from the API perspective, it's just an immutable property of the class. The next listing shows a slightly more fleshed-out `Details` snippet that makes use of these new stateful abilities.

Listing 4.6   Defining stateful instances in the `Details` snippet

```
import net.liftweb.http.StatefulSnippet

class Details extends StatefulSnippet with AuctionHelpers {
  ...
  val auction = Auction.find(                            ❶ Auction
    By(Auction.id,S.param("id").map(                        query
    _.toLong).openOr(0L)))

  def show = auction.map {
    single(_) &                                          ❷ Element
    "#current_amount" #>                                    binding
      <span>{leadingBid.toString}</span> &
    "#next_amount" #> <span>{minimumBid.toString}</span>
  } openOr("*" #> "That auction does not exist.")
  ...
}
```

If you're wondering why this looks like normal Scala code with no magic beans or such, that's because it's just that—plain Scala code! The interesting thing here is that the whole instance is kept around in a special state called `RequestVar[T]`, so the next time a snippet method is invoked (from AJAX, for example) the exact same auction value (as set at ❶) is reused, and the subsequent invocation has access to every property and function, just like the first invocation did.

This can have some very powerful uses in application development. Here we'll be using it so that each subsequent bid the user makes is attached to the correct auction. Interestingly, notice how `show` only binds the extra items needed for this specific snippet by *composing* the `single` method that was created earlier and inherited through the `AuctionHelpers` trait ❷. The call to `single(_)` yields a specialized CSS selector function, which can be composed together with other `CssSel` functions by way of the `&` operator. The net effect is that all the elements are bound to placeholders without the need to repeat the binding.

4.2.2   *The AJAX bidding interface*

The application can now list and display auctions, but there is no facility for customers to place bids. This needs fixing. We're going to implement a fairly simple bidding interface and touch on Lift's AJAX support during the process. But first, we need to modify the `Auction` class.

MODIFYING THE AUCTION CLASS

Before we start building the interface, we need to modify the `Auction` class and add some helper methods for common operations, such as finding the highest current bid, determining the minimum next required amount, and placing a bid on an auction.

Listing 4.7 shows three methods that assist in the calculation of auction values.

Listing 4.7   Auction value methods

```
class Auction extends LongKeyedMapper[Auction]
     with IdPK with CreatedUpdated {
  ...
  private def topBid: Box[Bid] = bids match {
    case List(first, _*) => Full(first)
    case _ => Empty
  }
  def currentAmount: Box[Double] = topBid.map(_.amount.is)
  def nextAmount: Box[Double] = currentAmount.map(_ + 1D)
  ...
}
```

The topBid method uses the bids relationship defined in chapter 3 to check whether there are any bids placed against this auction. There's a key thing to note here before we progress further: the return type of the topBid method is Box[Bid].

Box is a monadic type that exists in the Lift Common package, and it's an excellent way to work around programming to null, which is the typical idiom in imperative programming, such as Java, where the code is full of if statements checking for null or "". Understanding Box[T] isn't that difficult, and there's a great value in taking the time to do so. Box types and what they can do are explained in appendix C.

For now, just understand that boxes allow you to contain types in such a way that you can statically check for missing values and gracefully handle runtime exceptions that might occur by using the Box states listed in table 4.1.

Table 4.1   Possible states of the Box[T] data type

Subtype name	Description
Full	If you think of a physical box, when you place items in the box it becomes full, hence the name. Boxes that have a value are of type Full.
Empty	This is the opposite of Full—boxes that are empty.
Failure	This is a special type that's used to express and contain errors. For instance, if you try to convert a string to an int, Scala will throw an exception at runtime, and this can have some hazardous side effects. Wrapping the type in a Box lets you programmatically check for errors and chain errors together using Failure. We won't go into the details here; just understand that Failure wraps errors and provides a safe way of handling unexpected things during program execution.

The next method, currentAmount, builds on the topBid method and provides a helper to get the top bid if one exists. If no bids have been made on this auction, then the method will return 0. The nextAmount method is another helper that requires the next bid to be exactly one more than the current highest bid. In real terms, this perhaps isn't the most robust system, but it's adequate for the purpose of this tutorial.

We still have no way for people to bid on auctions, so let's add a helper method called `barter` that handles the process of creating a new bid in the database and runs some commonsense checks on the input, as shown in the next listing.

Listing 4.8   The `barter` helper method

```
def barter(next: Box[String]): Box[Bid] = for {
  ann <- next ?~! "Amount is not a number"
  amo <- tryo(BigDecimal(ann).doubleValue) ?~! "Amount is not a number"
  vld <- tryo(amo).filter(_ >= (nextAmount openOr 0D))
    ?~ "Your bid is lower than required!"
  } yield Bid.create.auction(this)
    .customer(Customer.currentUser).amount(vld).saveMe
```

This listing defines what is likely the most complex Scala code covered so far, so let's take a moment to review some of the more alien-looking symbols in the listing.

The first line uses the Scala keyword `for`. This is a Scala language feature and not like the imperative `for` loop you've likely seen before. This structure is covered in more detail in appendix A, but in broad terms it extracts the items on the right side of the arrow and projects them to the value on the left, which can be used without its containing type. For example, `Box[Double]` on the right is projected to `Double` on the left.

The next line uses a rather odd looking piece of syntax: `?~!`. This is a method on the `Box` class that, in the event of the parameter `next` being `Empty` will convert that `Empty` value into a `Failure` with the message `"Amount is not a number."` This is very helpful; rather than getting some zero-length error, or `NullPointerException`, we can expect the code to behave in a very predictable and manageable way in the event of something unexpected.

In the next few lines, we have two examples of one of Lift's built-in helper methods from `net.liftweb.util.Helpers`. It's called `tryo` and can be used instead of the `try { ... } catch { ... }` block that most imperative programmers will be familiar with. The difference here is that rather than returning exceptions or arbitrary values, it will always return one of the `Box` subtypes. In listing 4.8, we ensure that the value is a number and that it can be converted to a double. If someone passes a string or other value that would cause this to explode in an exception, `tryo` will catch it and convert it to a `Failure` with the specified message. This can be rather helpful in a large variety of situations.

Finally, the last couple of lines define a new `Bid` instance with the appropriate values extracted from the `for` comprehension. The previous section added code to the SiteMap that would mean only customers who were logged in could use this page, so it's completely safe to use `Customer.currentUser` to get the current customer instance to reference from this new bid—you know that they will always be logged in at this point.

ADDING A BIDDING SNIPPET

Next we need to add a small utility method to the `AuctionHelpers` trait in the snippet package. This method will let you apply JavaScript actions for different `Box` types and provide a notification to let the user know what happened. Specifically, when a Box is a Failure and contains an error, it will show an appropriately styled error message, and when the Box is Full it will show a success message. The next listing shows the utility method definition.

Listing 4.9 Notification utility method

```
trait AuctionHelpers {
  ...
    def boxToNotice[T](yes: String, no: String)(f: => Box[T]){
      f match {
        case Full(value) => S.notice(yes)
        case Failure(msg,_,_) => S.error(msg)
        case _ => S.warning(no)
      }
    }
  ...
}
```

The boxToNotice method lets you pass a string as a message for both the success and failure outcomes.

Now that this utility method is in the AuctionHelpers trait, let's get on with defining the bid method in the Details snippet, which will actually let users place bids on auctions. The modifications for the snippet class are shown in the following listing.

Listing 4.10 Adding the bid method to the Details snippet

```
import net.liftweb.http.{S,StatefulSnippet,SHtml}
import net.liftweb.http.js.JsCmds.{Noop}
import net.liftweb.mapper.{MaxRows,By,OrderBy,Descending,StartAt}
import example.travel.model.{Auction,Bid,Customer}

class Details extends StatefulSnippet with AuctionHelpers with Loggable {
  override def dispatch =  {
    case "show" => show
    case "bid" => bid
  }
  ...
  def bid = {
    var amount: Box[String] = Empty                     ① Set default
    def submit = boxToNotice(                              amount value
        "Your bid was accepted!",
        "Unable to place bid at this time."){
      for {                                             ② Define form
        a <- auction                                       submit action
        b <- a.barter(amount)
        c <- amount
        d <- tryo(c.toDouble)
      } yield AuctionServer ! NewBid(a.id.is, d,
        S.session.map(_.uniqueId))
    }
    "type=text" #> SHtml.text(
      amount.openOr(""), s => amount = Box.!!(s)) &
```

```
    "type=submit" #>
      SHtml.ajaxSubmit("Place Bid", submit _)
      andThen SHtml.makeFormsAjax
  }
  ...
}
```

❸ **Bind the Submit button**

For convenience's sake, we're using Lift's built-in notification system, which is part of the S object. Typically you can use S.notice, S.warning, and S.error to inform users of different outcomes after form submissions, AJAX events, or anything else you can think of. As notification is such a common idiom in web development, it makes sense to leverage Lift's notice system rather than reinvent the wheel by implementing something where you specify div IDs specifically (although that would have been possible by using the JsCmds system).

The bid method assigns an internal boxed variable called amount that will hold the value passed by the frontend AJAX ❶. It's of type String and not Double (or another numeric format) because at this point in the code you just want to hold the value that came in from the user; the processing of that input can be done later.

The internal submit method is the method that will be invoked when the user clicks the Submit button ❷. It calls the boxToNotice helper method defined previously in the AuctionHelpers trait, passing string parameters for both success and failure messages. The block (or second parameter group) calls the barter method that we created on the Auction class, passing in the value of amountBox, which will contain whatever input the user entered. The barter method will correctly execute the business logic to determine whether it's a valid value and so forth. If, for instance, the user enters a string, and not something that can be converted to a number, the barter method will return a Failure type with the appropriate message, which would then be presented as a notice to the user.

The last few lines within the barter method define form inputs required to place a bid. In brief, the SHtml object provides Lift's server-side representation of markup elements that provide some kind of user interaction. In this case, we want a form that submits its values via AJAX, so we use the ajaxForm method. We then bind a text input using SHtml.text and pass two arguments. The first can be thought of as the getter—the value the text box should use when it needs to obtain a value for display. In this example, it should just display the value of the amountBox, or an empty string if no value is present. The second parameter can be thought of as a setter function that should be executed when the form has been submitted—essentially you're defining what logic the value entered by the user will have performed on it at runtime. In this case, the value that the user enters will become the value assigned to amountBox.

The final component to make this work is the Submit button binding ❸. The first parameter is a text value for the button; the really interesting thing here is the function passed to the second parameter. This Submit button is no regular button. It's an AJAX button, so the result of the passed function must be a special Lift type: JsCmd.

What is a JsCmd?

JavaScript is a core part of modern web development, and during the creation and evolution of Lift, JavaScript has played and continues to play a critical role. Early on, the Lift team found that there's a disparity between coding JavaScript and coding Scala. To that end, several JavaScript abstractions were added to smooth the interaction between client and server code. This is where `JsCmd` comes into action.

A `JsCmd` can represent pretty much any arbitrary JavaScript code, and Lift has support for a whole raft of common operations, such as hiding markup divs or focusing on an input element. There are also extensions to `JsCmd` that cover some specific JQuery, YUI, and ExtJS library features.

You only need to display the bidding interface if the user is logged in, so you can leverage one of Lift's built-in snippets called `TestCond`. Lift has a built-in notion of a known user being logged in, so we only need to add one line of code to your Boot.scala:

```
LiftRules.loggedInTest = Full(() => Customer.loggedIn_?)
```

Here we're leveraging a special `loggedIn_?` method on the `Customer` Mapper that's inherited from `MetaMegaProtoUser`. This method stores the current user in session state as part of its login and logout functionality. No extra coding is required to provide this check— `LiftRules.loggedInTest` tells Lift that when it needs to determine if someone is logged in, this is the function it should evaluate.

With this in place, we can now alter the auction.html markup to look like the following listing.

Listing 4.11 Implementing the `TestCond` snippet

```
<lift:test_cond.loggedin>
  <div id="bidding-form" lift="details.bid">
    <label>Enter New Bid:</label>
      <div class="half">
        <form>
          <input type="text" id="amount" />
          <input type="submit" /><br />         Display if user
          <span class="small">                  is logged in
            (must be more than: &pound;
            <span id="next_amount" />)
          </span>
        </form>
      </div>
    </div>
</lift:test_cond.loggedin>

<lift:test_cond.loggedout>
  <label>Enter New Bid:</label>                  Display if user
  <div class="half">Log in to place a bid</div>  is unknown
</lift:test_cond.loggedout>
```

It would have been possible to achieve the same result with two or three other routes of implementation within Lift, but this is probably the most "Lift-esque" solution because you're defining two different templates that are selected based on a known server function: in this case, the `loggedInTest` defined in `LiftRules`.

This isn't the end of the story. If you run the code as it is now, you'll notice that it does indeed update the database and insert the new bid, complete with auction and customer references. The interface, however, isn't updated. This is intentional. In the next section, we'll be covering Comet, and the bidding values will be updated from the `CometActor`, along with a real-time countdown.

4.2.3   Real-time bidding

An auction is intrinsically a real-time event: users need to see what the highest bid currently is, and see if they're winning the auction in question. The user experience would be greatly enhanced if each user's bids were automatically propagated to the other users; the resulting interface then wouldn't need to be refreshed, and users would receive instant updates whenever someone else makes a successful bid on an item the user is viewing. It would also be good if the user were notified when an auction they had previously bid on but weren't currently viewing received another bid. Fortunately, Lift provides a mechanism to make this a reality: Comet.

What is Comet?

Comet differs from both the traditional style of web-based user experience and AJAX applications, because it's not an iterative cycle of request then response. In a Comet application, generally the page loads, and the page-rendering updates are pushed to the browser via a long-lived HTTP connection.

In practice, Lift uses long-polling for the majority of browsers, but it can automatically detect the ability of the client to use HTML5 web sockets[*], and it will use this newer technology if it's available. This model of Comet application programming is what allows Lift to make applications real-time because the application can arbitrarily update any part of the page or supply new data to a client-side visualization technology like JavaScript, Adobe Flash, or even Java applets.

[*] Currently not available in Lift 2.3, but should be available by the time 2.4 makes a final release.

Lift has one of the best Comet implementations available today, and it's built on a programming paradigm called *actors*. You can find a lot more information about actors on the main scala-lang.org site (specifically at http://www.scala-lang.org/node/242), so we won't cover it here other than to say that actors are a lightweight model for concurrent programming, and they generally remove the need to explicitly deal with threading and locking.

Actors send and receive information as messages, and this happens to be a very nice fit with the request and response cycle present in HTTP. To this end, Lift provides an abstraction for Comet programming called `CometActor`. Figure 4.2 illustrates how

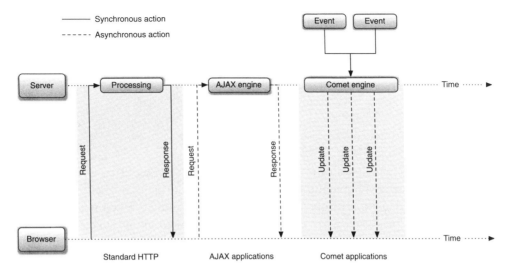

Figure 4.2   Comet workflow versus traditional HTTP request and response workflow. Notice how the
Comet application can asynchronously push information to the browser.

Comet-orientated applications typically differ from traditional request and response
workflows. Compared to both standard HTTP calls and AJAX calls, Comet doesn't
require a request to have a matched response. Once the page has been rendered and
Lift has an appropriate `CometActor` in the current session, said `CometActor` can arbitrarily push updates to the browser and pretty much alter the object model of the
markup in any way.

SETTING UP AUCTION FOR COMET

Before we get into the Comet implementation itself, let's take a moment to add two
helper methods to the `Auction` model so we can easily ask certain things about an auction without having to continually jump through hoops to get the right answers.

The following code shows the additional helper methods added to the `Auction` class:

```
def expired_? : Boolean = endsAt.is.getTime < now.getTime
def winningCustomer: Box[Customer] = topBid.flatMap(_.customer.obj)
```

The first of these methods checks whether the auction has expired and the second
determines the current auction leader.

It's also a good idea to add two convenience methods to the `AuctionHelpers` and
`AuctionInstanceHelpers` traits created earlier. The latter will ultimately be composed
with a `CometActor` so that it can easily access and update the browser based on an auction instance it obtains. Listing 4.12 details the changes to `AuctionHelpers`, and listing 4.13 shows the `AuctionInstanceHelpers`.

Listing 4.12   Additional helper methods for the `AuctionHelpers` trait

```
protected def hasExpired_?(a: Box[Auction]) : Boolean =
  a.map(_.expired_?).openOr(true)
```

```
protected def leadingBid(a: Box[Auction]): Double =
  a.flatMap(_.currentAmount).openOr(0D)

protected def minimumBid(a: Box[Auction]): Double =
  a.flatMap(_.nextAmount).openOr(0D)

protected def winningCustomer(a: Box[Auction]): NodeSeq =
  Text(a.flatMap(_.winningCustomer.map(_.shortName)
  ).openOr("Unknown"))

protected def winningCustomer(a: Auction): NodeSeq =
  winningCustomer(Full(a))
```

These helper methods either take `Auction` or `Box[Auction]` instances and serve as useful assessors for common auction aspects, ensuring that you don't continually need to unbox auctions throughout your code. You can merely compose the class or object with the `AuctionHelpers` trait and have these functions automatically.

Listing 4.13   Definition of the `AuctionInstanceHelpers` trait

```
trait AuctionInstanceHelpers extends AuctionHelpers {
  protected def auction: Box[Auction]
  protected def hasExpired_? : Boolean = hasExpired_?(auction)
  protected def leadingBid: Double = leadingBid(auction)
  protected def minimumBid: Double = minimumBid(auction)
  protected def winningCustomer: NodeSeq = winningCustomer(auction)
}
```

This is a very simple trait that builds on the `AuctionHelpers` trait, provides an implied `Box[Auction]`, and then calls the methods we just defined in `AuctionHelpers`. The reason for this is that in both the `CometActor` and the `Details` snippet, we'll want to be accessing a boxed instance of `Auction`, and as the auction is a member field, we might as well deal with it as an implied value rather than constantly passing it as an argument to methods. This is most certainly a style preference, but composing such a trait is more idiomatic Lift development and thus merits discussion.

PROVIDING A BACKEND

One of the things that makes Lift great for Comet-style development is the fact that it's highly stateful. For each `CometActor` you have in your application, Lift maintains one instance per session until its defined lifetime expiration (typically 10 minutes or so). This means that you need to have a design whereby the updating actor can obtain a list of other sessions watching a particular auction and receive updates from them about bidding information.

For example, suppose two users (*A* and *B*) are bidding on an auction. When *A* places a bid, this should immediately be updated on *B*'s screen. In order to achieve this sort of cross-session communication, we need to have some kind of auction server. As customers browse the site viewing different auctions, their `CometActor` will notify the `AuctionServer` object about the auction that the `CometActor` is currently updating. The `AuctionServer` then holds these values in a map so that when a user places a bid on a particular auction, `AuctionServer` can work out which other `CometActors` need to receive an update.

The next listing shows the definition of the global `AuctionServer` object.

Listing 4.14 Definition of the global `AuctionServer`

```
import scala.collection.immutable.Map
import net.liftweb.actor.LiftActor
import net.liftweb.http.CometActor

object AuctionServer extends LiftActor {
  private var cometActorAuctions =
      Map.empty[CometActor,List[Long]]
  private def auctionCometActors = cometActorAuctions        ❶ Map CometActors
    .foldLeft[Map[Long, List[CometActor]]](                     to auction IDs
      Map.empty withDefaultValue Nil){
        case (prev, (k, vs)) => vs.foldLeft(prev)(
          (prev, v) => prev + (v -> (k::prev(v))))
    }

  override def messageHandler = {
    case ListenTo(actor,auctions) =>
      cometActorAuctions =                                   ❷ Handing incoming
        cometActorAuctions + (actor -> auctions)               messages
    case msg@NewBid(auction,amount,session) =>
      auctionCometActors(auction).foreach(_ ! msg)
  }
}
```

The most important thing to note about this listing is that this is the backend actor, not the `CometActor` itself. This is the global singleton object that holds information about which `CometActors` are viewing which auctions, and which `CometActor` instances need notifications about which currently active auctions.

The first thing that this object defines is a pair private variables that contain a mapping between a specific `CometActor` instance and a list of auction IDs ❶. This is useful because if a user is bidding on more than one auction at a time, you can send updates about the status of all the user's auctions in a unified manner.

Although the definition of `auctionCometActors` looks somewhat complicated, you don't need to understand the specifics of what's going on here; you just need to understand that it's a section of what transforms the `Map[CometActor,List[Long]]` to `Map[Long,List[CometActor]]`. In this auction application, this is eminently helpful, because when a user bids on an auction, the ID for that auction is passed along so the `AuctionServer` can then figure out exactly who needs to be notified of this new bid. Again, it's important to stress that this isn't Lift-specific code; it's just regular Scala code that inverts a `Map` in a very specific way, which is useful for this auction application.

The `messageHandler` is really where all the work happens ❷. It defines the handlers for what the actor should do upon receiving a message. (The messages will be detailed in listing 4.16.) This handler allows the `AuctionServer` to receive new auction IDs for a particular `CometActor` instance and keep track of which auctions are of interest to which sessions.

When a customer places a new bid, the `AuctionServer` dispatches the `NewBid` message to every `CometActor` that has expressed an interest in that auction. You might be wondering what the exclamation mark syntax here is actually doing. When dealing with actors, the `!` means to send the message (on the right side of the exclamation mark) to the actor instance (on the left side of the exclamation mark). This message sending is asynchronous, so there's no need to wait for a reply of any kind.

Here are the messages used in the application's Comet components. For the moment, just understand that these are simple Scala *case classes*, and there's no Lift intervention happening here:

```
case object CountdownTick
case class ListenTo(actor: CometActor, auctions: List[Long])
case class CurrentAuction(auction: Box[Auction])
case class NewBid(auction: Long, amount: Double, sessionid: Box[String])
```

These messages are immutable and throwaway; once they've been received and handled by their destination actor, they'll just disappear into the ether and be garbage-collected by the JVM automatically.

ADDING THE AUCTIONUPDATER COMETACTOR

Now that we have the backend in place, it's time to add the Comet implementation that will update the customer's browser. First, let's add the markup in the auction.html file to load the `CometActor` when the page renders:

```
<lift:surround with="wide" at="content">
  <lift:comet type="AuctionUpdater" />
  ....
<lift:surround>
```

One important point to note here is that the `CometActor` has been placed before the call to the `Details` snippet. There are many scenarios where the placement wouldn't matter, but in this case, because we're going to be sending messages from the `Details` snippet to the `AuctionUpdater`, we need to be sure that the `AuctionUpdater` has already been instantiated. There are ways to programmatically ensure that within Lift, but for the sake of keeping this tutorial straightforward for newcomers, we've kept the Comet call at the head of the template.

Calling `CometActors` from markup differs from calling snippets because you have to use the special postfix `comet` and then pass the name of the `CometActor` subtype. In this case, `AuctionUpdater` is the name of the `CometActor`.

The following listing shows a trimmed down `CometActor` that we can work through and add the other methods to.

Listing 4.15   Basic auction countdown `CometActor`

```
import scala.xml.{NodeSeq,Text}
import net.liftweb._,
```

```
      common.{Full,Empty,Failure,Box},
      util.Schedule, util.Helpers._,
      http.{CometActor,S},
      http.js.JsCmds._,   http.js.jquery.JqJsCmds.FadeOut
import example.travel._,
      model.{Auction,Customer},
      lib.AuctionInstanceHelpers

class AuctionUpdater extends CometActor
      with AuctionInstanceHelpers {
      private lazy val countdownId = "time_remaining"
      private val server = AuctionServer
      private var _auction: Box[Auction] = Empty
      protected def auction = _auction
      private def auctionId = auction.map(_.id.is).openOr(0L)

      private def countdown =
        if(hasExpired_?) Text("This auction has ended.")
        else Text(TimeSpan.format(
          (auction.map(_.ends_at.is.getTime).openOr(
            now.getTime) - now.getTime) / 1000L * 1000L))

      override def lowPriority = {
        case CountdownTick => {
          partialUpdate(SetHtml(countdownId, countdown))
          if(!hasExpired_?)
            Schedule.schedule(this, CountdownTick, 5 seconds)
        }
        case CurrentAuction(a) => {
        _auction = a
         registerListeners
         }
      }

      def registerListeners {
      auction.map(a => server ! ListenTo(this,(a.id.is :: Customer.currentUser
        .map(_.participatingIn).openOr(Nil)).removeDuplicates))
      }

      override def render = {
        registerListeners
        Schedule.schedule(this, CountdownTick, 2 seconds)
        NodeSeq.Empty
      }
}
```

❶ Implement CometActor trait

❷ Define DOM IDs for updating

❸ Calculate remaining auction time

❹ Increment countdown

❺ Render CometActor

Here we have a basic `CometActor` that reads the `ends_at` date from the `Auction` instance, does a short computation to figure how much time is remaining until the auction ends, and updates this to the user's browser every 5 seconds.

All `CometActors` in a Lift application must be a subtype of the `CometActor` class and live in the `comet` subpackage of any package you add to Lift's search path by invoking `LiftRules.addToPackages` ❶.

Within `CometActors`, it's typically idiomatic to assign the element IDs of the content you want to update to some private values ❷, as these IDs can then be referenced throughout the rest of the actor definition. To start with, you only need the ID of the

<span> element containing the countdown, and its new value is computed using Lift's TimeSpan time helper class ❸.

The lowPriority block is essentially a delegate for the messageHandler from LiftActor. In this implementation, it can receive two types of message: Countdown-Tick and CurrentAuction ❹. CountdownTick is a case object that periodically tells the CometActor to update the browser with the new time. It does this by determining whether the auction has finished. Upon finding a live auction, it uses a special utility in Lift Util called Schedule, which lets you set a time in the future when a message will be sent to a particular actor. In this case, it sends itself an arbitrary message to update the clock, and upon receiving that message, it reschedules itself for the next update. Upon receiving the second type of message—CurrentAuction—the CometActor updates its internal _auction variable with this new instance. The result is that when the user is moving around the site viewing different auctions, this instance can be passed by the Details snippet when needed.

When the CometActor is rendered for the first time during page load, the contents of the render method ❺ will execute and be presented to the user. In this case, we don't have any content that the actor needs to render, so we can return NodeSeq.Empty, telling the compiler that no content should be rendered.

As the render method is normally only executed upon the initial page load, this is an appropriate place to tell the AuctionServer that this CometActor will be listening to this particular auction, and merge that auction with any other active auctions that can be determined from the database. You can facilitate this step by adding a participatingIn helper method to the Customer class:

```
def participatingIn: List[Long] = (for {
    b <- Bid.findAll(By(Bid.customer, this.id))
    a <- b.auction.obj
  } yield a.id.is).distinct
```

This helper method allows you to obtain a list of the entire range of auction IDs that a customer is currently participating in. This is then added to the auction they're currently viewing, and the updated list is passed to the AuctionServer.

As it stands, this won't actually update the countdown timer because its internal _auction variable will continually be Empty. The following code snippet shows a minor modification to the show method in the Details snippet: when the page is rendered, it notifies the CometActor with the current auction instance.

```
def show = {
  S.session.map(_.findComet("AuctionUpdater"))
    .openOr(Nil).foreach(_ ! CurrentAuction(auction))
  ...
}
```

This may look somewhat complicated, but its function is quite straightforward. Using the Lift state object, S, you obtain a reference to the current session, and then iterate through it calling the findComet method, which will in turn yield a list of Comet-Actors. With this list in hand, the foreach call iterates through the list, sending the

CurrentAuction message with this new Auction instance. This is how the Auction-Updater instance knows which is the current auction being viewed by the customer. With this modification in place, the AuctionUpdater will function perfectly and update the auction countdown every five seconds.

This is all very nice, but it's really only the base for the main functionality we want to achieve using this CometActor. We still want to update the current auction value, the minimum bid value, and the current auction leader. To get the full functionality, we only need to add a few more lines of code. The following listing shows the additional methods needed.

Listing 4.16 Enhancements to `AuctionUpdater`

```
class AuctionUpdater extends CometActor with AuctionInstanceHelpers {
  ...
  private lazy val nextAmountId = "next_amount"
  private lazy val currentAmountId = "current_amount"          More DOM IDs
  private lazy val winningCustomerId = "winning_customer"      to update
  private lazy val amountId = "amount"

  private def notifyOtherAuctionUpdate {
    warning("""You have been outbid on an                 ❶ Deliver notification
            auction you are participating in""")              that you've been
  }                                                           outbid

  private def notifyThisAuctionUpdate {
    partialUpdate {
      SetHtml(currentAmountId,
        Text(leadingBid.toString)) &
      SetHtml(nextAmountId,                               ❷ Update and reset
        Text(minimumBid.toString)) &                        auction GUI
      SetHtml(winningCustomerId, winningCustomer) &
      SetValueAndFocus(amountId,"")
    }
  }

  override def highPriority = {
    case NewBid(auctionId,amount,fromsession) =>
      notifyThisAuctionUpdate
      if((S.session.map(_.uniqueId)                       ❸ Handle receiving
          equals fromsession) == false)                     a NewBid
        notifyOtherAuctionUpdate
  }
  ...
}
```

First, notifyOtherAuctionUpdate ❶ defines a utility method that's very similar in function to the S notices covered earlier in the chapter and is simply a convenience method for displaying notices to the user. The main part of this listing, however, is notifyThisAuctionUpdate, which defines what's known as a partialUpdate—these deliver JsCmds to the browser ❷. Here we've specified a chain of commands that will update the various IDs with new values and then focus on the input field after clearing its value so it's ready for the next customer bid. Finally, the highPriority message dispatcher receives the `NewBid` message, updates the current user's browser with the new values, determines whether this session was the sending session, and, if not, notifies the user that they were outbid by another customer ❸.

This concludes the implementation of the bidding interface. We've looked at a range of Lift's interactive components and how they can play together. Chapter 9 provides some more in-depth AJAX and Comet examples that will give you a more complete picture on these features.

4.3   Summary

We've covered a lot of ground in this chapter and advanced the application significantly. Hopefully you're now starting to appreciate how many parts of Lift slot together seamlessly to make your life as a developer easier. We've covered how to retrieve information from the database using Mapper queries and subsequently display that information in a nice list with automatic controls for paging. We also touched on URL rewriting and Lift's awesome AJAX support.

The real takeaway from this chapter, however, is the flexibility that Lift allows and how it encourages you to use idiomatic Scala code that's highly functional and highly composable. Whether you're writing snippets or `CometActors`, you can compose and reuse functionality in many ways with no to little overhead. We also took our first plunge into real-time Comet applications and actor-orientated programming by implementing an automatic notification system for concurrent auction bidding.

In the next chapter, we'll be implementing the classic shopping basket functionality and ensuring that when an auction ends, it's attributed to the correct user by implementing Lift's `ProtoStateMachine`. To finish off, we'll add a basic checkout process and collect payments with Lift's built-in PayPal support.

Shopping basket and checkout

5

This chapter covers

- Order creation and processing
- Attributing auctions to customers
- Creating a shopping basket
- Collecting payment through PayPal

So far our booking application is missing a couple of very important aspects that any online retail system must have to complete orders. First, it's missing the workflow that attributes an item—or in this case an *auction*—to a particular order for a particular customer. This notion of an order is something that was included in the original entity-relationship diagram (ERD) shown in figure 3.5 (in chapter 3). The order portion of the ERD is shown here in figure 5.1. It exists in the application already, but it currently does nothing.

To enable this workflow, we'll utilize one of Lift's lesser-known features called Machine to automatically assign expired auctions to the winning customer—the next time they load the shopping basket, they'll see the completed auction ready for checkout.

Secondly, we'll be building a checkout process to collect delivery information from customers. To implement this, we'll be utilizing `LiftScreen`, Lift's high-level abstraction on building forms and input screens.

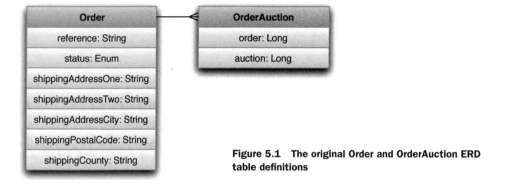

Figure 5.1 The original Order and OrderAuction ERD table definitions

Finally, no online shopping system would be complete without some mechanism to collect payment from users. To this end, we'll be leveraging Lift's built-in integration with PayPal, the online payment gateway.

5.1   Order creation

Before addressing any of the technical issues around order creation and processing, let's take a moment to clarify the term *order*. In the context of this booking application, you should think of an order as a logical group of auctions that have all been won by a single user. This order exhibits the following properties:

- One customer might have multiple orders over a period of time
- One order could contain multiple auctions
- At any particular moment a single user can only have one *active* order

Technically speaking, this means that we'll require two Mapper models to implement the functionality:

- Order—to represent the order itself
- OrderAuction—to act as a join table between the orders and auctions tables

Let's now take a look at the implementation of these order models in detail.

5.1.1   Order models

Having outlined in broad terms what the overall ordering process should achieve, let's look at some specific implementation details.

The Order class will need to hold information about its current status (open, pending, complete, or failed), and it will need to know which customer this order is for, along with which auctions are attributed to it. Another class, OrderAuction, will handle the auction references. We'll explore it after the Order implementation.

With these things in mind, let's take a look at the Mapper code that will implement the Order class, as shown in the following listing.

Listing 5.1 Definition of the `Order` class

```
import net.liftweb.common.{Full,Box,Empty,Failure}
import net.liftweb.mapper._
import net.liftweb.util.Helpers.randomLong

object OrderStatus extends Enumeration {
  val Open = Value(1,"open")
  val Pending = Value(2,"pending")
  val Complete = Value(3,"complete")
  val Failed = Value(4,"failed")
}

object Order extends Order with LongKeyedMetaMapper[Order]{
  override def dbTableName = "orders"
  override def beforeCreate = List(
    _.customer(Customer.currentUser)
    .status(OrderStatus.Open)
    .reference(randomLong(99999999L)))
}

class Order extends LongKeyedMapper[Order]
    with IdPK with OneToMany[Long, Order]
    with CreatedUpdated {
  def getSingleton = Order
  object reference extends MappedLong(this)
  object status extends MappedEnum(this, OrderStatus)
  object customer
    extends LongMappedMapper(this, Customer){
    override def dbColumnName = "customer_id"
  }
  object order_auctions extends MappedOneToMany(
    OrderAuction, OrderAuction.order)
    with Owned[OrderAuction]
}
```

1 Create OrderStatus enumeration

2 Add post-creation functions

3 Define foreign key to customers table

4 Reference OrderAuction Mapper entity

First, you define an enumeration of statuses that a given order can move through; for this simple use case you only need to extend `scala.Enumeration`. A user always needs to have an `Open` order in case they win one of the auctions they bid on. Upon winning an auction, it can then be assigned to the user's currently open order, and then their order progresses to the `Pending` state and then to the `Complete` state upon successful payment (or `Failed` if their payment was declined). The `OrderStatus` enumeration is then applied to a special field type called `MappedEnum`—any value being assigned to this field must be a value from the `OrderStatus` enumeration **1**.

Mapper offers a set of lifecycle methods that let you define functions that allow an order instance to be modified before it's persisted to the underlying database. In this instance, if a new order is being created, its initial status must be `Open` and it requires a new order reference number that can be included in any communication with the customer **2**.

Finally, the `Order` class utilizes Mapper relationship classes that you've already seen in implementing other models in the application **3** and **4**.

The next listing shows the definition of the join-table Mapper class, `OrderAuction`.

Listing 5.2 Definition of the `OrderAuction` class

```
import net.liftweb.common.{Full,Box,Empty,Failure}
import net.liftweb.mapper._

object OrderAuction extends OrderAuction with
LongKeyedMetaMapper[OrderAuction]{
  override def dbTableName = "order_auctions"
}

class OrderAuction extends LongKeyedMapper[OrderAuction]
with IdPK with CreatedUpdated {
  def getSingleton = OrderAuction
  object order extends LongMappedMapper(this, Order){
    override def dbColumnName = "order_id"
  }
  object auction extends LongMappedMapper(this, Auction){
    override def dbColumnName = "auction_id"
  }
}
```

❶ Join table to reference auctions and orders

This listing defines the entire `OrderAuction` class, along with the companion object ❶. Although this implementation is quite small, it's key in the application, as without it there's no way to effectively assign auctions to a specific customer order and determine what that customer needs to pay.

With both the `Order` and `OrderAuction` models in place, the next thing we need to do is ensure that when the customer logs into the application, and they don't have a currently `Open` order, that an order is assigned to them. Fortunately, `MetaMegaProto-User`, from which the `Customer` model descends, already has a hook for executing functions when the user successfully logs in (and logs out). With the following small modification to the `Customer` class and companion object, we can ensure that the user always has a valid `Order` instance, as shown in the next listing

Listing 5.3 Providing a login hook on the `Customer` class

```
class Customer extends MegaProtoUser[Customer] with CreatedUpdated {
  ...
  def order: Box[Order] =
    Order.find(By(Order.customer, this.id),
      ByList(Order.status,
        OrderStatus.Open, OrderStatus.Pending)
    ) or Full(Order.create.saveMe)
  ...
}


object Customer extends Customer with MetaMegaProtoUser[Customer]{
  ...
  onLogIn = List({ _.order })
  ...
}
```

❶ Give customer an order

❷ Execute on login

This modification to the `Customer` class provides a method that looks in the database for a currently open `Order` for this particular customer, and if it doesn't find one, it creates a new one ❶. This happens by way of the `or` operator that's part of `Box`. In short, if the left-hand expression results in `Empty`, the right-hand expression is used as a fallback. In this case, the fallback is to create a new order and return it.

To ensure that a customer always has an `Order`, no matter what their situation, the `order` method is appended to a `ProtoUser` hook that executes functions when the user logs in ❷.

You now have the underlying structure for the ordering process. The next section will take you through the application logic that facilitates the ordering process. In the process, you'll implement a basic state machine using Lift Machine and collect payment through Lift's built-in PayPal support.

5.1.2 Attributing auctions to customers

Currently, when an auction reaches its predefined expiry time, nothing happens. The auction will just sit there, still active but not accepting any new bids. What's required is that when the auction reaches completion, it must be attributed to the winning customer's currently open order—this has to be done irrespective of the customer's browser being open or not.

Fortunately, Lift has a solution for this in its state machine implementation: Lift Machine. Machine is one of the lesser-known modules in Lift's toolkit, and it's a great tool that can be used for all sorts of operations that run asynchronously to the browser or standard user workflow. It's not widely used because there isn't a great deal of understanding about what it can actually do.

What is a state machine?

A state machine is an abstraction that allows the developer to define a set number of states, including any transitions between those states and subsequent actions that need to be executed during that process flow.

For example, we could assign a running auction a state called *active* and define a transition to a state called *expired*. This flow or transition could have an action applied to it, so that upon reaching the expired state, a particular function is executed.

For more information on finite state machines, see Wikipedia's "Finite-state machine" article: http://en.wikipedia.org/wiki/Finite-state_machine.

In exactly the same way that Lift provides prototypical traits to assist in your user-orientated development, Lift also has two proto-traits for its state machine: `Meta-ProtoStateMachine` and `ProtoStateMachine`. To implement these traits, you first need to make a few choices about the states that you're going to have and the actions that will be attached to them.

For the auction use case, there are only two states that we're concerned about: when the auction is active and when it has expired. There is, of course, a strong conceptual coupling between the countdown in the auction and the transition from an active state to an expired one. Within the state machine, we can easily schedule the transition to expired.

The following listing shows the implementation that extends the machine proto-traits.

Listing 5.4   Implementation of Lift Machine

```
import net.liftweb.common.{Loggable,Full,Empty}
import net.liftweb.machine.{ProtoStateMachine,MetaProtoStateMachine}
import net.liftweb.mapper.MappedLongForeignKey
import net.liftweb.util.Helpers._

object AuctionStates extends Enumeration {              ❶ Enumeration of
  val Initial, Active, Expired = Value                    auction states
}

object AuctionMachine extends AuctionMachine
  with MetaProtoStateMachine[AuctionMachine, AuctionStates.type]{
  def instantiate = new AuctionMachine
  val stateEnumeration = AuctionStates
  def initialState = AuctionStates.Initial
  def globalTransitions = Nil                            ❷ State machine
  def states = List(                                       required
    State(AuctionStates.Initial,                           methods
      On({case _ => }, AuctionStates.Active)),
    State(AuctionStates.Active,
      After(Auction.duration,
      AuctionStates.Expired)))

  case object FirstEvent extends Event                   ❸ Initial event to
}                                                          kick things off

class AuctionMachine
    extends ProtoStateMachine[AuctionMachine, AuctionStates.type]{
  import AuctionStates._
  def getSingleton = AuctionMachine

  object auction
    extends MappedLongForeignKey(this, Auction){        ❹ Foreign key to
    override def dbColumnName = "auction_id"               auction table
  }

  override def transition(
    from: AuctionStates.Value, to: StV, why: Meta#Event){
    (from, to, auction.obj) match {
      case (Active, Expired, Full(auc)) => {
        auc.attributeToWinningCustomer                   ❺ State transition
        auc.close                                          actions
      }
      case (from,to,why) =>
    }
    super.transition(from, to, why)
  }
}
```

There's a lot of code to digest in this listing, so let's look at the key methods and their functions. First, `ProtoStateMachine` is a subtype of Mapper, so the state is persisted in your database of choice.

As was briefly touched on in the preceding paragraph, a state machine is all about the transition of one state to another. In order to define those states programmatically, it's necessary to first define the types of states ❶ and then the transitions between them ❷. All instances start with the `Initial` state but are automatically promoted to `Active`. The only transition that matters in this example, however, is moving from `Active` to `Expired`.

In order to execute some meaningful code upon the transition taking place, `transition` uses a pattern match to call two new helper methods on the `Auction` instance: `attributeToWinningCustomer` and `close` ❺.

In addition to the code that controls the state machine actions, listing 5.4 also defines two items that you'll need in order to hook up the state machine to the `Auction` model. Specifically, the `FirstEvent` object ❸ will be used later to set up an `AuctionMachine` instance for a given auction; more on that shortly. Second, as `Auction-Machine` instances should always be related to a given `Auction` instance, the `AuctionMachine` needs a foreign key ❹.

You might be wondering how it knows to call these action methods at a particular point in the future. Well, the real key is this line of code:

```
State(AuctionStates.Active,After(
    Auction.duration, AuctionStates.Expired))
```

In essence, this says "move to the `Expired` state after the time defined by `Auction` `.duration` has passed." For simplicity's sake, and to not lose clarity in the example, we set the duration of auctions in the system to 24 hours. In this example, we're using Lift Machine to demonstrate the stateful nature of Lift and how powerful that concept can be. A more typical use case for Lift Machine might be something like reminding a user to validate their account one day after registering; essentially, anything that requires some action to be asynchronously executed at a given point in the future. The real take-away here is that Lift Machine can perform actions away from the browser, resulting in multifaceted workflows.

To complete the functionality, it's also necessary to modify the `Auction` class to include some new helper methods and lifecycle hooks. As it stands, there's nothing to instantiate the `AuctionMachine` instances and initialize the state. Fortunately, because all `AuctionMachine` instances have a close relationship with `Auction` instances and their subsequent lifecycles, it makes sense to instantiate a new `AuctionMachine` instance when a new `Auction` is added to the system. Listing 5.5 shows the revised `Auction` definition.

Listing 5.5 Revised `Auction` class definition

```
object Auction
  extends Auction
```

```
    with LongKeyedMetaMapper[Auction]
    with CRUDify[Long,Auction]{
      ...
      override def beforeCreate =                  ❶  Auction ends
        List(_.endsAt(duration.later.toDate))          24 hrs. later

      override def afterCreate = List(
        a => new Bid().amount(a.starting_amount.is)  ❷  Auction setup
                    .auction(a).save,                    operations
          a => AuctionMachine.createNewInstance(
            AuctionMachine.FirstEvent, Full(_.auction(a)))
        )
      val duration = 24 hours                      ❸  Duration of
      ...                                              auctions
    }

class Auction extends LongKeyedMapper[Auction]
  with CreatedUpdated with IdPK {
  ...
  def expired_? = if(!is_closed.is)               ❹  Is auction
    ends_at.is.getTime < now.getTime else true        expired?

  def expires_at: TimeSpan =                      ❺  When does
    TimeSpan(((ends_at.is.getTime -                   auction expire?
      now.getTime) / 1000L * 1000L))

  def close: Boolean = this.is_closed(true).save  ❻  Close this
                                                     auction
  def attributeToWinningCustomer {
    winningCustomer.map(_.order.foreach(o => {     ❼  Assign auction
      o.order_auctions.+:(OrderAuction.create          to winner
        .order(o).auction(this)).save
      o.status(OrderStatus.Pending).save
    }))
  }
  ...
}
```

Similar to the lifecycle additions made previously to the Customer definition, here we add a couple of different functions that will be executed before and after the row has been persisted to the database. First, beforeCreate sets the auction to end 24 hours (the value defined by duration, ❸ from the current time ❶. Then, afterCreate creates an initial bid and a new instance of the AuctionMachine ❷.

In order to streamline some operations for a particular Auction instance, the modifications in listing 5.5 add three utility methods: expired_? ❹, expires_at ❺, and close() ❻. These methods help in removing some of the boilerplate from the calling code. The attributeToWinningCustomer definition ❼ is a bit more complicated: when an Auction expires, it's first necessary to determine which customer had the highest bid and obtain the related Order instance. With this Order in hand, you then need to create a new OrderAuction and reference this Auction instance.

With these methods implemented, the auctions will expire and automatically be assigned to the correct customer.

With the auction process now in place and operational, the next component of functionality to implement is the basket and checkout—an auction is no good if users can't pay for it! The next section implements a rudimentary checkout function and allows people to pay via PayPal.

5.2 Implementing the basket and checkout process

Now that orders are successfully being attributed to the right customers, we need to give the customers a method to provide their shipping details so the tickets and collaterals can be dispatched to them successfully.

The first thing that's missing is what would traditionally be referred to as a shopping basket or cart to hold the user's won auctions and where they can see the items that they have pending payment.

The second component that you'll be building is a very basic checkout form to collect the user's shipping information. To achieve this we'll be looking at another aspect of Lift, `LiftScreen`, which is designed specifically to make constructing forms and user input simple.

5.2.1 Implementing the basket

The basket is quite straightforward and inherits a lot of its functionality from things that have already been defined, such as the `AuctionHelpers` trait. The goal is to create a simple snippet that reads the contents of the database based upon which the customer is currently logged in. If there is no current customer session, it should display a friendly message requesting that the user log in to see the contents of their basket.

Once again, we'll use the built-in `TestCond` snippet to present the correct content depending on whether the user is logged-in or not. That will keep this logic separate from the snippet controlling basket rendering. The basket itself only has to decide whether the current basket has any contents or not. The next listing shows the `Basket` snippet.

Listing 5.6 The `Basket` snippet

```
import scala.xml.NodeSeq
import net.liftweb.util.Helpers._
import example.travel.model.Customer
import example.travel.lib.AuctionHelpers

class Basket extends AuctionHelpers {
  private lazy val contents = Customer.currentUser.flatMap(      ❶ Load items
    _.order.map(_.order_auctions.all)).openOr(Nil)                   from basket

 def items = ".basket-row *" #>
  contents.map(x => single(x.auction.obj)) andThen             ❷ Render items
   "%s ^*".format(                                                  template
     if(contents.isEmpty) "empty"
     else "full") #> NodeSeq.Empty
}
```

❶ Load items from basket

❷ Render items template

The whole `Basket` class inherits from `AuctionHelpers` so that you don't need to rede-fine the bindings for a single `Auction` to obtain its name and so forth. The first thing to do is load the current user's completed auctions from the database ❶. This is done by using the helper methods that were previously defined on both the `Customer` and `OrderAuction` classes earlier in this chapter. The result here is a `List[OrderAuction]` if auctions exist; if the current user hasn't won any auctions, the method returns an empty list, or `Nil`.

The items snippet itself ❷ uses a different CSS-style selector that might look a little strange. This selector takes the input markup and selects a specific child node. In this case, it allows you to select either the `<full>` element if the `contents` value isn't empty, or the `<empty>` node in the markup if the `contents` list is empty. You can find more detailed information about the available CSS-style selectors in section 6.1.2.

When it comes to the actual binding for the content, the `items` snippet reuses the `single` method from the `AuctionHelpers` trait that has been used elsewhere in the application.

The next listing shows the view code—note how part of the content is contained in the `<full>` and `<empty>` nodes. This allows the designer to explicitly decide what should be displayed for each scenario without needless coupling to the server-side code.

Listing 5.7   Basket markup from _basket.html

```
<div class="bg3 basket">
  <h2>Your Basket</h2>

  <lift:test_cond.loggedin>                    ❶ Start of logged-
    <lift:basket.items>                          in content        ❷ Invoke Basket.items
      <full>                                                          snippet
        <div class="basket-row">
          <h3 class="name">Name</h3>
        </div>                                                     ❸ Define template
        <div>                                                        for full baskets
          <input type="button"
                 name="checkout"
                 value="checkout" />
        </div>
      </full>

      <empty>                                                      ❹ Define template for
        <p>You have not won any auctions</p>                         basket when empty
      </empty>
    </lift:basket.items>
  </lift:test_cond.loggedin>

  <lift:test_cond.loggedout>
    <p>Please log-in to see the contents of your basket</p>
  </lift:test_cond.loggedout>

  <br />
</div>
```

Once again, this template uses the `TestCond` snippet to determine whether the user is logged in or not **❶**. From there, the `Basket.items` snippet determines the appropriate content node in the XHTML **❷**. Specifically, if the basket has items, it renders the `<full>` node **❸**; otherwise it renders the content to be displayed if the user's basket is empty **❹**.

Note that neither `<empty>` nor `<full>` are valid HTML tags; they're simply used as markers in the template, and they're removed by the snippet during page rendering. The markup also defines a link to the checkout page so that users can enter their shipping information for that order and pay via the online payment provider PayPal.

5.2.2 *Implementing the checkout*

With the basket complete, the frontend needs to receive some shipping information from the customer so their tickets can be sent out. In addition, you'll also add functionality to pass the customer to PayPal so they can pay for the auctions and complete the transaction.

As this section makes use of Lift's PayPal integration, so you'll need to make sure you add the `lift-paypal` artifact as a dependency to your project. Add the following line to your SBT project:

```
val paypal = "net.liftweb" %% "lift-paypal" % liftVersion % "compile"
```

Be sure to call `reload` and `update` from the SBT shell before continuing.

In the current Mapper models, there's nowhere to hold shipping details in the database, so first you'll need to add some extra fields to the `Order` model. The following listing shows the required additional fields and convenience method.

Listing 5.8 Additions to the `Order` model

```
class Order extends LongKeyedMapper[Order]
    with IdPK with OneToMany[Long, Order] with CreatedUpdated {
  ...
  object shippingAddressOne
      extends MappedString(this,255){
    override def displayName = "Address One"
  }
  object shippingAddressTwo
      extends MappedString(this,255){
    override def displayName = "Address Two"
  }
  object shippingAddressCity
      extends MappedString(this,255){
    override def displayName = "City"
  }
  object shippingAddressPostalCode extends
    MappedPostalCode(this,shippingAddressCounty){
    override def displayName = "Postcode"
  }
  object shippingAddressCounty
      extends MappedCountry(this){
    override def displayName = "Country"
  }
```

❶ Extra fields for shipping

```
...
def totalValue: Double = (for(
  oa <- order_auctions.all;
  au <- oa.auction.obj;
  av <- au.currentAmount
) yield av).reduceLeft(_ + _)
}
```

❷ Helper for order value

This listing defines a simple set of additional addressing fields that should be familiar to anyone who has shopped online before ❶. The `totalValue` helper method determines the overall value of the auctions attributed to this order ❷. Essentially, this method just maps through the auctions invoking the `currentAmount` helper we defined in the previous chapter.

With the changes to the `Order` model complete, we can now focus on creating the basic checkout. The checkout process itself will consist of two screens:

- The first to input the shipping information
- The second to confirm the basket and shipping information, with a link to conduct the transaction through PayPal

In order to implement the form for the shipping details, we could quite happily use a snippet and code it manually with the bind statements and so forth, exactly as we've done with everything else in the application. But there's another component in Lift WebKit called `LiftScreen` that can help us with this.

Web applications typically have complex flows for form completion and collection of user input. To this end, `LiftScreen` makes building forms super simple and provides a way to test forms programmatically without involving any form of HTTP simulation. `LiftScreen` also has a bigger brother called `Wizard` that can link lots of different screens together and control complex page flow and validation. To keep things simple here, we'll be implementing a single screen, but making a more complex multi-screen flow based on user selection would be a simple extension of the `LiftScreen` code. `Wizard` is covered in more detail in chapter 6.

The purpose of using `LiftScreen` is to ease the creation of user input flows and reduce code bulk. The following listing shows the whole `LiftScreen` implementation for the checkout.

Listing 5.9   Input for collecting shipping details using `LiftScreen`

```
import net.liftweb.http.{LiftScreen,S}
import example.travel.model.{Customer,Order}

object Checkout extends LiftScreen {
  object order extends
    ScreenVar(Customer.currentUser.flatMap(
      _.order) openOr Order.create)

  addFields(() => order.shippingAddressOne)
  addFields(() => order.shippingAddressTwo)
  addFields(() => order.shippingAddressCity)
```

❶ Define internal variable

❷ Register specific fields

```
  addFields(() => order.shippingAddressPostalCode)
  addFields(() => order.shippingAddressCountry)

  def finish(){
    if(order.save) S.redirectTo("summary")
    else S.error("Unable to save order details")
  }
}
```

2 Register
   specific fields

3 Finish
   action

The first thing to say about this `LiftScreen` is that it sits alongside the other regular snippets in the application. `LiftScreen` is a subtype of `DispatchSnippet`, so it can be thought of as an abstraction over the normal snippets that you're familiar with. The next point of note is that the `Checkout` implementation is a singleton, rather than a class like the other snippets in the application.

Within the object itself, the first item is a local `ScreenVar` used to hold the order instance that's retrieved via the logged-in customer **1**. `ScreenVars` are local to the screen and can't be shared directly. The next group of method calls **2** registers specific model fields for receiving input in the UI. Had you wanted to construct inputs for the entire model, you could simply pass the model reference itself, and `LiftScreen` would automatically construct inputs for *all* the fields on the specified model. Finally, the `finish` method definition takes the order instance and saves it with the updated values from the form **3**. It couldn't be easier!

Of course, it's necessary to invoke this screen from checkout.html, but as its rendering methods are already plumbed in just like any other snippet; you only need to do this:

```
<lift:checkout />
```

In order to make this screen appear in an application-specific style, you can provide a customized template so that when Lift renders the screen, it does so in a manner that suits your application. The wizard and screen template you can customize is located at webapp/templates-hidden/wizard-all.html. This special template ensures that any rendering completed by either `LiftScreen` or its bigger brother `Wizard` will be styled in a manner that's appropriate to your specific application. `LiftScreen` and `Wizard` are very powerful user input abstractions, and they save heaps of time when building user forms and workflows.

With these things in place, your input form should look something like figure 5.2.

When the user clicks the Finish button, the input is saved to the database and the user is redirected to an overview page where they can see their cart contents and its value, along with the shipping details they entered. To make this work, we need to add an `OrderSummary` snippet to display the shipping information and grab some summary information about the order, such as its total worth. The purpose is to let the user review what they're purchasing, confirm their information, and give them the option to amend any details before being transferred to PayPal to collect payment.

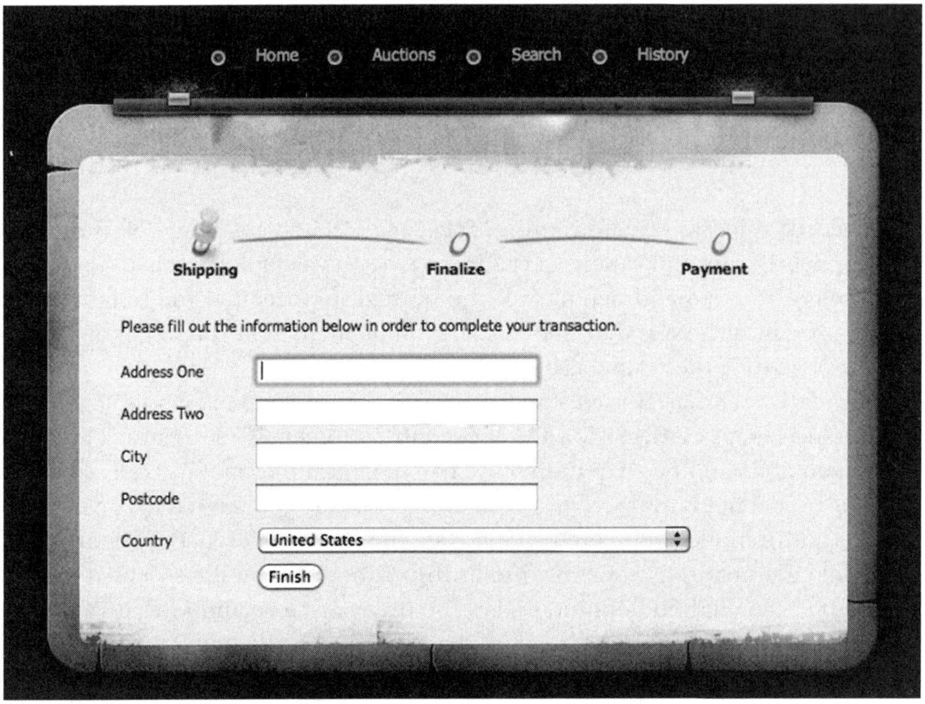

Figure 5.2 User input form for collecting the shipping information

Listing 5.10 shows the OrderSummary snippet.

Listing 5.10 The OrderSummary snippet

```scala
import scala.xml.NodeSeq
import net.liftweb.util.Helpers._
import net.liftweb.paypal.snippet.BuyNowSnippet
import example.travel.model.Customer

class OrderSummary extends BuyNowSnippet {
  override def dispatch = {
    case "paynow" => buynow _
    case "value." => value
    case "shipping" => shipping
  }

  val order = Customer.currentUser.flatMap(_.order)
  val amount = order.map(_.totalValue).openOr(0D)
  val reference = order.map(
    _.reference.is.toString).openOr("n/a")

  override val values = Map(
    "business" -> "seller_XXXXX_biz@domain.com",
    "item_number" -> reference,
    "item_name" -> ("Auction Order: " + reference))

  def value = "*" #> amount.toString
```

1 Wire up BuyNowSnippet

2 Configure PayPal

3 Get order value for auction

```
def shipping = order.map { o =>
  "address_one" #> o.shippingAddressOne.is &
  "address_two" #> o.shippingAddressTwo.is &
  "city" #> o.shippingAddressCity.is &
  "postcode" #> o.shippingAddressPostalCode.is
} openOr("*" #> NodeSeq.Empty)
}
```

❹ Bind shipping info from order

This class extends the Lift PayPal integration snippet, `BuyNowSnippet`, which provides a mechanism for automatically generating the relevant markup required to post transaction information to PayPal. By connecting the dispatch table to the `buynow` method in the `BuyNowSnippet` ❶, buynow becomes callable from your template markup. In addition, the `BuyNowSnippet` allows you to define extra configuration parameters that will be transferred to hidden inputs in the resulting PayPal form. This is done by providing a simple key-value `Map` ❷.

In addition to the PayPal setup, the `value` snippet method ❸ obtains the overall value of the order using the `totalValue` helper method that was added to the `Order` model earlier in the chapter.

The shipping method reads the values that were entered in the `Checkout` screen and binds them for display using the familiar CSS-style selectors. Had this example been using a full `Wizard`, you wouldn't need to reload the values in this way, but for the sake of simplicity, we chose to do it this way rather than complicate the example with even more new content ❹.

With this snippet code in place, you need to implement these snippets and add the checkout and summary pages to the sitemap. The next listing shows the markup required for the summary page.

Listing 5.11 XHTML for checkout summary

```
<lift:surround with="wide" at="content">
  <div>
    <h2>Order Summary</h2>
    <lift:basket.items>
      ...
    </lift:basket.items>

    <div class="basket-row">
      <p class="bold">Total purchase value: &pound;
        <em lift="order_summary.value" /></p>
    </div>

    <h2>Shipping Details</h2>
    <p>Details of travel will be sent to the
       following address: (<a href="checkout">
       Edit</a>)</p>
    <p class="bold" lift="order_summary.shipping">
      <address_one /><br/>
      <address_two /><br/>
      <city /><br/>
      <postcode /><br/>
    </p>
```

❶ Reuse basket markup

❷ Display total value

❸ Display shipping details

```
    <h2>Payment</h2>
    <p>Please pay for your items using the PayPal button below</p>
    <lift:order_summary.paynow />
  </div>
</lift:surround>
```

4 Render PayPal form

This markup should look fairly familiar. It's just implementing the snippet methods as you've done in the past couple of chapters. First it reuses the Basic snippet from the previous section ❶, and then it displays the total order value ❷. In addition, it renders the customer's shipping information ❸ and finally generates the Buy Now button ❹, which sends the transaction to PayPal.

The only other point of note here is the static link back to the checkout page. The checkout screen is clever enough to figure out what it needs to do in order to obtain the values, so the same screen serves as both an input and editing form with no extra work. The final result should look like figure 5.3.

A couple of visual features have been added in this screenshot, such as the stage pin to indicate what phase of the transaction the user is at, but these are just standard HTML and CSS tricks, so they don't warrant discussion here. As this screen is near the end of the user's journey through the application, the only thing remaining is to transfer them to PayPal for payment.

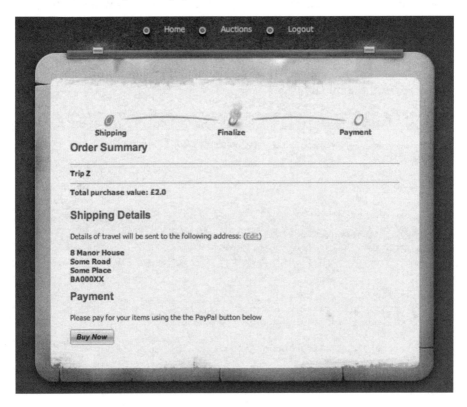

Figure 5.3   The completed checkout summary page

5.3 Collecting payment with PayPal

As it stands, there's no way for the user to actually send the funds for their orders. This is somewhat problematic and wouldn't make for a very good ecommerce site! Fortunately, the Lift module that you added to the project dependency earlier in this chapter provides out-of-the-box support for the online payment service provider PayPal. The integration supports the two most common forms of electronic payment used by PayPal: Payment Data Transfer (PDT) and Instant Payment Notification (IPN).

> **NOTE** You can read more about PDT and IPN on the PayPal site. PDT is discussed at https://mng.bz/3gvM and IPN is covered at https://mng.bz/5tOy.

The PayPal integration means you don't have to set up your own dispatch functions for handling the responses from PayPal and parsing their postback to your application. Typically, all you need to do is create a handler object that implements methods required by the `PaypalIPN` and `PaypalPDT` traits, and hook up the dispatchers supplied by those traits in your application boot.

5.3.1 Environment setup

Before we cover the PayPal implementation, there are several things you must know about PayPal and their developer process. First, you'll need to register yourself on developer.paypal.com. Then you should do some background reading on PDT and IPN. The online documentation is very comprehensive, and as this is a book about Lift, and not about PayPal, we won't repeat it here other than to touch on some high-level configuration instructions.

With your account created and logged in to developer.paypal.com follow the steps in table 5.1.

Table 5.1   Process of configuring the PayPal sandbox environment

	Configuring your PayPal sandbox	
	Action	**Result**
1	Set up both a "preconfigured seller" and "preconfigured buyer" account in the sandbox.	PayPal generates random account names and allows you to log in as those "people." ⦿ seller_1278962623_biz@getintheloop.eu Business Verified ▶ View Details ◯ buyer_1278962189_per@getintheloop.eu Personal Verified ▶ View Details [Enter Sandbox Test Site] [Delete]

Table 5.1   Process of configuring the PayPal sandbox environment *(continued)*

Configuring your PayPal sandbox		
	Action	**Result**
2	Log into the sandbox as the seller account you just created, and enable Auto Return in the selling preferences. The PayPal documentation can be found here: http://mng.bz/M8NJ.	Enabling Auto Return ensures that the user is sent back to the application when their transaction is completed. Your autoreturn URL will now be http://YOUREXTERNALHOST/paypal/pdt.
3	Enable PayPal Data Transfer (it's on the same screen as the Auto Return configuration).	Enabling PDT will ensure that when the transaction completes, PayPal passes back a few details about the order, such as the transaction token.
4	Edit the IPN callback URL and enable IPN. The PayPal documentation can be found here: https://www.paypal.com/ipn.	IPN is an asynchronous call back to your server with all the specific details about a given transaction.

Now that your environment is set up, you need to wire up the Lift side of things, or the communications from PayPal will disappear into the ether. As I mentioned, there are two main traits in the PayPal package to take responsibility for the two supported transaction systems: `PaypalIPN` and `PaypalPDT`. In this example, let's create a handler that implements these traits called `PaypalHandler` with the implementation shown in the following listing

Listing 5.12   The `PaypalHandler` implementation

```
import net.liftweb.common.{Loggable,Full,Box,Empty,Failure}
import net.liftweb.paypal.{PaypalIPN,PaypalPDT,
  PaypalTransactionStatus,PayPalInfo}
import net.liftweb.http.DoRedirectResponse
import net.liftweb.mapper.By
import example.travel.model.{Order,OrderStatus}

object PaypalHandler extends PaypalIPN with PaypalPDT with Loggable {
  import PaypalTransactionStatus._
  val paypalAuthToken = "yourtokengoeshere"          ◁─┐   ❶ PDT token key
  def pdtResponse = {
    case (info, resp) => info.paymentStatus match {
      case Full(CompletedPayment) =>                        ❷ Successful
        DoRedirectResponse.apply("/paypal/success")           PDT action
      case _ =>
        DoRedirectResponse.apply("/paypal/failure")         ❸ Failure PDT
    }                                                           action
  }

  def actions = {
    case (CompletedPayment,info,_) =>
      updateOrder(info,OrderStatus.Complete)
    case (FailedPayment,info,_) =>                          ❹ IPN response
      updateOrder(info,OrderStatus.Failed)                    handlers
    case (status, info, resp) =>
  }
```

```
    private def updateOrder(info: PayPalInfo,
                            status: OrderStatus.Value){
      Order.find(By(Order.reference,
          info.itemNumber.map(_.toLong)
        .openOr(0L))) match {
        case Full(order) => order.status(status).save
        case _ =>
      }
    }
  }
}
```

⑤ **Find and update order by ref**

In short, this code block composes the two PayPal traits supplied by the Lift PayPal integration and implements the required methods to handle the various responses PayPal might provide. It goes without saying, however, that this is only an example. In a real production system, you'd account for a lot more responses and intelligently handle them. This, in comparison, is a mere stub to illustrate the process and ease of implementing ecommerce in Lift.

When you enabled PDT in the PayPal sandbox, you were assigned a security token to use in the PDT request. It needs to be entered in this code so PayPal can know that it's your application calling back to it for information on the transaction **❶**. In this implementation, PDT serves only to display the correct response screen back to the user; the pdtResponse cases **❷** and **❸** dictate which URL the user should be redirected to based on the result of the transaction.

The actions are somewhat more complex **❹**, because when the PayPal servers make the IPN callback to the application, it contains much more data and is generally considered the best way to then update order information with the transaction data. The updateOrder helper method **❺** will look up an order by the order reference number that was generated when the order was created; then, depending upon the status received from the IPN data, the order has its status set appropriately.

Although this code is functional, it's currently not wired into the application boot cycle, so it won't ever be invoked by Lift. In order for Lift to be able to call the PayPal Handler you need to add the following code within your Boot class:

```
import net.liftweb.paypal.PaypalRules
import example.travel.lib.PaypalHandler

class Boot extends Loggable {
  def boot {
    ...
    PaypalRules.init
    PaypalHandler.dispatch.foreach([LiftRules.dispatch.append(_))
    ...
  }
}
```

The PaypalRules and PaypalHandler lines of code first initialize the PaypalRules object that contains configuration information used to determine a range of factors about the transaction. For example, it contains a function configuration that lets you dynamically determine which currency should be used when communicating with

PayPal. In this case, it uses the defaults, so it will select a currency based upon the locale of the JVM running the example. Second, they take the dispatch functions in the `PaypalHandler` object (inherited from the two Lift PayPal traits), which respond to the IPN and PDT callbacks, and map them into the application using Lift's dispatching mechanism. We'll discuss Lift's dispatching mechanism in chapter 8.

5.3.2 *The Buy Now button*

With the backend all wired up and ready to go, you need to supply the user with a simple one-click button to instantiate the transaction process in the familiar PayPal way: a bright orange button! In Lift's PayPal support there's a mechanism for automatically generating these buttons. You simply need to implement the `BuyNowSnippet` trait into one of your snippet classes and populate the required methods so it knows the value and other metadata you wish to send to PayPal.

Earlier in the chapter, listing 5.10 detailed the `OrderSummary` snippet that computed the overall value of the order and presented the user with a rundown of what they were going to purchase. As this already has the data we need for the button, the simplest approach is to just compose the `BuyNowSnippet` with the existing class. The next listing shows the changes made to the class.

> **Listing 5.13 Implementing the `BuyNowSnippet` trait**

```
import net.liftweb.paypal.snippet.BuyNowSnippet

class OrderSummary extends BuyNowSnippet {
  ...
  override val values = Map(                          ❶ Configure
    "business" -> "me@business.com",                    PayPal fields
    "item_number" -> reference,
    "item_name" -> ("Auction Order: " + reference))

}
```

As you can see in the listing, very few lines of code are required to implement the button. The main code overrides the `Map[String,String]` of the key-value pairs that need to be included in the form submission to PayPal ❶, but these parameters are detailed in the PayPal documentation (https://mng.bz/YnC1).

Finally, ensure that you add the PayPal response pages to the `SiteMap` in the `Boot` class:

```
Menu("Transaction Complete") / "paypal" / "success"
  >> LocGroup("public") >> Hidden,
Menu("Transaction Failure") / "paypal" / "failure"
  >> LocGroup("public") >> Hidden,
```

For simplicity's sake, we've populated these two files with a friendly message so the user is aware of the transaction's outcome. You might also want to customize the pages with customer information about their order; you have everything at your disposal in the PDT and IPN responses supplied by PayPal.

5.4 Summary

The application is now functioning with a good degree of functionality, and during its implementation you've seen various parts of Lift—some parts at a high level, and others in more detail. This chapter has made use of several Lift modules, including the state machine and PayPal integration. The real take-away here is that Lift has numerous modules for many aspects of web development, and they can often enhance your development cycle and cut the time to market for your application. Specifically, Lift Machine can be a very useful tool when you need to execute actions after or at a particular time in the future. This is a very common idiom in modern web applications, whether you're sending reminder emails or triggering some kind of notification in an application. Lift's stateful nature lends itself to this kind of sophisticated functionality.

In the next chapter, we'll start looking at the various aspects of Lift in far more detail than we've done so far. In the next chapter you'll be taking a deep dive into Lift's powerful templating and snippet mechanism, handling state with sessions and request variables, and looking at examples of how you can implement Lift's frontend components like `LiftScreen`. In the templating discussion, you'll see how you can make use of HTML5 and automatic validation of your markup templates while also utilizing powerful CSS-style element transformations to bind dynamic content to your design templates via Lift's snippet mechanism.

Part 3

Lift in detail

We've swept through several of Lift's features during the construction of the example booking application; it's now time to take a more extensive tour of the Lift toolset. This part of the book aims to act as a guide and in-depth reference and to provide helpful bits of advice along the way that should smooth your learning curve with Lift.

Chapter 6 covers common techniques for implementing applications with Lift, including templating, views, sessions, and multipage input structures. Chapter 7 covers Lift's excellent SiteMap module, which provides a lightweight access control mechanism and slick way to componentize logic within your applications. Chapters 8 and 9 cover Lift's HTTP feature set—from REST web services, through dispatching and URL rewriting, right up to advanced Comet usage. Chapters 10 and 11 cover persistence within Lift. They demonstrate both the Mapper module for working with RDBMS with an Active Record pattern, and the Record module, which provides a context wrapper around a store-agnostic provider system for working with backends from RDBMS to NoSQL.

The final three chapters in this part of the book cover topics usually associated with complex enterprise applications. Chapter 12 covers localization within Lift. Chapter 13 covers distributed programming and messaging. These technologies are increasingly becoming a part of application requirements in the enterprise. Chapter 14 explains how you can leverage Lift's test kit and the other Scala testing frameworks to ensure your code is of high quality before getting it ready for a production deployment. Finally, chapter 15 shows how you can take your Lift application into deployment, and covers some strategies for scaling and performance, including complicated topics like state handling and monitoring.

Common tasks
with Lift WebKit

This chapter covers

- Templates, views, and snippets
- Session and request variables
- Forms with `LiftScreen` and `Wizard`
- Widgets

There are many ways to achieve similar results in Lift, especially with templating and rendering. This chapter will show different ways that templates can be composed together and how you can control the rendering of dynamic content in your applications. Lift's view system, for example, is perfect for generating markup content from anything other than a standard template while still maintaining full access to the application state.

We also look at how you can effectively utilize Lift's type-safe session and request variables to hold on to important pieces of application state. From there we move on to look at Lift's stateful page flow mechanisms, `LiftScreen` and `Wizard`. Finally, we touch on what are known as Lift's *widgets*, which are a group of ready-made components that provide an easy API for adding things like autocomplete text boxes to your apps.

The first things we cover are Lift's templates, views, and snippets, because these are typically where most users will spend the majority of their time working with Lift.

6.1   *Templates, snippets, and views*

Any web framework, irrespective of language or implementation style, will ultimately need to generate markup to pass back to the browser. With this in mind, the templating system must be flexible but also easy to use because it's highly likely that developers and designers will spend a lot of time using the template system. Lift takes this to heart and recognizes that templating should not just be an afterthought to flush markup to the client side.

In the following subsections, we look at how you can implement different templating strategies in Lift, and we highlight some of the best practices for designing your snippets.

6.1.1   *Templates*

At its core, you can think of Lift's entire template system as a mechanism for replacing XML nodes. The markup templates are essentially simple indicators to Lift that it ought to replace the markers with something dynamic from a particular snippet, a view computation, or another template. This kind of system allows for a high degree of reuse within templates, and Lift provides a selection of additional utilities to further reduce the amount of repetition in your applications.

This section covers the core components and strategies you'll need to wield Lift's template system in the vast majority of situations: from building common templates to avoiding repeating regularly used elements through to handling Lift's HTML5 support.

SURROUNDS

When dealing with presentation markup and templates, the same rules apply, and it's unfortunately all too easy to repeat yourself and create a maintenance nightmare. Developers by their very nature hate to repeat themselves; we're always looking for ways to reuse this, that, or the other. To that end, Lift provides a mechanism called *surrounds* that allow you to build hierarchies of templates, with grandparent, parent, and child relationships, where the child inherits from both the parent and the grandparent. You can have as many levels in this hierarchy as you require. The most common use case for such a technique is to save repeating the <head> elements and other bits of page furniture that are common over all your pages.

To give this concept a little more substance, suppose the following listing shows the contents of a parent template called default.html found in webapp/templates-hidden.

Listing 6.1   Example of a parent template

```
<!DOCTYPE html PUBLIC "-//W3C//DTD HTML 4.01//EN"
  "http://www.w3.org/TR/html4/strict.dtd">
<html xmlns:lift="http://liftweb.net" xmlns="http://www.w3.org/1999/xhtml">
<head>
```

```
  <title>My Application</title>
</head>
<body>
  <lift:bind name="content" />     <- 1 Bind placeholder
</body>
</html>
```

For the most part, this is pretty standard markup. But you'll notice that there's a special Lift element called `bind` ❶. This marks a location in your template where child templates will be merged in place. The name attribute must be unique, but otherwise you're free to name these bind locations whatever you like.

You might be wondering how you can actually get content into this placeholder. That's simple. For child templates binding to a single placeholder, the `surround` element is your friend. Consider this example of using `surround`:

```
<lift:surround with="default" at="content">
  <p>Will be displayed in the placeholder position</p>
</lift:surround>
```

As you can see, the `at` attribute denotes the name defined in the parent template. When the page containing the `surround` is loaded, Lift wraps the content defined in the page template with that of the parent, defined by the `with` attribute. By default, it's assumed that parent templates are located in the templates-hidden directory in the webapp folder, but if you'd rather place the template somewhere else, you simply have to do something like this:

```
<lift:surround with="/path/from/webapp_dir/template" at="content">
```

Be sure to not place .html at the end of the `with` attribute value, though.

This simple system covers a lot of use cases, but what if you need to bind to multiple placeholders in the parent template? In that case, there's a handy helper called `<bind-at>` that's perfect for such a situation. Lift templates can only have a single root element because they must all be well-formed XML markup, so when you want to use `bind-at`, your implementing template would look like the next listing.

Listing 6.2 Using multiple bind placeholders in a child template

```
<lift:surround with="default" at="content">
  <lift:bind-at name="another_placeholder">
    <p>Wow, I am going elsewhere!</p>
  </lift:bind-at>
  <p>Will be displayed in the placeholder position</p>
</lift:surround>
```

The `<bind-at>` element sits within the surround, and the content defined therein is placed at the named bind point, irrespective of where that lives on the page.

As a side note, if you have a template that's only updating fragments of pages utilizing `<lift:bind-at>`, but you attempt to supply a template that effectively has more than one root node, the markup parser will explode with an error because well-formed XML must have a single root node. In this situation, you may not want to wrap your fragments with a `<div>` or other erroneous markup as it would impact your CSS implementation, so there's a helpful wrapper called `children`. Simply wrap the group of nodes with `<lift:children>` and the template will pass markup validation—this won't cause any adverse impact on the ultimate rendering in the browser.

> **NOTE** You may be wondering if all this processing of markup and templates has a performance impact. To a degree, it does, but Lift is clever enough to realize that when you're running in production mode you're unlikely to be changing your templates, so by default Lift caches the templates. If, for whatever reason, you want to alter this behavior or stop the caching, just look at `LiftRules.templateCache`.

Using layers of surrounds can be an extremely effective technique for reducing markup duplication. But there are some use cases that would be somewhat cumbersome with surrounds, and an embedding strategy would be more effective for directly reusing content.

CONTENT EMBEDDING AND PARTIAL TEMPLATES

One of the things that `<lift:surround>` doesn't give you is the ability to easily reuse a segment of markup in multiple places in an ad hoc fashion. It's doable, but it wouldn't be overly elegant, and you'd certainly be better served by an alternative solution. This is exactly what content embedding was designed to do.

Let's assume that you have the following markup, and it represents something that you want to repeatedly use in your application:

```
<div style="amazing">
  <p>Did you realize quite how amazing this is</p>
</div>
```

If you wanted to embed that markup in an ad hoc fashion in any template, all you need to do is place it in the templates-hidden directory and then call `<lift:embed>` in the template where you'd like that content to be imported. Here's an example:

```
<lift:embed what="_amazing" />
```

As a general convention, we recommend denoting your partial templates in some way so that it's immediately obvious that they're different from your main surround templates. Typically, I prefix their names with an underscore, but this is just a suggested convention; it's not a hard and fast rule required to make the system work.

HEAD RESOURCES

It's very common to want to externalize the surrounding `<head>` content and other global resources into a single template. Doing this can really cut down on maintenance, but it does, like most things, have a downside too. Let's assume that you have a single page that requires some extra CSS and JavaScript that deviates from the standard `<head>` you have elsewhere, and that it's an unacceptable weight to include in the main parent surround. Lift provides the solution in a feature called a *head merge*.

In essence, head merge looks in your child (page) templates for the <head> element, and, upon finding it, will merge that together with the <head> from the surround template, giving you a rendered page that's an amalgamation of the resources from child and parent templates. It couldn't be simpler.

Lift also provides the reverse mechanism so you can insert content just before the closing </body> tag, which a lot of frontend developers like to do to boost page-loading speeds. Unsurprisingly, being the opposite of <head>, this mechanism is called tail, and it can be used like any other Lift tag:

```
<lift:tail>
  <!-- stuff you want before the closing body -->
</lift:tail>
```

Both during the development cycle and after moving an application into production, you can get strange results when the client-side browser has cached the CSS, JavaScript, and perhaps even image files. Lift provides a simple helper to prevent the browser from using an incorrectly cached resource: <lift:with-resource-id>. Simply wrap the element you want to have a specialized ID appended to with the with-resource-id tag like this:

```
<lift:with-resource-id>
  <script type="text/javascript" src="js/example.js"><script>
</lift:with-resource-id>
```

Then when Lift renders your page, you'll get a consistent URL that will only change when the application is rebooted. If you were wondering, the URL would be something like this:

```
<script
  type="text/javascript"
  src="js/example.js?F1142850447932JLI=_"></script>
```

Altering the String => String function that lives in LiftRules.attachResourceId can easily modify this appended string.

DOCTYPES AND MARKUP VALIDATION

As Lift runs all your template markup through its rendering pipeline, it will automatically strip off any Document Type Definition (DTD) information you apply directly in the template, and it will render your pages with XHTML Transitional document type by default. In order to set the DocType to your preferred type, you need to apply the following in your Boot class:

```
import net.liftweb.common.Full
import net.liftweb.http.{LiftRules,Req,DocType}

LiftRules.docType.default.set((r: Req) => Full(DocType.xhtmlStrict))
```

Because the LiftRules.docType configuration parameter is a FactoryMaker, you can set a different document type based upon information in the request. For example, if the request was from an iPhone, you might want to render the content with a mobile

DocType rather than the standard default. `FactoryMakers` are covered in detail in chapter 14 (section 14.2.2).

Table 6.1 details the available `DocType` declarations that Lift provides and shows examples of their usage.

Table 6.1   DocType declarations in Lift

DocType	Usage
XHTML Transitional	`DocType.xhtmlTransitional`
XHTML Strict	`DocType.xhtmlStrict`
XHTML Frameset	`DocType.xhtmlFrameset`
XHTML 1.1	`DocType.xhtml11`
XHTML Mobile	`DocType.xhtmlMobile`
HTML5	`DocType.html5`

Because your application could feasibly end up with a large number of templates, validating that they're all correct can often be difficult. With this in mind, Lift supports automatic validation of application markup in the normal course of development. If any validation errors exist, a notice is pushed out to the browser explaining the error.

To enable a validator, configure the following option in your `Boot` class:

```
import net.liftweb.common.Full
import net.liftweb.http.{LiftRules,StrictXHTML1_0Validator}

LiftRules.xhtmlValidator = Full(StrictXHTML1_0Validator)
```

This example employs the XHTML Strict validation during development. Lift supplies a couple of validators by default; these are listed in table 6.2.

Table 6.2   Default template validators in Lift

Validator	Usage
XHTML Strict	`LiftRules.xhtmlValidator =` `   Full(StrictXHTML1_0Validator)`
XHTML Transitional	`LiftRules.xhtmlValidator =` `   Full(TransitionalXHTML1_0Validator)`

If you want to implement your own validator, just extend `net.liftweb.http.Generic-Validator` and provide the location of the relevant XSD.

HTML5 SUPPORT

When Lift was first conceived, XHTML was lined up to be the successor for the HTML standard, and as such XHTM required all templates to be valid XML documents. At the time of writing, HTML5 was starting to make a large impact on the web development world, and HTML5 appeared to be slowly but surely overtaking the XHTML standard, which was not adopted as broadly as the W3C might have hoped. All versions of Lift still fully support XHTML, and it's the default mode for Lift applications, but as of version 2.2 onward, Lift fully supports HTML5. There is a parser for HTML5 templates and support within Lift's own rendering pipeline for emitting HTML5 to the browser.

In order to enable HTML5 support in Lift, just add the following line to your `Boot` class:

```
import net.liftweb.http.{LiftRules,Req,Html5Properties}

LiftRules.htmlProperties.default.set((r: Req) =>
  new Html5Properties(r.userAgent))
```

This configuration comes with a couple of oddities that relate to the strictness of HTML5. Specifically, HTML5 has some incompatibilities with XHTML templates and doesn't like self-closed tags, like `<lift:menu.builder />`. It also doesn't function with mixed-case tags, which are frequently used for snippets in Lift.

But there's a solution; if you want HTML5 output but would prefer XHTML templates, you can implement the following configuration in your `Boot` class:

```
import net.liftweb.http.{LiftRules,Req,XHtmlInHtml5OutProperties}

LiftRules.htmlProperties.default.set((r: Req) =>
  new XHtmlInHtml5OutProperties(r.userAgent))
```

This configuration can be exceedingly helpful if you're migrating an existing application to HTML5 from XHTML, or if you'd simply prefer to continue to build your templates in the way you've become accustomed to. More information about Lift's `HTMLProperties` system can be found on the Lift wiki: http://www.assembla.com/spaces/liftweb/wiki/HtmlProperties_XHTML_and_HTML5.

DISPLAYING MESSAGES

If you've been reading this book from the beginning, you'll be familiar with the `S.notice`, `S.warning`, and `S.error` methods. You can implement these methods in your snippet and pass them a `String` that represents a message you wish to pass back to the user.

In order to allow the designer to position and style these messages, Lift provides the `<lift:msgs />` and `<lift:msg />` helpers. These have a variety of options to allow you style the message and interface precisely.

The following listing shows an example of applying custom styles to the built-in notice system through `<lift:msgs />`.

Listing 6.3 Applying custom styling to the `Msgs` helper

```
<lift:msgs>
  <lift:error_msg>Error! The details are:</lift:error_msg>
  <lift:error_class>errorBox</lift:error_class>
  <lift:warning_msg>Whoops, I had a problem:</lift:warning_msg>
```

```
    <lift:warning_class>warningBox</lift:warning_class>
    <lift:notice_msg>Note:</lift:notice_msg>
    <lift:notice_class>noticeBox</lift:notice_class>
</lift:msgs>
```

The sequence of nodes enclosed by <lift:msgs> allows you to control various aspects of the messages. Each type of notification has a pair of styling elements. The nodes ending in _msg denote the text to be prefixed to each type of notice display, whereas nodes ending with _class allow you to customize the CSS class that's applied to the relevant display type.

One other interesting point about the notification system is that irrespective of whether it's displaying notifications after a hard page reload or notifications in response to some AJAX function, they operate in exactly the same way and can be styled through a single mechanism. You can even get the message to dynamically fade out after a defined period of time. In your application Boot, simply define the following:

```
import net.liftweb.http.{LiftRules,NoticeType}
import net.liftweb.common.Full
import net.liftweb.util.Helpers._

LiftRules.noticesAutoFadeOut.default.set(
    (notices: NoticeType.Value) =>Full(2 seconds, 2 seconds))
```

For any messages that are defined in your application, this configuration will automatically fade them out after displaying for a period of 2 seconds, and it will take 2 seconds to conduct the fade out.

Despite the significant differences between all these methods, they're all implemented using the same mechanism: snippets. Snippets are essentially sections of rendering logic, and the only difference between them and other rendering logic is that they're shipped with Lift and are automatically made available to the template mechanism, so they appear to be built in. Otherwise, they aren't leveraging anything that you couldn't implement yourself. This should give you a good indication of how powerful the snippet idiom can actually be.

6.1.2   *Snippets*

Way back in chapter 1 (section 1.2.2), we first discussed Lift's model of snippet operation, and in the previous section you saw how Lift itself, builds on the concept of snippets to provide a rich templating system. In this section, we spend some time comparing and contrasting the different types of snippet you can create and cover some useful things to know when making your own snippets.

CSS TRANSFORMERS

Snippets are essentially a way of generating dynamically rendered content, and having a clean and effective way to actually work with the template markup is key. This is where Lift's *CSS transformers* come in. Generally speaking, when you're building interactive content in Lift, you create server-side controls via the SHtml object and then bind that to a particular sequence of XML nodes. In order to choose which nodes have which server controls, Lift supplies a CSS-style selectors API; these are also collectively known as CSS transformers because they take template markup as input and *transform* that to rendered output markup. Let's take a look at a few examples of using SHtml and Lift's CSS transformers to understand the interplay between these two pieces.

The SHtml object has methods for creating text fields, check boxes, AJAX content, and much, much more. Most of the user interaction components you might want in your application can be found in SHtml. With this in mind, let's take a look at a basic example of attaching a text box and submit button, along with the template code used to call it, as shown in the following listing.

> **Listing 6.4 Basic binding snippet**

```
import net.liftweb.util.Helpers._
import net.liftweb.http.SHtml

class BasicExample {
  def sample = {
    var message = "Change this text"
    "type=text" #>SHtml.text(message, message = _) &      ❶ Make SHtml
    "type=submit" #>SHtml.onSubmitUnit(                      controls
      () =>println(message))
  }
}
```

This listing shows a very simple class that has a lone method called sample. This method has a single variable inside called message that will temporarily hold the value that's entered by the user before it's printed to the console by the submit function. The really important parts here are defined at ❶. At first look, this may look like rather strange syntax, but bear with me while we step through it.

CSS selector statements are defined in the following fashion:

```
"selector" #> thing-to-bind
```

The left-hand selector could be a variety of things, examples of which are detailed later in table 6.3. On the right side of the #> symbol is the content that you want to bind to that selector; this content could be a NodeSeq or some type that's implicitly *promotable* via implicit conversion to CssSel. All the default implicit conversions are imported into scope via the import Helpers._ statement, so be sure to include that or the selectors won't work as anticipated.

In this example, the elements being bound are SHtml controls for the required form. As this form only has two elements, we can just use the CSS-style selectors to grab the two elements from the template markup that have the attributes type="text" and type="submit". The template code in this instance would look like this:

```
<p class="l:basic_example.sample?form=post">
<input type="text" /><br />
<input type="submit" /></p>
```

You can almost think of the surrounding <p> element as invoking the class and calling the method, with anything contained in that block essentially being the markup that your selectors will address. Finally, but importantly, in order to make the form function correctly, you must add the ?form=post attribute to the snippet. This tells Lift that the element should be surrounded with a <form> tag, which enables the HTML submit to work as expected and submit the form when the users hit the Submit button.

Before we move on to a slightly more complicated example, let's first take a closer look at the SHtml call in listing 6.4. As previously mentioned, SHtml has a lot of different methods—far too many to cover in this section—but there are some important concepts that apply to all the different methods and that should help you. Consider figure 6.1.

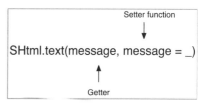

Figure 6.1 Typical SHtml usage patterns

As a general rule, most of the HTML element controls, such as inputs and non-AJAX interactions (AJAX controls are covered in chapter 9), will have two parameters:

- A getter function that reads an initial value (for example, from a Mapper model)
- A function that's of type String => Any and that's used to set the target's value (in listing 6.4, the value of the message var)

> **TIP** Lift has a built-in garbage collection system that intelligently cleans up any functions that have not been seen on the page in the past 10 minutes. This ensures that your application remains tight and doesn't become unduly bloated. You'll notice that each page is assigned an identifier like var lift_page = "F6205612861985YP"; that's inserted just before the </body> tag, and this is used by Lift to identify the currently active page of functions, essentially allowing Lift to detect when you browsed away from a particular page. You can turn Lift's garbage collection mechanism off if you want to, but that isn't recommended.

Consider table 6.3, which details some specific examples of using CSS selectors. If you aren't too keen on the #> method and would prefer something a little more regular, you can use replaceWith instead of #> and all the examples in the table will work just as well.

Table 6.3 Examples of implementing Lift's CSS-style transformers

Selector	Description
Subordinate selection	"*" #><p>Replace all</p>
	Global selectors replace all child nodes with the content defined on the right side of the function. Every element is replaced.

Table 6.3 Examples of implementing Lift's CSS-style transformers *(continued)*

Selector	Description
ID selection	`"#thing" #><p>Replaced</p>` Given an element that has an `id="thing"` attribute, this selector will replace the whole node with the content on the right side of the function.
Class selection	`".amazing" #><p>WOW</p>` Given an element with `class="amazing"`, this selector will replace the whole node with the content on the right side of the function. This will be applied to all elements meeting the condition in the template markup.
Attribute selection	`"type=text" #>SHtml.text(thing, thing = _)` Attribute selection chooses a node based upon the `attribute=key` syntax. In this example, it would select all text input nodes in the markup.
Name selection	`"@signup" #>NodeSeq. Empty` Given an element with a `name` attribute, you can use the `@nameofthing` syntax to select that element. Name selection is essentially a shorthand for `name=signup`.

Specialized selection	`":button" #>SHtml.button ("Hit me",`
	`    () =>println("w00t"))`
	
	Like some JavaScript libraries, Lift provides convenience selectors for commonly used elements. At the time of writing, the following shorthand selectors were supported: `:button`, `:checkbox`, `:file`, `:password`, `:radio`, `:reset`, `:submit`, and `:text`.

The base selectors give you functionality for selecting elements in a wide variety of scenarios and replacing their content. But this is only useful for some operations; there are times when you want to select something more specific than just one node, such as if you want to dynamically alter the class attribute of a given node to change its styling. CSS transformers also have a range of modifiers that work in conjunction with the straightforward element selectors, as detailed in table 6.4.

Table 6.4 CSS transformation modifiers and their usage

Selector modifier	Description
Replace element subordinates	`"li *" #> List("monday", "tuesday", "wednesday")` Transform the children of a given node by mixing together the element selector with the subordinate selector. This example will iterate through the list and replace all the `<li>`elements with `<li>{{list element}}</li>`.

Table 6.4 CSS transformation modifiers and their usage (continued)

Selector modifier	Description

Append element subordinates	`"#apd *+" #> "Timothy"`
	
	Appends content to existing nodes children. For example,
	
	`<div id="apd">Welcome, </div>`
	would become
	`<div id="apd">Welcome, Timothy</div>`

Prepend element subordinates	`"#prepend_target -*" #> "Timothy"` Prepends the content on the right side of the function to the start of the child nodes.
Element attribute replacement	`"type=text [class]" #> "textinput"` Selects an element and then uses the `[attribute]` modifier to change a particular attribute. This example adds the `textinput` class to all text inputs in the input content.
Element attribute append	`".foo [class+]" #> "bar"` Similar to the attribute replacement, but this modifier appends to the existing content. The classic use case here is to dynamically append a specific CSS class to a given element.
Root template selector	`"#content ^^" #> NodeSeq. Empty` Commonly, you'll need to only display a segment of content to a particular user. For example, if they're not logged in, you need to render a login form, but if they're already logged in, you might need to show them some other content. The `^^` modifier takes the selected element, removes all the other nodes in scope of this snippet, except for the one identified by the selector, and uses the remaining nodes as the display content. This allows you to select template content dynamically; in this example, the `id="content"` node would be used as the root node for that snippet's content.
Child template selector	`"#content ^*" #> NodeSeq.Empty` Provides identical functionality to the root template selector, but the specified node is dropped and only the children are used for the template content.

This idiom of replacing elements can be exceedingly powerful, as you can chain the use of CSS selectors with the `&` operator. This allows you to build up chained transformation functions in any given block. Also, because the CSS transformations derive from a `NodeSeq => NodeSeq` function type, you can compose function blocks together using `compose` and the `andThen` methods, giving you blocks of functions that feed input through one set of chained transformations to another. Here's an example of a render function we look at in more detail in chapter 10:

```
def render =
    "#value_one" #> doubleInput(one = _) &
    "#value_two" #> doubleInput(two = _) andThen SHtml.makeFormsAjax
```

Note how the first two declarations define input fields, and that's *composed* with another NodeSeq => NodeSeq function from the SHtml object: makeFormsAjax. For the moment, don't worry about what this function does; just understand that the content from the first two declarations is processed and then passed to the secondary function. The result is that elements can go for a second round of processing, or, in this case, be wrapped with an AJAX form element.

Armed with this new information, let's create a slightly more complex example that's more indicative of what you'd likely want to code in a real-world application. Let's construct two case classes that model the simple relationship between authors and the books they've written.

```
case class Book(name: String)
case class Author(name: String, books: List[Book])
```

This is a simple relationship but one that can be used to create a list of authors and their works. Given a List[Author], you could create the snippet shown in the following listing.

Listing 6.5   A more complex iteration

```
import scala.xml.NodeSeq
import net.liftweb.util.Helpers._             ❶ Supply
                                                 sample data
object Library {
  case class Book(name: String)
  case class Author(name: String, books: List[Book])
  val books = List(
    Author("JK Rowling", List(
      Book("Harry Potter and the Deathly Hallows"),
      Book("Harry Potter and the Goblet of Fire"))
    ),
    Author("Joshua Suereth", List(
      Book("Scala in Depth"))
    )
  )
}

class Authors {
def list =                                    ❷ Iterate through
    "ul" #> Library.books.map { author =>       authors
      ".name" #> author.name &
      ".books" #> ("li *" #> author.books.map(_.name))   ❸ Iterate through
    }                                                       books
}
```

In this example, the Library object is used purely for the purpose of example ❶. The really interesting part of this example is the list method ❷.

The first thing this list method does is *map* the List[Author] and implement the right CSS transformations based upon the markup supplied by the designer. In this case, the display is going to be an unordered list containing a nested unordered list that displays the books of the given author. As the `Author` type is a `case class`, this means that the parameters are automatically made immutable properties of that class, so it's possible to access them directly, as in the case of `author.name`, without the need to write the boilerplate `getXXX`-style methods that are commonly found in Java code.

Finally the nested iteration bound to the `.books` selector is used to display a given author's books ❸. You may remember from table 6.4 that the CSS transformers can automatically render list types, so in this example it's possible to *map* the `List[Book]` into a `List[String]` to obtain the titles, and then Lift takes care of the rest!

The picture would not be complete without the markup—the following listing shows the template code that implements the snippet in the next listing.

Listing 6.6   Markup for complex iteration snippet

```
<ul lift="authors.list">
  <li><span class="name">Author</span>
    <ul class="books">
      <li>Book title</li>
    </ul>
  </li>
</ul>
```

Here you can see the nested lists that were referred to in the snippet code. Specifically, notice that in the nested list, the elements all have dummy placeholder values, such as the book title in this example, that are replaced at runtime by the snippet.

EAGER EVALUATION AND SNIPPET ATTRIBUTES

When you have a page that encompasses a selection of distinctly different snippets, you may end up with a scenario where you explicitly need to nest snippets inside of each other. Consider this example:

```
<lift:example.one>
  ...
  <lift:example.two>
  ...
  </lift:example.two>
</lift:example.one>
```

By default, `example.one` would execute first, followed by `example.two`. Depending on your circumstances and the actual actions of these snippets, you may want to reverse this execution so that the inner snippet, `example.two` in this context, executes and yields its markup as part of the input for the outer snippet, `example.one`.

To trigger this behavior, you simply need to add the `eager_eval="true"` attribute to the outer snippet. This attribute indicates to Lift that it should evaluate the inner markup before evaluating this snippet. In this example, the first line would look like this:

```
<lift:example.one eager_eval="true">
```

That's all there is to it.

It's also possible to add your own custom attributes to snippets and readily access those attributes from your Scala code. This can be a helpful idiom for making reusable snippet code, and it's something you'll see in the Lift codebase itself. Assume you have the following snippet call:

```
<lift:attribute_example.thing extraStuff="true" fictionalCount="1" />
```

The two attributes here—extraStuff and fictionalCount—would, in the normal course of processing, be totally ignored. In order to access these attributes in your snippet code, you can call the S.attr method. The following listing shows a complete example.

Listing 6.7 Accessing snippet attributes

```
import scala.xml.{NodeSeq,Text}
import net.liftweb.http.S
import net.liftweb.util.Helpers._

classAttributeExample {
  def thing(xhtml: NodeSeq): NodeSeq = {
    val stuff = S.attr("extraStuff", _.toBoolean)     ❶ Get attribute
        .openOr(false)                                   and convert
    val count = S.attr("fictionalCount", _.toInt)        type
        .openOr(0)
    Text("extraStuff: %s fictionalCount: %s".format(stuff,count))
  }
}
```

As you can see, the attributes are accessed and then a converting function is applied to create the correct type ❶. Generally speaking, this is my preferred method of accessing attributes unless I'm simply accessing a string. This way you end up with a value that's the appropriate type, and you can provide a nice default value if the attribute is either not supplied or had problems during the type conversion.

METHOD DISPATCHING

Before we get into anything more detailed, let's take a moment to consider how Lift resolves template markup to server-side classes and methods.

Given a template snippet call like this,

```
<lift:my_snippet.some_method />
```

Lift will, by default, use reflection to resolve this to a class in a package called snippet that lives in whichever package you have defined in your application Boot.scala with a call to LiftRules.addToPackages. In this default scheme, Lift will translate snake_case naming conventions to CamelCase ones. In the preceding example, Lift would go looking for MySnippet.someMethod. If it can't find the snippet, Lift will throw an exception and present you with a nice red box where the snippet content should be, informing you that the class or method doesn't exist. (Note that the red box only appears in development mode.)

The alternative to loading snippet methods via reflection, and the one that's generally recommended when your application starts to grow, is what's known as a dis-

> ### Reflection snippet gotchas
>
> When using snippets loaded via reflection, class methods that are inherited from any applicable supertypes won't automatically be available as callable methods. For example, if you had `class MySnippet extends CommonSnippet`, any methods that were in `CommonSnippet` would not automatically be available when called from the template. If you try to make such a call, you'll be told by Lift that the snippet method you tried to call doesn't exist.
>
> If you want to reuse code and build a compositional snippet structure, all you need to do is implement a dispatch snippet and directly map a snippet dispatch name to the supertype method.

patch snippet. Dispatch snippets differ slightly from reflection-loaded snippets in that they determine which template markup invokes which class method by way of an explicit dispatch table that defines a string and then the appropriate `NodeSeq => NodeSeq` function. The enclosing class itself can still be resolved using reflection.

The following listing demonstrates an example of a basic dispatch snippet.

Listing 6.8   Basic dispatch snippet

```
class Example extends DispatchSnippet {
  def dispatch = {
    case "example" => render _
  }
  def render(xhtml: NodeSeq): NodeSeq = Text("sample")
}
```

You may well be wondering why you'd want to have the class discovered via reflection and yet do this manual dispatching. The answer is quite simple. When your application starts to grow, it will often make more sense to break your snippet classes into more manageable traits and compose the snippet entirely from traits. In such a situation, wiring up the dispatch map to invoke methods in the supertype is extremely helpful. Among the Lift community, using dispatch snippets would certainly be considered a best practice for this very reason, not to mention that you get some compile-time checking on the map between template snippet names and your actual method names.

The other situation that `DispatchSnippet` is useful for is when the operation that the snippet conducts is completely stateless, and it makes sense to use an object rather than a class, saving the need for the same thing to be instantiated in multiple sessions. As it happens, nearly all of the built-in snippets (`surround`, `msgs`, `bind-at`, and so on) are object snippets. Of course, as objects are by their very nature singletons in Scala, reflection won't work because the class instance already exists in the classloader.

To that end, if you have a completely stateless, object dispatch snippet, you can let Lift know about it by making a call to `LiftRules` like this:

```
LiftRules.snippetDispatch.append {
  case "example" => Example
}
```

As you can see, you simply need to give the snippet a name that will be used in the template and tell Lift where to find the object in question.

STATELESS OR STATEFUL?

Lift provides two different types of snippet: the normal and most common variety is what can generally be thought of as a stateless snippet, and the second is highly stateful and a subtype of `StatefulSnippet`.

Before going any further, we must be clear about the term *stateful*, because it's all too easy to misunderstand when terms like *state* are tossed around. When your snippet class is a normal Scala class, the instance is essentially discarded after the request has completed, so any class members or state in that instance are lost. But if in that snippet you make calls to Lift elements that create function bindings for things such as form submissions, the snippet itself is still stateless, but it causes a stateful action to occur in Lift. In contrast, when creating a snippet that's a subtype of `Stateful-Snippet`, the whole instance is kept around after the request cycle, so any variables or values that you have living in the instance are still accessible by subsequent calls in that session.

With this definition of the two types, let's talk a little more about why you would choose one over the other, and when you would choose `class` versus `object` for stateless snippets. Using stateless class snippets is the most common kind of Lift code you'll see. For the most part, there's absolutely nothing wrong with that—it provides the path of least resistance, as it requires no wiring up or other configuration. Consider the two definitions of the same snippet in the following listing.

Listing 6.9 Class snippet and object singleton snippet

```
import scala.xml.{NodeSeq,Text}
import net.liftweb.http.DispatchSnippet

classExampleA {
  def howdy(xhtml: NodeSeq) = Text("Hello world")      Stateless class
}                                                        snippet

object ExampleB extends DispatchSnippet {
  def dispatch = {
    case _ => howdy _                                    Stateless object
  }                                                      snippet
  def howdy(xhtml: NodeSeq) = Text("Hello world")
}
```

You can see how the object snippet is slightly more verbose, but because everything is explicitly wired, you benefit from the compile-time checking and bypassing the need for loading snippets via reflection at runtime. For a lot of applications, this may never be an issue, but if you want to take your application into any serious production environment where you're under anything but trivial load, we recommend using a singleton `object` and manually wiring it up through `LiftRules`, as discussed in the previous subsection on method dispatching.

By contrast, `StatefulSnippet` subtypes must always be class (instance) based because they're exclusive to a particular session. As the name suggests, any state that you're handling in the snippet is preserved longer than the initial page request, so you can reference it on subsequent requests. As `StatefulSnippet` is actually a subtype of `DispatchSnippet`, you must once again implement the `dispatch` method to specify which method dispatches which template call. The powerful thing about snippets inheriting from the `StatefulSnippet` trait compared to their stateless counterparts is that they can retain information from the previous operations; you can even make conditional dispatching rules based upon some stateful variable to determine which internal method the template will display when it renders the next time around. Consider the following listing, which details a simple stateful snippet that increments a counter and conditionally displays a form if the value of that counter is less than 5.

Listing 6.10 Stateful snippet count incrementing

```
import scala.xml.{NodeSeq,Text}
import net.liftweb.util.Helpers._
import net.liftweb.http.{StatefulSnippet,SHtml}

class CountIncrement extends StatefulSnippet {
  def dispatch = {
    case _ if count < 5 => renderBelowFive        ❶ Conditional
    case _ if count >= 5 => renderAboveFive           dispatching
  }

  def renderBelowFive =
      "count" #>count.toString&
      "increment" #>SHtml.submit("Increment",      ❷ Increment
          () => count += 1)                            count

  def renderAboveFive = (xhtml: NodeSeq) =>
    Text("Count is five or more.")                  ❸ Executed if
                                                       more than five
    private var count = 0
}
```

This small example increments the private `count` variable each time the button is clicked. This provides a clear illustration that the same instance is being used for each subsequent request. In the explicit `dispatch` function, the logic determines which method it should use to render the snippet, based upon the value of the internal `count` variable ❶. Every time the user clicks the button, the form is submitted and the `count` variable is increased by the function attached to the Submit button ❷. When the value is greater than 5, the `renderAboveFive` method is used ❸.

LAZY LOADING AND PARALLEL EXECUTION

When you have a snippet implementation, you have the option to apply a couple of different processing techniques to that snippet, irrespective of what it does. Let's assume that you have a system that takes some time to process a particular element that you need to display. Rather than delaying the rendering of the page, you could instruct Lift to lazily load that snippet. Lazy loading is baked right into Lift, and you can easily apply it to any snippet in your application by wrapping the invocation in the template.

Consider the following example:

```
<div class="l:LazyLoad">
  <span class="l:LongTime">Started this computation
    at<span id="start">start</span> and it completed
    at<span id="end">end</span>.
  </span>
</div>
```

Notice how the LongTime snippet is wrapped with the LazyLoad snippet. LazyLoad is a snippet built into Lift, and it will automatically inject a Comet component into the page that renders a placeholder for this snippet (complete with loading GUI) while the processing happens asynchronously on the server. When the snippet finishes processing, the content is pushed to the server automatically via Lift's Comet mechanism, which is discussed in depth in chapter 9. That's all there is to it!

In addition to lazily loading snippets, Lift can also parallelize the processing of snippets. Suppose you were building a system in which you needed to communicate with several backend servers, such as an advertising server. If each server took one second to respond, that's would seriously damage the user experience, so it makes sense to run those operations in parallel. To let Lift know that a particular snippet should be executed in parallel, just pass the snippet the parallel flag with the value of true. Here's an example:

```
<div class="l:FetchAd?parallel=true">
  ...
</div>
```

Notice the addition of ?parallel=true to the regular snippet invocation. When executing this snippet, Lift will farm off the processing to another thread and continue to process the rest of the page in the original thread. When the second thread completes processing, that markup will be reconstituted into the main page markup before returning the content to the browser. This is different from the lazy loading technique, which continues the page rendering and defers only a small portion until it's ready, and then pushes the completed content at a later date. In contrast, parallel processing defers the rendering of the whole page until it's ready.

So far in this section, you've seen how to leverage Lift's snippet and template infrastructure, including how to use Lift's powerful CSS transformers to attach server-side controls to rendered content. The next section shows you another Lift mechanism for displaying content:views.

6.1.3   *Views*

So far we've covered snippets as a mechanism for generating HTML content. Views offer an alternative route to generating that dynamic content. So what do they do? In terms of the generated output, the functionality is identical to that of snippets. The difference between the two approaches is in how that output is generated. In this section we look at what views are for and when they should be used instead of their snippet counterparts.

Before we get into anything too specific, let's consider what views offer over snippets. In the abstract, a view is `Box[() => NodeSeq]`. This is different from the familiar `NodeSeq => NodeSeq` transformation that snippets offer, and as the function implies, views are generating content from scratch rather than using a template as a basis. In this way, views lend themselves nicely to a couple of different tasks.

WHAT ARE VIEWS GOOD FOR?

One of the nice things about snippets is that they provide the development team a structured idiom for separating template and rendering logic. Although this is the most common of all Lift practices, Lift is ultimately about choice. To that end, one of the things views can offer you is the ability to work with different types of template mechanisms. Out of the box, Lift provides a secondary templating engine powered by Scalate (http://scalate.fusesource.org/) that allows you to write type-safe templates that encompass both the markup and the rendering logic. This style of intermingling code and markup will be familiar to anyone who has used JSP or ERB previously. The takeaway point here is that views allow you to generate markup content, which can even be used for plugging in other styles of templating to complement the defaults Lift provides.

Secondly, views offer developers who are working alone or who are at the very beginning of a project and require a fast, iterative approach to development a way to build markup output directly from their Scala code without the subjective indirection of HTML templates. Alternatively, you may be building something like an RSS feed, where the content output is XML-based but there's no need to involve a designer template (because RSS is a machine-to-machine process and so is handled by developers).

Snippets or views?

No doubt you're wondering which option—snippets or views—is the right route to choose. Well, Lift development is largely about choices. Some are neatly abstracted away and appear as defaults that you rarely need to touch, but others are more intrinsic to the way you and your team work and can't really be decided for you. You must make the choices that best suit your environment and the task at hand. Views versus snippets are such a choice. Both solutions offer you a way of rendering content, but they do so through different approaches, and before making a selection one way or another, you should play with both options and see which fits your project best.

Experience tells us that projects that involve designers or larger, more complex templating requirements will opt for snippets and HTML templates, whereas another project may prefer using SCAML rather than traditional markup and utilizing the view system. Understand your goals and constraints and make your choice accordingly.

USING VIEWS

With this introduction in mind, let's consider a few small examples in order to explore the view dispatch system and illustrate the ways in which views can be utilized.

First and foremost, the view dispatch system is controlled via the `LiftRules` property `viewDispatch`. This property takes a `List[String]` that represents the incoming URL, and returns

```
Either[() => Box[NodeSeq], LiftView]
```

`Either` is a type from the Scala standard library that allows for two different value types; in this case either `() =>Box[NodeSeq]`, or `LiftView`. Ultimately this particular `Either` represents two ways of producing XML content. The `Left` part of the `Either` construct is the `() =>Box[NodeSeq]` function, and this can be thought of as a generator of content. The `Right` side of the structure is a special type called `LiftView`.

First, let's explore the `Left` side of the `Either` used in the view system by wiring a custom view into Lift's `viewDispatch` handler, as shown:

```
LiftRules.viewDispatch.append {
  case "viewthing" :: "example" :: Nil =>
    Left(() => Full(<h1>Manual Sample</h1>))
}
```

In essence, `viewDispatch` is a map of incoming URLs to match for. When a match is found, a function is returned that can later be called to generate markup that will be returned to the browser. In this example, the `/viewthing/example` URL is matched, and an extremely simple bit of markup is returned to represent a heading. This whole response is wrapped in a `Left()` call to tell the compiler which part of the optional return type you're going to yield. In this case, it knows to expect `() => Box[NodeSeq]`.

So what about `Right` and the `LiftView` type? The `LiftView` type is a special one in Lift because `LiftViews` are wired into the template lookup mechanism. In practice, that means that you can place `LiftView` subtypes in a package called `view` that has its parent defined by `LiftRules.addToPackage`. The real difference here is that no manual wiring is required to define the input URL by default. Lift calculates the URL the same way it resolves snippets. For example, consider the following listing.

Listing 6.11 Implementing a `LiftView` subtype

```
packagesample.view

import scala.xml._
import net.liftweb.http.LiftView          ❶ Extend
                                             LiftView
class MyView extends LiftView {
  override def dispatch = {                  ❷ Provide XML
    case "sample" => render _                  generator
  }
  def render: NodeSeq = <h1>Test</h1>
}
```

First, note that the `MyView` class is present in the `sample.view` package, and within the `Boot.boot` method there's a call like this:

```
LiftRules.addToPackages("sample")
```

From here, Lift goes looking for the view package below `sample`, and then locates everything that's a subtype of `LiftView` ❶. The class and dispatch names are then used to determine the URL that this item addresses. Given this example, you can see that the `sample` dispatch name maps to the `render` method ❷. The URL to access this view would be /MyView/sample. It's as simple as that.

> **TIP** In exactly the same way that you can choose between reflection-based snippet lookup and explicit wiring, you can make that choice with views by using the two techniques outlined here.

Now that you have seen how to command Lift's templating and view generation mechanisms, let's move on to another commonly used part of Lift's functionality: session and request variables.

6.2 *Managing state*

In the vast majority of web applications, you'll find yourself needing to retain a specific value or object in order to access it later. That "later" context might be to span a request cycle, or it may be later down the line in your application flow. Either way, having a succinct method of temporarily storing a value is extremely handy.

In Java web applications, information is held in the loosely typed `javax.http.servlet.HttpSession`. One of the issues with this approach is that everything is generically referenced as a `java.lang.Object` instance, so you lose a lot of the type safety developers are used to having elsewhere in their toolchain and end up with ugly looking Scala code that has to use `asInstanceOf[T]`. As Scala has a more sophisticated type system than Java, it made sense for Lift to provide a session mechanism that was also strongly typed and in keeping with the rest of Lift's infrastructure and strongly typed nature. To that end, Lift provides its own session backing called `LiftSession`. Layered on top of this strongly typed mechanism are two abstractions, `RequestVar` and `SessionVar`, to deal with storing values for the duration of the request and session respectively. In the following subsections, you'll learn how to manage state in Lift using the abstractions on top of `LiftSession` and also how to utilize cookies from your Lift code.

6.2.1 *Request and session state*

At a basic level, a request is something that's sent from the client to the web server and that's then serviced with a response. Unless you're using a stateful snippet, the instance of that snippet will be discarded after that response cycle. But what if you wanted to hold on to a key piece of information from that snippet, rather than holding on to the entire snippet? This is where `RequestVar` comes in.

For example, let's assume that you have two snippets that are rendered on a page, and you want to share a value between both of them. By default, there's no easy way of doing this because each snippet is contained in a separate instance that knows nothing of the other. RequestVar was designed for just such a situation (among others).

You have a general idea what RequestVar is for, but how does it work? Well, the common practice for any descendent of AnyVar—of which RequestVar and its brother SessionVar are subtypes—is for it to extend a singleton object and use its apply method to provide a neat syntax for setting the value.

Consider the following listing, which is an enhancement of listing 6.7, which used a stateless snippet with a private var.

Listing 6.12 Implementing a RequestVar[Box[String]]

```
import scala.xml.NodeSeq
import net.liftweb.common.{Box,Full,Empty}
import net.liftweb.util.Helpers._
import net.liftweb.http.{RequestVar,SHtml,DispatchSnippet}

object sample extends RequestVar[Box[String]](Empty)          ◁─ ❶ Make RequestVar
                                                                     object
object RequestVarSample extends DispatchSnippet {
  def dispatch = {
    case _ => render
  }
  def render = {
    "type=text" #>SHtml.text(                                  ❷ Get and set
    sample.is.openOr(""),                                        RequestVar
      v => sample(Box.!!(v))) &
    "type=submit" #>SHtml.onSubmitUnit(
      () => println(sample.is))
  }
}
```

The key thing to note in this example is that even when the form is submitted, the text box doesn't lose its present value because it was held in the RequestVar defined at ❶. Specifically, the value held in the RequestVar is read out, if it exists, by the sample.is call, which returns a Box[T], where T is the value of the RequestVar type. In this case, T is a String, so calling openOr on the resulting value allows you to provide a sensible default if the RequestVar is empty ❷.

You may be thinking that the outcome of this example is similar to that of the earlier example using the StatefulSnippet trait in listing 6.10. But these two examples only *appear* to do similar things. In practice, the applications are quite different.

Typically, StatefulSnippet is great when you want to keep that instance around and access its state on a subsequent request or function execution (such as with AJAX). But what stateful snippets don't allow you to do is share that state over more than one snippet. In effect, when using StatefulSnippet, the whole instance is in a private RequestVar[Map[String, DispatchSnippet]], so your other application snippets can't access its state: it's a self-contained instance.

In contrast, `RequestVar` can be extremely useful when you wish to contain a piece of state that you either need to keep around without the weight of keeping the whole snippet instance, or when you need to share the state with another snippet or application process.

Unsurprisingly, because `SessionVar` is also a subtype of `AnyVar`, it takes on exactly the same usage semantics as `RequestVar`, except that its lifetime isn't limited to the page request cycle—it persists until the session is ultimately torn down by Lift or the container is shut down.

6.2.2 Cookies

Cookies have been with us in internet computing since 1994, when Netscape added them to their browser to give it a sort of memory. To that end, it's no surprise that Lift also has an abstraction for managing cookies as part of its state-handling system.

Lift is fully decoupled from the Java servlet API by way of a provider API, and it can be deployed in non-servlet environments, such as Netty. To that end, Lift has a layer on top of the various request and response components one would usually find in web applications: `HTTPRequest`, `HTTPContext`, `HTTPParam`, and `HTTPCookie`. With the exception of `HTTPCookie`, you'll likely never need these classes. Cookies are a little special because it's common to want to interoperate with them, but you don't have to worry about how they're implemented in the environment—you just deal with `HTTPCookie` instances.

The next listing shows the basic setting and getting of a cookie value.

Listing 6.13   Getting and setting a cookie value

```scala
import scala.xml.{NodeSeq,Text}
import net.liftweb.common.{Full,Empty,Box}
import net.liftweb.util.Helpers._
import net.liftweb.http.{DispatchSnippet,S,SHtml}
import net.liftweb.http.provider.HTTPCookie

class CookieSample extends DispatchSnippet {
  def dispatch = {
    case "add" => add
    case "delete" => delete
    case _ => display _
  }

  private val cookieName = "liftinaction.sample"

  private def action(does: String, using: () => Any) =      ❶ Form helper
    "*" #> SHtml.submit(does,
      () => {using(); S.redirectTo(S.uri)})

  def delete = action("Delete Cookie",                      ❷ Delete the
    () => S.deleteCookie(cookieName))                          cookie

  def add = action("Create Cookie", () => S.addCookie(      ❸ Create the
    HTTPCookie(cookieName,"I love cookies")))                 cookie
```

```
def display(xhtml: NodeSeq) =
  S.findCookie(cookieName).map { cookie =>
    Text("Cookie found!: %s".format(cookie))
  } openOrText("No cookie set.")
}
```

Check and display cookie content

This listing demonstrates how to control cookies via the S object. Here, the snippet is a straightforward dispatch snippet, resolved via reflection.

First, note that the class provides an internal cookieName value so that you don't have to repeat the name of the cookie continually. Next, the action helper method is defined to generate the form buttons for adding and deleting the cookie ❶. Don't worry too much about this helper; it's there purely to save on code duplication in the add and delete snippet methods. The second argument of the action method is a function that can return Any. This is where the cookie-modifying code is passed, and you can see in the delete method that the second argument includes S.deleteCookie(cookie-Name) ❷. As you might imagine, based upon its method name, deleteCookie removes a cookie with the given name from the response. The add method does the opposite; it creates a new cookie and adds it to the response state ❸. Note here that the HTTP-Cookie type is from Lift's environment-agnostic provider API and that this two-parameter method is essentially an instance factory that lives in the companion object of the case class, HTTPCookie. For the sake of this example, we're only really concerned with the cookie name and its subsequent value. If you want to control the expiry or valid domains, for example, you can use the full case class and pass the various boxed arguments. See the Lift scaladoc for more information on valid parameters.

With cookies, RequestVar, and SessionVar, you have a robust toolbox for constructing complicated applications with sophisticated state handling. As your application grows, you may want to add some kind of state-dependent page-flow; fortunately Lift builds on its state abstractions and provides a neat API for building page flows and forms. It's called LiftWizard.

6.3 Forms with LiftScreen and Wizard

The more code you write in your Lift applications, the more you may find that you have some loose conceptual relationships between the various snippets within your application in order to create some kind of flow, or a particular way of servicing user input and making application choices therein. In such a situation, neither having these as separate snippets nor converting them to one large stateful snippet feels like the right solution, and this is where LiftScreen and Wizard can help.

Consider a user interaction flow like that detailed in figure 6.2.

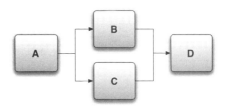

Figure 6.2 Page flow requiring user input on page A, which dictates the following page, B or C, both of which lead to D. An example would be choosing a delivery type at an ecommerce checkout, where different couriers require different information.

This kind of simple page flow is common in a lot of applications. What is typically very tricky is managing the relationships and state between each logical section. `Wizard` provides a structured system for defining these screen relationships, and `LiftScreen` provides a mechanism for implementing the contents of each screen.

6.3.1 *LiftScreen*

When you require a page flow in your application, it isn't uncommon for it to be hard-coded in one aspect or another, be it templating, snippets, or something else. This is obviously less than optimal; it would be far better to have well-defined stories that you could test in a single environment, devoid of a HTTP environment. `Wizard` provides such a construct by allowing you to knit together multiple `LiftScreen` instances in a unified and declarative fashion.

Let's take a moment to manually construct a single, isolated `LiftScreen` to collect some user input, validate it, and then serve a response based upon the user input. The next listing shows the most basic type of `LiftScreen`.

Listing 6.14 Basic `LiftScreen` implementation

```
import net.liftweb.http.{LiftScreen,S}

object AskAboutIceCreamBasic extends LiftScreen {
  val flavor =
    field("What's your favorite Ice cream flavor", "")
  def finish(){
    S.notice("I like "+flavor.is+" too!")
  }
}
```

This small example shows the smallest `LiftScreen` you can make, with a single field and an action function to be executed upon the submission of the form. In this case, the `finish` method simply reports a notice via the message infrastructure.

NOTE Both `LiftScreen` and `Wizard` support AJAX operations right out of the box. Chapter 9 covers this AJAX support in full with all the necessary background information.

All `LiftScreen` implementations must descend from the `net.liftweb.http.Lift-Screen` trait and implement a set of fields either manually—as in this example—or by registering a `Mapper` or `Record` type. You must also implement the `finish(): Unit` method so that the screen has a final action, even if that action does nothing.

In order to manufacture a field in the output, this listing calls the `field` method and assigns it to a value called `flavor`. The `field` method is essentially a factory method for the internal `Field` type, and it takes two mandatory parameters and one optional one:

- The label for the field (mandatory).
- The default value for the field (mandatory). Importantly, the type and subsequent rendering of the field is, by default, asserted from the type of the default

value. `String` gets a text box, `Boolean` gets a check box, and so forth. If you use a custom type, you can override the rendering of the field by implementing a custom `FormBuilderLocator` and appending that to `LiftRules.appendGlobal-FormBuilder`.

- A `varargs` of `FilterOrValidate` functions that are applied for validation (optional). `LiftScreen` ships with several basic validation helpers for rudimentary operations, such as non-null values, matching to a regular expression, and ensuring minimum and maximum lengths.

Currently, the example in listing 6.14 will take in a string value and report a notice upon submission, but it would be helpful to apply some validation rules and do some kind of computation based upon the field input. The following listing shows the original example with some modifications and with basic validation.

Listing 6.15 Applying validation to the `LiftScreen` sample

```
object AskAboutIceCreamTwo extends LiftScreen {
  val flavor = field("What's your favorite Ice cream flavor", "",
  trim, valMinLen(2,"Name too short"),                                  ❶ Validation
  valMaxLen(40,"That's a long name"))                                      functions

  val sauce = field("Like chocolate sauce?", false)        ⟵
                                                            ❷ Checkbox field
  def finish(){
    if(sauce){
      S.notice(flavor.is+" tastes especially good with chocolate sauce!")
    } else S.notice("I like "+flavor.is+" too!")
  }
}
```

As you can see, this version has a few modifications to add validation options to the `flavor` field. These simply aggregate together so you can apply whatever validation you require ❶. There's also a new field called sauce that demonstrates a different type assertion around display elements, and as field has been passed a `Boolean`, Lift will automatically create a check box ❷.

You may be wondering how all of this actually gets displayed. Handily, `LiftScreen` takes care of all the rendering by using the following template resolution path:

1 Look for the template located at `allTemplatePath` in the context of that `Lift-Screen` object.
2 Look for the wizard-all.html template in the webapp/templates-hidden directory.
3 Use the built-in markup defined by `allTemplateNodeSeq`.

Given the template markup resolved by the aforementioned search path, all the fields, labels, and validations will be correctly rendered. All you need do is style it to your own tastes, and because it's essentially just snippet markup, there's no limit upon how you can position items or sections on the screen. It's very much up to you.

CUSTOM FIELD TYPES

As discussed earlier in this section, `LiftScreen` automatically determines what kind of user interface element it should render based upon the type of the value it's instantiated with. Although this is helpful for the default use cases, there are times when you'll want to customize that behavior, such as in the case of a password. The password is a string, so it does need a text input, but it must be a password input and not a regular text input field. Another example would be rendering a text area instead of a one-line text input.

Fortunately, it's simple enough to create an ad hoc field type in your `LiftScreen`. Implementing a custom field allows you to build a field for a type that isn't supported by Lift directly, so you can present your own domain classes however you wish. That's demonstrated in the following listing.

Listing 6.16   Implementing an ad hoc custom field type with `LiftScreen`

```
object ScreenWithCustomField extends LiftScreen {
  val password = new Field {
    type ValueType = String
    override def name = "Password"
    override implicit def manifest = buildIt[String]
    override def default = ""
    override def toForm: Box[NodeSeq] = SHtml.password(is, set _)
  }
  def finish() = println("Submitted")
}
```

This implementation of `LiftScreen` includes a custom field type called `ValueType`. The key thing about this is that the `ValueType` lets the `Field` know what type the content is. Finally, the `toForm` method provides the customized implementation of the UI control itself. In this example, supplying `SHtml.password` will result in a password input being presented to the user.

This is exceedingly helpful for a one-time implementation, but it can result in duplication of code if you have a specialized type that you need to display in several screens. In this case, it's much better to use a global form builder so that every form in which you need to represent a particular type doesn't need a repeat implementation of the display logic. The following listing shows an example of this global form building.

Listing 6.17   Implementing a custom form build

```
import net.liftweb.common.Empty
import net.liftweb.util.FormBuilderLocator
import net.liftweb.http.{SHtml,LiftRules}

case class Book(reference: Long, title: String)
➥LiftRules.appendGlobalFormBuilder(FormBuilderLocator[List[Book]](
  (books,setter) => SHtml.select(books.map(b =>
    (b.reference.toString, b.title)), Empty, v => println(v))))
```

This listing defines a custom type: `Book`. In practice, this might be one of your custom domain types or something similar, but it will suffice for this example. When `Lift-Screen` is presented with a `List[Book]` type, it will automatically render it as a drop-down list with no additional configuration or input at the call site. By calling to `Lift-Rules.appendGlobalFormBuilder`, you only define this functionality once and it becomes available globally within your application.

Form builders are functions that `LiftScreen` uses to create the interface elements for any given form, and in this example the code just takes the list of books and constructs the drop-down list by using `SHtml.select`. In order to use this in conjunction with a field, you just need to do this:

```
val book = field("Choose book", books)
```

Now you know how to make single-page forms with `LiftScreen`, but what if you wanted to create a multipage wizard, as we suggested in the introduction to this section? Well, you can take what you learned about `LiftScreen` and wrap that in a `Wizard`, which is a collection of `LiftScreen` definitions.

6.3.2 *Wizard*

Lift's `Wizard` system builds on the base of `LiftScreen` and allows you to build complex, stateful workflows with only a few lines of code. In this example, we build a small form that simulates a registration system. On the first screen, users enter their name and age, and depending on whether they're under 18 or not, they will be presented with a second screen asking them to populate their parents' names. Of course, this isn't applicable to users who are over 18, so in that case the parents screen is skipped and the final screen is displayed right away.

Before diving into the code, don't forget to add the wizard dependency to your project. Unlike `LiftScreen`, which is generic and lives in the main WebKit JAR, Wizard carries more infrastructure, so it's in a separate JAR called lift-wizard. Add the following definition to your SBT project class:

```
val wizard = "net.liftweb" %% "lift-wizard" % liftVersion
```

The following listing shows the example wizard.

Listing 6.18 Using Lift's `Wizard`

```
import net.liftweb.http.S
import net.liftweb.wizard.Wizard                          ◁— ❶ Extend Wizard type

object PetSurveyWizard extends Wizard {
  object completeInfo extends WizardVar(false)

  val you = new Screen {                                   ◁— ❷ Define screens
    val yourName = field("First Name", "",
      valMinLen(2, "Name Too Short"),
      valMaxLen(40, "Name Too Long"))
```

```
    val yourAge = field("Age", 1,
      minVal(5, "Too young"),
      maxVal(125, "You should be dead"))

    override def nextScreen =                    ❸  Define link to
      if (yourAge.is< 18) parents                   next screen
      else pets
  }

  val parents = new Screen {                                        ◁─┐
    val parentName = field("Parent or Guardian's name", "",          │
      valMinLen(2, "Name Too Short"),                                │
      valMaxLen(40, "Name Too Long"))               ❷  Define screens│
  }                                                                  │
  val pets = new Screen {                                          ◁─┘
    val pet = field("Pet's name", "",
      valMinLen(2, "Name Too Short"),
      valMaxLen(40, "Name Too Long"))
  }

  def finish(){
    S.notice("Thank you for registering your pet")
    completeInfo.set(true)
  }
}
```

In this listing, you can see that with the `lift-wizard` package on the classpath, you can import the `Wizard` type and create a singleton called `PetSurveyWizard`, which is a subtype of `Wizard` ❶. In this object, several `Screen` instances are defined ❷. As the name suggests, these define the screens (and fields) that the end user will interact with. The fields themselves are defined exactly the same as for `LiftScreen`, so we won't cover them again. Interestingly, you can see the `nextScreen` method ❸; overriding this and providing your own implementation gives you the flexibility you need to define very complex workflows through linked screens. The `Screen` type itself also has other things you can override, such as the `confirmScreen_?` method to tell Lift that this screen is for confirmation only.

More broadly, the `Wizard` type has several helpful features that can assist in making sophisticated user interaction flows. For example, a `Wizard` can have a snapshot taken of its state at any given time, and you can restore that snapshot at a later date in the same session. At the time of writing, these snapshots were not serializable, but that's certainly on the roadmap, so check the wiki or scaladoc for up-to-date information. Although you can't currently save the `Wizard` state directly, it's possible to persist form data to the database, such as by calling the `save` method on a `Mapper` instance you might hold in a `WizardVar`.

As you can see, `Wizard` provides you with a helpful out-of-the-box frame for creating multipage user interactions, whatever they might be. In the next section, we look at another module of Lift that provides functionality for certain common web components.

6.4 Widgets

There are often times in web development when you might want to add an autocomplete text box, or perhaps a Gravatar icon. These are fairly common things to want in your application, and Lift provides a group of ready-made *widgets* to fill this need. As there are quite a number of widgets, we'll only cover two here. The others follow similar patterns of implementation.

Note that the term *widget* is essentially an arbitrary term referring to what is essentially a cluster of JavaScript, CSS, and Scala class files that make up individual units of functionality.

Before we get started, don't forget to add the Lift Widgets dependency to your project, as shown:

```
val widgets = "net.liftweb" %% "lift-widgets" % liftVersion
```

The lift-widgets JAR holds all the JavaScript, CSS, and markup required by the various widgets.

6.4.1 AutoComplete widget

The first widget we look at is called `AutoComplete`. As the name suggests, this is a widget wrapper around completion JavaScript that makes an AJAX request to the server while you type and presents a list of possible options based upon the current input. As with most of the widgets, it carries its own resources that need to be served to the browser. In order to automatically wire this up, the general idiom for widgets is to call an `init` method in your `Boot` class.

For example, the following lines are needed to enable the `AutoComplete` widget:

```
import net.liftweb.widgets.autocomplete.AutoComplete

class Boot {
  def boot {
    ...
    AutoComplete.init
    ...
  }
}
```

With this wired up in your application `Boot` class, all the resources required to make the widget work are now available to Lift. The following listing shows how you would implement the `AutoComplete` helper in your snippet code.

Listing 6.19 Implementing the `AutoComplete` snippet helper

```
import scala.xml.NodeSeq
import net.liftweb.util.Helpers._                           ❶ Import
import net.liftweb.widgets.autocomplete.AutoComplete           widget

class AutoCompleteSample {
  private val data = List(                                  ❷ Define
    "Timothy","Derek","Ross","Tyler",                         sample data
    "Indrajit","Harry","Greg","Debby")
```

```
def sample = "*" #> AutoComplete("", (current,limit) =>
  data.filter(_.toLowerCase.startsWith(
    current.toLowerCase)),
  x => println("Submitted: " + x))
}
```
❸ Bind autocomplete

This listing here shows a normal snippet class that includes the specially imported `AutoComplete` class from lift-widgets ❶. For the purpose of this example, this listing just uses a static `List[String]` as the data source to search ❷, but in practice you'd probably use a database or similar source to obtain the matched results.

This class is a regular snippet, but rather than binding to some straight text or markup content, it calls the `AutoComplete` class from the widget ❸. Under the hood, this returns `Elem` (a `NodeSeq` subtype) so it's bindable in terms of Lift's templating system. The first parameter is the default value, whereas the second and third parameters are functions that have a little more going on.

The second parameter is the function invoked when the AJAX call is made to the server when the user makes a keystroke. This example simply lowercases the input and looks for a string that starts with whatever the user entered. It's certainly crude, but the purpose here is to show how you can seamlessly evaluate user input with a function. The third parameter is a simple handler to be executed when the form is submitted. In this case, the `value` is just output to the console.

Just to be clear, this is a normal snippet and its implementation only requires the regular style of invocation:

```
<lift:auto_complete_sample.sample form="post">
  <p>Type a name here: <f:find_name /></p>
</litt:auto_complete_sample.sample>
```

When these three things are in place—the line in the `Boot` class, the snippet class, and the HTML—you should see an outcome similar to figure 6.3.

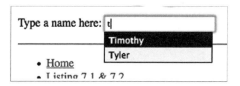

That really is all you need to do. This short example shows how powerful widgets can be, and it should give you some ideas about how you can wrap up your own code into reusable widgets. Before closing this

Figure 6.3   The finished `AutoComplete` widget as seen in Firefox

section, let's look at one more widget—the Gravatar, which doesn't have any JavaScript or CSS and is a straight snippet helper.

6.4.2   Gravatar widget

Gravatar is an online service for what they call *globally recognized avatars* that follow you from site to site based upon your registered email address. Simply pass the helper object an email address, and it will generate the correct markup for you in order to fetch the right image from gravatar.com.

The following listing shows just how simple this is.

Listing 6.20   The `Gravatar` widget

```
import scala.xml.NodeSeq
import net.liftweb.widgets.gravatar.Gravatar

class GravatarSample {
  def display(xhtml: NodeSeq): NodeSeq =
    Gravatar("your.email@domain.com")
}
```

This is very straightforward. It returns a `NodeSeq`, which, like other widgets, allows it to sit within a bind statement.

That pretty must rounds up our discussion of widgets. The key things to remember when working with widgets are, first, that if a widget uses any kind of JavaScript or CSS, you'll likely have to call `init` from in your `Boot` class to allow the resources to be served by Lift. Second, nearly all widgets have some kind of markup-producing component so you can use them in nearly all Lift templating situations.

6.5   *Summary*

Wow, we covered a lot in this chapter! Hopefully you're still with us and managed to follow along for the duration. This chapter should have given you a good insight into how Lift differs from other frameworks and how you can go about implementing common operations in Lift, from the aspects of templating, through to making complex multiscreen forms. Ultimately, Lift is a rich infrastructure for doing many things, and these are just some of the items that are important to cover.

In this chapter, you've seen how to utilize Lift's built-in snippets to perform common operations, and you've seen when and where the different types of snippets should be used when designing your own applications. Snippets can come in many different forms, but it's generally better to use manually wired dispatch snippets when you can, so you have the safety of compile-time checks on the snippet-to-template mapping. You've also seen how to make use of session and request variables, right through to using full blown stateful snippets to retain entire snippet instances for further computation.

You've also seen how to wield `LiftScreen` and `Wizard` to build complex, stateful page flows. Using these tools, you can construct sophisticated flows with a minimal amount of code and still have complete control over the rendering. `LiftScreen` can also automatically assert the appropriate input control based upon the type it's passed. For example, it will automatically generate a check box when passed a Boolean type.

You may be wondering why we didn't cover anything to do with persistence. Unsurprisingly, there are several ways to handle the issue of persistence in Lift, and we didn't want to introduce any more topics into this chapter. Persistence is covered in depth in chapters 10, 11, and 12.

The next chapter looks at Lift's HTTP system in depth and at how you can handle rewriting to create friendly URLs and build REST web services using Lift's dispatching API.

SiteMap and
access control

This chapter covers

- Access control functionality
- Menu generation
- Building custom location parameters
- HTTP authorization

SiteMap offers you granular page-level security, a tidy DSL for defining application structure, and an automatic way to generate user navigation. Bearing in mind Lift's view-first architecture and the way in which snippets are executed in a given page request, there's nothing to effectively control access or execute code before the page (and its snippets) start to load. This is where SiteMap fits in, architecturally speaking.

Everything within the SiteMap is related to what is known as a *location*, or Loc for short. These locations typically represent pages that have a corresponding markup template in your application, but more broadly these locations are resources within your application, something that will be accessed by your application's users. As SiteMap is executed before any page rendering takes place, it can effectively execute access control rules, or even short circuit the whole rendering of that resource and return a response directly.

In this chapter, you'll first use SiteMap's high-level DSL, then learn about location parameters, and finally create your very own componentized custom location for generating a wiki. SiteMap is perfectly positioned for defining access control rules or even just executing arbitrary code before a page loads. Whichever you want to do, you can typically bolt on functionality for a given location via *location parameters*, which are discussed in section 7.2.

The idea of locations is fundamental in SiteMap, and the next section will show you how to use the Menu class to define these locations, and how to define the functionality associated with each location.

7.1 Menus and locations

A *location* can be either a page or a view—it's usually something that renders HTML output. These locations within your application can be grouped into logical sets, and in SiteMap terminology these are called *menus*.

Menus and locations form the base of SiteMap's functionality. Within your application, the pages and views can be arranged into these two abstract concepts quite neatly. In this section, we look at how you can construct menu hierarchies that include all the locations in your application. You'll also see how the Lift SiteMap can be extended in various ways to either apply your own application functionality to a given location, or provide encapsulated components of logic that can be reused in wholly different applications.

To illustrate the concept of locations, imagine the site structure in any shopping or catalog site. More often than not, you'll have a menu called *products* (or something indicative of the content), and when you interact with that menu, either by clicking it, rolling over it, or performing some other UI action, it will display the submenu content, which usually has location links to take you to whichever product item you select. This notion of locations is an important one, because SiteMap really only deals with the locations of template files in your application deployment, and not, as many new users think, with the URLs that access those templates.

Consider the folder structure in figure 7.1. By default, the application will respond to the following URLs:

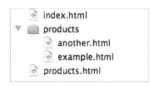

- /
- /index
- /products
- /products/another
- /products/example

Figure 7.1 Example layout of a webapp folder. Listing 7.1 defines a SiteMap for this folder.

If the user visited /products/another in their browser, they would see the content held in another.html. This would work by default, and it's fairly obvious given the folder structure why that specifically works: the URLs being accessed correspond *directly* with the layout in the webapp directory.

If you were to define a `SiteMap` for an application structure like that in figure 7.1, it would look something like the following listing.

> **Listing 7.1 `SiteMap` definition to match figure 7.1**

```
import net.liftweb.sitemap.{SiteMap,Menu,**}

val pages = List(
  Menu("Home") / "index",
  Menu("Products") / "products" submenus(          ❶ Create location
    Menu("Another") / "products" / "another",         with submenus
    Menu("Example") / "products" / "example"
  )
)

LiftRules.setSiteMap(SiteMap(pages:_*))
```

Let's just pause for a moment to inspect what's happening in this code block. One of the key notions in SiteMap is the `Menu`. A `Menu` is a logical grouping of locations, and each `Menu` can have any number of submenus, and so on. In this instance, all the lines except one define a location entry in the SiteMap for their individual page, whereas the products location defines a menu that groups the two subordinate locations together, in addition to having its own location ❶.

The code in listing 7.1 leverages the SiteMap domain-specific language (DSL) to make the construction of the SiteMap easier and less verbose. You may come across SiteMap examples online that look quite different, but there's no difference in behavior. The difference is purely cosmetic. For example, this line,

```
Menu("Home") / "test"
```

can also be written as

```
Menu(Loc("Home",List("test"),"Home"))
```

The latter is more verbose but possibly more easily understood. As you can see, the first parameter of the `Loc` (the location) is its title, the second is the path to the template, and the final parameter is the text to be used for the link in any navigation generated by Lift.

Being able to nest menus allows you to build complex and detailed hierarchies that define your application structure, often referred to as a site map (hence the SiteMap name). You can use this structure to control access to individual locations or groups of locations, generate dynamic navigation, and execute arbitrary code early in the incoming request cycle. For example, had you wanted to group everything under the products directory in one simple expression, you could have replaced the `Menu` lines in listing 7.1 with this one:

```
Menu("Products") / "products" / **
```

The `**` syntax denotes a wildcard for any location subordinate to products—the use of `*` as a wildcard idiom is quite commonplace in most programming languages. Typically it makes sense to use the `**` wildcard syntax when you would prefer to allow access to all pages within a site hierarchy. A common example of this is when you just want to allow access for a bunch of static files. The only downside of using the wildcard is that without an explicit entry, Lift won't know what information to assign those submenus in the navigation structure that's rendered by the built-in Menu snippet which is discussed in section 7.1.2 of this chapter. Just understand for the moment that the Menu snippet can only generate nested links for the locations explicitly defined in the SiteMap.

7.1.1 Understanding and implementing locations

At the beginning of this chapter, we briefly introduced the idea of locations. This section expands on that introduction and covers some of the finer details and goes into the concrete implementation of a location: the Loc.

Each and every Loc has a swath of information associated with it, such as basic properties (page title and text for a generated link) and more advanced properties (a breadcrumb trail through the hierarchies and custom templates the Loc will be rendered with).

By default, a Loc must be unique in your application. You can't have two entries that define a menu item for the same resource location. You can't, for example, have two entries in different parts of your menu structure that point to the contact page. While this is fine for the majority of applications, you may occasionally run across a situation where you need to define the same resource location in multiple parts of your SiteMap. By default, Lift will throw an error if you try to define the same location twice, but you can disable this restriction with the following call in Boot:

```
SiteMap.enforceUniqueLinks = false
```

Now that you know the purpose of Menus and Locs, you might be wondering how to instruct Lift to generate a set of navigation menus from the SiteMap. Lift has a built-in snippet to do this; it too is called Menu.

7.1.2 Rendering menus

The Menu snippet is a regular DispatchSnippet, and it functions in exactly the same way as one of your own snippets. Its purpose is to extract the hierarchical information from the defined SiteMap and render it.

To render the default navigation, include the following line in one of your templates:

```
<lift:menu.builder />
```

This then generates the following markup, providing the browser is currently viewing the home page (by default, the Menu snippet does not generate links for the page it's currently displaying):

```
<ul>
  <li><span>Home</span></li>
  <li><a href="/sample">Sample</a></li>
</ul>
```

It generates the following HTML when selecting the products link. If you recall from listing 7.1, the products location had two subordinate locations, and when the browser is displaying the products location, it expands to display the menus of the next tier down in the tree of submenus (if they exist):

```
<ul>
  <li><a href="/index">Home</a></li>
  <li>
    <span>Products</span>
    <ul>
      <li><a href="/products/another">Another</a></li>
      <li><a href="/products/example">Example</a></li>
    </ul>
  </li>
</ul>
```

This is straightforward HTML code for unordered lists, and it's completely out-of-the-box markup rendering for the Menu snippet.

You'll probably often want to apply CSS styling to the current page or do some other customization that will affect the way the menu will be displayed. To this end, the Menu snippet allows you to pass a raft of different attributes to it to customize the markup. Table 7.1 lists the valid attributes that can be passed to the Menu snippet. As you can see, the Menu snippet gives you a good degree of control over how the menu is rendered, and you're free to style the markup however you please with little or no constraints from Lift.

Table 7.1   SiteMap's `Menu.builder` attribute options

Attribute namespace	Description	Usage

ul	Attributes that feature the ul prefix will be merged onto every ul list node irrespective of menu depth.	`<lift:menu.builder ul:class="sample" />`
		
		Will render this:
		
		`<ul class="sample">...</ul>`

li	Like ul, the li prefix merges attributes with every list node recursively.	`<lift:menu.builder li:class="sample" />`
		
		Will render this:
		
		`<ul>`
		`<li class="sample">...</li>`
		`</ul>`

li_item	These attributes will *only* be merged with the currently selected menu item.	`<lift:menu.builder li_item:class="me" />`
		Will render this:
		
		`<li class="me">...</li>`

Table 7.1 SiteMap's `Menu.builder` attribute options *(continued)*

Attribute namespace	Description	Usage
`linkToSelf`	This attribute specifies whether the currently selected page should be an active link or not.	`<lift:menu.builder linkToSelf="true" />`
`level`	This attribute renders the menu from a specific starting level based on a zero index. If you specify a level deeper than is currently being displayed, the menu will be blank (not displayed).	`<lift:menu.builder level="1" />`
`expandAll`	Setting this attribute will expand the entire menu statically rather than have each set of submenus be rendered dynamically after the selection of their parent.	`<lift:menu.builder expandAll="true" />`
`outer_tag`	If you don't want the menu to render using the normal list markup, you can change the element rendered by passing it to `outer_tag` to replace the default `ul`.	`<lift:menu.builder outer_tag="div" />`
`inner_tag`	This is like `outer_tag` but it replaces the default `li` node with the specified value.	`<lift:menu.builder outer_tag="div" />`

`top`	Merges the specified attribute and its value into the very first (root) element of the menu markup. Typically used to define an element ID for the menu tree markup.	`<lift:menu.builder top:id="something" />`
		 Will render this:
		 `<ul id="something">,, </ul>`

There are a couple of other things to note about the Menu snippet. Not only can it render the menu structure, it has a built-in method for getting the title of the currently active page:

```
<title>My Application &ndash; <lift:menu.title /></title>
```

All you need to do is insert this line into your template, and all the pages will automatically be assigned the title that you defined in your SiteMap Menu structure.

Finally, the Menu snippet can also render your whole SiteMap navigation structure as JSON if you want to do some fancy navigation with JavaScript or Adobe Flash, for example. To illustrate this functionality, calling `<lift:menu.json />` on the menu from listing 7.1 would generate output like this:

```
{"menu": [
{ "text": "Home",
   "uri": "/index",
```

```
        "children": [],
        "current": false,
        "placeholder": false,
        "path": false
    },
{ "text": "Products",
    "uri": "/products",
    "children": [
{ "text": "Another",
        "uri": "/products/another",
        "children": []}
      ...
    ]
  }
  ...
]}
```

You might be wondering what to do if you want to allow access to a page, but still apply some special rule or condition to it so that it would be omitted from the main navigation. This might be necessary for an editing page that requires parameters to be passed to it in order to function correctly. SiteMap's solution to this is location parameters—LocParam.

7.2   *Location parameters*

Location parameters allow you to add an aggregated set of rules to a given menu. For example, suppose you have a selection of menu locations, one of which is an edit screen with a form that's populated with data by loading a specific item from the database, based upon a URL parameter. Obviously, the parameter must be present, and SiteMap provides location parameters, which are simple declarative mechanisms for ensuring that this page can't be accessed without that parameter.

These location parameters typically come in the form of small, self-contained case classes, and in this section, we demonstrate Lift's default LocParam instances, which augment both control and rendering functionality for any location in your SiteMap.

To continue with the edit page example, it's highly unlikely that such a screen would be displayed in the menu structure because, without the appropriate parameter the page would not operate correctly. To that end, the location needs to be both hidden within the rendered output of the Menu snippet, and it also needs to block access if the necessary request parameters are missing. These use cases are exactly the types of situations that Lift's location parameters are designed for.

First, let's deal with hiding the menu item. Consider the following menu definition:

```
Menu("Edit Something") / "edit" >> Hidden
```

As you can see, appended to the normal menu definition, by way of the << operator, is the Hidden location parameter. This instructs Lift that it must not include this menu entry as part of the larger menu structure that's rendered with the Menu snippet.

That's fairly straightforward, but what about ensuring that the URL parameter is always present? Lift provides a collection of LocParams right out of the box (listed in tables 7.2 and 7.3), one of which is `Unless`. Let's look at how you could use this `LocParam`:

```
Menu("Edit Something") / "edit" >> Hidden
  >> Unless(
    () => S.param("id").isEmpty,
    () => RedirectResponse("index"))
```

In this example, the additional location parameter is aggregated into the existing menu and parameters. This concept of parameter aggregation is an important one to note, because as your applications grow in complexity, it allows you to remain very granular about controlling the flow of pages and access control. Essentially, you can layer `LocParams` on top of each other as you need to in order to achieve the desired functionality. With the `Unless` class, specifically, you need to supply two component functions, as you can see in the preceding code: a function yielding a `Boolean` based on some information about that request, and a function that yields a subtype of `LiftResponse`.

In this example, the page requires that the `id` attribute be set. If it's not (if `isEmpty` evaluates to `true`), the second function is executed. This second function can essentially return any subtype of `LiftResponse` (more on this in chapter 8), so you could present a page informing the user of the error, or as in this case, just direct the user back to the index page.

> ### Ahhh, symbols make my head hurt!
> Symbols acting as function identifiers are something that's quite prevalent in Scala and functional programming in general. This is because math and computer science have had a large influence on the functional community, and they share many things in common.
>
> In this instance, `>>` represents the aggregation of location parameters. But if you aren't comfortable using these symbols, you can replace `>>` with `rule` and get the same functionality (`rule` is an alias of `>>`).

Location parameters are fairly unassuming, but they're a powerful means for controlling a lot of different user experience aspects, from controlling menu visibility, right through to rendering an entire dynamic page with snippets. Lift provides a selection of default location parameters that can make your development process smoother, and we look at them next.

7.2.1 Default location parameters

Lift ships with a raft of location parameters that solve typical use cases, such as the `Hidden` and `Unless` classes that were covered in the previous subsection. There are a variety of parameters with different functions, so we go over them and look at their usage in this section.

Rails and Django users: think controller filters

If you have previously used either Ruby on Rails or Python Django (or any other framework that has filters), you're likely to be familiar with the concept of a before filter. Because Lift is a view-first framework, the snippet mechanism is tightly coupled with the markup rendering, and it wouldn't make sense for that process to play a part in executing code before a page renders (technically, it can't do that anyway). This is where `SiteMap` can step in.

If you're familiar with the `before_filter` style of working, your use case may enable you to use one of the default parameters or simply extend `LocParam` to do your bidding before the request processing gets underway. It's also important to note that `LocParam` does have access to the current request and session state.

With the exception of the authentication parameters that will be covered in the next section, there are two distinct groups of location parameters:

- *View-affecting parameters*—These parameters have a direct effect on the output or rending of the view. The *view* in this context is the UI that users are operating. An example of such a location parameter would be the `Hidden` parameter, which hides a menu item from rendering.
- *Control-affecting parameters*—These parameters affect the user's experience. For example, the `Unless` class affects `LocParam`.

Why make this distinction? It helps to distinguish the two types based on the task that the `LocParam` will be performing. Moreover, their usual patterns of usage are quite different. View-affecting parameters will usually yield a `NodeSeq`, whereas control-affecting parameters will usually return a `Box[LiftResponse]`.

Table 7.2 lists and describes the view-affecting parameters. As you'll see, there are quite a number of ways to manipulate the view that's ultimately rendered for the user. Table 7.3 lists and describes the control-affecting location parameters.

Table 7.2   Default location parameters that affect view rendering

Parameter type	Description
Hidden	Hides the current menu from being rendered with the rest of the `SiteMap`. Usage: `>> Hidden`
HideIfNoKids	If the menu has no child menus, drops this menu from the `SiteMap` rendering. Usage: `>> HideIfNoKids`

Table 7.2 Default location parameters that affect view rendering *(continued)*

Parameter type	Description
PlaceHolder	This menu item is purely for structural purposes within the SiteMap. Typically this is useful for grouping subordinate menus when rendering the menu as a JSON representation. Usage: `>> PlaceHolder`

Title	Overrides the name of a page defined in the menu definition, perhaps with something more dynamic.
	
	Usage:
	
	`>> Title(x =>`
	`    Text("Some lovely title"))`

Template	Provides an XHTML template that this location will use to render the display.
	
	Usage:
	
	`>> Template(() =>`
	`TemplateFinder.findAnyTemplate(`
	`    List("example")) openOr`
	`<div>Template not found</div>)`

Snippet	Registers a single snippet for use in this location. You specify a name (what the snippet will be called from the template) and then the `NodeSeq => NodeSeq` function as you would for a normal snippet definition.
	
	Usage:
	
	`>> Snippet("sample", xhtml =>`
	`    bind("l",xhtml,"sample" -> "sample"))`
	
	Markup (only valid for the given SiteMap location the `LocParam` is applied to):
	
	`<lift:demo><p><l:sample /></p></lift:demo>`

DispatchLocSnippets	Registers multiple snippets on a single location (building on the single snippet registration method). In this case, the `DispatchLocSnippets` parameter lets you apply snippets based on a partial function.
	
	Usage:
	
	`lazy val MySnippets = new DispatchLocSnippets {`
	`  def dispatch = {`
	`    case "demo" =>xhtml =>`
	`      bind("l",xhtml,"sample" -> "sample")`
	`    case "thing" =>xhtml =>`
	`      bind("x",xhtml,"some" -> "example")`
	`  }`
	`}`
	`...`
	`>> MySnippets`

Table 7.3 Default location parameters that affect control

Parameter type	Description

EarlyResponse	Lets you serve any `LiftResponse` subtype to the browser before any other processing has taken place. This is useful for several reasons, such as redirecting old content URLs to new content URLs.
	
	Usage:
	
	`>> EarlyResponse(() =>`
	`   RedirectResponse("newstuff"))`

If / Unless	Does the same thing as `Unless` but with a reversed testing polarity. The test function must evaluate to `true`, not `false` as is the case with `Unless`.
	
	Usage:
	
	`>> If(`
	`() => S.param ("something").isEmpty,`
	`() => PlainTextResponse("missing"))`

LocGroup	Allows you to group different menus together in a virtual way. The user has no idea about these groups; they're purely for developer convenience and operations. Usage: `>> LocGroup("admin")`

Location parameters offer you a robust and flexible way to aggregate functionality in your application, even at the individual page level. The selection presented in tables 7.2 and 7.3 are the defaults supplied by Lift. If you need to make your own `LocParam`, all you need to do is extend `UserLocParam` and implement whatever functionality you need.

Now it's time to look at controlling page access. Lift ships with several rather helpful authentication parameters that allow you to both test for access in a general way and also use HTTP authentication modes.

7.2.2 *Authentication parameters*

We've touched on using `SiteMap` for access control, but we haven't demonstrated any of that functionality yet. Broadly speaking, Lift has three location parameters that are used for access control: `Test`, `TestAccess`, and `HttpAuthProtected`. (If and Unless can also be used quite successfully.) These names are a little confusing, so let's take a moment to outline their functionality.

TEST AND TESTACCESS

There are two ways of thinking about results from access control systems in web applications. One is that if the user doesn't have permissions for that part of the application, it shouldn't even appear to exist for them; anything they don't have access for should resolve to a HTTP 404 Not Found page. This is the route that `Test` takes. The other line of thought is that it's OK to admit that the application is there, so as not to baffle the user, but you should direct the user to a login screen or some other friendly landing screen. This is the approach `TestAccess` adopts. Depending on your application's requirements, you can choose either implementation.

`Test` differs from `TestAccess` in that it takes a `Req` instance as its function argument so you can check any aspect of the request that you like. For example, perhaps the incoming request must have a particular cookie, or can only be accessed under a certain host (like localhost). All these things are easily tested for with the `Test` parameter.

Consider the following usage:

```
>> Test(req => req.hostName == "localhost")
```

In this example, unless the URL is being accessed under http://localhost/, Lift will yield a 404. You can try this out by visiting http://127.0.0.1/ and then http://localhost/. The former will get a 404 page, but the latter will give you the page as expected. Pretty neat.

`Test` has its uses in certain applications, but you'll likely use `TestAccess` more because it removes items from the menu that yield a `Full[LiftResponse]` from the function. `TestAccess` allows you to check any resource you like within your function, to verify that the current user has access to that aspect of the application. For example, it's common to check whether a user is logged in, and if they are a particular value will exist in the current session. If the user then happens to navigate to that page without logging in (perhaps the page was saved as a bookmark), you can safely redirect them to the login URL.

Here's an example of forcing a user to log in to a page:

```
object LoggedIn extends SessionVar[Box[Long]](Empty)

>> TestAccess(() =>LoggedIn.is.choice(
     x => Empty)(Full(RedirectResponse("login"))))
```

There are several things going on in the preceding code. First, an object called `LoggedIn` that holds a user ID is set by a page called `login`. The `TestAccess` parameter then checks for the existence of the properly set `SessionVar` before allowing access to the page. If `TestAccess` is `Empty`, the menu is displayed and all is well. If it yields the redirect response, the link is removed from the rendered menu and any attempt to access the page will result in a redirect to `login`. On the login page, the user could enter their credentials and the code there would properly set the value of `LoggedIn`, allowing them to successfully access the page in question.

HTTPAUTHPROTECTED

In order to use Lift's HTTP authentication, you must first define something like listing 7.2 in your `Boot` class to define the type of HTTP authentication you wish to use. You can currently choose between HTTP basic authentication and the more sophisticated HTTP digest authentication. Currently the choice between the two mechanisms is global in your application, but this generally isn't an issue because it would likely be problematic to mix the two authentication formats.

Listing 7.2 Configuring HTTP authentication in Boot

```
LiftRules.authentication = HttpBasicAuthentication("yourRealm"){
  case (un, pwd, req) =>
    if(un == "admin" && pwd == "password"){
      userRoles(AuthRole("admin")); true
    } else false
}
```

> **NOTE**   For more information on the difference between HTTP basic authenti-
> cation and digest authentication, see the Wikipedia articles at http://en.wiki-
> pedia.org/wiki/Basic_access_authentication and http://en.wikipedia.org/
> wiki/Digest_access_authentication.

Listing 7.2 shows how to configure HTTP basic authentication within your application, but the implementation is nearly identical for HTTP digest authentication; for
the digest authentication, just replace `HttpBasicAuthentication` with `HttpDigest-`
`Authentication`.

Whichever scheme you choose, credential checking in real-world code would be
significantly better than this, but the point is that you just need to check what the user
has actually entered by pattern matching on the request input (as seen here in the
`case` statement). Whether you look that up in a database, in some configuration file
in your app, or any other way, it's not the concern of Lift. Ultimately you only have to
return `true` to allow the user access to the page, or `false` to deny access.

With that in mind, the implementation of the `HttpAuthProtected` parameter is
very simple. Consider the following:

```
>> HttpAuthProtected(req => Full(AuthRole("admin")))
```

You might be wondering about these roles, which were also used in listing 7.2.
Essentially the `userRoles` and `Role` types allows you to define a simplistic role structure: `userRoles`, in listing 7.2, is just a `RequestVar` with a `List[Role]`. In listing 7.2,
we assigned everyone to the `admin` role, and then in the `LocParam`, the `Full(AuthRole`
`("admin"))` tells Lift that users must qualify as `admin` in order to gain access to
the page.

EXTERNAL SECURITY MODELS

Finally, let's take a look at external security models. Many people coming to Lift from
an enterprise Java background wonder why Lift doesn't ship with integration for products such as Spring Security. The reason for this is mostly ideological.

The model that's provided by Lift allows you to use the following security construct:

```
(Session, Resource) => Boolean
```

Consider for a moment that such a function can be applied to pages, locations,
URLs, and even field-level access in Mapper. The Lift ethos is that this construct can
be applied throughout your application to whatever degree of granularity you
require. With integrated access control, you always know what the access rules are
for a given resource.

Lift is evolving constantly, and modules for things such as OpenID are continually being added and improved upon. Technically speaking, there are no difficulties in using an external security model. But with `SiteMap` protecting your pages, you'll never present the user a link that isn't accessible for them, nor do you have to worry about parallel logic between your menu rendering and your external access control system, as would be the case with off-the-shelf-solutions. One such external security model that has been neatly integrated into Lift via a third-party module is Apache Shiro (http://shiro.apache.org/). This integration hooks into SiteMap and Lift's snippet pipeline, so you get all the functionality of Apache Shiro coupled with the power of Lift.

That pretty much covers controlling access with `SiteMap`. Lift provides you with a comprehensive set of tools for determining how and when a user should be allowed access to a page. If you require more control, you can always either write your own location parameter or extend `SiteMap` locations.

7.3 *Customizing SiteMap*

We've covered `SiteMap`, `Menu`, and `LocParam` in moderate detail and skimmed over the `Loc` class itself. `Loc` is a very powerful class that can do a lot more than an initial glance might reveal.

Consider what you have seen of `LocParam` (which essentially an add-on to `Loc`); it can add its own snippets, specify control flow rules, and supply its own template. To all intents and purposes, these `LocParam` are altering the `Loc` that they're attached to.

Given that, imagine what you could do if you were to subtype `Loc` and provide your own implementation. You would have a pretty powerful platform for providing dynamic content in a componentized way.

7.3.1 *Creating a custom Loc*

Nearly everyone who uses the internet will have come across a wiki at some point. Of course, the most well-known is Wikipedia, but the principles are pretty much the same in all wikis: the URL is the article name, and the content is pretty much free to edit. In this section, you'll see how to assemble a wiki component based upon a custom `Loc` implementation.

> **NOTE** A Mapper model called `WikiEntry` powers each page of the wiki pages you'll use in this section. The sample code for this chapter has all the basic Mapper configuration stuff set up, so rather than repeat all the configuration information here, please either check the sample code for reference or use your knowledge from previous chapters to make a simple `WikiEntry` class with two fields for the name (`MappedString`) and entry (`MappedTextarea`).

To get started, we'll create a simple `caseclass` to model each wiki page, and by *page* we're referring to some content from the database. Each wiki entry has two states that we care about: display and editing. Consider the definition of `Page`, which shows a simple case class that wraps the wiki content needed for each page:

```
case class Page(title: String, edit: Boolean){
  lazy val data: WikiEntry =
    WikiEntry.find(By(WikiEntry.name, title))
      openOr WikiEntry.create.name(title)
}
```

This is a fairly standard `caseclass` definition with one difference: it has a lazy value called `data` that will query the database looking for appropriate content, based upon the page name it's passed. If that content doesn't exist (as is often the case with wikis), a new `WikiEntry` will be created, and its name will be set to the name that was passed into the `title` parameter.

CREATING THE LOC

Making a subtype of `Loc` requires that you implement several different parameters. The following code listing demonstrates a `Loc` subtype with the required method implementations.

Listing 7.3   The most basic `Loc` implementation

```
import scala.xml.{Text, NodeSeq}
import net.liftweb.common.{Box,Full,Empty,Failure}
import net.liftweb.util.NamedPF
import net.liftweb.util.Helpers._
import net.liftweb.http.{SHtml,RewriteRequest,RewriteResponse,ParsePath}
import net.liftweb.sitemap.Loc
import net.liftweb.mapper.{OrderBy,Ascending,By}
import net.liftweb.textile.TextileParser
import net.liftweb.textile.TextileParser.WikiURLInfo
import sample.model.WikiEntry

object Wiki extends Loc[Page]{                          ❶ Location name
  def name = "wiki"
  def defaultValue = Full(Page("HomePage", false))      ❷ Default
  def params = Nil                                        page value
  val link = new Loc.Link[Page](
 ⇒List("wiki"), false){                                 ❸ Extra LocParam
  override defcreateLink(in: Page) =
    if(in.edit) Full(                                   ❹ Location link
 ⇒      Text("/wiki/edit/"+urlEncode(in.page)))
    else Full(Text("/wiki/"+urlEncode(in.page)))
  }
  val text = new Loc.LinkText(calcLinkText _)
  def calcLinkText(in: Page): NodeSeq =                 ❺ Location text
    if(in.edit) Text("Wiki edit "+in.page)
    else Text("Wiki "+in.page)
}
```

In order to create a custom Loc, first define a new class that's a subtype of `Loc` and that has a type to model pages with. In this example, the implementation makes use of the `Page` case class type discussed a moment ago. The body of the class contains a few parameters; some are more obvious than others. First, `name` defines the name of the location ❶ and `defaultValue` defines a default value for whatever this `Loc` does. In this case, the `Loc` loads wiki pages from the database, so we want to make sure that there's a default page to load—the `HomePage` ❷. Next is the `params` method, which lets you add additional `LocParams` to this custom `Loc` ❸. In this example, there are no `LocParams` required, so supplying a `Nil` (an empty list) will suffice.

The next method, `link`, is a rather important one; it manages how links for this location are created and handled ❹. Specifically, the first parameter for `new Loc.Link` provides a list representing the URL to match against. In this case, passing `List("wiki")` is sufficient as it will be the base URL for all pages in this `Loc`. The second parameter passed to `Loc.Link` is a `Boolean` that dictates whether the URL matching is only looking for a head match (so that anything within the incoming request path that fell after the aforementioned URL list being passed to `Link.Loc` would constitute a valid match). In this case, we're looking for absolute matches only, but a head-only match can be very useful, such as if you wanted to open up a whole directory structure for a help system.

Finally, `text` defines the text that should be used for this link in the menu rendering ❺. As you can see, depending upon the state of the `Page`—whether it's being edited or just displayed—different text content is returned.

The code in listing 7.3 just gets the `Loc` up and running with the compiler. It doesn't actually do anything helpful. Let's now add some methods to handle the display, editing, and listing of wiki entries. The following listing shows the additions required to the `Loc`.

Listing 7.4 Additions to the `Loc` to enable display, editing, and listing

```
object Wiki extends Loc[Page] {
  ...
  def showAll(in: NodeSeq): NodeSeq = WikiEntry.findAll(     ❶ List all pages
    OrderBy(WikiEntry.name, Ascending)).flatMap( e =>
      <div><a href={url(e.name)}>{e.name}</a></div>)

  def displayRecord(entry: WikiEntry) =
   "content" #>TextileParser.toHtml(                          ❷ Show wiki
     entry.entry, tcxtileWriter) &                              entry
   "a [href]" #>createLink(Page(entry.name, true)) &
   "view ^*" #>NodeSeq.Empty

  def editRecord(r: WikiEntry) = {
val isNew = !r.saved_?
val pageName = r.name.is
    "a [href]" #> url(pageName) &
    "form [action]" #> url(pageName) &
    "textarea" #>r.entry.toForm&                              ❸ Edit wiki
    "type=submit" #>SHtml.submit(                               entry
    isNew ? "Add" | "Save", () =>r.save) &
    "message" #>
      (if(isNew) Text("Create Entry '"+pageName+"'")
    else Text("Edit entry named '"+pageName+"'")) &
    "edit ^*" #>NodeSeq.Empty
  }
```

```
    def url(page: String) =
      createLink(Page(page, false))
    def stringUrl(page: String) =
      url(page).map(_.text).getOrElse("")
    private val textileWriter =
➥ Some((info: WikiURLInfo) => info match {
      caseWikiURLInfo(page,_) =>
        (stringUrl(page), Text(page), None)
    })
    ...
}
```

❹ **Define helper methods**

This is a fairly long code block, so let's take a look at what's going on in it. You'll be surprised how much of it will be familiar from working with snippets in earlier chapters.

First, `showAll` is simply retrieving all the `WikiEntrys` from the database and making a very list with links to the relevant entries ❶. The structure used here is exactly the same as in a standard snippet, in that it's a function of `NodeSeq => NodeSeq`.

The `displayRecord` method is what renders the contents of the `WikiEntry` ❷. Note, however, that the method has two parameter groups, the first taking a `WikiEntry` instance, and the second taking a `NodeSeq` for the incoming template markup. This is key, because it lets you use the `WikiEntry`, and in this instance read its data, to display that content to the user. Once again, the method makes use of Lift's CSS-style transformers functionality, which will be familiar from our earlier discussion of snippets.

The `editRecord` definition ❸ also sports two parameter groups for passing both the `WikiEntry` instance and HTML markup. The difference here is that we construct a form using the SHtml.submit helper; this form executes the save function upon being submitted.

Finally, the last section of the code ❹ defines some helper utilities that handle constructing URLs and converting the plain `WikiEntry` content into valid markup by using Lift's built-in Textile support.

The methods in this example are mostly doing the work of pulling information from and pushing it to the database and subsequently rendering the output. Your custom `Loc` can do anything you want—it doesn't need to use `Mapper` or anything else specific.

Let's now take a look at the actual `Loc` plumbing that makes this all work. We take a look at where the rendering methods are actually invoked and how that fits together in SiteMap. The following listing shows the final `Loc` methods that join the dots together.

Listing 7.5 Final Loc methods to implement the wiki

```
object Wiki extends Loc[Page] {
  ...
  object AllEntriesLoc extends Page("all", false)

  override val snippets: SnippetTest = {
    case ("wiki", Full(AllEntriesLoc)) => showAll _
    case ("wiki", Full(wp @ Page(_ , true))) =>
```

❶ **Internal wiki entry**

❷ **Snippet dispatch**

```
        editRecord(wp.record) _
     case ("wiki", Full(wp @ Page(_ , false)))
       if !wp.record.saved_? =>editRecord(wp.record) _
     case ("wiki", Full(wp: Page)) =>
       displayRecord(wp.record) _
   }
   override val rewrite: LocRewrite =
     ➥Full(NamedPF("Wiki Rewrite"){
     case RewriteRequest(ParsePath(
     ➥"wiki" :: "edit" :: page :: Nil,_,_,_),_,_) =>
       (RewriteResponse("wiki" :: Nil), Page(page, true))
     case RewriteRequest(ParsePath(
     ➥"wiki" :: page :: Nil, _, _,_),_,_) =>
       (RewriteResponse("wiki" :: Nil), Page(page, false))
     })
   ...
 }
```

② Snippet dispatch

③ Wiki rewrites

In section 7.2.2 we looked at providing location-specific snippets via the `LocParam` snippet. In listing 7.5, we're making a subtype of `Loc`, so we can add the snippet dispatching directly ②.

Interestingly, this implementation gives the wiki snippet several different functions. First, it responds to a specialized `Page` implementation called `AllEntriesLoc` ① that causes this location to list all the entries in the database. For example, if the URL is `/wiki/all`, it dispatches this to the `showAll` method that was defined in listing 7.4. Similarly, the next two function cases dispatch to the `editRecord` method, saving the record in the case that it's modified but not saved. Finally, if the URL is for the wiki, but it's not an editing URL, it displays the wiki entry itself by calling `displayRecord`.

Finally, the rewriting pattern tells Lift how to rewrite the URLs to the wiki.html file ③. We haven't covered rewriting in any detail yet, but you just need to understand that there are two URL schemes that both need to dispatch to the same template, `/wiki/edit/<page>` and `/wiki/<page>`, and this functionality is conveniently supplied by Lift's rewriting mechanism. For more information on rewriting, see section 8.2.

The following listing shows the markup required to make everything work.

Listing 7.6 Markup for the wiki.html template

```
<lift:surround with="default" at="content">
  <p><a href="/wiki/all">Show All Pages</a></p>
  <lift:wiki>
    <edit>
      <form action="" method="post">
        <p><message /><br /><textarea></textarea></p>
        <p><a href="">Cancel</a>
        <input type="submit" /></p>
      </form>
    </edit>
```

① Display template

```
    <view>
      <content />
      <p><a href="">Edit</a></p>
    </view>
  </lift:wiki>
</lift:surround>
```

❷ **Edit
   template**

The markup in this code should be familiar, given the fields that were bound in the `Loc` definition. There are only two points of note here: the template code for the editing page ❶ and the straightforward display code ❷. Because the content is being rendered with Textile, it will come complete with the correct tags, so just placing the `<content />` placeholder within the template is sufficient, as the element will be completely replaced by the snippet rendering.

The final thing to do is to register the custom location with the `SiteMap` itself:

```
Menu(Wiki)
```

As you can see, it wasn't too difficult to build a custom location that's essentially a self-contained component of functionality. There are many things that you can use custom locations for, and it's an underused idiom in Lift development.

7.3.2   *When to customize SiteMap?*

You may be wondering what the benefit of utilizing a `SiteMap` extension is over and above regular snippet functionality. There are several use cases that are a good fit for custom locations:

- *Shared state*—In some scenarios, you may want to have lots of separate snippets on a page that are rightly separate but that require a degree of shared state. Because a custom `Loc[T]` allows you to control the instantiation of snippets on that page, you can inject common data into the snippet's constructor. In this way, you could (if your use case demands it) have a mini-controller to centralize some shared state for a given page.

- *Help directory*—Consider a help directory that has lots and lots of pages that you'd like to be available under multiple URLs, based upon their content. In this situation, rather than having a single canonical URL, you may want the same content available at multiple URLs. Moreover, you could have a single location without the need to explicitly specify all the locations; for these this scenario using a custom Loc is often preferable to using the generic `**` notation within the `Menu` definition, because you would not want to lose the ability to set specific page titles, and so on.

- *Wiki*—As in this chapter's example, a wiki is a great use case for custom locations, because the content tends to be relatively fluid and thus driven directly by the URL.

- *Blog*—It's a fairly common idiom in blogging to use URLs that have the date embedded, such as /2010/01/30/some-article. In this case, the URL is carrying significant information about the resource that's being requested, so it makes sense to use a custom location.

Generally speaking, using a custom `Loc` works well when your URLs have meaning or metadata that's important for the page. In the wiki example, the URL itself is everything, as it denotes the page to be loaded. Likewise, the other three use cases in the preceding list have in common the notion of meaningful URLs. If your problem involves meaningful resource URLs, using a custom location in SiteMap is probably going to be a good solution.

7.4   *Summary*

SiteMap is an unassuming but powerful part of Lift. In this chapter, you've seen how you can leverage SiteMap's simplistic DSL to build sophisticated menu structures and apply granular security to those menu locations. Lift also provides a convenient way to render your application's navigation by using the built-in `Menu` snippet. The `Menu` snippet offers you a flexible way to dynamically generate your application's navigation and automatically ensure that your application displaying the correct menus for any given user.

The other important topic covered in this chapter was the notion of locations and location parameters. Locations give you a convenient way to build functionality that's highly componentized and pluggable between your applications. This was demonstrated by building a location that automatically adds wiki functionality to the sample application. Locations can also have location parameters associated with them to augment both the presentation and control flow. Lift's location parameter system provides a highly integrated way to add authentication either by using your own custom login system or using the built-in HTTP authentication providers.

In the next chapter, we cover Lift's HTTP feature set. At its very core, Lift is a highly capable abstraction on the HTTP request and response cycle. With the concepts of REST (Representational State Transfer) permeating all the corners of the web in recent times, it's important to understand what a good companion Lift can be for your adventures on the web. So far you've seen several fundamental classes that make up Lift's awesome HTTP support, such as `Req`. The next chapter covers the core of Lift and demonstrates how you can build applications that leverage sophisticated REST services, and that can respond with multiple formats, including XML and plain text.

HTTP in Lift

Because Lift uses its view-first architecture, it's often not clear to users who are not familiar with this setup how Lift handles requests. To that end, this chapter explains how to do everything related to request handling in Lift, such as rewriting to provide friendly URLs, dispatching to create REST web services, and understanding Lift's HTTP pipeline.

Lift's HTTP pipeline consists of numerous components, and it's often difficult to visualize where the things you configure during your application boot phase actually take effect in the request cycle. This chapter starts by positioning the various pipeline components and exploring some of the configuration points available during the process. After looking at the pipeline in moderate detail, we take a deeper practical look at both URL rewriting and dispatching.

Rewriting provides you a robust toolkit for defining content-resolution rules. For example, if you have a file called help.html in your application webapp folder, rewriting allows you to alter the URLs that can access this template. For example, you may decide at a later date that /support/ would be a better URL than simply /help.html, because you want to provide a more comprehensive set of support materials. In this case, you could internally alter the routing of /support/ to map to the help.html file. In broad terms, you can think of rewriting as being about routing and resolution. A more in-depth use case is discussed in section 8.2.

Conversely, dispatching is primarily about content generation. The content could be anything from markup through to PDF, or even some custom format. In essence, dispatching is the core of Lift's HTTP service, and plugging into it gives you as much control over the response as internal Lift operations have. It can be a very powerful and effective tool, and it's commonly used for building REST services. We discuss this more in section 8.3.

Without further ado, let's start our exploration of Lift's HTTP processing pipeline.

8.1 HTTP pipeline

It can be useful to understand the HTTP processing pipeline, where these facilities sit, and the classes involved in booting, servicing requests, and destroying a Lift application. Users coming to Lift from other Java frameworks often like to have this wider picture so they can understand the relationship between components and classes in the codebase. This section presents that overview.

With that being said, you can also safely skip this section and go straight to section 8.2 without missing any critical information if you're only interested in getting things done with Lift's HTTP feature set.

8.1.1 HTTP abstraction

Lift has an abstraction of the whole HTTP request-response cycle that completely decouples it from the Java servlet container specification. This means that Lift is actually capable of running on anything from a normal servlet container like Jetty or Tomcat, right up to next-generation high-performance networking stacks like JBoss Netty.

The abstraction is visualized in figure 8.1 with the Lift application running in a traditional servlet container and using Lift's implementation of a `javax.servlet .Filter`. Because Lift is a filter, you can mix and match your application stack without affecting any other applications in your service chain. If Lift is unable to service a particular request, or you configure it not to, it simply forwards the request to the next process in the chain. In this way, Lift can be seamlessly integrated into your existing application stack.

The HTTP abstraction covers all parts and services Lift interacts with on the given platform—everything from basic requests right through to asynchronous request APIs for native Comet support. The benefit of this is that whenever you're dealing with HTTP aspects in your application, you have a single unified API to deal with, which keeps your application portable by removing platform-specific dependencies. Moreover, if you then need to implement something that's vendor specific, you simply need to provide the thin provider layer that delivers the behavior you require.

With this in mind, let's look at how Lift boots up in this abstracted environment.

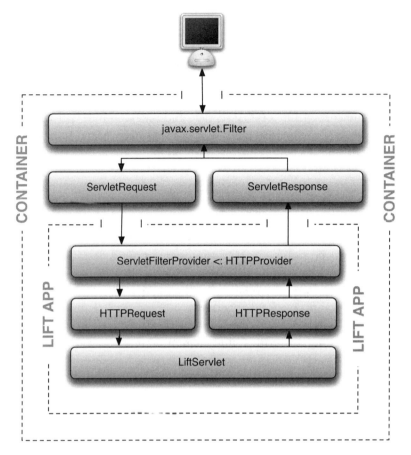

Figure 8.1 A visualization of Lift's HTTP abstraction as seen in the familiar Java servlet container. The request comes in a `ServletRequest` but is internally mapped in Lift to the `HTTPRequest` type.

8.1.2 *Application lifecycle*

Lift has three distinct phases in its application lifecycle: boot up, request handling, and shutdown. Request handling is where the vast majority of work is done, so it will be discussed separately in section 8.1.3. Here we'll cover the application lifecycle: boot up and shutdown. Section 8.1.1 outlined Lift's HTTP abstraction and the interface for talking to its container. That consistent interface means that Lift will always go through the same lifecycle process irrespective of its environment.

Let's assume that we have the most basic type of Lift application running in a standard Java servlet container. We look at configuration details in chapter 15, so here we just assume that the application is running under http://domain.com/myapp/, where myapp is the application context. Figure 8.2 shows the process Lift goes through during its boot cycle, when the container loads the application.

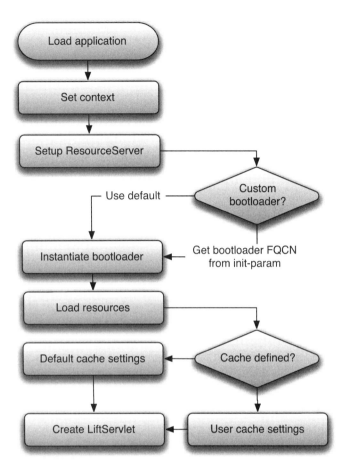

**Figure 8.2   Flow chart detailing the Lift application boot process.
During the startup sequence, Lift goes through a set number of tasks
to configure its environment. The main one to take note of here is the
invocation of the bootloader, because that's what actually starts
the application.**

As you can see, there are a few operations going on here. The container loads the web archive (WAR) file through the filter interface, and Lift assimilates the HTTP context passed to it via the container. In this case, the context is "myapp", so all URLs in the application are rewritten to be prefixed with that context. Then Lift configures the ResourceServer.

RESOURCE SERVER

The ResourceServer is a special object that can serve static content from the application classpath, allowing you to make (or simply use) portable components that include frontend content like CSS and JavaScript and wire those into your application.

During this early boot phase, Lift is configuring the `ResourceServer` to serve things that are bundled with Lift itself, such as JQuery and YUI JavaScript libraries. You'll notice that by default Lift applications can serve URLs such as this:

```
/classpath/jquery.js
```

The jquery.js file isn't coming from the webapp folder, as you might expect, but from the WAR classpath, in the lift-webkit JAR. If you wanted to make a reusable component of application logic and bundle some CSS styling inside the JAR file, all you'd need to do is place the CSS file that you'd like to serve inside the following folder: src/main/resources/toserve/css/. You would subsequently wire that up in your Lift application boot, as shown:

```
import net.liftweb.http.ResourceServer

ResourceServer.allow {
  case "css" :: "nameOfYourFile.css" => true
}
```

Any requests for /<context>/classpath/css/nameOfYourFile.css are serviced by the CSS content from the application classpath, rather than the webapp directory. This functionality is especially useful if you want to externalize some common user interface components, because it allows you to serve content from any JAR on the classpath.

Resources that are serviced via the `ResourceServer` are done so using Lift's stateless dispatch. We cover this in detail in section 8.3.

BOOTLOADER

The next phase of the boot process is for Lift to look for the application bootloader. That's the class that will contain your entire application configuration and setup, including such things as calls to `LiftRules` and other application-global configuration points. If you want to alter the environment Lift operates in, the bootloader is the place to do it.

By default, Lift will attempt to use the `bootstrap.liftweb.Boot` class. When running in a servlet container, you can override this by adding an additional `init-param` to the application web.xml as shown:

```
<filter>
  ...
  <init-param>
    <param-name>bootloader</param-name>
    <param-value>org.mycompany.Boot</param-value>
  </init-param>
</filter>
```

The only stipulation with this is that your custom bootloader must extend the type `net.liftweb.http.Bootable`.

Upon locating the bootloader, Lift makes a new instance of this class and calls the `boot` method.

TEMPLATE CACHE

When you're running your application in production mode, Lift optimizes the serving of page templates by using its `TemplateCache` system. Unless you specifically configured this value in your application bootloader, Lift will set up an in-memory cache that can hold 500 templates. This is perfectly acceptable for most applications, and more often than not you won't need to tune this value. With these boot operations completed, Lift creates an instance of the internal class `LiftServlet` and is now ready to start serving requests. Huzzah!

> **NOTE** Production mode is just one of Lift's *run modes*. They're covered in detail in chapter 15.

This is the end of the booting up phase. The next phase, the request lifecycle, is covered in detail in section 8.1.3. The opposite pole of booting up is the shutdown phase.

SHUTDOWN

Shutting down an application is always a sad time, but it's important to understand what happens when you do and how that can affect the service your application delivers. Figure 8.3 shows the shutdown process followed by Lift.

The application will receive the shutdown signal from the environment, and from there it will start to mark sessions on its internal session controller as shutting down.

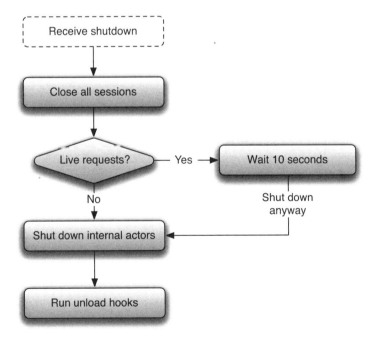

Figure 8.3 Lift's shutdown lifecycle gracefully stops taking requests and shuts down its internal operations before executing any user-defined functions prior to terminating.

Those sessions then start to be killed off and Lift checks to see if it has any currently active requests. In the interests of good service, Lift will give any requests in progress 10 seconds to close. Or, if the live request count is 0 under 10 seconds, Lift will continue to shut down its internal actors and operations before it moves to the final step—`LiftRules.unloadHooks`—which is typically used for shutting your connection to the database or cleaning up other services in a polite way.

That's the whole Lift application cycle—fairly short but sweet. The request cycle is where you'll likely find some interesting information and get a better appreciation for where the intercept points are, to which you can apply your executable functions.

8.1.3   *Request lifecycle*

Lift's request pipeline is made up of many facets and several nontrivial moving parts. In this section, you'll gain an appreciation for the parts and the process of this pipeline, rather than get a blow-by-blow account of method calls. At the very high level, you can visualize Lift's pipeline as a two-step process: the initial stateless processing and the subsequent state initialization and processing.

There are various intercept points in Lift where you can define URLs to be handled statelessly, either using a stateless dispatch (covered in section 8.3) or a stateless test. The latter is more complicated, so for now we stick with the notion of whether something is stateless or not.

Clarifying *state*

In the request lifecycle, we talk a lot about stateful and stateless processes, so it's important that you understand the practical difference and their implications.

A *stateless* request or component has no access to session variables, cookies, or other such items that can be categorized as *state*. By contrast, *stateful* requests have full access to request variables, session variables, and all the other goodies that are available from the S and SHtml objects.

State is very important for Lift, especially when using the built-in form helpers and secure AJAX, because Lift keeps a function around to execute later (such as when a form is submitted), and it can only do this function mapping when there's somewhere to store it for later use. Without access to state, these functions wouldn't be able to work.

We start by looking at the first part of the request lifecycle: stateless processing. Figure 8.4 details the stateless part of Lift's HTTP request pipeline.

Let's break this first part of the rather long workflow down into its most important components and look at some example code for the various configuration points.

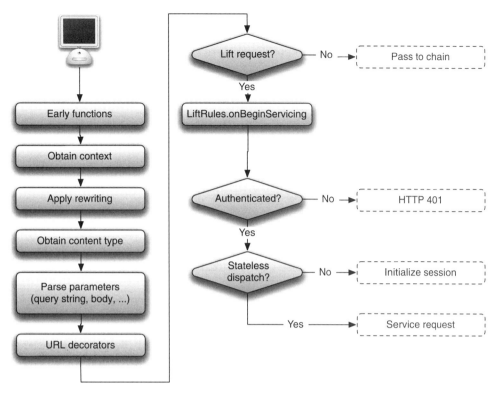

Figure 8.4 **The very first part of the Lift processing pipeline, illustrated here, is stateless. Once this part of the pipeline is complete, if the request isn't stateless, it proceeds to the steps in figure 8.5 for state initialization and further processing.**

EARLY FUNCTIONS

The early executing functions are user-defined function types of the form `HTTP-Request => Any`. This allows you to modify the request before it's passed to any other parts of Lift's processing chain. For example, you may want to alter the parameter parsing of the container like this:

```
LiftRules.early.append(_.setCharacterEncoding("UTF-8"))
```

The only point of note here is that if Lift is operating as one of many filters in your application stack, the other filters must be expecting UTF-8, or some unexpected things might ensue as different encoding schemes clash.

The next important stage is the application of rewriting rules. Because rewriting is a sizable topic in its own right, it's covered in section 8.2. The important thing to understand here is that the rewriting is applied recursively until there are no more matches with the specified rewrite pattern. Lift then assigns the incoming parameters from the query string or the request body. The request body itself is lazily evaluated, so until it's touched directly by the code, the body remains assigned but unparsed.

The final step in the stateless pipeline is to evaluate the URL for any parts that have been defined as decorators. This essentially means that the incoming URLs can have a fixed or static item suffixed to them. Here's an example:

```
LiftRules.urlDecorate.prepend {
  case url => if(url.contains("?")) url + "&srv=001" else "?srv=001"
}
```

In this example, all Lift requests will have the static suffix `srv` automatically applied, and some infrastructure configuration could be made to route requests to specific servers, for example. Decorators are essentially a mechanism that allows you to define static additions to the incoming URLs, in order to serve some application-specific purpose.

REQUEST VALIDATION AND EXECUTION

In the second column of processes in figure 8.4, Lift has to decide whether it should be servicing this request or not. This is once again configurable through `LiftRules` with a simple `Req => Boolean` function that you can use like so:

```
LiftRules.liftRequest.append {
  case Req("nolift" :: Nil,"xml",_) => false
}
```

When would you use such a function? There are several scenarios in which this can prove useful:

- A single Lift application is running in a container, and you want to serve a static file from the container directly rather than piping it through Lift.
- A Lift application is running as part of a set of filters, and you know that a particular incoming request needs to be serviced by a filter further down the chain from Lift, so piping it through Lift's pipeline doesn't gain you anything.

Assuming that the request is indeed for processing by Lift, the first hook available to you is the `LiftRules.onBeginProcessing` function list. This hook allows you to execute a side-effecting function with full access to the incoming `Req` instance. The final step before moving on to a stateless dispatch, is ensuring that this request doesn't have any HTTP authentication applied, based on the definition at `LiftRules.httpAuth-ProtectedResource`, which we touched on in chapter 7.

With the request now through the preservice validation, Lift checks to see if the request should be dealt with via the stateless dispatch mechanism (covered in section 8.3) or whether it should continue into phase two of the servicing and initialize a session, being a stateful request. Figure 8.5 shows the stateful request-processing pipeline.

Once again, there are several distinct components in this second phase of processing. All of the operations depicted in figure 8.5 have access to the application state, such as session variables. With this in mind, the first operation is to check whether this URL should be serviced directly using a stateful HTTP dispatch. This is an identical process to the stateless dispatch discussed in the previous section, but it has access to

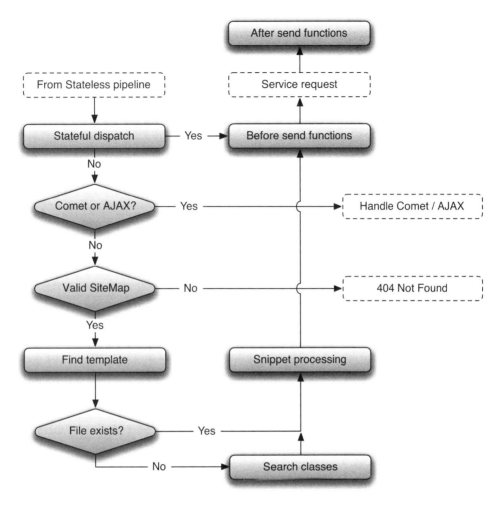

Figure 8.5 This is the second phase of the processing pipeline. If the request makes it to this stage, it's by definition stateful. The process here is concerned with loading the template content and processing any functions or state that are being used in the application logic.

all the current session state. Stateful dispatching is discussed in section 8.3. If the URL is not handled by dispatching, the request is then checked to see if it is an AJAX or Comet request; if it is, it's bounced to the appropriate handler for further processing and response to the browser.

Assuming this is a regular (non-Comet, non-AJAX, non-dispatch) request for a resource, the next check in the pipeline is the SiteMap, as discussed in chapter 7. If the page passes the SiteMap access control checks, it will return a 404 Not Found if the access control returned false, or it will continue with request processing and attempt to load the template and handle the dynamic page content.

TEMPLATE RESOLUTION

At this point in the request processing, all the access control is completed and Lift is only concerned with generating and serving the dynamic markup content. To that end, TemplateFinder goes looking for the appropriate template file in the application WAR by removing parts of the path that start with a period (.) or underscore (_) or that contain -hidden and then looking for a filename match. In addition to these rules about template resolution, Lift will also attempt to augment the filename with some rules for finding locale-specific templates, but this is discussed specifically in chapter 12.

There is also the possibility that a template doesn't exist for this URL, at least as a file. You may remember from chapter 6 that Lift also has the LiftView mechanism for generating content. If a template file doesn't exist on the classpath as a file resource, Lift will start looking in the class system for an appropriate view. Lift knows where to look for views, Comet, and reflection snippets because of the following configuration in the application boot:

```
LiftRules.addToPackages("com.mycompany.project")
```

Lift will subsequently look for an appropriate view in the com.mycompany.project .view package. Whether the template is a class view or a file template, the result will ultimately be a scala.xml.NodeSeq that a response can be generated from by executing the appropriate snippets, handling any content, and so forth. Whatever the output contains, it will be some form of markup, and Lift then converts that to a LiftResponse and flushes it to the browser. That's pretty much all there is to it!

Now that you've seen how Lift handles requests and controls its environment, it's time to look at two of the main HTTP features we touched on during this discussion of the pipeline: rewriting and dispatching. These are common components that you'll want to use in your application, and both come in stateless and stateful flavors. Section 8.2 will take you through the details of rewriting, and section 8.3 will walk you through creating a REST service with dispatching.

8.2 *URL rewriting*

When seeing a term like *URL rewriting*, you might think about .htaccess from Apache, or another frontend web server. Other frameworks on the market also call this functionality *routing*. Conceptually, Lift's URL rewriting is the same, in that it takes an input URL and maps that onto an output URL, which in the context of Lift is either a specific view or template.

We briefly touched on the rewriting of a response in chapter 7 with SiteMap .LocParam, and this is the same mechanism under the hood. In the LocParam use, however, the rewrite is often targeted for a single site component or piece of application functionality. Here we cover the global application rewriting and focus on specific details of the mechanism that you can use either here in the global context or when building a LocParam.

Consider the following situation: You have a template called *product* that displays a detailed view of a particular product, alongside some information about other products within the same category. By default, your URLs might look something like this:

```
/product?id=5678&category=1234
```

This is a little clunky because the product 5678 is in fact a subordinate resource of category 1234. That is, the product ID has no relationship with the category ID, and it would be nicer if the accessing URL were a better semantic representation of the resources being used.

By implementing rewriting, that URL could be changed to this:

```
/category/1234/product/5678
```

This is a trivial example, but the takeaway is that you can completely alter the incoming URL and still extract the component parts and issue them to the correct template or view. Let's take this use case and look at a basic example.

8.2.1 Defining a RewritePF

Most things in Lift are configured through the `LiftRules` object, and rewriting is no different. There are two different modes of rewriting with Lift: stateful and stateless. We encourage you to use stateless rewriting in most cases, unless you specifically have a use case that demands it be stateful. In my experience, there are only a few corner cases that truly require stateful rewrites, so you're generally better off not carrying that slight extra overhead with each request.

The following listing shows a full example of using stateless rewriting.

Listing 8.1 Example of stateless rewriting

```
import net.liftweb.http.{LiftRules,RewriteRequest,
                         RewriteResponse,ParsePath}

LiftRules.statelessRewrite.append {
  case RewriteRequest(ParsePath(
    ➥"category" :: cid :: "product" :: pid :: Nil, "",true,false),
      GetRequest, http) =>
    RewriteResponse("product" :: Nil,
      Map("cid" ->cid, "pid" -> pid))
}
```

This can be confusing as rewriting makes use of Scala's `unapply` functionality, which at first glance can seem somewhat mystical. Let's break this statement into its component parts.

NOTE For more information on Scala's unapply method, see the article on "Extractor Objects" in the "Tour of Scala": http://www.scala-lang.org/node/112.

All rewrites have two phases: the request, denoted by the `RewriteRequest` type, and the output, `RewriteResponse`. First, let's look at the input `RewriteRequest` and its parameters:

```
case class RewriteRequest(
  path: ParsePath,
  requestType: RequestType,
  httpRequest: HTTPRequest)
```

The first parameter is of type `ParsePath`. This is a special Lift type that lets you control elements of a request. In listing 8.1 the `ParsePath` definition is essentially going to match this:

```
/category/<variable>/product/<variable>
```

The first parameter of `ParsePath` is a `List[String]`. Listing 8.1 uses the cons notation to build that list, and where the URL parts should be variable, a placeholder is used instead of a static string, which at runtime will have its value set based on the incoming URL values. The second parameter defines the suffix this request should use. In this example, no suffix is used, so passing `""` is sufficient. But if you wanted to only allow requests that ended in .xml, you would specify `"xml"` as the value, or if you didn't care what the extension was, you could simply pass an underscore, and any suffix would be considered a match. The final two parameters are simple `Boolean` values: the first is a switch to specify whether this must be an absolute match from the root context, or whether any URL matching this pattern will do; the second specifies whether this URL has a trailing slash or not.

ParsePath is the biggest part of the input `RewriteRequest`, so you should take a little bit of time to understand the options it provides. With the request aspect under control, let's look at the second part of the partial function, the `RewriteResponse`. The purpose of this class is to define which template file is servicing this request. In listing 8.1, for example, the URL itself isn't going to match any template path by itself, so you have to tell Lift which resource it should use to service this request and detail how to map the URL parameters so they can be accessed later from your snippets using the `S.param` method.

In listing 8.1, the following `RewriteResponse` is implemented:

```
RewriteResponse("product" :: Nil, Map("cid" -> cid, "pid" -> pid))
```

This line tells Lift that when handling this request, it should use the webapp/ product.html template and map the product ID in the URL that was denoted by the `pid` placeholder to a parameter called `pid`. This parameter can be named whatever you want, but it's idiomatic to name the mapped parameter the same as the placeholder. This mapping allows you to access the value of the `pid` URL parameter in any state-initialized part of your application using `S.param("pid")`.

The `RewriteResponse` object has several overloaded methods that support different use cases. For example, you have seen how rewriting can be used to make friendly URLs and map parameters into your application, but there are situations where you may want to alias a resource, or perhaps alter the rewrite based upon an HTTP verb. The overrides are listed in table 8.1.

Table 8.1 List of `RewriteResponse` overloaded `apply` methods

Method	Usage

`def apply(path: ParsePath,`
`    params: Map[String, String])`
	`RewriteResponse(`
	`ParsePath("sample" :: Nil,`
	`    "xml",true,false),`
	`    Map("pid" -> id))`

	Rewrites the incoming `RewriteRequest` to use the template located at src/main/webapp/sample.html.
`def apply(path: List[String])`	`RewriteResponse("sample" :: Nil)`
	Rewrites the incoming `RewriteRequest` to use the template located at src/main/webapp/sample.html.
`def apply(path: List[String],` `    suffix: String)`	`RewriteResponse("sample" :: Nil,` `"xml")`
	Rewrites the incoming `RewriteRequest` to /sample.xml.
`def apply(path: List[String],` `    params: Map[String, String])`	`RewriteResponse("sample" :: id :: Nil,` `    Map("pid" -> id))`
	Rewrites the incoming `RewriteRequest` to use the template at src/main/webapp/sample.html and map the `<id>` parameter in the URL pattern to a parameter that's accessible via `S.param("pid")`.

These overloads provide you with enough flexibility to support the vast majority of things you'll likely want to do in your applications. However, there are some more advanced use cases that require you to build custom parameter extractors. We look at those next.

8.2.2 Advanced rewriting

In the previous section, we looked at examples of rewriting that will cover a lot of what you might want to do in the course of normal application programming. But rewriting (and dispatching, for that matter) makes extensive use of Scala's partial functions and pattern-matching features, and as mentioned in the previous section, you can use `unapply` functions in conjunction with these match statements.

The rewriting examples you've seen so far have exclusively dealt with strings. This is all well and good if you're working with string values like words, but it's a little cumbersome when you're working with numeric values, such as a reference or identification number. Moreover, consider a rewrite request pattern like this:

```
RewriteRequest(ParsePath("account" :: aid :: Nil,_,_,_))
```

This would match both /account/rubbish and /account/12345, so how can we determine the difference between them?

Scenarios like this are a perfect use case for unapply. In the net.liftweb.util .Helpers object there is an object called AsInt that sports the following definition:

```
def unapply(in: String): Option[Int] = asInt(in)
```

Without getting into the specifics of how unapply actually works and is handled in pattern-matching statements, you can see that this method takes a string argument and converts it to an integer value, if it can be converted. Helpfully, we can drop this into the RewriteRequest pattern and Lift will automatically check the type of the incoming URL and only match on those it can successfully convert to integers, meaning that the /account/rubbish URL simply won't match and will yield a 404 Not Found error.

This listing demonstrates such a use of the AsInt helper:

Listing 8.2 Using `AsInt` unapply to add type checking to rewrites

```
LiftRules.statelessRewrite.append {
  case RewriteRequest(
    ParsePath("account" :: AsInt(aid) :: Nil,"",true,false),_,_) =>
    RewriteResponse("account" :: Nil, Map("aid" -> aid))
}
```

The listing should look very similar to what you have seen previously, but with the key difference being in the ParsePath method. As you can see, the AsInt helper has been applied as a specific part of the URL List[String] match. It's this component that ensures that incoming URLs are integer values rather than any old string.

Using unapply with rewriting can provide you with a flexible system for doing all manner of interesting things. For example, given a situation where you have a page with several snippets, you could feasibly initialize a RequestVar from the rewriting and have that ready for use in all your snippets featured on that page, thus negating the issue of having a main snippet that must load the item from the database. This technique is certainly something to bear in mind when building your own applications—it may well come in handy.

At the beginning of this chapter, we talked about rewriting being all about content resolution, and its counterpart being dispatching, which was all about content creation. Now that you've had a good introduction to resolving application resources, let's take a deep dive into dispatching and content creation.

8.3 *Dispatching and web services*

In this section, we look at how you can hook into Lift's HTTP dispatching, which is the system that lets you return any subtype of LiftResponse. This could be a markup response, some kind of binary response such as a PDF, or pretty much anything else you can transport via HTTP. It's fairly common practice in other web frameworks to use strings to set the headers, content type, and other response parameters, and then just flush this heap of strings to the browser. Lift takes a slightly different approach and provides an extensible, strongly typed mechanism for servicing content. This is known as the `LiftResponse` trait, and Lift has a raft of premade subtypes that give you, as the developer, a simple API for putting together structures that will be sent to the browser.

A common use case for dispatching is the creation of web services, and often those services follow a RESTful Resource Orientated Architecture (ROA) design. Here you will see the high-level DSL that can assist you in creating basic web services and also cover the lower-level dispatch table, so you can implement your own dispatchers and even conduct content negation to deliver the right content to the right client (you could deliver HTML content to a browser, but PDF content to a mobile eReader, for example).

> **NOTE** Resource-oriented architecture (ROA) is discussed in the Wikipedia article: http://en.wikipedia.org/wiki/Resource_oriented_architecture. For more information about content negotiation, see the discussion in RFC 2616 at http://www.w3.org/Protocols/rfc2616/rfc2616-sec12.html.

Before we get started, it's important to understand that Lift can service HTTP dispatching in either stateful or stateless modes. There is a slight overhead in using stateful dispatching, because it's creating a session if one doesn't already exist, but the key thing that should decide your implementation route is the use case in which it's being applied. For example, if you need to use session variables to hold information over multiple requests, then stateless dispatching won't work for you, but otherwise stateless dispatching should be good for most use cases. Either way, it's a fairly minimal difference, and the only change in implementation is the `LiftRules` property that you append to. For stateful dispatching, use

```
LiftRules.dispatch.append(...)
```

and for stateless dispatching, use

```
LiftRules.statelessDispatchTable.append(...)
```

All of the examples we cover here will work well irrespective of which dispatcher you wire things up to—it's completely down to your use case.

In terms of its implementation, all HTTP dispatching in Lift is based upon two things: a request, or `Req` instance, and a response, which is a `LiftResponse` subtype. As we just mentioned, there are a couple of different ways to interact with this process, and both have their respective merits. We cover more specific details of both `Req` and `LiftResponse` later in the chapter, but, for now, just understand that these are the input and output types used by Lift to service the process.

Let's get on with looking at how to implement a small example using the high-level dispatching DSL.

8.3.1 *Using the HTTP dispatch DSL*

Before we get into anything more complicated, such as REST and content negotiation, let's first check out how you can create simple services using Lift's dispatch DSL. The next listing shows the most basic example.

Listing 8.3 Using the HTTP dispatch DSL

```
import net.liftweb.http.rest.RestHelper

object BasicDispatchUsage extends RestHelper {
  serve {
    case "my" :: "sample" :: _ Get _ => <b>Static</b>
  }
}
```

This small example implements the `RestHelper` trait in a singleton object called `BasicDispatchUsage`. Inheriting from `RestHelper` delivers a whole set of functionality via special helper types and implicit conversions to keep your implementation code as light as possible. The main method inherited from the `RestHelper` is the `serve` method, which allows you to define `case` statements and use specialized helpers like `Get` to define your HTTP resources. As you can see, the `case` statement in listing 8.3 defines a URL using a `List[String]` (via the `::` cons operator) that will match `/my/sample/**` and serve it with the most basic XML response.

With this definition in place, the only thing that must also be done is to tell the appropriate dispatcher about this service definition object:

```
LiftRules.dispatch.append(BasicDispatchUsage)
```

This is rather nice, you'll probably agree. All you need to do is reference the singleton object that extends `RestHelper`, and no other wiring is needed. Of course, this example is rather trivial, but it illustrates the point at hand rather nicely. At compile time Lift is able to determine the type of response conversion it should be doing. In this instance, it defines an XML literal in the code, which the Scala compiler sees as type `scala.xml.Elem`. It also sees that within the `serve` block there are implicit conversions in scope that can take a `scala.xml.Elem` and convert it to the correct `LiftResponse` subtype, which in this instance is a `NodeResponse`, because we're serving XML.

Let's just pause for a moment to review the `LiftResponse` mechanism that we've briefly touched on in the past couple of paragraphs. All dispatch methods in your Lift application, no matter how they're constructed, must return a subtype of `Lift-Response`. Out of the box, Lift comes with a whole raft of response types for serving XML, JSON, Atom, and so on, and each response type typically takes care of any appropriate options that need setting; nevertheless, you can override any behavior as you see fit.

In Lift's dispatching system, anything that will ultimately return something to the browser must yield a subtype of `LiftResponse`. With this in mind, it's useful to be aware of the wide variety of prebaked `LiftResponse` types available. Table 8.2 details some of the types you'll likely find yourself using fairly regularly, with examples of their usage. There are other types that fill the whole spectrum of HTTP response possibilities—these are just the common usages. Also bear in mind that several of these response types have companion objects with overloaded `apply` methods, meaning that they can often be used with different arguments to control behavior in a more specific way or to provide a more simplistic API.

Table 8.2 Commonly used `LiftResponse` subtypes

Response type	HTTP code	Usage
OkResponse	200	OkResponse()
JsonResponse	200	JsonResponse(JString ➥("This is JSON"))
PlainTextResponse	200	PlainTextResponse("Your message")
XmlResponse	200	XmlResponse(<sample />)
AcceptedResponse	202	AcceptedResponse()
PermRedirectResponse	301	PermRedirectResponse("/new/ ➥path", req)
RedirectResponse	302	RedirectResponse("/new/path")
BadResponse	400	BadResponse()
UnauthorizedResponse	401	UnauthorizedResponse("Magical ➥Realm")
ForbiddenResponse	403	ForbiddenResponse("No access ➥for you")
NotFoundResponse	404	NotFoundResponse()
InternalServerErrorResponse	500	InternalServerErrorResponse()

The syntax of the DSL relies quite heavily on Scala currying and implicit conversions to achieve its construction, so let's look at a few examples that illustrate how the types are built up into the bare metal `LiftRules.DispatchPF` that all of Lift's dispatching is based upon.

> **NOTE** Broadly speaking, curried functions are those that have multiple argument lists. Currying can be a fairly deep subject in and of itself, but for more in-depth information on currying, see Joshua D. Suereth's *Scala in Depth*.

At a very base level, the dispatching mechanism boils down to this:

```
PartialFunction[Req, () => Box[LiftResponse]]
```

That is to say, a request comes in and your code will return a `Function0` that has a boxed `LiftResponse`. The DSL makes this whole process easier for you by abstracting and providing sensible defaults via implicit conversions. For example, if you're returning an XML response, the `RestHelper` has conversions that translate the `scala.xml.Node` into `() => Box[Node]`.

There are many conversions to make working with the DSL as seamless as possible. The following listing demonstrates four different statements that all create XML responses but make use of the `RestHelper` at different levels of abstraction.

Listing 8.4   Understanding dispatch DSL type hierarchy

```
object SecondDispatchUsage extends RestHelper {
  serve {
    case "sample" :: "one" :: _ XmlGet _ => <b>Static</b>
    case "sample" :: "two" :: Nil XmlGet _ => <b>Static</b>
    case XmlGet("sample" :: "three" :: Nil, _) => <b>Static</b>
    case Req("sample" :: "four" :: Nil, "xml", GetRequest) =>
      <b>Static</b>
  }
}
```

Listing 8.4 defines four cases that illustrate the various routes you can use with the dispatching DSL. The first shows a basic implementation that simply services /sample/one/*/*.xml and is very similar to what was defined in listing 8.2, but as this version uses the `XmlGet` helper, so the incoming request must present an .xml extension and the content accept header must be `text/xml`. If these conditions aren't met, Lift will return a 404 Not Found response to the calling client. This is an important difference from the definition in listing 8.2, which would serve XML irrespective of what the caller could actually accept.

The second case is nearly identical to the first, with a subtle difference; the request URL that's defined is suffixed with `Nil`. The result of this is that the incoming URL must match /sample/two.xml exactly, or a 404 Not Found will be returned. To clarify this a little further, the URL in the first case was defined as follows:

```
"sample" :: "one" :: _
```

This trailing underscore essentially means *any other pattern*. Behind the scenes, this uses Scala pattern matching and a language feature called extractors to determine the resulting types, which in this instance are (`List[String]`, `Req`). Extractors are a fairly complex topic, so we don't dwell on them here—just understand how you can use the underscore to ignore parts of the pattern.

NOTE   For more information on extractors, see the "Extractor Objects" page in the "Tour of Scala": http://www.scala-lang.org/node/112.

The third case utilizes the exact same extractor, `XmlGet`, but you may find this usage a little easier to get your head around. Here you can see that the exact same syntax is in play for the URL, followed by another underscore to ignore the `Req` instance and satisfy the extractor pattern.

Finally, the fourth case involves the most verbose DSL usage. So far, we've been ignoring the `Req` instance with these patterns, in favor of the prebaked extractors supplied by the `RestHelper` trait, but here we're using the raw `Req` instance directly to match on.

You may be wondering what the advantages are of accessing the `Req` directly, as compared to using the built-in extractors. There are a couple of considerations when choosing a route of implementation:

- The `Req` instance has a whole bunch of helper methods. For example, if you wanted to service a particular request only if the incoming request came from an iPhone, you could put a guard on the match statement with `req.isIPhone`. Depending upon your use case, these helper methods may be something you want to access, but otherwise the prebaked DSL extractors may be the ticket for you.

- It's a matter of preference. The DSL uses a fair amount of currying and what is known as infix operation pattern (http://www.scala-lang.org/docu/files/ScalaReference.pdf, section 8.1.10); some people really like this, and others don't. Ultimately, with choice comes personal preference.

The dispatch DSL gives you the tools to quickly create HTTP services, so let's look at a more concrete example. In the next section, we make a base REST service.

8.3.2 Basic REST service

We've spent some time looking at the `RestHelper` dispatch DSL, and hopefully you can see how this can quickly assist you to construct HTTP services. Let's create a short and very basic example with a couple of services to put that overview into practice. This example will be based on the premise of a bookstore and creating a simple read-only web service that you can use to get a list of stock and to query the stock by publisher.

To get started, let's define some simple domain objects to model and store the stock list. To implement this simply, create a case class that can model a `Book` at the most simplistic level, and a singleton `Bookshop` object that contains the actual list of books. This listing shows the appropriate code.

Listing 8.5 Bookstore domain classes

```
case class Book(publisher: String, title: String)

object Bookshop {
  val stock = List(
    Book("Bloomsbury", "Harry Potter and the Deathly Hallows"),
    Book("Bloomsbury", "Harry Potter and the Goblet of Fire"),
    Book("Manning", "Scala in Depth"),
    Book("Manning", "Lift in Action")
  )
}
```

This is an extremely simple example, where `Book` is the model and the singleton `Bookshop` object holds a list of books, which represents the stock. Although this may seem trivial, this example is really about the dispatching, rather than a complex domain model or persistence system, so we just need some data to interact with. In practice, you'd likely be accessing a database or domain model to grab live data and serve that to the client.

Let's get on with creating the basic service. The goal here is to create two services with the following HTTP resources:

```
GET - /bookshop/books.xml

GET - /bookshop/books/<publisher>.xml
```

Having earlier constructed an XML dispatching service in section 8.3.1 by using the `RestHelper`, you can probably guess how to implement the first resource in this task. The following listing shows an implementation for retrieving a list of all the books in stock.

Listing 8.6   Retrieving a list of bookstore stock items

```
import net.liftweb.http.rest.RestHelper

object BookshopHttpServiceBasic extends RestHelper {
  serve {
    case "bookshop" :: "books" :: Nil XmlGet _ =>
      <books>{Bookshop.stock.flatMap{b =>
        <book publisher={b.publisher} title={b.title}/>}
      }</books>
  }
}
```

Here again the `RestHelper` trait is used as a base for the implementation object. And again, the definition in the `case` statement should be pretty familiar from the preceding section. As this is to be an XML service, you simply implement the `XmlGet` type. The `<books>` definition is the interesting part here, though, because you pull the list from the static `Bookshop` object and iterate through that list, creating XML elements. The `RestHelper` brings an implicit conversion into scope that converts `Elem` to Lift's `NodeResponse`. Simple enough.

Right now, this service can tell the caller what books are currently in stock, but it gives the client no way to filter or query the bookstore's stock. To remedy this, let's add another service that allows the caller to filter the stock by publisher. We need to refactor a touch so that we don't duplicate the XML generation. The following listing shows the updated implementation.

Listing 8.7   Adding the filtering resource

```
object BookshopHttpServiceBasic extends RestHelper {
  serve {
    case "bookshop" :: "books" :: Nil XmlGet _ =>
      response(Bookshop.stock)
```

```
    case "bookshop" :: "books" :: publisher :: Nil XmlGet _ =>
      response(Bookshop.stock.filter(
        _.publisher equalsIgnoreCase publisher))
  }

  private def response(in: List[Book]) =
    <books>{in.flatMap(b =>
      <book publisher={b.publisher} title={b.title}/>
    }</books>
}
```

❶ Response builder

The `List[Book] => NodeSeq` function has been moved into a separate method called `response`, which is detailed at ❶. More importantly, because the query by publisher URL requires some dynamic input (name of publisher), you specify this in the second case statement ❶. Notice how `publisher` is unquoted—it's not a static `String` value but a placeholder for a variable value of type `String` for the value that makes up that URL. Handily, this placeholder can be used on the right side of the case statement, so you can simply pass the value directly into the creation of the `filter` predicate ❶, which removes all items from the list that don't match the input.

To give a concrete example, if you accessed the URL,

```
GET - /bookshop/books/manning.xml
```

the response would be

```
<books>
  <book title="Scala in Depth" publisher="Manning"/>
  <book title="Lift in Action" publisher="Manning"/>
</books>
```

That's all there is to it. This kind of implementation works well for most circumstances because it's very simple, very straightforward, and quick to create.

DISPATCH GUARDS

Lift also has a rather nice mechanism that allows you to apply *guards* to your dispatch services by defining a partial function to check the incoming request. In short, this gives you the following style of syntax:

```
LiftRules.dispatch.append(onMondays guard BookshopService)
```

Parts of this declaration should look familiar, but it's likely that the `onMondays` and `guard` appear to be somewhat undefined. In this context, `onMondays` is a simplistic partial function that defines the parameters under which this service should operate. Consider the definition of `onMondays`:

```
import net.liftweb.util.Helpers._
import java.util.Calendar

val onMondays: PartialFunction[Req, Unit] = {
  case _ if day(now) == Calendar.MONDAY =>
}
```

Notice that the partial function simply compares today's day of the week to see if it's Monday, with the result being that this will only evaluate to `true` when it's actually

Monday. As a result, when onMondays is applied to the service definition with the guard keyword, the service will only respond to requests on Mondays.

In practice, it would be more likely that you'd be checking for authentication or something else meaningful, but the same pattern holds true. In order to make this work, it's necessary to have the Helpers._ import statement so that the required implicit conversions are available to the compiler.

Let's throw another requirement into the mix: what if you needed to represent a single set of logic in multiple formats? You could perhaps use function passing, or maybe even some kind of workflow system to determine the output, but neither of those solutions feel very Scala-ish. Scala's type system is incredibly powerful and can do quite amazing things. In the next section, we show you a rather advanced technique for producing REST services in multiple representation formats while utilizing only a single implementation of a service method.

8.3.3   *Advanced multiformat REST service*

Before we dive into this section, we need to add a slight disclaimer: this section is *advanced*. It may be some time, if ever, before you feel comfortable with this kind of implementation, but we really want to show you some of the amazing things that can be done with Scala and Lift to yield a nice clean API.

This advanced example builds on the simple bookstore example from the previous section; the Bookshop and Book types are exactly the same. In this case, though, we add the requirement of multiple service representations, so we go through a very different route of implementation.

Let's step back and consider the problem. We only want to write the actual service method once, but we need to have multiple response representations. In a broad sense, this can be modeled as T =>LiftResponse. That is to say, an input type is converted to a LiftResponse. If this input type was the output from our single method definition, we could design an API that implicitly converts the single method output to a given LiftResponse. The API we'll end up with is going to look like this:

```
case "bookshop" :: "books" :: Nil XmlGet _ => list[XmlResponse]
```

where the list method looks like this:

```
def list[R : Return[List[Book]]#As]: R = Return(Bookshop.stock)
```

You don't need to worry about this right now. Just be aware that what we're driving at here is to make an implementation that doesn't care about the resulting output format.

The following listing shows a simple structure we can use to start modeling the input => output relationship this section started with.

Listing 8.8   Modeling representational types

```
trait ReturnAs[A, B]{
  def as(a: A): B
}
```

```
object ReturnAs {
  implicit def f2ReturnAs[A, B](f: A => B): ReturnAs[A, B] =
    new ReturnAs[A, B]{
      def as(a: A) = f(a)
    }
}
```

This is a non-trivial piece of code, so don't worry if it looks intimidating: it is. First, the ReturnAs trait defines a method called as that can be used to essentially say "here's type A; give me it as type B."

Next, the ReturnAs object defines the companion that takes a function A => B and yields the input/output structure by creating a new instance of the ReturnAs trait. So what's the reason for this? Well, this section lets you define the conversion methods as simple functions. In practice, the service method itself will yield a List[Book], and a representation conversion could be a List[Book] => XmlResponse function. To that end, this implicit f2ReturnAs converts that A => B type (or, if it helps you grasp it mentally: Function1[A,B]) to a ReturnAs[A,B].

Let's jump ahead for one second and look at the service implementation, or central point of logic, and then work backwards to fill in the blanks. This listing shows the service implementation for the same two operations implemented in listing 8.7: they list all books and list all books for a specific publisher.

Listing 8.9 Advanced service implementation

```
trait BookshopService {
  def list[R : Return[List[Book]]#As]:R =
    Return(Bookshop.stock)

  def listByPublisher[R : Return[List[Book]]#As](publisher:String):R =
    Return(Bookshop.stock.filter(_.publisher equalsIgnoreCase publisher))
}
```

First, you probably recognized the operation code that gets the entire stock list and also queries the bookshop stock by publisher from the previous example in listing 8.7. What likely looks rather crazy are the type signatures for both the list and listByPublisher methods. This specialized notation, A : B, is a Scala feature called *context bounds*, which are brand new in Scala 2.8 and are rather awesome. We won't explore them fully here, as it's out of the scope of this book but do check out Joshua D. Suereth's *Scala in Depth* if you'd like to know more.

In short, given the following definition,

```
def sample[T : Bound]
```

the compiler would expand that to the following:

```
def sample[T](implicit a: Bound[T])
```

What does that have to do with this exercise? Well, the goal with this implementation is to push the representation type out to the method call site and leave a generic service method that's agnostic to representation. Bearing in mind the information you just read about context bounds, consider the following listing in conjunction with the type signatures in listing 8.9. Listing 8.10 is the missing piece of the type puzzle!

Listing 8.10   Implementing the `Return[A]` trait and type projection

```
trait Return[A] {
  type As[B] = ReturnAs[A, B]
}
object Return {
  def apply[A, B](a: A)(implicit f: ReturnAs[A, B]) = f.as(a)
}
```

Notice how in listing 8.9 the type signature isn't complete because the #As declaration is missing the type parameter: Return[List[Book]]#As. The actual implementation of the Return[A] trait requires that As take a type parameter and that the apply method take an implicit parameter. The compiler fills these in for you by way of the context bound notation, which is awesome.

You may be wondering about the actual conversion, as currently there is no code to make the List[Book] into a representation. Here we can also get the compiler to fill in some blanks for us by providing the conversions as implicit once again. These methods live in the companion object of the Book type and are detailed in the next listing.

Listing 8.11   Convert domain to response types

```
object Book {
  implicit val booksAsXml:                          ❶ Implicit with
    Return[List[Book]]#As[XmlResponse] =              projection syntax
      (books:List[Book]) => XmlResponse(
        <books>{books.flatMap(b =>
          <book publisher={b.publisher} title={b.title}/>)
        }</books>)

  implicit val booksAsPlainText:                    ❷ Generate XML
    ReturnAs[List[Book],PlainTextResponse] =          response
      (books:List[Book]) => PlainTextResponse("Books\n"+
        books.map(b => "publisher: %s, title: %s"
          .format(b.publisher, b.title)))
}
```

Earlier we discussed the implicit method that converted Function1[A,B] to a ReturnAs[A,B] in the ReturnAs companion object. This is the implicit conversion that's at play here; the booksAsPlainText function shows this as a straightforward example ❷. Conversely, one of the awesome things you can do in Scala is use a type projection to yield the ReturnAs from the Return trait, which can be seen in the booksAsXml function type signature ❶. A nice byproduct of this is that it gives you a cool type-level grammar that describes this conversion method! The actual method implementations here are nearly identical to those in listing 8.7, but with the addition of delivering a plain text version as well.

The last part of this jigsaw is wiring up the HTTP dispatch through the dispatch DSL. If you remember from section 8.3.1, the right side of the dispatch DSL match statement only needs to return a subtype of `LiftResponse`, which we have here, so they should fit together like peas in the proverbial pod. The following listing demonstrates the wiring and use of the service implementation.

Listing 8.12 Wiring up the advanced REST sample

```
object BookshopHttpServiceAdvanced
    extends BookshopService with RestHelper {
  serve {
    case "bookshop" :: "books" :: Nil XmlGet _ =>        ❶ Define list all
      list[XmlResponse]                                     services
    case "bookshop" :: "books" :: Nil Get _ =>
      list[PlainTextResponse]
    case "bookshop" :: "books" :: pub :: Nil XmlGet _ =>  ❷ Define list
      listByPublisher[XmlResponse](pub)                       by publisher
    case "bookshop" :: "books" :: pub :: Nil Get _ =>        services
      listByPublisher[PlainTextResponse](pub)
  }
}
```

Once again, you only need to make an object that extends the `RestHelper` but in addition composes the `BookshopService` trait from listing 8.9. Doing this provides both the methods that will conduct the service operation (`list` ❶ and `listBy-Publisher` ❷) and the dispatch DSL. Notice that in order to call a format-specific response, you just pass the *type* of response required, like this:

```
list[XmlResponse]
```

That's all there is to it. I quite like this pattern of implementation as it keeps the logic and representation code nicely separated and gives you a really sweet syntax when you understand what it is you're looking at. Scala is a powerful language, and I think it's important to be able to leverage such abstractions in your applications. Lift won't stop you or make life difficult in the vast majority of situations, so learn the advanced Scala and go crazy!

8.4   Summary

At its core, Lift is a simple abstraction on HTTP. Hopefully in this chapter, you've seen how to leverage the tools and structures that build on that base abstraction and that enable you to quickly and effectively get things done. Early in this chapter, we demonstrated the various processes and flows that make up the HTTP pipeline in Lift and highlighted the important intercept points where you can inject your own code or functions to really customize Lift for your requirements. You have also seen how to control URL resolution using rewrite partial functions and how to build REST services using dispatching.

Lift's lifecycle is made up of three distinct parts: application boot, the request-handling pipeline, and application shutdown. The boot and shutdown are in many respects similar to normal Java servlet applications, but Lift provides configuration points through both processes. Request handling, on the other hand, is broken down into two distinct parts: the initial stateless part and then stateful initialization with further processing. The whole cycle has injection points for you to control the behavior and output that Lift ultimately serves to the client.

Part of Lift's HTTP pipeline is rewriting. Lift's rewriting system can be used to tightly control the incoming URL and map its structure to templates, parameters, or pretty much any other type you can create. Rewriting can operate in two modes: stateful and stateless. Generally speaking, using stateless rewriting is recommended as it ensures that the rewrite and mapping is done early in the processing pipeline.

Finally, section 8.3 explored Lift's dispatching mechanism, which is commonly used for building web services or providing a direct API into Lift's response and servicing system. You've seen how to utilize the `RestHelper` trait to quickly assist you in making HTTP services, and you created a very basic XML service that checks the incoming request to see if it can accept a text/xml response and that the incoming request features an .xml extension. You then saw how to build on a simple example and leverage the full power of the Scala language to service multiple media formats from a single service definition.

In the next chapter, we build on the base HTTP knowledge covered here and explore Lift's JavaScript, AJAX, and Comet support. Lift has one of the best Comet implementations available today, and it sits upon a lightweight actor concurrency model.

AJAX, wiring, and Comet

This chapter covers

- Lift's JavaScript abstraction
- Using AJAX controls
- AJAX wiring
- Server-push with `CometActors`

This chapter covers Lift's advanced support for AJAX, connected AJAX components, known as *wiring*, and Comet, or *server-push* architectures. Creating highly interactive content with Lift is often easier or more intuitive than creating "normal" web applications. Pretty much everything in Lift's interactive toolkit boils down to writing Scala functions, and AJAX is no different. As Harry Heymann, the lead engineer from Foursquare.com, puts it, "Writing AJAX style code is actually easier in Lift than writing traditional forms... All web programming should work like this."[1]

Over the past few years particularly, the internet has seen a mass popularization of extremely interactive online experiences. People no longer tolerate green screen experiences and demand rich user interfaces that are slick and responsive.

---

[1] Harry Heymann, "Foursquare.com & Scala/Lift" (1/11/2010). http://mng.bz/1eX6

For developers, this creates several different challenges, but it primarily means using AJAX and Comet programming paradigms to create these rich applications.

AJAX is increasingly well supported by the web programming ecosystem, but Comet, or server-push style programming, where data is dynamically sent to the browser without the user explicitly requesting it, has remained elusively difficult to implement for many developers. Lift provides powerful abstractions for both of these technologies.

9.1   AJAX

Before getting into the specifics of how to build AJAX components with Lift, let's take a few moments to explore the actual purpose of AJAX. AJAX provides developers a technique they can use to load parts of a page on demand, typically in reaction to a user event such as the click of a button. An example that many readers have likely experienced is that of the Gmail user interface. When clicking on an email you wish to read, the browser makes a request to the server asynchronously to fetch the required content. Such techniques have several material bonuses.

First, AJAX supplies an increase in the *perceived* speed of an application. When the page loads, it can contain only a bare bones structure or the base level of information required to fulfill the initial request. Any subsequent content that's needed for the page would be loaded on demand in reaction to a user operation. The perfect example of this is Google Maps (http://maps.google.com/). Each fragment of the map is a relatively expensive download in terms of bandwidth, so you couldn't download the entire world every time you browsed Google maps. Instead, Google Maps loads only the fragments of the map that are being displayed at the time. Scrolling around the map prompts the client-side JavaScript to make asynchronous requests to the server to obtain any additional map fragments that are now visible in the user's browser window.

Second, AJAX allows you to offload elements of processing to the client-side machine. The average computer these days has far more power than a regular user makes use of, and modern browsers can do many things at once. Bolster this with the ever-increasing sophistication of JavaScript applications, and you have an environment in which many operations can be executed on the client side, saving the server a degree of load for each connection that exists. This is a small saving in one instance, but over tens or hundreds of thousands of requests, this can really mount up.

AJAX gives the web a richer model of programming. In the majority of other frameworks, or in static HTML, this is accomplished by using a client-side JavaScript library, such as JQuery (http://jquery.com/) to specify a server URL from which a response will be fetched and subsequently processed. Even in the most basic example, you typically have to conduct three separate operations to get a single AJAX call set up:

1   Define the client-side request with JavaScript.
2   Set up the server-side handler, controller, or component that will retrieve the content you need for that page.
3   Implement the response handling in the client-side JavaScript.

Although this does work, it sucks time, which is often the most valuable commodity a developer has. Moreover, many developers are more familiar with either the server side or client side, and they may not be familiar enough with both sides of that programming fence to implement this. Fortunately, Lift has a solution for this.

Lift has a pair of abstractions that you can work with from your Scala code that distances you from the process of programming in JavaScript. For instance, if you're dealing with a process that alters the client-side user interface, you won't need to worry about which URLs need to be invoked to handle the request, nor do you have to write JavaScript code to trigger an element effect such as a fade out. The keys to this whole process are two subset abstractions known as JavaScript commands (`JsCmd`) and JavaScript expressions (`JsExp`). These types allow you to program client-side interactions from within your server-side Scala code. Ultimately, these implementations do boil down to JavaScript, but you don't have to deal with that if you don't want to. But with that being said, it's important to note that you can write your own JavaScript code and invoke that from the server side as well.

Given that these abstractions result in JavaScript code that's executed on the client side, you may be thinking that this sounds a lot like reinventing the wheel, but Lift actually leverages existing JavaScript libraries and uses them to do the client-side legwork. Lift calls this system of leveraging existing libraries `JSArtifacts`. At the time of writing, there were three implementations of `JSArtifacts` that used JQuery, YUI (http://developer.yahoo.com/yui/), and ExtJS (http://www.sencha.com/products/extjs/) respectively. JQuery is used in all Lift applications unless you override this default in your application `Boot`.

9.1.1 JavaScript abstractions

In chapter 8, you saw how Lift configures something called the `ResourceServer` in order to serve resources that are bundled in the classpath JARs. Some of the things that ship with Lift by default are the implementations of the JavaScript libraries. In practice, this means that you can simply include the following link in your HTML template and get the JQuery library:

```
<script src="/classpath/jquery.js" type="text/javascript"></script>
```

If your application is running in a different context than the root, this URL will be automatically rewritten to include the contextual prefix. As JQuery is the default JavaScript artifact for Lift applications, we assume in all of the examples going forward that this is the library in use. But all the fundamental abstractions will work irrespective of the library, so if you want to configure a different artifact, here's what you need to do:

```
import net.liftweb.http.js.yui.YUIArtifacts

class Boot {
  def boot {
    ...
```

```
    LiftRules.jsArtifacts = YUIArtifacts
    ...
  }
}
```

Configure the appropriate JavaScript library within the application `Boot` class by passing a `JSArtifacts` subtype to the `LiftRules.jsArtifacts` setting. In this example, the Yahoo! YUI library is specified explicitly.

NOTE During development, Lift will use the uncompressed version of the JavaScript library, but in production mode it will automatically use the minified version without you having to change any URLs in your templates. (Lift's run mode system is discussed in section 15.4.1 of chapter 15.)

Now that you have your JavaScript library all configured and ready to go, let's explore the `JsCmd` and `JsExp` abstractions.

BASIC JAVASCRIPT COMMANDS

In order to illustrate the JavaScript abstraction, we look at a couple of examples that highlight particular features of the API.

Let's begin by creating a very simple example that displays a JavaScript alert box when opening the page. For this, you'll need a snippet. You can use the Lifty tool to do this with the following command:

```
> lift create snippet MySnippet
```

Or you can make a new snippet class and configure it however you like, using either convention-based reflection or by manually wiring it up. Add the code to your snippet as shown in the next listing.

> **Listing 9.1   Basic JavaScript alert using JsCmds**

```
import scala.xml.NodeSeq
import net.liftweb.http.js.JsCmds.{Alert,Script}

class AbstractionExamples {
  def alert(xhtml: NodeSeq): NodeSeq =
    Script(Alert("Important Alert Goes Here!"))
}
```

This is a super-simple snippet that implements the `Alert` JsCmd. It has a single parameter for the message that will be displayed in the alert dialog box. For anyone who is familiar with JavaScript at all, it should be fairly obvious what the outcome will be. Perhaps less obvious is the `Script` class that's wrapping the call to `Alert`. You've seen throughout this book that you always need to return a `NodeSeq` subtype from snippet methods, and the `Script` tag ensures this.

To clarify that, take a look at the rendered code that reaches the browser:

```
<script type="text/javascript">
// <![CDATA[
```

```
alert("Important Alert Goes Here!");
// ]]>
</script>
```

As you can see here, the call to the `alert` method is wrapped in a well-formed `<script>` tag, including a CDATA block. This ensures that the snippet method returns a `NodeSeq`-compatible type and that the JavaScript is correctly presented to the browser.

> **NOTE** Using a CDATA block essentially escapes any HTML entities or tags when received by the browser. The contents of the CDATA block are not literally converted into HTML entities, but rather the surrounding CDATA instructs the browser to parse the contents as escaped entities, as opposed to literal HTML. For more information, see the CDATA article on Wikipedia: http://en.wikipedia.org/wiki/CDATA.

There are lots of different commands that you can import from the `JsCmds` object, and invoking them individually would be verbose and litter your rendered source code with `<script>` blocks. Fortunately, `JsCmd` subtypes are chainable. This means that you can link together multiple JavaScript commands, and they'll all be flushed to the browser as a single `<script>` block. This kind of functionality is very helpful when you want to create more complex user interactions, and it's an idiom you'll see a lot throughout this chapter. The following listing shows an example of chaining two `JsCmd` instances together.

Listing 9.2 Chaining JsCmd types together

```
import scala.xml.{NodeSeq,Text}
import net.liftweb.http.js.JsCmds.{Alert,Script,SetHtml}

class AbstractionExamples {
  ...
  def two(xhtml: NodeSeq): NodeSeq = Script(           ❶ First JsCmd
    SetHtml("replaceme", Text("I have been replaced!")) &
    Alert("Text Replaced")                             
  )                                                     ❷ Second JsCmd
}
```

This listing is a direct extension of the previous example, and you can see the usage of the `JsCmd` instances `SetHtml` and `Alert` ❶ and ❷. The real point of note, however, is the `&` at the end of the first `JsCmd` ❶. This is actually a method defined as part of `JsCmd`, and it allows you to combine an arbitrary depth of `JsCmd` instances to create a single output.

The other aspect of the JavaScript abstraction is `JsExp`. It differs from `JsCmd` in that `JsExp` is an abstraction of JavaScript expressions, such as an array or an if/else statement, whereas `JsCmd` is really focused on statements such as "fade this div out" and so on.

Here's an example of using one of the `JsExp` subtypes:

```
import net.liftweb.http.js.JE.{JsNotEq,Num}
```

```
Script(Run(
  JsIf(JsNotEq(Num(1), Num(2)), Alert("3: 1 does not equal 2!")).toJsCmd
))
```

Here the `JsNotEq` `JsExp` is used to create an expression that does a simple `if` statement comparison on the two passed values. The `JE` object holds most of the `JsExp` subtypes, and here, because the expression is simply comparing two integers, they're wrapped in the `Num` expression. The two integer values will never be equal in this example, so the body `JsCmdAlert` will fire. The resulting JavaScript rendered in the browser source code is as follows:

```
<script type="text/javascript">
  // <![CDATA[
  if ( 1 != 2 ) { alert("1 does not equal 2!"); };
  // ]]>
</script>
```

Although this use case is exceedingly trivial, a common use case for `JsExp` is when you want to check a value from within an AJAX callback. Also, many of the AJAX elements in `SHtml` have an optional `Call` expression, which allows you to call an arbitrary JavaScript expression before executing that interaction.

For more complex JavaScript statements, the `JsExp` API would likely become somewhat unwieldy, and using the `Call` and `JsRaw` commands can often be more elegant. `Call` simply takes the name of your preexisting JavaScript function and a set of arguments (if any):

```
Call("nameOfFunc", Str("arg1"))
```

By using `Call`, you can keep the client-side logic on the client side. Alternatively, if you simply want to pass some arbitrary JavaScript to the client to execute, you can make use of `JsRaw`. Here's an example:

```
JsRaw("alert('Passed from lift!')")
```

The clear downside with `JsRaw` is that your actual JavaScript is embedded in the Scala code, but for certain operations or situations it can be a useful tool.

Broadly speaking, if the JavaScript you need to execute is fairly complex, leave it on the client side and use `Call` to invoke and pass any required data to that function.

JSON HANDLING

Another technology that's extremely prevalent in client-side programming is JavaScript Object Notation (JSON). JSON has pretty much become the ubiquitous interchange format for many different aspects of the web, and it's often used in AJAX solutions to serialize data back and forth between client and server. Because of this, Lift has excellent JSON support, including a DSL for constructing JSON structures in type-safe Scala.

Lift JSON is a fairly standalone library in the Lift project, and it's utilized by many other projects in the Scala ecosystem because it's extremely fast and reliable. Let's look at an example of parsing and creating some JSON using this toolkit.

All of Lift's JSON handling types are packaged in `net.liftweb.json`, so you can parse a JSON string by doing this:

```
scala> import net.liftweb.json._

scala> val json = parse(""" { "numbers" : [1, 2, 3, 4] } """)
res2: JValue = JObject(List(
JField(numbers,JArray(List(
JInt(1), JInt(2), JInt(3), JInt(4))))))
```

In this example, the `parse` method comes from Lift JSON and it's passed a literal JSON string. This string is then parsed and returned as a `JValue` subtype with all the component parts broken out into strongly typed representations, such as `JInt`. This then allows you to interact with the JSON in an intuitive manner.

Let's assume that you wanted to get the list of integers from this JSON. You could simply do

```
json \ "numbers" children
```

This would give you `List[JValue]`, and you could operate on it however you please.

The JSON structures have several convenience features, like the backslash (\) method that allows you to traverse the JSON structure programmatically from the root of the document. Alternatively, you can use the \\ method to find a given object anywhere in the document.

Parsing is straightforward enough, but what about construction? Well, that too is pretty easy to get to grips with. Consider the following example:

```
scala> import net.liftweb.json.JsonDSL._

scala> val json = ("name" -> "joe")

scala> compact(render(json))
res1: String = {"name":"joe"}
```

Here the members of `JsonDSL` are imported into the current compilation scope, which includes a set of implicit conversions that allow you to supply regular Scala types like tuples to the JSON `render` method. The result of the `render` method is then passed to `compact`, which does the serialization to a string. As the name implies, the `compact` method will create a compacted JSON string so it takes up as little room as possible. Alternatively, if you'd prefer nicely structured output, you can replace `compact` with `pretty`, and it will render a pretty printed version of the JSON output, complete with structured spacing.

With these basics laid down, the number of things you'll want to do with JavaScript when the page loads is limited. Most of the cool things you can do with Lift's AJAX and JavaScript system are driven by user interaction. To that end, let's move on to look at using the JavaScript abstraction in conjunction with Lift's AJAX system.

9.1.2   AJAX 101

You've now heard about the overall benefits of Lift's AJAX implementation and how it conceptually works, and you've seen some examples of using Lift's server-side JavaScript abstractions. It's now time to build on this understanding and apply it to user interaction.

In Lift, the vast majority of concepts can be condensed into a functional representation. Snippets, for example, are `NodeSeq => NodeSeq`, and views are `() => NodeSeq`. Lift's AJAX system is no different in this regard, and generally it can be thought of as the function type `() => JsCmd`. Let's take a moment to evaluate this in more detail and understand exactly what the process is when using AJAX function binding. Figure 9.1 outlines a basic AJAX request process from the initial request through to a secondary asynchronous request and response.

This illustration has several related points but let's begin with the solid black duration line that goes from time marker 1 to *A* to 2. This line indicates the initial request coming from the user's browser going to the server. At marker *A*, Lift does a bunch of processing to generate the in-memory function mapping for any bound elements and returns content to the browser with session-specific opaque GUIDs. That may sound a little cryptic, but it's like the form processing covered in chapter 6 where each rendered `<input>` on a page was automatically assigned a random GUID for a name. The same is happening here, but rather than it being a form input, the GUID is passed from the client to the server so the server knows which callback function it should execute when the AJAX request is triggered by a particular user interaction.

At time marker 2, the page has loaded completely. For argument's sake, let's assume the user is reading the page and they click a button on the page. If this button is a Lift AJAX button, a second asynchronous request is made to the server. In the illustration, this is the line from time marker 2 to *B* to 3. When the request is made from 2 to *B*, the JavaScript call on the client side will pass the function GUID back to

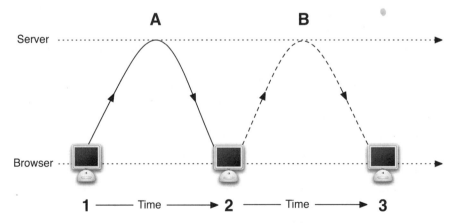

Figure 9.1   An example of an AJAX request and response cycle, including the original HTTP request and detailing the touchpoints with the server over time

the server, and Lift will then look up that GUID in its function map to figure out what needs executing. After completing the server-side callback, Lift will return the response, and that often (but not always) includes some `JsCmd` that's subsequently executed on the client side.

Given this process diagram in figure 9.1, let's now implement a basic snippet that performs exactly this functionality. The following listing details the code required to make an anchor link that, once clicked, fires an AJAX call to the server.

Listing 9.3   Basic AJAX example with clickable anchor

```
import scala.xml.{NodeSeq,Text}
import net.liftweb.http.SHtml
import net.liftweb.http.js.JsCmds.Alert

class BasicAjax {
  def one(xhtml: NodeSeq): NodeSeq =
    SHtml.a(() => Alert("You clicked me!"),       Create AJAX
      Text("Go on, click me"))                    text link
}
```

This is a simple AJAX link. The first parameter is a `() => JsCmd`, and for familiarity's sake we used `JsCmds.Alert` once more as the command to execute upon returning a response to the client side. The second parameter here denotes the text or `NodeSeq` that the link will display to the user. In practice, it might not be particularly useful to display an alert after clicking a link, but if you watch the traffic between your browser and the server with a tool such as Firebug (http://getfirebug.com/), you'll see the AJAX event occurring and the response being handed back to the browser. Neat!

That was a pretty trivial example, so let's now look at something that has a little more functionality. The `SHtml` object has many helpers for creating AJAX elements, and the previous example covered the `a` method. The next example makes uses of `SHtml.ajaxEditable`, which is a helper that creates a field type that has both a *read* component and a *write* component. The write aspect is an in-place editor for which the value is submitted via AJAX.

To clarify this, consider the definition of `ajaxEditable`:

```
def ajaxEditable(
  displayContents: => NodeSeq,
  editForm: => NodeSeq,
  onSubmit: () => JsCmd)
```

The important thing to note here is that both the first and second parameters are by-name functions that return `NodeSeq`. These `NodeSeq`s represent the two states that the item can have: read and write, as mentioned before.

To illustrate this functionality, let's create a session variable to hold a simple text field that will be updated via this AJAX component. The following listing demonstrates the use of `ajaxEditable`.

Listing 9.4   Implementing `SHtml.ajaxEditable`

```
import scala.xml.{NodeSeq,Text}
import net.liftweb.http.{SHtml,SessionVar}
import net.liftweb.http.js.jquery.JqJsCmds.FadeIn

class BasicAjax {
  ...
  object ExampleVar extends SessionVar[String]("Replace Me")

  def two(xhtml: NodeSeq): NodeSeq =
    SHtml.ajaxEditable(Text(ExampleVar.is),
    SHtml.text(ExampleVar.is, ExampleVar(_)),
    () => FadeIn("example_two_notice"))
}
```

❶ Define success JsCmd

This listing defines a `SessionVar` called `ExampleVar` that will act as a placeholder for the value on the server. It's important to note that this could be anything or any server-side action; most frequently it would be a Mapper or Record persistence object, but here it's simply storing the string value to and from the `ExampleVar`. The first argument to the `SHtml.ajaxEditible` control is a `Text` (or any other `NodeSeq`) instance, and it defines what will be displayed to the user initially. In this case, the value of the session variable is loaded and passed as text content to the browser.

Looking to the second argument of `SHtml.ajaxEditible`, you can see the use of the (by now) familiar `SHtml.text` for creating and binding input fields with getter and setter arguments. Here, the input simply displays the value of the user and executes the set function to insert the value back into the session when the OK button, which is automatically rendered next to the display, is clicked by the user.

Finally, the `SHtml.ajaxEditible` control requires a `() => JsCmd` function as its final argument; something that will be executed upon completion of editing ❶. In this example, a specialized type of JavaScript abstraction that we haven't looked at before is being used. Earlier in this section, you saw how `JSArtifacts` acted as an intermediary between the various JavaScript libraries. Although these abstractions give you a baseline of functionality, Lift has library-specific operation abstractions, and here you can see the use of one of the JQuery implementations: `FadeIn`. As the name and first parameter suggest, upon the AJAX request being successful, this function is executed and it fades in a hidden DOM element called `example_two_notice`.

If you're an eager reader and have just tried out this code, you may have noticed that there is a slight lag between clicking the OK button and the start of the fade operation. That's because the frontend JavaScript is making the AJAX call, Lift is doing the processing, and then the browser interprets the result. Although this happens fairly quickly, you'll often want to display a loading spinner or some other page furniture to keep the user happy. Lift provides some nice built-in hooks for this, so that any time an AJAX call is being made, it will automatically show the content you define, wherever you want on the page. Simply add the following lines to your Boot definition:

```
LiftRules.ajaxStart =
  Full(() => LiftRules.jsArtifacts.show("loading").cmd)
```

```
LiftRules.ajaxEnd =
  Full(() => LiftRules.jsArtifacts.hide("loading").cmd)
```

These two `LiftRules` configurations should be fairly self-explanatory. The first executes a particular `JsCmd` when the AJAX request is started, and the latter executes when the response is completed. In this particular illustration, there's an element ID within the template markup called `loading`, and this JavaScript essentially toggles whether it will be displayed or hidden. Provided your function is of type `() => JsCmd`, you can essentially get Lift to execute whichever JavaScript functions you would like surrounding AJAX requests.

You've now seen two examples of fairly basic AJAX in Lift. All AJAX operations revolve around simple function passing, and at no point have you had to deal with request URLs, HTTP verbs, or any other such plumbing. Lift makes it very simple for you to construct slick AJAX interfaces and provides hooks in the Life cycle to customize its display behavior.

But although they've been informative, these two isolated examples don't tell you anything else in specific terms. In the next section, you'll see how to create a more complex AJAX example that's closer to the real-world scenarios you may be faced with.

9.1.3 *Sophisticated AJAX*

In this section, you'll see how to construct an entire AJAX form with some more funky AJAX goodness, building on the example introduced in the previous section. Before we get to the code, though, let's look at the workflow you'll need to create.

This example will display a simple list of books with an Edit link beside each item. When the user clicks the link, the browser will make an AJAX request to the server to retrieve an update form that will then appear on the same page. The user can then update the title of the book, and when they click Submit, the browser will make an AJAX request to the server, which in turn responds with JavaScript to update the list with the new value.

There are many times where you'll want to update a value, or provide some kind of form or editing functionality, and this example will give you a base on which to build. Of course, in reality you'd likely be interacting with some kind of persistent storage, like Mapper or Record, but to keep this example focused on the AJAX elements, we simply use the session as the data store.

The next listing shows the code to create the editable AJAX list.

Listing 9.5   Editable AJAX list

```
import scala.xml.{NodeSeq,Text}
import net.liftweb.util.Helpers._
import net.liftweb.http.{SHtml,SessionVar}
import net.liftweb.http.js.JsCmds.SetHtml
import net.liftweb.http.js.jquery.JqJsCmds.{Show,Hide}

case class Book(reference: String, var title: String)
```

① Sample model type

```
class MoreAjax {
  object stock extends SessionVar[List[Book]](List(
    Book("ABCD", "Harry Potter and the Deathly Hallows"),
    Book("EFGH", "Harry Potter and the Goblet of Fire"),
    Book("IJKL", "Scala in Depth"),
    Book("MNOP", "Lift in Action")
  ))

  private val editFormDiv = "edit_display"

  def list =
    ".line" #> stock.is.map { b =>
      ".name *" #> b.title &
      ".name [id]" #> b.reference &
      ".edit" #> edit(b)
    }

  def edit(b: Book): NodeSeq => NodeSeq = { ns =>
    val form =
      "#book_name" #> SHtml.text(b.title, b.title = _) &
      "type=submit" #> SHtml.ajaxSubmit("Update",
        () => SetHtml(b.reference, Text(b.title))
      ) andThenSHtml.makeFormsAjax

    SHtml.a(() =>
      SetHtml(editFormDiv, form(ns)) &
      Show(editFormDiv, 1 seconds),
      Text("Edit"))
  }
}
```

2 Dummy data set

3 Initial listing bind

4 Update for binding

5 AJAX edit link

You'll notice that the first thing this code listing defines is the simple `Bookcase class` that you'll use to model the list of stock with **1**. The `stock` object details the list of books that are stored in the session **2**. Again, this is really not advisable for production usage and is simply for example purposes as it gives you a simple route to update a dataset without the need to setup a database and associated overhead.

The real meat of this class begins at **3**. As `stock` is a `List[Book]`, you can use Lift's CSS transformer binding mechanism to create many copies of a single template element by passing a list of promotable types. In this instance, each element that's assigned the template class `.line` will have several other transformations applied to both that element and its children. (In order to make sense of this definition, consider the template code in listing 9.6 along with the code in listing 9.5.)

Currently this is very similar to any kind of binding or listing that you'd create with Lift; you're simply iterating through a `List[T]` and implementing the bound properties. The primary difference here is the call to the `edit` function, which contains both a binding for the update form **4** and the AJAX link that dynamically inserts the form on the page **5**. The `edit` function is really the key to this whole process, as it binds the elements that feature the `.edit` class with an AJAX link: essentially, these elements will have their values replaced with an AJAX anchor, which you'll remember from the first AJAX example in listing 9.3. The interesting part here is that rather than simply using an `AlertJsCmd` type, the function makes use of the `SetHtmlJsCmd`.

As the name suggests, this JsCmd is all about setting the content of a specific DOM node, and here SetHtml is passed editFormDiv, which holds the name of the element that will be displaying the form. The second parameter for SetHtml is the NodeSeq (HTML markup) that will be displayed. As you can see, in order to generate the form markup, a call to the internal form function is made. The form value is a NodeSeq => NodeSeq function, nested inside the edit method, which is also a NodeSeq => NodeSeq function, which means that the incoming markup bound to the edit function can be passed down to the form function in order to generate the correct form markup using the template HTML as its input.

To recap the process, the user will click the Edit link that will make an AJAX call to the server and retrieve an AJAX form that's subsequently rendered in editFormDiv. The reason that the edit elements aren't bound in the initial CssBindFunc is that otherwise each element in the list would have a form attached to it, when we really only want to create a form for a particular item when the user requests it. Finally, do note that SetHtml is actually a JsCmd chained via the & operator, and here it has been coupled with a Show instance that will cause the element to fade in, presenting the form to the user.

With the form displayed, the contents are now bound to server-side actions, so the field itself, will update the value of the book title when the form is submitted ❹. SHtml.ajaxSubmit is the function that does the legwork to update the original list of books, thus negating the need for a page refresh. For simplicity's sake, each item in the list had its ID attribute set to the book reference, which allows you to simply call the specific DOM element by reference and update its content value with the latest user input.

The next listing shows the template code that goes with listing 9.5.

Listing 9.6   Template markup to accompany listing 9.5

```
<lift:surround with="default" at="content">
  <ul id="list" lift="more_ajax.list">
    <li class="span-12 clear line">
      <div class="span-7 name" id=""></div>
      <div class="span-3 edit">
        <p>Name: <input id="book_name" /></p>          Form
        <p><input type="submit" value="Update" /></p>  template
      </div>
    </li>
  </ul>
  <div id="edit_display"                               Form display
  ➥ style="display: none;"></div>                     node
</lift:surround>
```

As you can see, the elements here make use of the terse designer-friendly templating mechanism discussed in chapter 6, whereby the snippet is invoked at the start of the <ul> tag and the <div id="edit_display"> element is where the AJAX-rendered content will be displayed.

9.1.4   *Using JSON forms with AJAX*

Lift has several different ways to interact with forms and AJAX, and as you saw in the previous section, you can quite easily configure Lift to create an AJAX form by using SHtml. SHtml contains many useful methods and should be your main port of call for all of the out-of-the-box AJAX functionality.

One of the other interesting facilities that the SHtml object offers is the ability to create forms that are serialized and sent to the server using JSON. The following listing shows an example of using a JSON form.

Listing 9.7   Implementing `JsonForm`

```
import scala.xml.NodeSeq
import net.liftweb.util.JsonCmd
import net.liftweb.util.Helpers._
import net.liftweb.http.{SHtml,JsonHandler}
import net.liftweb.http.js.{JsCmd}
import net.liftweb.http.js.JsCmds.{SetHtml,Script}

class JsonForm {                                          ❶ JSON serialize
                                                            function
  def head = Script(json.jsCmd)

  def show =                                              ❷ JSON form
    "#form" #> ((ns: NodeSeq) =>                            wrapper
      SHtml.jsonForm(json, ns))

  object json extends JsonHandler {
    def apply(in: Any): JsCmd =
      SetHtml("json_result", in match {
        case JsonCmd("processForm", _,
            params: Map[String, Any], _) =>               ❸ Parameter
          <p>Publisher: {params("publisher")},              handling
            Title: {params("title")}</p>
        case x =>
          <span class="error">Unknown error: {x}</span>
      })
  }
}
```

You can see that this is once again a basic class with a few snippet methods. First, this class defines a snippet that adds a JavaScript element to the page that will handle the form serialization ❶. Typically, you would call this method from within the <head> tag in your template, so that the head is merged into the main page template. The point of this is that the JsonHandler implementation (in this instance the json object) contains JavaScript that registers a function to serialize the passed object to JSON.

The show method ❷ is the familiar snippet method setup, which binds to the jsonForm method, passing the JsonHandler instance and the passed NodeSeqfrom the template. This generates a <form> element that will wrap the fields in your template. A point to note here is that the fields in your template won't have randomized names because they aren't generated with SHtml helpers; they're raw from the template, so, from a security perspective, this is something to bear in mind. Listing 9.8 shows the full contents of the markup template.

The guts of this class are really the implementation of the `JsonHandler`, but the specific point of interest is the `match` statement that determines what content to serve ❸. This defines the handling of parameters passed from the browser. Because `params` is a `Map`, you must be careful to only request keys that actually exist. This could throw a runtime exception if the key you're expecting doesn't exist.

Listing 9.8   Template implementation for `JsonForm`

```
<lift:surround with="default" at="content">
  <head>
    <script type="text/javascript"
      ➥ src="/classpath/jlift.js" />
    <lift:json_form.head />
  </head>
  <h2>JSON Form</h2>
  <div id="form" lift="JsonForm.show">
    <p>Book Name: <br />
    ➥<input type="text" name="title" /></p>
    <p>Publisher: <br />
      <select name="publisher">
        <option value="manning">Manning</option>
        <option value="penguin">Penguin</option>
        <option value="bbc">BBC</option>
      </select>
    </p>
    <p><input type="submit" /></p>
  </div>
  <hr />
  <h2>JSON Result</h2>
  <div id="json_result"></div>
</lift:surround>
```

❶ Include Lift JSON functions

Input fields

Result element

Lift provides a specialized client-side JavaScript library with a set of helper functions for conducting operations such as serializing forms, handling collections, and so forth, called `jlift.js`. Here it's included at within the `head` element ❶, which is important, because otherwise the JSON form functionality won't operate as expected.

When the library is included and the `head` method in the `JsonForm` class is called from the template, you'll be left with something similar to the following:

```
<script src="/classpath/jlift.js" type="text/javascript"></script>
<script type="text/javascript">
//<![CDATA[
function F950163993256RNF(obj){
  liftAjax.lift_ajaxHandler('F950163993256RNF='+
  encodeURIComponent(JSON.stringify(obj)), null,null);
}
//]]>
</script>
```

As you can see, it's important to call the head method from your template so the rendered output includes this function.

9.1.5   AJAX with LiftScreen

Back in chapter 6, you were introduced to Lift's support for creating forms and interactive input elements: LiftScreen and its bigger brother Wizard. AJAX was deliberately left out of that earlier discussion because it requires knowledge of the JsCmd infrastructure, which you've now seen in operation in several scenarios. This section builds on chapter 6's introduction to LiftScreen and AJAX'ifies the example we looked at then.

The following listing recaps the LiftScreen implementation from chapter 6.

Listing 9.9   A recap of the base LiftScreen example

```
import net.liftweb.http.{LiftScreen,S}

object LiftScreenExample extends LiftScreen {
  val flavour = field("What's your favorite Ice cream flavor", "",
    trim, valMinLen(2,"Name too short"),
    valMaxLen(40,"That's a long name"))

  val sauce = field("Like chocolate sauce?", false)

  def finish(){
    if(sauce)
      S.notice("%s goes great with chocolate sauce!"
        .format(flavour.is))
    else S.notice("I like %s too!".format(flavour.is))
  }
}
```

Currently, this form will force a hard refresh every time it's submitted. This is functional, but it's somewhat clunky. Fortunately Lift supports AJAX in LiftScreen right out of the box, and enabling this is a simple two-step process.

First, in the invoking markup, you need to indicate to Lift that this form will use AJAX:

```
<lift:LiftScreenAJAXExample ajax="true" />
```

Specifically note the addition of the ajax="true" parameter. This is the simplest way to add AJAX to an existing form, but you can also override the defaultToAjax_? method in the screen definition if you'd prefer to keep all the configuration in Scala code.

Second, it's likely that you'll want to fire some client-side activity when the form is submitted, so be sure to add the following line to the screen definition:

```
override def calcAjaxOnDone = Alert("Form submitted!")
```

This example is not particularly practical, as it just throws up an alert box, but you just need to supply some kind of JsCmd subtype to this method and it will be executed when the form is successfully submitted. If you don't override this method, the default functionality is to redirect the user back to the page that referred them, which is likely not what you want when using an AJAX user interface.

So far in this chapter, you've seen how to construct JavaScript commands in your Scala code and how Lift's seamless AJAX system provides you a secure and flexible way to write interactive apps with simple function constructions. With that being said, there is a point where having a slightly higher level of abstraction is most useful, because you can then focus more on the interactivity you're building rather than "update XYZ div element here." This is exactly what Lift's wiring mechanism can help you with. When you have several components on the page and you want them to have a related set of UI interactions, wiring is a great fit.

9.2 Wiring

Lift 2.2 brought with it many great enhancements, and one of those was the wiring feature. Wiring provides a high-level abstraction for building AJAX-rich pages in which you can wire together different page elements.

For example, imagine a spreadsheet that calculates the tax and total value of a product when given its unit cost minus tax. There would be two formulas at work: one to calculate the tax field, and a second to calculate the value of the item plus the tax. By using Lift's wiring system, you could set up a scenario where the user would enter a value into the input field, and the two other components on the page that displayed the output calculations would automatically update. Wherever you have user interaction resulting in more than one simple DOM update, wiring is more often than not a good fit.

In this section, you'll build a basic formula wiring example that delivers the functionality we just outlined. This example uses wiring to conduct multiple page-content updates based upon user input.

9.2.1 Formula wiring

The formula wiring example involves a simple set of snippets whose behavior is wired together. As the name implies, there is a distinct relationship between these snippets; when the value of the input field is updated, the two wired snippets will also update.

Before getting into the code for this example, take a look at figure 9.2. This is the result of the example you'll be building; it illustrates the output and how the automatic updating will operate. Without further ado, let's start constructing this example.

The first thing that you need to consider is how to handle the input data. The values of the Tax

Figure 9.2 Rendered output of the formula-wiring sample. The Product Value field ❶ is the field for input, whereas the Tax and Total fields ❷ and ❸ are automatically updating values based on the input.

and Total fields are designed to change based upon the user's input into the Product Value field. Typically, sharing the state between several snippets can be tricky to do safely. Simply using a global, mutable var can be a nightmare because you must bear in mind the synchronization and thread safety of that particular variable. Fortunately, it's common to have a variable that has volatile state, that must remain thread safe, and whose value you'll need to transform—Lift provides what is known as a ValueCell to handle this use case.

Consider the following:

```
import net.liftweb.common.{Box,Empty}
import net.liftweb.util.ValueCell

val sample = ValueCell[Box[Double]](Empty)
```

Here, the value sample is assigned a ValueCell that takes Box[Double]. You may be wondering what the purpose is of putting Box, which is a sort of container, into seemingly another container. In this instance, Box affords us the ability to initialize the value without a concrete value of its own, and ValueCell gives us some additional functionality. For example, if you call the currentValue method of sample, you're returned a Tuple2 of Box[Double] (or whatever T you passed the ValueCell), and a Long of the timestamp when that value was specified. The purpose here is that the timestamp acts as a clock for that value and allows you to resolve conflicts if you were in a scenario where you had two of the same ValueCell and needed to determine the latest value to use.

Getting back to the formula-wiring example, you'll be using ValueCell to hold the user input and then to determine resulting output values. The next listing shows the starting implementation for this example.

Listing 9.10 Setting up the `ValueCell` holders for the formula wiring example

```
import scala.xml.{NodeSeq,Text}
import net.liftweb.common.{Box,Full,Empty}
import net.liftweb.util.ValueCell
import net.liftweb.util.Helpers._
import net.liftweb.http.{SHtml,WiringUI}
import net.liftweb.http.js.JsCmds.Noop
import net.liftweb.http.js.jquery.JqWiringSupport

class FormulaWiring {

  private val productValue =                                ❶ User input
    ValueCell[Box[Double]](Empty)                             cell

  private val taxValue = productValue.lift(_.map(x =>       ❷ Tax calculation
    (x/100d*17.5d))).openOr(0d))

  private val totalValue = productValue.lift(_.map(x =>     ❸ Tax plus
    (x+taxValue.currentValue._1))).openOr(0d))                product value
}
```

Here we set up the various `ValueCells` for this example. First, you define a `Value-Cell` to contain the product value entered by the user ❶. Next, you make two `ValueCells` to calculate the tax and total values. These are the interpreted cells that both calculate their own values by lifting the `productValue` cell value given by the user ❷ and ❸. These two cells do fairly simple calculations; `taxValue` does a straightforward sum to determine 17.5 percent of the original product value, and `totalValue` adds the value entered by the user with the computed tax amount.

> **TIP** "Lifting" is a term you'll sometimes see when discussing data structures within Scala and other functional programming languages. Typically, lifting a structure means you create another version of it by applying the given function to the structure. With regard to wiring, the values are lifted to the new values by applying the tax calculations.

With these value holders in place, you now have a mechanism to collect and compute the values to be used in the example. But currently there's no way for the user to interact with this. Let's fix that now by adding the methods shown in the following listing to the base class implementation.

Listing 9.11   Adding snippet methods to the formula wiring example

```
class FormulaWiring {
  ...
  def product =
    "#value" #> SHtml.ajaxText(              ❶ Bind input
      productValue.map(_.toString).openOr(""),   field
      v => { asDouble(v).pass(
        productValue.set(_)); Noop })
  def tax(xhtml: NodeSeq): NodeSeq =       ❷ Wire up
    WiringUI.asText(xhtml, taxValue,          tax text
      JqWiringSupport.fade)
  def total(xhtml: NodeSeq): NodeSeq =     ❸ Wire up
    WiringUI.asText(xhtml, totalValue,        total text
      JqWiringSupport.fade)
}
```

To complete this example, add the three rendering methods to the `FormulaWiring` class. The `product` definition implements `SHtml.ajaxText` ❶, which is used to collect the input from the user.

> **TIP** If your output doesn't update, you should be aware that, by default, the second parameter, `SHtml.ajaxText`, which defines the action to update the values, is only executed when the field is blurred somehow—when the field is deselected. Usually the user does this either by pressing Enter or by deselecting the field with the mouse.

The thing to focus on here is how the user input is actually sent to the `productValue` instance in the function definition that's defined within the second parameter passed to SHtml.ajaxText. The function is passed the value entered by the user and represented here by v. Using the asDouble method from util.Helpers, Lift will try to convert the text input to a Double and return a Box[Double]. Conveniently, this is the same type as the productValue cell, so by using the pass method from Box you can pass the result of asDouble to be set into the ValueCell. Doing so protects you from exceptions, in the case of the user entering something like a text string that can't be converted to Double, as it will simply be set to Empty.

The calls to the wiring infrastructure are defined at ❷ and ❸. These are the snippet methods for tax and total respectively. Like regular snippets, they're NodeSeq => NodeSeq functions, but they call the WiringUI object to connect the wiring.

The WiringUI.asText method takes several arguments: the markup consumed by the snippet, the Cell instance, and the JavaScript effect that will be executed when updating the UI. In this example, the effect is a fade, so that the text fades out, the value is updated, and the new value fades back in. There are several out-of-the-box effects to choose from, and if you'd prefer something custom, you can construct your own effect that conforms to the following type signature: (String, Boolean, JsCmd) => JsCmd.

Now that you know how to set up the wiring, the last piece of the puzzle is the template markup The relevant code is shown in the next listing.

Listing 9.12   Template markup for the formula wiring example

```
<lift:surround with="default" at="content">
  <h2>Simple Wiring Example</h2>
  <div lift="formula_wiring.product"
    <p>Product value (minus tax):                    ❶ User input
    <input id="value" /></p>
  </div>
  <h2>Output</h2>
  <p>
    Tax: <span lift="formula_wiring.tax">
      unknown</span><br />                           ❷ Wired
    Total: <span lift="formula_wiring.total">          output
      unknown</span>
  </p>
<lift:surround>
```

This template is a very regular one; the input ❶ is a simple placeholder, and it's replaced with the correct AJAX form element at runtime. The other interesting thing in this template is that the two output elements that are wired are exactly the same as any other snippet call ❷. Lift does the right thing, without any specific input from you.

Both the manual AJAX and automatic wiring systems in Lift provide rich models for interactive programming. But there is a change afoot as users demand more and more interactivity—over the past few years, the web has been a constantly shifting landscape, with user behavior transitioning to a more social model. This puts a whole different set of technical requirements on developers, as they have to contend with the move from read-orientated or broadcast-style applications to very write-orientated application designs with users constantly demanding instant gratification. These are tough challenges, and this change requires more interactivity than AJAX can reasonably supply without things becoming clogged up. This next step requires Comet.

9.3 *Comet*

Although AJAX supplies a great model for interactive programming, it still requires the sending of a request from the browser before you can obtain any data or content to render a display or create an interactive element for the user. This is where Comet differs; the content can be pushed to the browser as the application dictates. An example of such a technique is the Gmail online email portal: when an email is received, it's a much better user experience if the new email simply appears in your inbox as opposed to you having to manually refresh the page or poll with AJAX. The user doesn't experience any slowness or batching, so it's a lot more like a desktop user experience.

With Comet, the page has been requested by the client, and the server is then able to push content back to the browser with no additional requests from that same browser, asynchronous or otherwise. That means no secondary AJAX requests, no page refreshes, nothing. This is a totally different model than most developers are used to, and it really lends itself to building event-based systems: when something happens (an event) you can act upon it and shunt data to the browser without the need for the client to ask for it. In Lift's implementation of Comet, when an event occurs for which you'd like a response pushed to the browser, you simply send a message to the Lift abstraction that deals with Comet, and the message is passed down to the client.

Comet as a programming concept, however, isn't specific to Lift. Alex Russell is widely credited as having first coined the term on his blog in 2006.[2] He drew common patterns from services at the time that were leveraging long-lived HTTP connections to push data in an event-driven manner.

Consider figure 9.3, which illustrates the Comet request and response workflow. At time marker 1, the browser makes the initial request to the page that has the Comet component present. The server responds to the browser at time marker 2 and renders the page. But the server also keeps that initial request active using a technique called long polling. With the request still open, the server can then push data to the browser whenever it needs to, as illustrated at *B*.

This approach opens the door to building applications that truly operate in real time, because page furniture can be dynamically altered via events occurring on the server. There are several Comet applications in the public eye today—one of the most well-known is Facebook chat. As users input messages to each other, they're relayed via the Facebook servers and are pushed to the other user's browser.

---

[2] Alex Russell, "Comet: Low Latency Data for the Browser," in his blog, *Infrequently Noted.* http://infrequently .org/2006/03/comet-low-latency-data-for-the-browser/

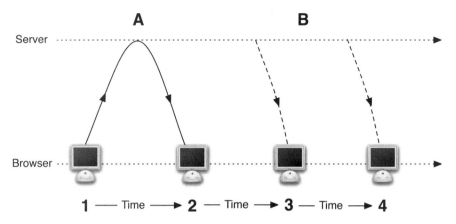

Figure 9.3   A Comet request requires no secondary request in order to push data to the browser.

> **NOTE**   Long polling keeps the request active, but this means that there are potential scalability issues with high numbers of connections. This issue is addressed in chapter 15, along with the more general topic of scaling Lift applications.

Because Comet can be thought of primarily in terms of events and messaging, the abstraction in Lift that deals with Comet is primarily based around the Actor programming paradigm. Lift comes with its own actor implementation called (unsurprisingly) `LiftActor`.

9.3.1   *What are actors?*

Actors are a high-level abstraction on concurrency and parallelism. Using manual threading and locking to create programs that execute concurrently or that use parallel processing is exceedingly difficult to get right, so that's why concurrent programming has been difficult over the past decade or so. Actors provide a convenient model for parallelizing code and neatly encapsulating logical operations that exchange state via lightweight messages. This sounds like a really great new idea, but actors are nothing new; they were invented in the 1960s and were popularized in the 1980s in the telecom industry, where having highly parallelized, fault-tolerant code was key to achieving the scalability and reliability required by their problem domain. With commodity computing hardware operating more and more processing cores, developers now must start to parallelize their code to achieve the best results from the available resources.

Actors encapsulate both state and behavior into lightweight processes, but these processes don't share any kind of state. They communicate via lightweight, asynchronous messages that are sent and then forgotten: fire and forget, if you will. Each actor has an inbox for messages that can be thought of as a message queue, and each message the actor receives is operated on by that process or thread.

Consider the basic actor example in the next listing.

```
import net.liftweb.actor.LiftActor

object Example extends LiftActor {
  def messageHandler = {
    case s: String => println("Sent '%s'".format(s))
  }
}
```

This is the simplest `LiftActor` you can make. Lift actors differ from other implementations available in the Scala ecosystem in that you never explicitly call start or shutdown. The instance is simply dereferenced and is garbage collected by the JVM when it's no longer being used. After implementing an actor by extending the `LiftActor` trait, you must implement the `messageHandler` method. This essentially tells the actor how it should respond to the different messages it receives. In this case, this `Example` actor only knows how to deal with `String` messages, and upon receiving a `String` instance, it will simply print out a message to the console.

Now that you have this shiny new actor, how do you call it? Well, the Actor pattern was popularized through languages like Erlang, and the Scala implementations follow very similar syntactic idioms. You send messages to actors using the bang (`!`) method, like so:

```
Example ! "w00t"
```

If you try this out in the SBT console shell, you'll notice that this command doesn't appear to finish. That's because the command is processing in a thread independent from the one running the console. Actors are generally thread-safe because there's no shared state to speak of. Nevertheless, actors typically operate from a thread pool, so although you don't need to use thread-blocking synchronization or similar techniques, the execution may still happen on the same thread.

Actor-based programming is a very broad subject, and one that this book can only give a cursory introduction to, so if you'd like more information on actors, check out Joshua D. Suereth's *Scala in Depth*, which provides more specific information on the actor pattern in Scala.

Now that you have an appreciation for the event-based nature of actors and how you can communicate via asynchronous messages, let's get back to seeing how that relates to using Comet in Lift.

9.3.2   *Basic Comet usage*

Lift's Comet implementation builds upon this actor foundation, so the semantics of sending messages to Comet components are exactly the same as sending messages to a regular actor. The main difference is that the messages are piped out via the appropriate HTTP connection and are executed in the client's browser.

In the same way that the basic actor example in listing 9.13 extended Lift-Actor, Lift provides a specialized trait for Comet components called CometActor. This trait contains all the plumbing required to implement a Comet element, so you simply need to implement this in your own class and you can start building a real-time component!

In this section, we create a simple Comet component that simulates a basic clock that pushes the time to the browser every five seconds. Comet components are actually resolved in the template via reflection, and the class is looked up and instantiated once per session. The only exception to this is if you have manually overridden the CometActor lifecycle method so the instance expires after a certain period of time, causing the lapsed CometActor to be re-instantiated.

The next listing shows the basic Clock implementation.

Listing 9.14 Basic Comet clock implementation

```
import scala.xml.Text
import net.liftweb.util.ActorPing
import net.liftweb.util.Helpers._
import net.liftweb.http.CometActor
import net.liftweb.http.js.JsCmds.SetHtml

case object Tick

class Clock extends CometActor {                          ❶ Schedule
  ActorPing.schedule(this, Tick, 5 seconds)                  first ping

  def render =                                            ❷ Render to
    "#clock_time *" replaceWith timeNow.toString             DOM

  override def lowPriority = {
    case Tick => partialUpdate(SetHtml("clock_time",      ❸ Update time,
      Text(timeNow.toString)))                               schedule next update
      ActorPing.schedule(this, Tick, 5 seconds)
  }
}
```

This listing shows a simple class that implements the CometActor trait. The first thing you'll notice is the call to ActorPing lurking in the body of the class ❶. Scala classes don't define constructors in the same way Java classes do, so this will only be called when the class is instantiated. When the class is instantiated, the CometActor will send a message of Tick to itself ❷, subsequently getting the time and flushing that to the browser and critically kick-starting the ticking of the clock—each time the Tick message is received, another Tick is schedule in five seconds' time ❸.

You may be wondering why in a CometActor there is no messageHandler but rather a lowPriority method that defines the message dispatcher. Well, the CometActor provides three levels of message handling: highPriority, mediumPriority, and lowPriority.

The different priorities essentially allow you to control which messages are more important and should be handled over and above others in a high-load environment.

For the vast majority of situations, using `lowPriority` dispatching will be fine. In the implementation of `CometActor`, the `messageHandler` is a fall-through set of partial functions that will all get evaluated eventually; unless you're operating with very high loads and the message inbox of a particular actor which is very full, causing some delay on the fall-through processing of handlers, any handler you use will be fine.

The `render` method is mandatory for all `CometActor` subtypes and must be implemented. When the page loads, the `render` method is called to render the initial value, and in this instance it uses the `timeNow` method from `util.Helpers` to grab the current time.

Last, but not least, is the construct that does the updating: `partialUpdate` ❸. This method takes a by-name function that yields a `JsCmd`. In this example, it uses the familiar `SetHtml` method to update the correct DOM element with the new time.

The markup for using the `Clock` within your template is equally simple:

```
<div lift="comet?type=Clock">
  Current Time:<br /><span id="clock_time">Missing Clock</span>
</div>
```

Here, the `lift="comet?type=Clock"` command causes Lift's templating mechanism to find and load the correct `Clock` instance if one doesn't already exist in the current session. By default, Comet instances will last for the duration of the session in which they are created, but if your use case demands it, you can specifically set a lifespan for a given Comet actor implementation by overriding the `lifespan` method:

```
override def lifespan = 2 minutes
```

Additionally, it's worth noting that, just like snippets, more than one way exists to instantiate them. The other template markup that you may well see in examples is this:

```
<lift:comet type="Clock"> ... </lift:comet>
```

The effect is identical; this is just a different way of achieving the same thing.

The only other way to create Comet components is programmatically using `LiftRules.cometCreation`. This method allows you to specify how you want to create particular types, and it requires passing a set of properties to the class, such as the current session and the default markup, among other things.

This `Clock` example is one of the simplest `CometActor` implementations you could build, and because data is only ever being pushed to the browser, there is very little coding that needs to be done. It's a simple repeat broadcast in the scope of a single session. In order to explore some of the more complex facilities Lift's Comet support has to offer, we build a much more complicated example in the next section: a game of rock-paper-scissors.

9.3.3   *Comet-based rock-paper-scissors*

In order to properly explore Lift's Comet support, we take a meander down memory lane and play rock-paper-scissors. No doubt nearly everyone will be familiar with this game, but if not, rock-paper-scissors is a game in which each player chooses to be rock, paper, or scissors, where certain properties of each can defeat their opponents:

- Paper defeats rock by wrapping it
- Rock defeats scissors by blunting them
- Scissors defeat paper by cutting it

NOTE   For everything you ever wanted to know about rock-paper-scissors, see the Wikipedia article: http://en.wikipedia.org/wiki/Rock-paper-scissors.

The nice thing about this game for the purpose of this example is that it's totally event- based. Both players make a move, which can be modeled as an event, and the game logic is fairly simplistic so it isn't overly complex to model using Scala case classes and objects.

Before starting to code anything, let's define a few parameters: first, you must have two human players. AI would be fairly simple to implement, but it clouds the example of utilizing Comet, so we exclude it. Moreover, a player must only be able to play one game at a time, and when a game is won, it will automatically reset after 5 seconds so you can continue playing. In a real-life implementation, it would be sensible to include some kind of *return to lobby* type of functionality, but again, that will simply complicate matters in this example.

Getting down to the implementation details, actors communicate with immutable messages, so let's first define a set of objects that model the basic parts of the game functionality. The following listing details these classes and objects.

Listing 9.15   Classes and objects required for the rock-paper-scissors game

```
sealed trait Move
final case object Rock extends Move                       ❶ Game move
final case object Paper extends Move                         types
final case object Scissors extends Move

sealed trait Outcome
final case object Tie                                     ❷ Possible
final case class Winner(is: CometActor)                     outcomes

final case classAddPlayer(who: CometActor)
final case classRemovePlayer(who: CometActor)
final case object PairPlayersInLobby
final case classNowPlaying(game: Game)                    ❸ Game events
final case class Make(move: Move, from: CometActor)
final case object HurryUpAndMakeYourMove
final case object ResetGame
final case object Adjudicate
```

These sets of messages are all that the actors will use to communicate between themselves. The first block of classes ❶ defines the possible moves that a player can make in the game, and they all inherit from the sealed `Move` trait. The purpose here is that when implementing the message handler, the actor can simply match on the `Move` type rather than on the specific type of move.

The second set of classes ❷ defines the available outcomes: a tie if there's a stalemate or someone wins. The third and final set ❸ of types defines the messages that are actively interchanged between the actor instances. This may seem a little abstract at the moment, but it will come into focus shortly.

The next things that need to be modeled are the actors that will be doing the sending and receiving of these messages. There are going to be four main actors in order to model the problem domain, as listed in table 9.1.

Table 9.1 Actor models used in rock-paper-scissors

Actor	Description
RockPaperScissors	This will be the actor that extends `CometActor` and thus deals with all the presentation issues, such as updating the display and sending any communication back to the user. There can only be one instance of `RockPaperScissors` in any given session, so it's essentially representing a player.
Lobby	When a player becomes active, they're registered with the `Lobby`. The `Lobby` pairs players together and creates enough games for people to play. If there is a lone player in the `Lobby`, it will wait until someone else joins before creating a game.
AskName	Before a player can join the lobby, they must enter a nickname. This allows you to experience the rather powerful ask/answer paradigm supported by Lift `CometActors`.
Game	Finally, the game itself, When the players are paired off into a game, they're sent a reference to the `Game` actor so they can communicate directly with it. This allows you to neatly encapsulate the game functionality for logic, such as determining the winner of any particular match.

It can often be tricky to visualize the relationships between actors, especially when the concept is a new one. To that end, consider figure 9.4, which details the first-stage relationships between the three main types: RockPaperScissors, Lobby, and Game.

This diagram may seem a little strange at first. Each circle represents an actor, and the whole figure assumes that the RockPaperScissorsinstance (RPS) has just been instantiated for the first time in this session—this is the first page visit. As depicted at *A*, the RockPaperScissors instance first creates a new instance of AskName, at which point the user is prompted to input a nickname. As you might imagine, this is the ask stage of the ask/answer workflow. After the nickname is entered, the AskName instance sends an answer back to the RockPaperScissors actor with the relevant answer, and the user's nickname is saved into a local private variable.

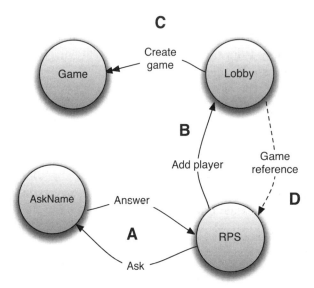

Figure 9.4 **Illustrating the message passing between the three main operational types in the rock-paper-scissors game**

After receiving the nickname, the RockPaperScissors instance is registered with the Lobby object, as shown at *B*. The Lobby holds a list of players that are currently not participating in a game, and every time a new player joins, it will check to see if it has *n* pairs of players that it can create games for, as shown at *C*. In a real-life use case, it would probably be wise to add some kind of upper limit to this, or to add more sophisticated logic for assigning users to games, but for the purpose of this example it works well. Upon finding users that it can pair, the Lobby will create a new instance of the Game actor, and assign these two users to that Game.

Finally, *D* shows each player being asynchronously notified about the game they're being added to, so they can notify the game of their moves later on.

Listings 9.16 through 9.18 demonstrate the segments of functionality described so far, starting with the RockPaperScissors actor.

Listing 9.16 Part one of the `RockPaperScissors` actor

```
import scala.xml.Text
import net.liftweb.common.{Box,Full,Empty}
import net.liftweb.http.{CometActor,SHtml}

class RockPaperScissors extends CometActor {

  private var nickName = ""                        ❶ Internal
  private var game: Box[Game] = Empty                  variables

  ...

  override def localSetup(){
    askUserForNickname
    super.localSetup()                              ❷ Lifecycle
  }                                                    methods
  override def localShutdown() {
```

```
    Lobby ! RemovePlayer(this)
    super.localShutdown()
  }

  private def askUserForNickname {
    if (nickName.length == 0){
      ask(new AskName, "What's your nickname?"){
        case s: String if (s.trim.length> 2) =>
          nickName = s.trim
          Lobby !AddPlayer(this)
          reRender(true)
        case _ =>
          askUserForNickname
          reRender(false)
      }
    }
  }
}
```

❸ **Ask/Answer construct**

The RockPaperScissors actor is essentially representing the player. First, this CometActor defines some internal state you want to keep about this session-scoped instance; namely, the player's nickname and the reference to the game in which they're participating ❶.

The important parts to note about the class at this phase are at ❷. The local-Setup and localShutdown methods are implemented in the CometActor trait and allow you to hook into the lifecycle of the CometActor instance. In this case, you use the localShutdown method to remove this particular player from the Lobby. The localSetup method is used to jump into the ask workflow defined at ❸.

The ask/answer paradigm can be thought of much like a person-to-person conversation, except that here the CometActor asks a new instance of AskName the question "What's your nickname?" and AskName gets that answer from the user and responds.

The second parameter group, or block, in ❸, processes the subsequent answer. The next listing shows the simple definition of the AskName actor.

Listing 9.17 Definition of the `AskName` actor

```
import net.liftweb.http.{CometActor,SHtml}

class AskName extends CometActor {
  def render = SHtml.ajaxForm(
    <p>What is your player nickname? <br />{
      SHtml.text("",n => answer(n.trim))}</p> ++
      <input type="submit" value="Enter Lobby"/>)
}
```

The implementation of AskName is super simple. In this case, its only task is to get the name from the user and pass that to the answer method. The awesome thing about this ask/answer paradigm is that you don't have to manage the relationship between the two actors. Lift does that for you, and as soon as the asking actor has its answer, Lift will shut down the redundant partner for you.

In the response handling of the original `ask` block in `RockPaperScissors` (listing 9.16), you can see that if it receives an acceptable answer, it tells the `Lobby` to add this player to the lobby state by sending the `Lobby` object an `AddPlayer` message. This brings us neatly to the `Lobby` object itself. What does the `Lobby` actor do upon receiving an `AddPlayer` message? How does the `Lobby` handle the state and assign games? The following listing shows the `Lobby` implementation.

Listing 9.18 Creating the Lobby actor

```
import net.liftweb.actor.LiftActor
import net.liftweb.http.CometActor

object Lobby extends LiftActor {                          ❶ Maintain
  private var games: List[Game] = Nil                        state
  private var lobby: List[CometActor] = Nil

  def messageHandler = {
    case PairPlayersInLobby => {
      for(i <- 0 until (lobby.size / 2)){                 ❷ Iterate lobby
        val players = lobby.take(2)                          players
        val game = new Game(players.head, players.last)
        games ::= game                                    ❸ Notify players
        players.foreach(_ ! NowPlaying(game))                of game
        lobby = lobby diff players
      }
    }
    case AddPlayer(who) =>
      lobby ::= who                                       ❹ Register/remove
      this ! PairPlayersInLobby                              player
    case RemovePlayer(who) =>
      lobby = lobby.filter(_ ne who)
  }
}
```

The `Lobby` actor object is essentially a dispatcher that creates games and assigns players. The `Lobby` first defines some private variables that hold state about the ongoing games and players that are waiting in the lobby ❶. Next, the `Lobby` implements the mandatory `messageHandler` so that upon receipt of a `PairPlayersInLobby` message, the `Lobby` actor will execute the necessary logic to assign players to a game. If the `Lobby` has a player count that's evenly divisible by 2, it will iterate through the list of waiting players and assign pairs of players to a new `Game` instance ❷ and ❸. Then, with this new `Game` instance, it notifies both players which instance of `Game` they've been assigned to and removes these players from the `Lobby` ❹.

The next step is to implement the `Game` actor that actually handles the processing of `Rock`, `Paper`, or `Scissor` moves made by the user. As this is really the next part of the actor implementation, consider figure 9.5, which details the way players send moves to the `Game` instance.

After the game has been initialized and players are in position to make their moves, one eventually will make the first move, as indicated at *A*. The `Game` actor then checks to see if the other player has made their move, and if not, sends them a hastening

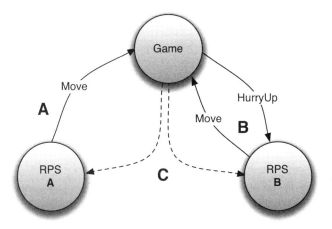

Figure 9.5 The event cycle depicting users making moves in the game, and the notifying of players as to which participants were the winners and losers

message, after which the second user will also make their move (*B*). Finally, *C* illustrates the point at which the game adjudicates the match and notifies both parties of the winner. Each instance then displays a witty message appropriate to the user's winning or losing status.

Having the game itself be an actor allows for all the logic relating to the match to be encapsulated in the Game actor's message handlers. The Game actor implementation is as follows.

Listing 9.19 Implementing the Game actor

```
import scala.collection.mutable.Map
import net.liftweb.common.{Box,Full,Empty}
import net.liftweb.util.Helpers._
import net.liftweb.util.ActorPing
import net.liftweb.actor.LiftActor
import net.liftweb.http.CometActor

class Game(playerOne: CometActor, playerTwo: CometActor)
    extends LiftActor {

  private var moves: Map[CometActor, Box[Move]] = Map()      ◁─
  clearMoves()                                                  ❶ Player moves

  private def sendToAllPlayers(msg: Any){
    moves.foreach(_._1 ! msg)
  }

  private def clearMoves() {
    moves = Map(playerOne -> Empty, playerTwo -> Empty)
  }

  def messageHandler = {
    case Adjudicate => {                                      ❷ Determine
      val p1move = moves(playerOne)                              match outcome
      val p2move = moves(playerTwo)
      if(p1move == p2move)
        sendToAllPlayers(Tie)                                 ◁─ ❸ Notify players
                                                                   of a tie break
```

```
      else {
        (p1move, p2move) match {
          case (Full(Rock), Full(Scissors)) |
               (Full(Paper), Full(Rock)) |
               (Full(Scissors), Full(Paper)) =>
            sendToAllPlayers(Winner(playerOne))
          case _ =>
            sendToAllPlayers(Winner(playerTwo))
        }
      }
      Schedule.schedule(this, ResetGame, 5 seconds)
    }
    case Make(move, from) => {
      moves.update(from,Full(move))
      if(moves.flatMap(_._2).size == 2)
        this ! Adjudicate
      else
        moves.filter(_._1 ne from).head._1 ! HurryUpAndMakeYourMove
    }
    case ResetGame =>
    clearMoves()
    sendToAllPlayers(ResetGame)
  }
}
```

② **Determine match outcome**

④ **Notify the winner**

⑤ **Reset current game**

⑥ **Hastener for the opponent**

Unlike the other actors in this setup, the Game actor can only be instantiated with two players. This cuts down on the amount of mutability and ensures that any game always has the correct number of players it requires to operate. That being said, the current implementation could benefit from some additional logic to handle session expiry, users opting to leave a game, and so forth, but that's somewhat out of scope for this example.

The Game actor first defines an internal Map that relates a particular player to the move they made ❶. Due to the simple nature of rock-paper-scissors, this is really easy to implement. All you need to do is make the Move itself boxed, so that you can initialize the value with Empty. Later on, when you receive the message with their move, you can update this internal map ❻.

In addition to updating this internal map upon receiving a player's move, the game will check to see if the other player has already made a move as well. If not, the game sends an asynchronous message to the player to remind them to make a move. Assuming the other player then makes a move, a message is sent to itself to trigger the adjudication of the match, as detailed at ❸, ❹, and ❺. This block of code is really the core of the game because it computes the outcome and then sends messages out to the relevant actors notifying them of their next action.

In order to adjudicate a given match, the Game actor assigns both players' moves to a value ❷ and first checks to see if the moves are equivalent, which would result in a tiebreak ❸. It's perfectly fine to check for equality on these values. They're case objects, meaning that there can only ever be one instance of that value in a single classloader, so the equality check is valid here. If the result is not a tie, the Game does a basic pattern match using a `Tuple2` of the move values and notifies all the players of the winner **❹**.

Finally, let's complete the picture of the `RockPaperScissors` actor, which is handling the receipt of all these different events and the subsequent rendering to the browser. The next listing shows the remaining parts of the implementation.

Listing 9.20   Part two of the `RockPaperScissors` actor

```scala
import scala.xml.Text
import net.liftweb.common.{Box,Full,Empty}
import net.liftweb.util.Helpers._
import net.liftweb.http.{CometActor,SHtml}
import net.liftweb.http.js.JsCmds.{SetHtml,Run}

class RockPaperScissors extends CometActor {
  ...
  private def showInformation(msg: String) =                      ❶ Message
    partialUpdate(SetHtml("information", Text(msg)))                  display helper

  override def mediumPriority = {
    case NowPlaying(g) =>                                          ❷ Initialize the
      game = Full(g)                                                  game
      reRender(true)

    case HurryUpAndMakeYourMove =>
      showInformation(
        "Hurry up! Your opponent has already made their move!")

    case Tie =>
      showInformation("Damn, it was a tie!")

    case Winner(who) =>
      if(who eq this)                                             ❸ Am I the
        showInformation("You are the WINNER!!!")                     winner?
      else
        showInformation("Better luck next time, loser'")

    case ResetGame ->
      reRender(true)
  }

  def render =
    if(!game.isEmpty)
      "#information *" #>
      ➥ "You're playing! Make your move..." &
      ".line" #> List(Rock, Paper, Scissors).map(move =>
        SHtml.ajaxButton(Text(move.toString), () => {            ❺ Notify      ❹ Render
          game.foreach(_ ! Make(move, this))                      move and        game or
          Run("$('button').attr('disabled',true);")               disable UI      lobby
      }))
    else
      "#game *" #>
      ➥ "Waiting in the lobby for an opponent..."
  ...
}
```

This is the final part of the implementation of the game's actors. As `RockPaper-Scissors` is the only `CometActor` in play here, the entire rendering and communication of user-bound information must pass through it in order to be pushed to the browser. For example, when the instance receives the winner notification, it determines what text it should display ❸. Note that the `showInformation` private helper has been defined to alleviate the duplication for displaying messages by supplying a simple wrapper around rendering updates to the browser ❶. If the GUI were more complex, it would probably be better to read content from a template using `S.runTemplate`, but for this example it works perfectly.

Upon receiving the `NowPlaying` message, which contains a game reference, the `RockPaperScissorsCometActor` sets its internal game variable to the passed reference ❷. Critically though, notice the call to `reRender(true)`. When a page that features a `CometActor` loads up, its `render` method is called and the output is displayed. `CometActor`s have two main ways to update the page: either redraw themselves using `reRender`, or use `partialUpdate` to alter a specific part of the DOM. In this example, the internal state of the game has changed from waiting in the lobby to playing, so rather than updating specific DOM elements that would be lost if the user refreshed their page, the render method produces something different based upon whether or not the user is participating in a game, so calling `reRender(true)` from the `NowPlaying` message handler is a simple way to have the page display correctly. The important thing to remember here is that there is not a huge difference between `partialUpdate` and `reRender` in small `CometActor` examples. But in a larger, more complex examples, redrawing the whole component could be a costly operation, so using `partialUpdate` would be a better strategy in that situation.

Finally, the `render` method uses a pretty standard binding syntax that's the same as you would use in a snippet invocation ❹. The point of note in this section is where the buttons are being created ❺. Given a list of moves, a `SHtml.button` is created with a callback function that sends the appropriate `Move` message to the game actor before executing some custom JavaScript code on the client side via the `Run` JsCmd. The `Run` command essentially lets you pass a string through as a `JsCmd`, and Lift will then run this for you on the client side. The only caveat is that the JavaScript code must execute and be valid, or it simply won't work!

Last, but certainly not least, the final piece of the puzzle in this rock-paper-scissors example is the template markup. The complete template is shown in the next listing.

Listing 9.21 Template markup for the rock-paper-scissors example

```
<lift:surround with="default" at="content">
  <h2>Rock, Paper, Scissors</h2>
  <div lift="comet?type=RockPaperScissors">            Call Comet
    <div id="game">                                ❶  component
      <p id="information">Pending information...</p>
      <ul id="button">
```

```
        <li class="line"></li>
      </ul>
    </div>
  </div>
</div>
```

By now you should be familiar with the general feel of template markup in Lift. The main differentiator here is the call to the Comet component in the first instance ❶. As was touched on in section 9.3.2, you can invoke components from the view in several ways, but you always have to tell Lift to use the Comet snippet and give it the name of the `CometActor` it should use at that location within the markup.

This concludes the rock-paper-scissors game and our exploration of using Lift's Comet support to build real-time applications and leverage the powerful event-based architectures that actors lend themselves to so well.

9.4   *Summary*

AJAX and Comet are two areas that Lift really excels in. Throughout this chapter, you've seen how Lift provides a set of server-side abstractions for working with JavaScript, in the form of the `JsCmd` and `JsExp` types. These JavaScript abstractions provide you with a flexible and straightforward way to affect client-side behavior, all from within your Scala code.

As these calls on the server side result in JavaScript being generated on the client-side rendering in the browser, Lift has a decoupled interface for JavaScript libraries called `JSArtifacts`. Due to this loose coupling, you can use whatever client-side library you like and implement the appropriate `JSArtifacts` trait to tell Lift about certain parts of that library. Moreover, Lift ships with three popular library integrations out of the box: JQuery, Yahoo UI (YUI), and ExtJS, so you can get up and running quickly and make use of all that these popular libraries have to offer. In addition, Lift has several library-specific server-side representations, so you can have access to particularly popular parts of a given library. For example, fading a div out is a popular operation in JQuery, and Lift lets you call `JqJsCmds.FadeOut` and you're all set.

These JavaScript abstractions are used throughout Lift, and we also looked at how you can leverage the `SHtml` AJAX builder methods to create elements on the page that trigger server-side actions. The powerful thing about Lift's AJAX system is that you can capture the logic to be executed upon making the specific callback in a Scala function. This gives you a flexible system that can pretty much execute whatever you'd like when an AJAX event occurs.

When an AJAX element is used, Lift automatically assigns it a random GUID. Each AJAX element then has a session-specific and opaque name, much in the same way Lift does with every input on regular forms. This is important, because it prevents large-scale request tampering or cross-site request forgery. Lift lets you focus on the logic and completely hides the request and response workflow. In short, you can spend more time focusing on getting things done rather than worrying about how or where the AJAX call is being sent.

With more and more AJAX elements being added to pages, it can often be tricky creating complex interactions between these dynamic AJAX elements. This is where Lift's wiring mechanism comes into play. Using wiring, you can automatically update different user interface elements without having to explicitly specify a change or action to occur. You simply wire them together, and Lift takes care of the rest.

The next step in interactivity from AJAX and automatic wiring is Comet. With Comet you no longer need to have a request coming from the browser to push data or content back to the client. Once the page featuring a Comet component has loaded, your application can push data to the browser whenever the need arises. This yields an extremely dynamic and event-driven systems architecture that makes great use of the actor-programming paradigm. As examples, we looked at both a simple clock that pushes the new time to the browser every 5 seconds, and a rock-paper-scissors game that included a game lobby and the ability for two players to play each other in a match via the web.

In the next chapter, we cover Lift's SQL persistence system: Mapper. You'll learn how to create queries and relationships and how to implement validation for your application models. Mapper is one of the oldest parts of Lift, but it has lots of functionality and is widely used by many applications in production. See you in the next chapter!

Persistence with Mapper

10

This chapter covers
- Connecting to a database
- Query constructs
- Relationships
- Entity validation

The vast majority of web applications that do anything semiuseful will ultimately need to store their data somewhere. Over the past decade or more, the relational database management system (RDBMS) has been the solution of choice for most developers, and the ANSI Structured Query Language (SQL) has become a standardized dialect for interacting with these databases. Although many database vendors have added and extended the ANSI version of SQL in several different directions, the core operations are still pretty much the same in any engine you choose to work with.

In the beginning, developers would construct their SQL statements as strings in their application code and then ultimately pass that to a database driver for execution. This approach worked fine and was used by many, many applications. But as time progressed and the object-oriented (OO) revolution took hold, there was a desire to interact with the underlying data store in a more OO manner. At this point, object-relational mapping (ORM) systems were born.

Today, you can find ORM implementations in nearly every programming language, and they often take different forms and routes of design. In this regard, both Scala and Lift are no different. The Scala ecosystem has numerous ORM-style interfaces to SQL stores, and Lift provides two implementations: Mapper and its younger brother Record.

This chapter will demonstrate how to leverage Mapper to create, query, update, and delete records in a database, including how to pull back the covers and write some more granular SQL if the need arises. It will also cover how to define relationships between tables to abstract SQL joins so they're simply lazy collections available on a given Mapper entity. Moreover, you'll see how to define validation for individual data fields and ensure that all the necessary requirements have been satisfied, before trying to flush the instance back to the store.

Before moving on to interacting with the database, you need to get set up and configured with a database system. The following section walks you through setting up PostGreSQL but also provides configuration information for other database types if you'd prefer to use one of the other options supported by Mapper.

10.1 Setting up a database

Before diving into the specifics of how to use the Mapper abstractions, you need to have a database to work with. Two databases have proven to be particularly popular in the open source space—MySQL (http://www.mysql.com/) and PostgreSQL (http://www.postgresql.org/)—whereas in the commercial fields, Microsoft SQL Server (http://www.microsoft.com/sqlserver/) and Oracle (http://www.oracle.com/us/products/database/index.html) are still very prevalent. Despite each of these products making use of extensions to the SQL standard and implementing a slightly different dialect for commonly used operations, Mapper ships with drivers for each of these database stores and a whole set of others (Derby, H2, MaxDB, Sybase, Sybase ASE), so you can move platforms with the minimum of fuss.

With that being said, this chapter is written on the assumption that you'll be using PostgreSQL, but the examples should still perform admirably with MySQL, SQL Server, and others. PostgreSQL is a great choice as a relational database. It's very fast, very stable, and has a lot of advanced features that will see you through from small startup applications right up to large-scale enterprise usage.

10.1.1 Installation and connectivity

There are many convenient ways to install PostgreSQL, no matter what platform you're using. The primary route is to head over to the official download page (http://www.postgresql.org/download/) and grab the one-click installer for your operating system. If you're using Mac OS X, there are also packages available for both the Homebrew (http://mxcl.github.com/homebrew/) and Mac Ports (http://www.macports.org/) installation systems, which make getting up and running a breeze. Where possible, I would suggest that Mac users install via Homebrew because it will give you the most seamless experience and will require no additional compilation or configuration of dependent libraries. Linux users should also consider looking in their package manager for the appropriate database packages, which will likely be the simplest route of installation.

In order to start utilizing the Mapper persistence system with your application, you must first add the correct dependencies to your SBT project. Mapper is a separate module of Lift because not all applications require database access, so to have the classes load in your project you need to add the following dependency to your project definition:

```
val mapper = "net.liftweb" %% "lift-mapper" % liftVersion
```

Depending upon your choice of database access, you may require an additional dependency for the database driver itself.[1] This is true for nearly every database type, and in the case of PostgreSQL, the dependency should be as follows:

```
val postgresql = "postgresql" % "postgresql" % "9.0-801.jdbc4"
```

Don't forget that if you're already running SBT, you'll need to call the `reload` and `update` commands so that SBT will fetch the new dependencies for you and apply them to the classpath. If you see errors about Mapper types not being available, it's highly likely you need to update your dependencies.

Once you've installed and booted PostgreSQL and applied the necessary dependencies to your project, you must configure the application to connect to the backend database upon booting up. If you have been following along from the beginning of the book, you may remember from chapter 3 (section 3.2) that there are two mechanisms for obtaining a connection to the database.

The first connectivity route is to obtain a connection via JNDI. When taking an application into deployment, this is generally the preferred route because then all the connection management can be handled by the servlet container and can usually be configured either via a container GUI or the server configuration. All you then need to do on the Lift side is add the following line of code to your `Boot` class:

```
DefaultConnectionIdentifier.jndiName = "jdbc/liftinaction"
```

This line specifies which JNDI data source you'd like to connect to, and Lift will then resolve this connection, provided it exists with the same name in your container, and connect to it.

The second connectivity route is to set up a direct connection that's created by your application on startup and torn down at shutdown. Lift provides the plumbing for this in the form of `StandardDBVendor` from the Mapper module. This class wraps

---

[1] Table 10.1 lists the dependencies required for different database types.

up all the common aspects of making a database connection, such as connection pooling, and provides a single extension point that only needs the fully qualified driver class name, connection string, and credentials. Implement the following:

```
objectDBVendor extends StandardDBVendor(
  Props.get("db.class").openOr("org.h2.Driver"),
  Props.get("db.url").openOr("jdbc:h2:database/chapter_ten"),
  Props.get("db.user"), Props.get("db.pass"))
```

The interesting thing here is that rather than hard-coding the connection details, they're externalized into a properties file that can be altered for different deployment environments. Chapter 15 details the specifics of the run modes, but for the moment just understand that the db.class will have a set value from the external .props file, or if that value is missing, the application will fall back onto H2 and attempt to make a local database on the filesystem. This is a really common idiom in Lift development, because it allows you to use one type of database during development and another in production. For example, many people like to use H2 locally during development or testing and then swap to a server-based database in production.

It can often be confusing determining which connection strings and driver combinations to use with which databases, but table 10.1 lists some of the most popular configurations for the four most popular database types: H2 (often used in development), PostgreSQL, MySQL, and Microsoft SQL Server.

Table 10.1 Commonly used connection settings for server-based data sources. These were the latest versions at the time of writing, but newer versions will inevitably become available, so check with the driver vendor.

Database	Connection parameters
H2	Dependency:
	`val h2 = "com.h2database" % "h2" % "1.3.146"`
	Driver:
	`org.h2.Driver`
	Connection URL:
	`jdbc:h2:database/yourdb`
PostgreSQL	Dependency:
	`val pg = "postgresql" % "postgresql" % "9.0-801.jdbc4"`
	Driver:
	`org.postgresql.Driver`
	Connection URL:
	`jdbc:postgresql://localhost/yourdb`

Table 10.1 Commonly used connection settings for server-based data sources. These were the latest versions at the time of writing, but newer versions will inevitably become available, so check with the driver vendor. *(continued)*

Database	Connection parameters

MySQL	Dependency:
	
	`val mys = "mysql" % "mysql-connector-java" % "5.1.12"`
	
	Driver:
	
	`com.mysql.jdbc.Driver`
	
	Connection URL:
	
	`jdbc:mysql://localhost/yourdb`

MS SQL Server	Dependency:
	
	`val jtds = "net.sourceforge.jtds" % "jtds" % "1.2.2"`
	
	Driver:
	
	`net.sourceforge.jtds.jdbc.Driver`
	
	Connection URL:
	
	`jdbc:jtds:sqlserver://localhost:1433/`
	`yourdb;instance=Thing`

Once you have the database settings configured, the final step in database setup is actually getting the application to make the connection during the boot up part of the applications lifecycle.

```
if (!DB.jndiJdbcConnAvailable_?){
  DB.defineConnectionManager(
    DefaultConnectionIdentifier, DBVendor)
  LiftRules.unloadHooks.append(() =>
    DBVendor.closeAllConnections_!())
}
```

The first three lines of code check to see if an appropriate JNDI connection can be resolved, but if not, it will attempt to create a new connection to the database using the DBVendor object outlined earlier in this section. The last two lines instruct Lift to close all the database connections when Lift starts shutting down.

Now that you have an active connection to the database, let's start creating some entities to utilize it.

10.1.2 *Defining Mappers*

For the most part, Mapper follows what is known as the Active Record pattern. In practice, this means that each entity represents a concrete table in the database, and the inner objects of that entity define the columns in the table.

Each Mapper entity generally comes with two parts: the first is the `Mapper` instance, which typically represents the data rows that the table holds. This is a good place to include helper methods that operate on a given instance; for example, given a `Person` Mapper, a possible action method would be `wave`. The second part is the `MetaMapper`. The `MetaMapper` is defined as an object and typically provides additional services on top of the `Mapper` instance—things such as lifecycle hooks and methods to find datasets (more on this in section 10.2).

In order to demonstrate Mapper's usage in this chapter, you'll be working with a fairly straightforward three-table model that represents a simplified version of the relationship between publishers, authors, and books. Figure 10.1 visualizes this entity relationship.

Conceptually speaking, the diagram in figure 10.1 shows the two relationships at play. There's a one-to-many relationship from the `Publisher` entity to `Book`, because publishers nearly always release a wide selection of titles. The second relationship is the many-to-many relationship between the `Book` and `Author` entities. This relationship is due to the fact that authors often end up writing many titles, so to keep the data effectively normalized it's extrapolated into the additional table. Section 10.1.3 specifically covers how to make relationships with Mapper, but before that let's study the construction of the `Publisher`, `Book`, and `Author` entities.

As the simplest model in this example is `Publisher`, let's address it first. The next listing shows the definition for the `Publisher` entity.

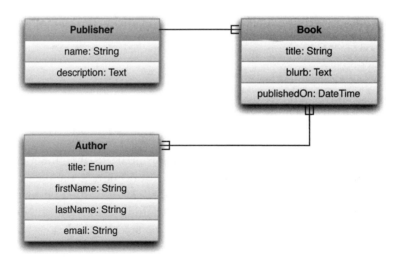

Figure 10.1   Relationship diagram for the entities deployed in this chapter. Any given publisher has many books in publication, and a single book can have many authors who may have contributed to many books. This diagram outlines the conceptual relationships; the implementation will differ slightly.

```
import net.liftweb.mapper._

class Publisher extends LongKeyedMapper[Publisher]
    with CreatedUpdated with IdPK {
  def getSingleton = Publisher

  object name extends MappedString(this, 255)
  object description extends MappedText(this)
}

object Publisher extends Publisher
  ➥with LongKeyedMetaMapper[Publisher]{
  override def dbTableName = "publishers"
}
```

1 Common traits

2 Specialized field types

3 Meta object

Earlier in this section we touched on the concept of having both an *instance* implementation and a companion, or *meta* implementation of any given Mapper entity. The first thing defined here is the instance implementation. It simply defines a Scala class and extends `Mapper[T]`. You may have noticed that in this instance `Publisher` actually extends a trait called `LongKeyedMapper[T]`, rather than a plain `Mapper[T]`; this is for convenience. It's common for an entity to have a field called ID that has an auto incrementing `Long` value, so rather than repeatedly add this field, it's inherited from the `LongKeyedMapper` trait. This is just one way that common idioms have been factored into compositional traits.

In addition to extending `LongKeyedMapper`, this example also mixes in the `CreatedUpdated` trait **1**, which will add two fields to this Mapper: a `DateTime` field called `createdAt`, which has its value set (unsurprisingly) when the entity is first persisted to the database, and a field called `updatedAt` that has its `DateTime` value updated automatically whenever changes are persisted. The second trait that's inherited here is `IdPk`. Given that this Mapper inherits `LongKeyedMapper`, it will have an ID column, so the `IdPk` trait applies a constraint to make that ID column the primary key in the database.

Next, the `Publisher` class defines the entity fields (database columns), and it's where the bulk of your Mapper instances will usually fall. You can see here that there are two separate fields defined as inner objects of the main class. All Mapper field types follow the naming convention `Mapped<Type>`; here `MappedString` and `MappedText` are used **2**. Under the hood, `MappedString` will boil down to a `varchar(max)` or similar column type, depending upon the database, whereas `MappedText` will save down to a text BLOB and thus is capable of handling far more data than a simple string.

Lastly comes the definition of the meta, or companion object, for this Mapper **3**. You create an object that extends the `LongKeyedMetaMapper` trait, which is the opposite number of the `LongKeyedMapper` inherited by the class definition. Notice how it extends the class definition, which gives you the `object Publisher extends Publisher` syntax. Some users find this a little confusing and prefer to name the companion `MetaPublisher` or something like that. There's no hard and fast rule you must obey here—the choice in naming is largely a matter of personal preference. In section 10.2, you'll see how to construct queries and use the functionality defined on the companion object, and there you'll see why many users find it more intuitive to give both the class definition and the companion the same type of name. Whatever you decide, the `getSingleton` method of the class instance must reference the appropriate companion object.

The `Publisher` type is a pretty simple implementation, so let's now consider the `Book` and `Author` entities, which use some additional Mapper features. The following listing shows the implementation for the `Book` and `Author` models.

Listing 10.2 Implementation of the Book and Author models

```
import net.liftweb.mapper._

class Book extends LongKeyedMapper[Book]
    with CreatedUpdated with IdPK {
  def getSingleton = Book
  object title extends MappedString(this, 255)
  object blurb extends MappedText(this)
  object publishedOn extends MappedDate(this)          ①  Using MappedDateTime type
}

object Book extends Book with LongKeyedMetaMapper[Book]{
  override def dbTableName = "books"
}

class Author extends LongKeyedMapper[Author]
    with CreatedUpdated with IdPK {
  def getSingleton = Author
  object title extends MappedEnum(this, Titles)         ②  Using MappedEnum
  object firstName extends MappedString(this, 255)
  object lastName extends MappedText(this)
  object email extends MappedEmail(this, 150)           ③  Using MappedEmail
}

object Author extends Author with LongKeyedMetaMapper[Author]{
  override def dbTableName = "authors"
}

object Titles extends Enumeration {
  val Mr, Mrs, Miss, Dr = Value
}
```

Here the implementation of `Book` is also pretty simplistic, and it follows a similar pattern of usage as the `Publisher` entity. The only notable difference is the use of a new mapped field type: `MappedDate` ①. As the name implies, this field type boils down to the date type supported by the backend database. Often this is a `datetime`, but the time element is ignored when saving the value.

Once again, the `Author` entity treads the same path as `Publisher` and `Book` by using a class definition and a companion object. The interesting thing with `Author` is that it uses two new field types: `MappedEnum` ② and `MappedEmail` ③. These types are specifically interesting because they model additional context over and above simply storing a string or value. `MappedEnum` allows you to define a strongly typed enumeration of values that are valid for use with this column. In this instance, it's a simple enumeration of salutations, but the database is only storing the identifier of the enumeration value, not the values "Mr" or "Mrs" and so on.

`MappedEmail`, on the other hand, is an extension of the standard `MappedString` implementation. You may well be wondering what the value of having a different concrete type for an email address verses a regular string is, because ultimately an email *is* a string. Although this is true, there are many things you might want to do with an email address, such as validating that it's an email address and not just a random string of numbers and letters. By using this approach, you can have rich column types in your entities and get access to a whole set of helpers, depending upon the abstraction. Table 10.2 shows a list of rich column types available at the time of writing and includes a short description and example usage for each.

Table 10.2 The `MappedField` subtypes available in the `Mapper` package

Field type	Description and usage
`MappedBirthYear`	Holds the year of a person's birth. The implementation must include a minimum page parameter, and the field will only accept years of birth that make the user older than the supplied value. `object birthday extends MappedBirthYear(this, 18)`
`MappedCountry`	A subtype of `MappedEnum` that is used to represent a single country from the list of countries defined in `net.liftweb.mapper.Countries`. There is also a utility method called `buildDisplayList` that will generate a select input element of the countries for you automatically. `object country extends MappedCountry(this)`
`MappedEmail`	Represents a string that's an email address. Supports out-of-the box validation for email patterns. The email regex itself is held in the companion object: `MappedEmail.emailPattern`. `object email extends MappedEmail(this, 200)`
`MappedGender`	Another extension of `MappedEnum` where `net.liftweb.mapper .Genders` provides the generic male or female enumeration of gender. `object gender extends MappedGender(this)`
`MappedLocale`	Saves a representation of `java.util.Locale`, and allows you to return the value as a `Locale` instance via `isAsLocale`. `object locale extends MappedLocale(this)`
`MappedPassword`	Stores user passwords as encrypted hash values. The underlying database will have two columns: the hash value and the random salt used to generate that hash. `MappedPassword` fields allow you to test a value against the stored value by using the `match_?("passwordinput")` method. `object password extends MappedPassword(this)`

Table 10.2   The `MappedField` subtypes available in the `Mapper` package (continued)

Field type	Description and usage

`MappedPostalCode`	Stores a postal code string value for a particular country. You must provide a `MappedCountry` member as a reference.
	
	`object postcode extends`
	`    MappedPostalCode(this, mappedCountry)`

`MappedTimeZone`	A stored representation of `java.util.TimeZone`. In much the same way as `MappedLocale` provides a method to obtain the concrete representation of the `Locale` type, `MappedTimeZone` can yield values as an actual `TimeZone` instance by using the `isAsTimeZone` method. `object timezone extends MappedTimeZone(this)`

In order to satisfy the original entity relationship diagram laid down in figure 10.1, you'll need to implement the relationships between the Mapper entities. As it stands right now, each entity lives in isolation with no way to communicate with its peers. It's time to add relationships to the Mapper implementations.

10.1.3 *Relationships*

The original proposition was to use two different types of relationships. The first was a one-to-many relationship with a publisher having many book titles, and the second was a many-to-many relationship because many authors could feasibly have authored or contributed to many different books. Table 10.3 summarizes the three most common types of relationships.

Table 10.3   Types of relationships commonly used with RDBMS

Relationship	Description
One-to-one	In a one-to-one relationship, the tables are associated in such a way that the record in the first table can only have a single corresponding row in the secondary table. An example of this sort of implementation would be having a list of capital cities and relating them to a country table. A capital city can only have *one* country and vice versa.
One-to-many	One-to-many is probably the most common of all relationship types and the most frequently used by developers. An example use case would be when modeling a book publisher: the publisher publishes many different titles, so *one* book publisher has *many* books.
Many-to-many	In a many-to-many relationship, it's said that each side of the relationship has and belongs to many of the other entity. For example, it's feasible for an author to have written many books with many different publishers. This means that there would be a many-to-many relationship between publisher and author because each side of the relationship can both have and belong to *many* instances of the other entity.

With this in mind, Mapper supplies a few different ways to make these relationships happen. Let's start by exploring the one-to-many structure between publishers and books.

ONE-TO-MANY

In order to facilitate the one-to-many relationship, you need to make a couple of changes to both the `Book` and `Publisher` models, as shown in the following listing.

> **Listing 10.3 Adding `OneToMany` to the `Publisher` model**

```
class Publisher extends LongKeyedMapper[Publisher]
    with CreatedUpdated with IdPK
    with OneToMany[Long,Publisher] {
  ...
  object books extends MappedOneToMany(Book, Book.publisher)
}

class Book extends LongKeyedMapper[Book]
    with CreatedUpdated with IdPK {
  ...
  object publisher extends LongMappedMapper(this, Publisher)
}
```

The first thing happening in this listing is the additional composition of the `OneTo-Many` trait into the `Publisher` class definition. The `OneToMany` trait provides an inner class called `MappedOneToMany` that can then be used as many times as needed within that class to define one-to-many relationships to other Mapper entities. In this instance, only the `Book` relationship exists, and you can see its definition as an object called `books`. `MappedOneToMany` takes two parameters: the entity that's the child collection of this entity (`Book` in this case), and the foreign key on the target entity that relates to the parent entity (in this case, `Publisher`). This should be a fairly familiar approach for anyone familiar with SQL.

Of course, with the `Publisher` model now looking for a foreign key on the `Book` instance, you need to add a `LongMappedMapper` to the `Book` definition to satisfy the relationship on both sides. You can see that it extends `LongMappedMapper` and passes a reference to the `Publisher` companion object.

> **TIP**   At the time of writing, Lift did not have a specific trait for handling one-to-one relationships, because the functionality can be encompassed by the `OneToMany` trait. If you require a one-to-one relationship, simply use the `One-ToMany` trait.

Out of the box, Lift ships with prebaked abstractions for making foreign keys that are of type `Long`, but in the unlikely event that you need to make a foreign key that's based on another type (like `String`, for example) you can make up your own `MappedForeign` type that extends both `MappedForeignKey` and `BaseForeignKey` and implements similar functionality to `MappedLongForeignKey`.

MANY-TO-MANY

The next relationship is the many-to-many relationship needed to model many authors having many books, and books potentially having multiple authors. The many-to-many relationship is implemented much like that in any other RDBMS-backed system, in that it requires a join table to operate. Put simply, an intermediate table is required to hold information that relates the authors with multiple books and vice versa. In this instance, the join table holds ID numbers for both sides of the relationship.

In practical terms, this means it's necessary to create a Mapper representation of this intermediary table. The following listing shows the intermediate table's definition.

Listing 10.4   Definition of the `AuthorBooks` join table

```
class BookAuthors extends LongKeyedMapper[BookAuthors] with IdPK {
  def getSingleton = BookAuthors
  object author extends LongMappedMapper(this, Author)
  object book extends LongMappedMapper(this, Book)
}

object BookAuthors extends BookAuthors
    with LongKeyedMetaMapper[BookAuthors]
```

This join table looks a lot like the other entities you've already defined. The only slight difference here is that it uses plain `Mapper` and `MetaMapper`, rather than the `LongKeyedMapper` and `MetaMapper`. The main points of interest are the `author` and `book` fields, as these fields reference the `Author` and `Book` entities using the already-familiar `LongMappedMapper`.

With the join table in place, you need to make a couple of adjustments to the `Author` and `Book` entities to make them both aware of the relationship set up between them via the join table. Mapper comes with a trait called `ManyToMany`, which (unsurprisingly) is a container for the field type that handles many-to-many relationships. Let's apply the `ManyToMany` trait to the `Book` and `Author` entities, as shown in the next listing.

Listing 10.5   Adding the `ManyToMany` trait to the `Author` and `Book` entities

```
class Book extends LongKeyedMapper[Book]
    with CreatedUpdated with IdPK
    with ManyToMany {
  ...
  object authors extends MappedManyToMany(         ❶ Implement
    BookAuthors, BookAuthors.book,                     authors
    BookAuthors.author, Author)
}
class Author extends LongKeyedMapper[Author]
    with CreatedUpdated with IdPK
    with ManyToMany {
  ...
  object books extends MappedManyToMany(           ❷ Implement
    BookAuthors, BookAuthors.author,                   books
    BookAuthors.book, Book)
}
```

Both classes in this listing now inherit the ManyToMany trait, which provides the correct MappedManyToMany field type needed to deliver the correct collection semantics. In order to implement MappedManyToMany, a field is added to each entity that references its opposite number in the relationship. For example, the Book entity has an authors object ❶ that passes four parameters to the MappedManyToMany field: the entity representing the join table, the foreign key for this entity, the target foreign key, and the target entity companion, which in this instance is Author. The same is true for the Author entity, but the parameters passed to MappedManyToMany instead reference Book ❷.

The three entities are now constructed in accordance with the original proposal outlined in figure 10.1. Now it would be most helpful if Lift could create the tables in the database for us. Fortunately, there's a solution for this in the form of Schemifier.

10.1.4 *Schema creation and control*

During the development phase of a project, the database schema can often be in moderate flux as fields are added or altered. To this end, it can be quite helpful for the corresponding database schema to be updated as well. Mapper provides a tool called Schemifier for exactly this purpose.

In order to use Schemifier, you need to register the relevant entities in your boot class, as shown:

```
if(Props.devMode)
  Schemifier.schemify(true, Schemifier.infoF _,
    Author, BookAuthors, Book, Publisher)
```

Provided this call is specified after the database connection call, this one line of code will attempt to connect to the specified database and create or alter the tables based upon changes to the passed entity definitions.

> **NOTE** The database will only be updated or affected when the application is running in development mode.

The first argument required by the Schemifier object is a Boolean that determines whether or not the tables will actually be written to the database. The second parameter is a logging function that comes with Schemifier by default, and there are two possible options: Schemifier.infoF, which will log the actual SQL statements that Schemifier is trying to use, and Schemifier.neverF which will disable logging of these creation statements. When logging is enabled, you'll see output like this in the console:

```
INFO - CREATE TABLE book_authors (author BIGINT , book BIGINT)
INFO - ALTER TABLE books ADD COLUMN publisher_id BIGINT
INFO - CREATE INDEX book_authors_author ON book_authors( author )
INFO - CREATE INDEX book_authors_book ON book_authors( book )
INFO - CREATE INDEX books_publisher_id ON books ( publisher_id )
```

As you can see here, Schemifier is creating tables and adding columns and even indices. By default, Schemifier uses the field names defined in the entity for the names of the database columns, but there are situations where you may not want this, or you may want to assign a different name for operational reasons. Mapper supports this with a combination of approaches.

Like the global `LiftRules` configuration object that controls Lift's WebKit, Mapper has its own configuration object called `MapperRules`. This object primarily controls the interaction with the backend database, and naming is one of those control systems. Consider the following:

```
import net.liftweb.util.Helpers
MapperRules.columnName = (_,name) => Helpers.snakify(name)
MapperRules.tableName  = (_,name) => Helpers.snakify(name)
```

These two lines essentially instruct Mapper to address the database using column and table names that use snake case—words separated by underscores in the place of spaces. For example, an object field called `updatedAt` would be translated to a column name of `updated_at`.

Although this covers many common practices, there are situations where you'd prefer the underlying database to differ entirely from a given field name. For example, in relationships, a lot of developers prefer to have the foreign key use column names suffixed with "_id". In the case of the many-to-many join table outlined in listing 10.3, you might prefer to keep the collection named `publisher` but have the column named `publisher_id` rather than just `publisher`. In order to do this, you can override the `dbColumnName` method on any given Mapper field as shown:

```
object publisher extends LongMappedMapper(this, Publisher){
  override def dbColumnName = "publisher_id"
}
```

The usefulness here should be apparent. This method is present in every `Mapped-Field` subtype, so you can override the actual column name on a field-by-field basis if you wish. As it happens, each field supplies several things that you might want to override. The available options are shown in the next listing.

Listing 10.6 Optional overrides to control common database interaction

```
object exampleThing extends MappedString(this, 50){
  override def dbColumnName = "custom_name"
  override def dbIndexed_? = true
  override def dbForeignKey_? = false
  override def dbNotNull_? = true
  override def dbPrimaryKey_? = false
  override def ignoreField_? = false
  override def writePermission_? = false
}
```

Here you can see some field methods provided by `MappedField` that change the behavior of the underlying database column during schemification and querying. The methods themselves are very self-explanatory so you shouldn't need too much additional information. There are other options available, but these are the most commonly used controls.

Now that you have an appreciation for designing and constructing Mapper entities, the next section will show how you can interact with Mapper, run queries on the database, and work with the resulting data set.

10.2 Interacting with Mapper

Now that the Mapper entities are defined and the database schema has automatically been generated, you're left with a fresh, empty database complete with all the necessary tables. This section covers the controls provided by Mapper for constructing, querying, updating, and deleting records in the backend database. Section 10.2.1 details how you can insert data into the database purely by interacting with the Mapper entities, and section 10.2.2 demonstrates the different ways in which you can use Mapper to construct type-safe queries, or even write your own SQL statements directly.

Let's start by inserting some data into the database using the Mapper entities.

10.2.1 Creating data

Given a Mapper entity, there are some standard mechanisms for inserting content into the backend database. In order to demonstrate this Mapper functionality, you'll need to use the SBT `console` command. In practice, this means you'll be able to interact with the database live, right from within the terminal window.

To get started, type `console` at the SBT shell. Provided all your code compiled without errors, this will load the Scala REPL with all your entities on the classpath. Once that's loaded, you'll first need to run the following command to configure your Lift environment and then import the model classes (assuming you used the package name `sample.model`).

```
scala> new bootstrap.liftweb.Boot().boot
scala> import sample.model._
```

There will be a slight pause while the `Boot` class executes, and depending upon your setup, you may see console output from the `Schemifier`. When that's complete, consider the first entity you created, `Publisher`, and enter the following command:

```
Publisher.create.name("Manning").description("What a great company")
```

This creates a new instance of the `Publisher` class with the specified field content. Every call to the `apply` method on a field returns the instance of the Mapper entity, which allows you to write this chained-field notation. The REPL will likely output something similar to this:

```
res3: sample.model.Publisher = sample.model.Publisher={createdAt=Sun,
➥2 Jan 2011 17:05:25 UTC,updatedAt=Sun, 2 Jan 2011 17:05:25 UTC,
➥id=-1,description=What a great company,name=Manning}
```

Notice specifically how the values of `createdAt` and `updatedAt` have been set. This is due to the `CreatedUpdated` trait that was composed into the entity earlier, in listing 10.1.

This is all well and good, but at this point the instance hasn't been saved, and the database is still untouched. There are a couple of ways to save the instance:

```
scala>Publisher.create.name("Manning").description("Great company").save()
res5: Boolean = true

scala>Publisher.create.name("Manning")
➥.description("Great company").saveMe()
res6: sample.model.Publisher = sample.model.Publisher={...}
```

The first command here saves the entity to the database and returns a true value if the operation is successful. The second command calls saveMe, which returns the resulting instance as opposed to a Boolean. This can be helpful if you need to continue to work with the same entity after it has been saved. Both of these operations are capable of throwing exceptions if there was a fatal error in conducting the insert operation.

You can see that adding a single record to a table is pretty straightforward, but you may be wondering how you can add to the collections representing OneToMany and ManyToMany. That's fairly simple too:

```
scala> val manning = Publisher.create.name("Manning").saveMe
manning: sample.model.Publisher = sample.model.Publisher={...}

scala>Book.create.title("Lift in Action").publisher(manning).saveMe
res14: sample.model.Book = sample.model.Book={...}
```

Continuing the example of creating records here, the first command creates a new Publisher and persists it to the database. The returned instance is assigned to the value manning. The second command creates a new Book instance and explicitly assigns the publisher field, with the Publisher instance saved in the manning value.

Although this is fairly explicit, you may prefer a more collection-oriented API. The exact same process can be expressed with the following alternate syntax:

```
scala>manning.books += Book.create.title("Another book")
scala>manning.books.save
```

The LongMappedMapper field (books) defined on the Publisher instance defines the += method, which allows you to append Mapper instances of the foreign key type—in this case, Book. This collection-style syntax is exactly the same for many-to-many relationships.

Now that you've seen how to create data and insert it into the database, let's start exploring how you can query for specific records and load data dynamically.

10.2.2 *Querying data*

The vast majority of applications spend time doing reads rather than writes, and there are many different ways that you can obtain data using raw SQL. Mapper supports several of these mechanisms, but as with nearly all ORM systems, there is a point when writing SQL directly is a more practical approach. This section covers the various methods you can use to access data with Mapper, and it also touches upon how you can write SQL directly if you so wish.

For the most part, all querying for an object of a specific type is done via the entity companion object, and there are two primary methods that facilitate queries: `find` and `findAll`. The former will only ever find a single record and will always return a `Box[YourMapper]`, whereas `findAll` returns a `List[YourMapper]`.

To start, let's use the `find` method and assume you know the primary key for the record you're looking for:

```
scala>Publisher.find(10)
res26: Box[sample.model.Publisher] = Full(sample.model.Publisher={... })
```

Using the `find` method on the companion object, it's possible to find the record by its primary key. This is nice, but perhaps not all that useful because you'll often want to find a row by one or more field values. For this, Mapper has `By` parameters.

Let's assume you want to find a publisher by the name field alone, and only return a single result:

```
scala>Publisher.find(By(Publisher.name, "Manning"))
res28: Box[sample.model.Publisher] = Full(Publisher={...,name=Manning})
```

Notice here that the `find` method is passed the `By` instance that first takes the field type for which this constraint is based upon, and secondly takes the constraining value. The `By` parameter (and its negative counterpart, `NotBy`) will work with any field type; you just have to supply the right type of expected value.

Here are some more examples:

```
import java.text.{DateFormat => Df}

Book.find(By(Book.title, "Wind In The Willows"))

Book.find(By(Book.publishedOn, Df.getDateInstance.parse("March 10, 1908")))

Author.find(NotBy(Author.email, "demo@demo.com"))
```

The key thing to observe here is that the constraint system is completely type-safe; you couldn't look for a string field and accidentally pass it a `java.util.Date` or other type.

In addition to the regular `By` class, there are other types of `By` parameters, as outlined in table 10.4.

Table 10.4 Details of the other `By` parameters available in Mapper query constructs

Type	Description and usage

ByList	Often when retrieving something from the database, you'll need to address multiple columns in order to obtain the correct result. Mapper lets you pass several fields in addition to the regular `find` syntax:
	
	`Book.findAll(ByList(Book.title,`
	`    "Lift in Action" :: "Scala in Depth" :: Nil))`

Table 10.4 Details of the other `By` parameters available in Mapper query constructs *(continued)*

Type	Description and usage
`By_>` and `By_<`	Another common idiom is operating on records that are either less than or greater than a certain constraint. The `By_<` and `By_>` methods get you exactly that. `Book.findAll(By_<(Book.publishedOn, date))`
`ByRef` and `NotByRef`	The `ByRef` mechanism looks for equality in two field values *on the same entity*. This can sometimes be helpful for creating tree-like structures or self-referencing table joins. For example, given a tree structure, you could do the following: `TreeNode.findAll(ByRef(TreeNode.parent, TreeNode.id))`

`BySql`	There are times when it makes more sense to write the SQL for the WHERE clause directly, such as if you have a calculation best expressed in SQL. With this tool, you can retrieve Mapper instances however you like, provided it returns a compatible result with the calling Mapper entity. This means that you can't return a `List[Dog]` from the `Cat` Mapper. Note that the second parameter is the special IHaveValidatedThisSQL type. This forces the developer to check that the SQL is operational and secure, and to put their name and date by it for accountability purposes.
	
	`Book.findAll(`
	`BySql("created_at > (CURRENT_DATE - interval '2 days')",`
	`IHaveValidatedThisSQL("tperrett", "2010-01-02")))`

`BySql` (with parameter values)	The other method for using `BySql` allows you to use placeholders in the SQL statement, so that the passed values are properly escaped and your code stays safe from SQL injection attacks. The placeholders in the SQL statement are question marks (?). You must still pass the `IHaveValidatedThisSQL` type, and then your parameter values in the order that you wish them to be replaced in the SQL statement.
	
	`Book.findAll(BySql("id BETWEEN ? AND ?",`
	`IHaveValidatedThisSQL("tperrett", "2010-01-02"),`
	`  start, end))`

However you choose to implement your query, the resulting instance of the `find` method will always have a `map` and `flatMap` function, either from the `Box[Mapper]` or `List[Mapper]` result type, and as such, the usage pattern is very similar for either `find` or `findAll` Mapper query constructs coupled with any of the `By` locators.

Let's now investigate how to actually use the resulting values once you've retrieved an instance from the database. The following listing details such an example.

Listing 10.7 Accessing values of a Mapper instance returned from the database

```
import net.liftweb.mapper.By

val manning = Publisher.find(
  By(Publisher.name, "Manning"))
```
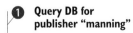 **❶** Query DB for publisher "manning"

```
val name = manning.map(_.name.is).openOr("unknown")

for {
  publisher <- manning
  book <- publisher.books.all
} yield book.title.is.openOr("No Name")

val book = Book.find(By(Book.title, "Lift in Action"))

book.flatMap(_.publisher.obj.map(_.name)).openOr("No Publisher")
```

This listing demonstrates a couple of different operations using a specific publisher instance once it has been retrieved from the database ❶. The first technique is for accessing a specific field (or set of fields) but that provides a default value in case the database call was not successful or yields no results. Note the specific use of the `is` method on the `name` field. All `MappedField` subtypes have an `is` method for obtaining the value they contain, which in this case is a `String`.

The second, and slightly more complex example, utilizes a *for comprehension* to grab the list of book titles this publisher has available. By calling the `all` method on the `books` `MappedOneToMany` collection, Mapper will retrieve the list of book entities. There is a slight hitch with this, however, in that Mapper will retrieve the list of books in an arbitrary way, with no particular ordering. You can apply a `QueryParam` to the `MappedOneToMany` definition to ensure that it always pulls back the results in alphabetical order (for example); this is more efficient than sorting the results in memory with a Scala `sortBy` call. To achieve this, adjust the `books` collection like so:

```
object books extends MappedOneToMany(Book, Book.publisher,
OrderBy(Book.title, Ascending))
```

You can append any number of query parameters to the definition to control the returned result.

> **WARNING**   There is a slight gotcha with using the `all` method, in that once it has been called for the first time in the scope of a given execution, the result is cached. Any updates you make to the child collection won't be represented until you call the `refresh` method to repopulate the result set.

The final example in listing 10.7 demonstrates the reverse method for traversing up the collection and determining the publisher's name given only a `book` instance. The `Book` entity has a `LongMappedMapper` defined called `publisher` that acts as the foreign key to the `Publisher` entity. You can just ask the `publisher` field for the corresponding instance by using the `obj` method. The `obj` method will return a `Box[Mapper]` instance of the parent type.

Now that you have the basics of retrieving records, let's explore some of the other query parameters that are available, like `OrderBy` and `Distinct`, by using the `findAll` method in some more examples.

QUERY PARAMETERS

Earlier in this section, you briefly saw how you could use query parameters to apply additional behavior to the Mapper relationships. But that isn't the end of the story for query parameters, because they encapsulate a lot of additional functionality you might want to apply to a SQL statement, both in terms of value comparison and control. Table 10.5 details the available query parameters and relevant samples of how you can use them in the context of a Mapper query statement.

Table 10.5   Optional query parameters for controlling the query your Mapper entity will execute

Query parameter	Description and usage

In	The In query parameter allows you to control the selection of records in exactly the same way you usually would with the IN SQL keyword.
	
	`Book.findAll(`
	`   In(Book.publisher, Publisher.id,`
	`      Like(Publisher.name, "Man%"))).map(_.title)`

InRaw	The InRaw parameter allows you to specify your own SQL for the subquery part of the IN *only*. The offshoot of this is that there are usually some additional massaging steps required to get the exact result you want. If you'd rather push this back to the database engine and write more complex queries, see listing 10.7 for information on `findAllByInsecureSql` and `findAllByPreparedStatement`.
	
	`Book.findAll(InRaw(`
	`Book.publisher,`
	`   "SELECT id FROM publishers`
	`    WHERE created_at >`
	`       (CURRENT_DATE - interval '2 days')",`
	`IHaveValidatedThisSQL("tperrett", "2010-01-02")))`

Like	Once again, this query parameter is a direct representation of the SQL keyword and is used to retrieve wildcard patterns from your data set. Assuming you had a list of Manning books in the database, you could search for all the "in Action"-style books using this simple expression: `Book.findAll(Like(Book.title, "% in Action"))`
StartAtandMaxRows	It's often useful to create systems that have a paginated view, or perhaps you need to collect a ranged subset of data. StartAt and MaxRows provide you an abstraction for specifying limited ranges of data. `Book.findAll(StartAt(10),MaxRows(10))`

OrderBy	OrderBy does exactly what it says on the tin and sorts the result set by the passed field in ascending or descending order.
	
	`Book.findAll(OrderBy(Book.title, Ascending))`
	`Book.findAll(OrderBy(Book.title, Descending))`

OrderBySql	If the regular OrderByQueryParam doesn't give you what you want, you may wish to use OrderBySql instead to gain some additional control.
	
	`Book.findAll(`
	`   OrderBySql("created_atDESC, title DESC",`
	`      IHaveValidatedThisSQL("tperrett", "2010-01-02")))`

Table 10.5 Optional query parameters for controlling the query your Mapper entity will execute *(continued)*

Query parameter	Description and usage
PreCache	Finally we come to `PreCache`. When Mapper loads an entity that has a foreign key defined, the foreign key isn't usually evaluated until it's requested. That is to say, it's lazily loaded. There are situations where you may know that you're going to be accessing this collection so preloading the results of the foreign key can be advantageous instead of executing additional queries later on. `Book.find(By(Book.id, 5), PreCache(Book.publisher))`

Although working with query parameters provides you a fair level of control, this may still not quite be enough, or perhaps the SQL being generated isn't optimal for your particular data set. In this situation, you can execute SQL directly on the underlying database.

DIRECT SQL EXECUTION

The entities you've defined so far are essentially type-safe abstractions on a low-level access to the JDBC data store. There are a couple of different levels at which you can execute your own, custom SQL. The first involves using the `findAllByInsecureSql` method on your entity companion object. For the second, you throw away your entities and interact with the `net.liftweb.mapper.DB` object instead. The `DB` object is far "closer to the metal" than the entity abstractions shown thus far, but there are pros and cons to both approaches.

When you need to retrieve a particular set of data that fits into an already defined entity, using `findAllByInsecureSql` is probably your best bet. A good use case would be if you needed to find a group of records by using some complex aggregated function, but ultimately the result was compatible with (for example) the Book entity. In that case, having a `List[Book]` is quite helpful, because you can achieve the lookup you want but still retain the Mapper helpers and all the functionality therein. The following listing shows an example.

Listing 10.8 Using the `findAllByInsecureSql` method

```
Author.findAllByInsecureSql("""
    SELECT *
    FROM authors
    WHERE email LIKE '%@demo.com'
    OR email LIKE '@another.co.uk'""",
  IHaveValidatedThisSQL("tperrett","2010-1-2"))
```

As you can see in the listing, this SQL specifically deals with authors, so it makes sense to return `Author` instances. The complexity here was more in the specific SQL expression for retrieving the desired data set, rather than it being an ad hoc query that didn't fit into the predefined entities.

If the query you want to execute was not directly related to a specific entity, or if it encompasses several tables in the result, you may consider using the DB object directly to run the SQL statement. The only downside here is that you get a raw Tuple2(List[String], List[List[String]]) as the result, which means you have to fish the values out of the structure accordingly. The following listing shows an example of using the DB object to execute a query.

> **Listing 10.9   Running a query directly using the DB object**

```
importnet.liftweb.mapper.DB

val result = DB.runQuery("""
    SELECT * FROM authors
    WHERE email LIKE '%@demo.com'
    OR email LIKE '@another.co.uk'""")
```

This listing details the same SQL query as listing 10.8, but this time it's being run directly with the DB object by using the DB.runQuery method. The DB object is essentially the core of all database connections in Mapper, and later in section 10.3 you'll see how you can use it to build transactions and talk to multiple databases.

Now that you have a good understanding of how to read records from the database using Mapper's query constructs, let's move on to updating and deleting.

10.2.3 *Updating and deleting data*

There will come a time when you want to update or delete some data in your application. Fortunately, this is pretty simple and builds on what we've already covered with regard to reading data.

The first thing you need to do in order to update a particular database entry is to obtain an entity instance to make changes to, and from there you can set new values into the fields and call save or saveMe, exactly as you did to create the records in the first place. Consider the following console session:

```
scala> val manning = Publisher.find(By(Publisher.name, "Manning"))
manning: Box[Publisher] = Full(Publisher={...})

scala>manning.map(_.name("Manning Publications").saveMe)
res88: Box[Publisher] = Full(Publisher={..., name=Manning Publications})
```

That's all there is to it! Simply obtain the Mapper entity instance that you wish to modify, pass the data to the appropriate fields, and call save.

Deletion is a little different. Let's consider a basic example:

```
scala> val manning = Publisher.find(By(Publisher.name, "Manning"))
manning: Box[Publisher] = Full(Publisher={...})

scala>manning.map(_.delete_!).openOr(false)
res94: Boolean = false
```

The important thing to note here is the delete_! method. The _! suffixed to the end of the method is an indication that it's a dangerous method and should be used with care.

Deleting a single record is quite straightforward. But what if you needed to delete lots of records? Well, each entity companion has a method called `bulkDelete_!!` just for this kind of task:

```
Book.bulkDelete_!!(Like(Book.title, "% in Action"))
```

As you can see, the usage is simple and once again makes use of the query parameters to define the subset of records that should be deleted. In this example, the query would delete all records from the `books` table where the `title` was an *in Action* book.

You may be wondering what happened to other records that referenced these rows. As it stands, they're effectively orphaned because there is no constraint to cascade delete operations to dependent rows. This is an easy fix, though, because you can add some additional code to the foreign key constraints in the `Publisher` entity, as follows.

Listing 10.10 Adding cascading deletes to the `Publisher` entity

```
class Publisher extends LongKeyedMapper[Publisher]
    with CreatedUpdated with IdPK
    with OneToMany[Long,Publisher] {
  ...
  object books extends MappedOneToMany(Book, Book.publisher,
      OrderBy(Book.title, Ascending))
    with Owned[Book]
    with Cascade[Book]                        ❶ Define cascade
}                                                requirement
```

In order to properly cascade the deletion from `Publisher` down to `Book`, you need to compose the `Owned` and `Cascade` traits into the `books` `MappedOneToMany` collection ❶. With this change in place, whenever you delete a `Publisher`, their books will also be removed.

> **TIP** At the time of writing, there is a slight gotcha with the way cascading deletes work. The `MappedOneToMany` field isn't actually a field, so there's nothing to initialize it before it has been touched by your calling code, because all object initialization in Scala is lazy. Just ensure that you touch the books field before calling `delete_!` in order to see the cascading delete operate as intended.

That's pretty much all you need to know about updating and deleting entity records with Mapper. It's surprisingly straightforward.

You've now got the Mapper relationships set up, and you're freshly versed in create, read, update, and delete operations, so the next things to look at are validation and lifecycle callbacks.

10.2.4 *Validation and lifecycle callbacks*

Most applications require validation, whether it's something simple like ensuring that a field has a value, or something more complicated like applying a custom regular expression to ensure that an entry conforms to a specific pattern. Mapper supports a set of validations out of the box for common use cases, such as minimum string length and regular expressions, but creating your own validation methods is trivial.

The second thing this section covers is the lifecycle of Mapper entities. Each Mapper can specify functions that should be executed at different stages in its own lifecycle. For example, you could specify functions that run beforeSave, afterSave, and a whole lot more. By defining these functions, you're passed the current Mapper instance and can then create any function you want.

VALIDATION

To get started, let's add a minimum-length validation to the Author firstName field. The following listing shows the changes required for the Author entity.

Listing 10.11   Adding validation to the Author entity

```
class Author extends LongKeyedMapper[Author]
    with CreatedUpdated with IdPK
    with ManyToMany {
  ...
  object firstName extends MappedString(this, 255){
    override def validations =                          ❶ Apply validation
      valMinLen(3,                                         function
        ➥ "Name must be at least 3 characters") _ :: Nil
  }
  ...
}
```

In this listing, you override the validations method ❶ and supply one of the prebaked validation functions: valMinLength. As the name suggests, this function validates the minimum length of the string value the field contains. Some of the other field types will automatically validate themselves: for example, MappedEmail will validate itself as an email address. But given a type such as MappedDouble, you'd need to construct your own validation method to suit your business logic.

The following listing shows an example of building your own validation function. This one can be applied to book titles to ensure users can only add books that have a title ending with *in Action*.

Listing 10.12   Adding custom validation to Mapper fields

```
import net.liftweb.util.{FieldIdentifier,FieldError}

object Validations {
  def onlyInActionBooks(field: FieldIdentifier)
    ➥ (string : String) =                               ❶ Custom
    if(!string.toLowerCase.endsWith("in action"))          method
      List(FieldError(field, "Not an in action book?"))
    else List[FieldError]()
}

class Book extends LongKeyedMapper[Book]
    with CreatedUpdated with IdPK with ManyToMany {
```

```
...
object title extends MappedString(this, 255){
  override def validations =
    Validations.onlyInActionBooks(this) _ :: Nil
}
...
}
```

❷ Apply validator

In this listing, you create another object called `Validations` and build a method called `onlyInActionBooks` ❶. The custom validation is then applied by overriding the `validations` method on the field ❷. As you can see, the method does a very basic bit of logic to check that the string value ends with "in action". Note that if the string doesn't end with "in action", the method returns a `List[FieldError]` containing a message that would be displayed to the user on the frontend. Although trivial, this same approach would work well for any custom validation you might want to apply in your own applications.

To round off this section, let's take a tour of the lifecycle functionality each Mapper supports and implement an example to demonstrate the idiom used for all callback points.

LIFECYCLE CALLBACKS

Each and every Mapper entity has a set of lifecycle callbacks that can be used to execute a list of functions at different points in the entity's lifecycle. Figure 10.2 shows the various points you can hook into.

There are five lifecycle states, each of which has a before and after hook. Table 10.6 details the various states.

Table 10.6 Mapper lifecycle states

State	Description
Create	Whenever a call to `YourEntity.create` is made, the before and after hooks are executed at the appropriate time.
Save	When a new record is added to the database; essentially surrounding the `INSERT` procedure.
Update	When a record for the given Mapper instance already exists in the database, and the content is modified and saved. Equivalent to a table `UPDATE` procedure.
Validation	Strictly speaking, `validate` can be called at whatever point is best for your application. Calling the `validate` method triggers all the validation rules for each field within the entity and the lifecycle methods wrap this operation.
Delete	Whenever there is a call to `delete_!` for this Mapper instance.

With this in mind, listing 10.13 demonstrates how to implement the lifecycle hook for `beforeSave` and `afterSave` in the companion object of `Book`.

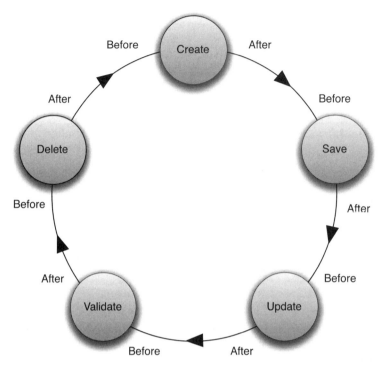

Figure 10.2 **Illustration of the different phases a Mapper can go through and where you can execute different functions around this process. Strictly speaking, the process doesn't flow from one to another in such an intrinsic way, but this details the lifecycle effectively.**

Listing 10.13   Implementing the `beforeSave` and `afterSave` lifecycle hooks

```
object Book extends Book with LongKeyedMetaMapper[Book]{
  ...
  override def beforeSave = List(book =>
    println("About to save '%s'".format(book.title.is)))

  override def afterSave = List(book =>
    println("I've saved!"))
}
```

The lifecycle hooks are implemented in the companion object of Book, and you can see here in the listing that the method override defines a list of functions, with each function being passed the correct instance of the entity in turn. After implementing this, whenever you save a new record, you should see the messages print to the console.

10.2.5 *Display functionality*

In addition to being a frontend to your database, Mapper also provides richer abstractions for data types than your typical database allows. Earlier in section 10.1.2, you heard about the richness of field types and how they can represent more than just plain types, such as string—you can add meaning to a field by using `MappedEmail`, for example, which provides some context about what that string actually does or means. As an extension to this idea, Mapper also allows these rich fields to render themselves as form types.

For example, imagine a `MappedEnum`. It knows right out of the box that its default course of action is to render itself as a `<select>` element with the options from the enumeration. `MappedString`, on the other hand, generates a generic `<input type="text />`. In essence, you can quickly create frontends to Mapper entities by utilizing their ability to render themselves as HTML markup. In addition, Mapper has close integration with `LiftScreen`—so much so that `LiftScreen` can render a complete form with only a couple of lines of code.

You'll be using the `Book` entity for this example, so before we look at how to implement the Mapper `toForm` method, make the change shown in the next listing to the `publisher LongMappedMapper`.

Listing 10.14 Generating a select box from a foreign key

```
import net.liftweb.common.Full

object publisher extends LongMappedMapper(this, Publisher){
    ...
    override def validSelectValues =
      Full(Publisher.findMap(                                      ❶ Build select
        OrderBy(Publisher.name, Ascending)){                        input
        case p: Publisher => Full(p.id.is -> p.name.is)
      })
  }
```

The small change to the model here ❶ essentially tells Mapper how it can obtain the correct information to display in a drop-down select input from the foreign reference object. In this case, it grabs a list of publishers ordered by name and makes the value of the select list their database ID field.

Now that this small bit of plumbing is done, you can implement the following snippet:

```
import net.liftweb.common.Full
import sample.model.Book

class Demo {
  def example = Book.findAll.head.toForm(Full("Submit"), { _.save })
}
```

This one liner is purely for example purposes. In reality, you'd likely obtain the Mapper instance by some slightly more useful means than grabbing the top one in the list, but the purpose here is to show that given a Mapper, you only need to call `toForm` to generate the form markup, inputs, and everything you need. Figure 10.3 shows what this code generates in the browser.

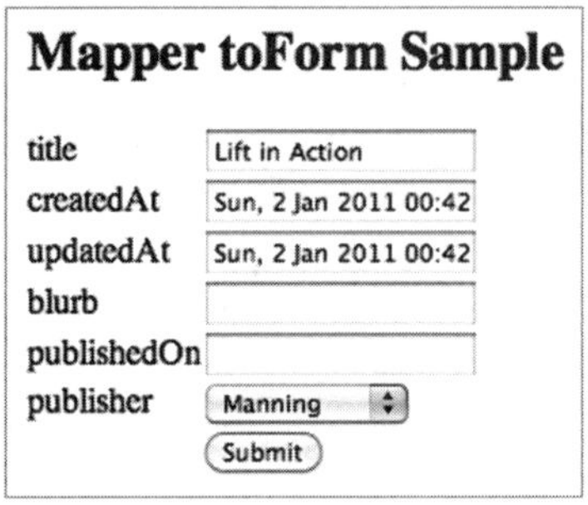

As you can see, with this one line of code you have a fully functioning update form. As it stands, the field names aren't ideal, but all that's required is to override the `displayName` method of the various form fields, and Mapper will use those instead of the raw field names.

Mapper toForm Sample

title	Lift in Action
createdAt	Sun, 2 Jan 2011 00:42
updatedAt	Sun, 2 Jan 2011 00:42
blurb	
publishedOn	
publisher	Manning ⬍

(Submit)

LIFTSCREEN INTEGRATION

In addition to the `toForm` support that Mapper has, it also has great integration with `LiftScreen` and `Wizard`, meaning that you can build fully functional forms with minimal code and get baked-in functionality, such as validation presented right next to the input fields.

Figure 10.3 Example of the one-line form generated by Mapper

The following listing shows how to implement `LiftScreen` just by using a Mapper.

Listing 10.15 Building a `LiftScreen` with only a `Mapper`

```
import net.liftweb.http.{LiftScreen,S}
import sample.model.Book

object BookScreen extends LiftScreen {
  object book extends ScreenVar(                    ❶ Load Mapper
    ➥Book.find(1) openOr Book.create)                 instance

  addFields(() => book)                              ❷ Register with
                                                       LiftScreen
  def finish(){
    if(book.save) S.notice("Saved!")
    else S.error("Unable to complete save...")
  }
}
```

This is a basic implementation of using Mapper with `LiftScreen`. First, the entity is loaded into a local `ScreenVar` ❶, though you wouldn't call `find(1)` in your code—you'd hopefully load something more meaningful!. Then that entity is registered with the screen ❷. This technique will subsequently display all the fields defined on that Mapper.

If, however, you only want to register certain fields, you can just register the ones you want rather than the top-level object:

```
addFields(() => book.title)
addFields(() => book.blurb)
```

The particular benefit of the `LiftScreen` approach over using the previously illustrated `toForm` is that you get better control over templating, validation, and a whole host of other things, so it's best to use `LiftScreen` over `toForm` where you can.

In the past two sections, you've seen the majority of the Mapper functionality. The next section takes a look at some of the more advanced features of Mapper, from query and performance logging, through to transactions and creating your own custom field types.

10.3 Advanced Mapper

When your development reaches a certain stage, you may find yourself needing to tune some of your queries or maybe create a custom field that represents part of your own problem domain as an intrinsic part of the Mapper model. This section addresses these types of concerns and shows you how to implement query logging with Mapper so you can see what SQL is being executed in the lifecycle of a request. You'll also see how to grab metrics from query executions, which you could either log or pass to a monitoring tool. In addition, you'll see how you can use Mapper to construct transactions containing operations that must all succeed or all roll back.

First up, though, let's take a look at the query logging support that Mapper offers and build a sample atop the entities you created earlier in this chapter.

10.3.1 Query logging

When structuring your application and migrating from development to production, it can often be important to get a handle on the queries that your ORM system is generating, because it may be making inefficient choices that aren't specifically tailored to your data set. Mapper provides hooks for logging the queries generated by Mapper and for delivering performance statistics on the length of any given query execution.

Like many things in Lift, functionality often boils down to simple functions. In this instance, Mapper isn't any different because it has the concept of logging functions. Each function is of type (DBLog, Long) => Any, where DBLog is an encapsulating type containing information about the query, and the Long is the time of execution.

Before exploring this any further, let's take a look at an example. The following listing shows how you can use the query log

Listing 10.16 Implementing a Mapper logging function

```
import net.liftweb.util.LazyLoggable
import net.liftweb.mapper.{DB,DBLogEntry}

class Boot extends LazyLoggable {
  def boot {
    ...
    DB.addLogFunc((query, time) => {
      logger.info("All queries took " + time + " milliseconds ")
      query.allEntries.foreach((e: DBLogEntry) =>
        logger.info(
          e.statement + " took " + e.duration + "ms"))
    })
    ...
  }
}
```

❶ Log all queries in this request

During the application boot phase, you can add your own custom logging functions so that every time Mapper makes a query, it will be logged as you see fit. In this example, notice that the Boot class inherits the LazyLoggable trait, and thus gains access to the logger value and the ability to send messages at different levels to the logging backend.

The important definition block starts with the DB.addLogFunc invocation. The DB.addLogFunc method expects the logging function discussed earlier as its argument. In this example, you can see that the query and time parameters pass to a block that executes the logging calls. The query object is actually an instance of DBLog, which is a special query logging type that contains information about the things Mapper is doing. Here the code calls the allEntries method, which returns a list of DBLogEntry. This list is subsequently iterated through using foreach, and each log entry has the statement executed and the duration of execution dumped to the log ❶.

If you boot up the console and start running queries, you'll see output similar to the following:

```
INFO - All queries took 52 milliseconds
INFO - Exec query "SELECT publishers.name, publishers.id,
    publishers.description, publishers.created_at, publishers.updated_at
    FROM publishers WHERE id = 1" :
    org.postgresql.jdbc4.Jdbc4ResultSet@2c3474d6 took 44ms
INFO - Closed Statement took 0ms
```

As you can see, this is a direct dump of the SQL query and specifically what Mapper is doing.

Many nontrivial applications require transactions to ensure consistency in their application data. We'll look at that next.

10.3.2 Transactions

A transaction is a process in which you have multiple queries to execute, but if one of the operations fails or for some reason can't be applied, all the other operations must be rolled back to their state before any query execution began, ensuring that the data set remains consistent.

The classic example is that of bank accounts. Suppose person A has 10 pounds in their bank account, and person B has 5 pounds in theirs. If person B had to pay person A 5 pounds, person A would have 15 pounds and person B would have none. This transaction would succeed, but consider a second transaction of another 5 pounds from person B to person A. Person B would be unable to pay this (assuming overdrafts aren't allowed), so you'd need to make sure that person A's bank balance wasn't updated if the debit from person B's account failed. This is exactly the kind of scenario that transactions were designed for. In the scope of any given transaction, the operations either all succeed or they all fail with no side effects.

Mapper supports transactions with the DB.use block. Operations are defined in the block, and unless an exception is raised, the block is committed to the database.

Implementing the `DB.use` block in the bank account scenario would look something like this:

```
DB.use(DefaultConnectionIdentifier){ connection =>
  account1.deposit(5)
  account2.withdraw(5)
}
```

In this example, the value of 5 pounds is being taken from `account2` and added to `account1`. Let's take a moment to look at the Mapper implementation for this `Account` entity, as shown in the next listing.

Listing 10.17   Implementing the Account entity

```
import net.liftweb.mapper._

object Account extends Account with LongKeyedMetaMapper[Account]{
  override def beforeSave = List(_.validate)                          ◁──① Apply
}                                                                          validation

class Account extends LongKeyedMapper[Account] with IdPK {
  def getSingleton = Account
  object balance extends MappedLong(this){
    override def validations =
      AccountValidations.notLessThanZero(this) _ :: Nil
  }
  def deposit(value: Long) = updateAndSave(value)
  def withdraw(value: Long) = updateAndSave(-value)        ② Implement helper
  def updateAndSave(value: Long) =                            methods
    balance(balance.is + value).save
}

import net.liftweb.util.{FieldIdentifier,FieldError}

object AccountValidations {
  def notLessThanZero(field : FieldIdentifier)
  ⇢ (amount : Long) =                                      ③ Define validation
  if(amount < 0) throw new Exception(                        method
  ⇢"Cannot be less than zero. You need money!")
  else List[FieldError]()
}
```

The `Account` entity is really no different from the other entities you've built throughout this chapter. First, this listing utilizes the lifecycle methods to automatically enforce validation upon saving the record ①. The validation it applies is a custom validation method defined separately in the `AccountValidations` object ③, which ensures that the balance value is greater than 0; if the validation fails, it throws a generic exception. This is important because the `DB.use` block should not commit if one of the balance values is lower than 0, and in order for this to take effect, an exception must be thrown. Finally, to make usage simpler the Account entity also implements two helper methods, `deposit` and `withdraw` that update the value of balance accordingly ②.

Let's load up the console and play with this new entity:

```
scala> val account1 = Account.create.balance(5).saveMe
account1: sample.model.Account = sample.model.Account={id=1,balance=5}

scala> val account2 = Account.create.balance(5).saveMe
account2: sample.model.Account = sample.model.Account={id=2,balance=5}

scala>DB.use(DefaultConnectionIdentifier){ connection =>
      |   account1.deposit(5)
      |   account2.withdraw(5)
      | }
res1: Boolean = true

scala>DB.use(DefaultConnectionIdentifier){ connection =>
      |   account1.deposit(5)
      |   account2.withdraw(5)
      | }
java.lang.Exception: Cannot be less than zero. You need money!
at sample.model.AccountValidations$.notLessThanZero(Account.scala:29)
```

Notice how two account records were created and their balance values were assigned as 5. The first attempt at the transaction completed without issue, because there were sufficient funds in the bank account to make the transaction, but the second attempt failed and the database value wasn't updated.

The last advanced topic to be covered in this section is creating your own custom field types. Mapper comes with a whole set of fields that will cover the majority of your use cases, but there may be situations where you want to go beyond those fields.

10.3.3 Custom mapped fields

Mapper ships with many different field types, but there may come a time when you'd like to construct your own representation of a field, perhaps either extending one of the regular types, like `MappedString`, or making something completely new. Whichever you want to do, most things should be possible, provided you can boil the type down to a SQL-compatible value and store the piece of data in an RDBMS.

Imagine if you will, a specialized field type that uses column aggregation to represent two database fields with a single `MapperField` subtype. Consider a field that represents a user's first and last names in a `name` field in the Mapper entity, but stores the values as two distinct columns. Figure 10.4 illustrates such a proposal.

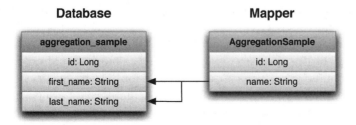

Figure 10.4   Field aggregation from the Mapper model (right) to the database table (left)

As you might imagine, this is more complex than a regular one-column, one-field save operation. But Mapper gives you a fairly reasonable abstraction with which to work. In order to execute the aggregation, you need to give Mapper some additional information about the columns and how they should be addressed. To that end, let's get started by making the implementation for `MappedSplitString`.

The following listing details an example of aggregation implemented in a Mapper entity.

Listing 10.18   Implementing column aggregation with Mapper, part 1

```scala
import scala.xml.Elem
import net.liftweb.mapper._
import net.liftweb.common.{Box,Full,Empty,Failure}
import net.liftweb.util.FatLazy
import net.liftweb.json.JsonAST
import net.liftweb.json.JsonAST.JString
import net.liftweb.http.S
import net.liftweb.http.js.{JE,JsExp}
import java.sql.Types
import java.lang.reflect.Method
import java.util.Date
abstract class MappedSplitName[T<:Mapper[T]](
  val fieldOwner: T,
  val maxLen: Int) extends MappedField[String, T] {      ❶ Specify class
                                                              types
  def dbFieldClass = classOf[String]

  override def dbColumnCount = 2
                                                         ❷ Specify column
  override def dbColumnNames(name: String) =                constraints
    List("first","last").map(_ + "_" + name.toLowerCase)

  def targetSQLType = Types.VARCHAR

  override lazy val dbSelectString =
    ➥dbColumnNames(name).map(cn =>
    fieldOwner.getSingleton._dbTableNameLC + "." + cn
    ).mkString(", ")

  override def jdbcFriendly(column: String) =
    if(column.startsWith("first_"))
      firstName.get
    else if(column.startsWith("last_"))         ❸ SQL converters
      lastName.get                                 and generators
    else null

  def real_convertToJDBCFriendly(
    ➥value: String): Object = value

  def fieldCreatorString(
    ➥dbType: DriverType, colName: String): String =
    colName+" "+dbType.varcharColumnType(maxLen) +
    notNullAppender()

  def defaultValue = ""
```

```
override protected[mapper] def doneWithSave(){}

protected def i_obscure_!(in : String) : String = ""

override def _toForm: Box[Elem] = Empty
override def toForm: Box[Elem] = Empty

def asJsExp: JsExp = JE.Str(is)

def asJsonValue: Box[JsonAST.JValue] = Full(is match {
  case null => JsonAST.JNull
  case str => JsonAST.JString(str)
})

  ...

}
```

As the code required to manufacture your own column is quite large, this listing has been split into two parts. This first dollop of code outlines the custom field and inherits from MappedField. This means there's a set of methods that you must implement in order to satisfy the MappedField abstract methods, and the first part is where you tell Mapper what type of class the value of this field will be ❶: in this case, it's a simple String. Second, you have to give Mapper some information about the columns and field types the database should use ❷. As this is an aggregate column, you can instruct Mapper to use two fields and make them of type VARCHAR (or whatever type is appropriate for your fields).

Now that Mapper is aware of the types on both sides (database and code), you must describe how this new field is to be addressed. It's feasible that your implementation might use some vendor-specific SQL. For example, if you wanted to wrap some special type up with SQL Server's embedded XML query language, you could then instruct Mapper how it should build that query using the methods defined at ❸.

You may have noticed that the code in listing 10.18 pretty much only deals with describing the fields and not with setting or handling values. The following listing contains the second half of the code.

Listing 10.19 Implementing column aggregation with Mapper, part 2

```
abstract class MappedSplitName ... {
  ...

  private var firstName = FatLazy(defaultValue)          ❶ Internal
  private var lastName = FatLazy(defaultValue)              state

  private def wholeGet = "%s %s".format(
    firstName.get, lastName.get)
  override def i_is_! = wholeGet                          ❷ Getters
  protected def i_was_! = wholeGet
  override def readPermission_? = true

  override def writePermission_? = true

  override def real_i_set_!(value : String): String = {   ❸ Setters
    value.split(" ") match {
      case Array(first, last) =>
```

```
        firstName.set(first)
        lastName.set(last)
      case _ => ""
    }
    this.dirty_?(true)
    wholeGet
  }

  override def setFromAny(in: Any): String = {
    in match {
      case JsonAST.JNull => this.set(null)
      case seq: Seq[_] if !seq.isEmpty =>
        seq.map(setFromAny).apply(0)
      case (s: String) :: _ => this.set(s)
      case s :: _ => this.setFromAny(s)
      case JsonAST.JString(v) => this.set(v)
      case null => this.set(null)
      case s: String => this.set(s)
      case Some(s: String) => this.set(s)
      case Full(s: String) => this.set(s)
      case None | Empty | Failure(_, _, _) =>
      this.set(null)
      case o => this.set(o.toString)
    }
  }

  def apply(ov: Box[String]): T = {
    ov match {
      case Full(s) => this.set(s)
      case _ => this.set(null)
    }
    fieldOwner
  }

  override def apply(ov: String): T = apply(Full(ov))

  private def wholeSet(in: String){
    real_i_set_!(in)
  }
}
```

❸ **Setters**

❹ **Set via apply**

This listing defines all the getting and setting operations for the field, essentially defining how it should handle different types and values. First, this class contains two internal variables that will hold the first and last parts of the person's name in this trivial example: `firstName` and `lastName` ❶. Next it defines the methods that will read the value whenever it's requested in calling code with the `is` method ❷. Finally, the rather large block methods that form the bulk of the class define how the field should respond on receipt of various types ❸.

Finally, to complete the listing, the `apply` methods allow fields to be set with `nameOfField("value")` notation ❹. These methods are essentially just proxies to the `set` methods defined earlier in the class ❸.

This section has shown you how you can create your own custom field types and even present aggregate columns as a single Mapper field that saves data into multiple

> **Why use setFromAny?**
>
> If you're looking at the code and wondering why the `setFromAny` method is set up like it is, there's a partly good reason for that. Mapper is one of the oldest parts of Lift, and like all projects that have been around for a while, the earlier parts have a different design than the newer components because trends and styles evolve over time. `setFromAny` may not be particularly idiomatic of Scala's type-safe approach, but it's idiomatic for Mapper and follows the conventions in other fields. Perhaps it's not ideal, but it's a solidified and supported API for now.

database columns. By providing Mapper with the information it needs to properly create the query for the underlying data store, you can essentially store whatever you like in a custom field type.

10.4 *Summary*

Throughout the course of this chapter, you've seen how you can utilize Mapper in your Lift project and how it can be quickly utilized to build effective applications, thanks to its close integration with other parts of the Lift framework.

The first thing to be explored was how to configure various types of database connections with Lift, and you also created a whole set of Mapper entities and explored the relationship constructs available, including the `OneToMany` and `ManyToMany` traits. By composing these traits into your Mapper entity definitions, you can gain access to other field types, such as `MappedManyToMany`, that abstract away what would otherwise be manual querying between objects. The entities defined here were also applied to the `Schemifier`, so that during development Lift will automatically adjust the schema of the database in accordance with the additions in your model, saving you the task of migrating tables by hand.

You also saw examples of Mapper's query syntax and how to make range queries, single queries, and build expressions that encompass custom constraints to retrieve specific batches of data. This section also covered how to execute raw SQL on the database via `DB.runQuery`.

The next chapter covers Record. Mapper predates Record by a couple of years, and Record brings with it support for modern NoSQL data stores, such as MongoDB, as well as a completely different approach to dealing with relational databases via the awesome Squeryl library.

Persistence with Record

11

This chapter covers

- Common Record anatomy
- Using Record for relational databases
- Using Record for NoSQL data stores

The previous chapter discussed Mapper and how you can use it to define an active-record style of interaction with a relational database. Mapper is one of the oldest parts of the Lift framework, and some of the ideas that were born in Mapper eventually evolved into another persistence system called Record and Field, or Record for short.

Record builds upon the idea of having contextually rich fields in your data model, but allowing you to interact with any data storage mechanism. This data storage could be a relational database, a NoSQL solution such as MongoDB, or even something as primitive as a filesystem. Record is ultimately a specialized persistence facade designed to make the development of web applications more intuitive, no matter which system is actually doing the persistence.

This chapter discusses the anatomy that all Record facades share, irrespective of their storage mechanism or actual function. Many parts of Record have been influenced directly by its initial vision of "keeping the meaning with the bytes." You'll see how Record shares and improves upon concepts from Mapper and gives you a contextually rich wrapper around different persistence technologies and libraries.

One of the backends currently shipping with Record is called Lift-Squeryl, which provides the ability to interact with relational database systems via a Scala JDBC library called Squeryl (http://squeryl.org/). Squeryl provides a type-safe syntax for statements, and you can be sure that if your code compiles, the statement will successfully execute. This negates the all- too-common runtime issues that plague other ORM or database abstraction systems.

> **NOTE** Over the past three years, the so called NoSQL movement has become increasingly prevalent as many developers building web applications face both the issue of applications becoming write-oriented (resulting from the prevalence of social media), and the move to solve the inherent impedance mismatch between the application domain and ORM tools.

One of the major advancements of Record over Mapper is its ability to address both relational and nonrelational backend systems. With such nonrelational systems now being more widely adopted, Record comes with interfaces for the popular MongoDB (http://www.mongodb.org/) and CouchDB (http://couchdb.apache.org/) databases.

Before getting into any specific backend implementation of Record, though, let's walk through the common anatomy of a Record and see some of the functionality you get right out of the box.

11.1 *Common Record functionality*

In order to get started with Record, it's important to understand its package structure and its derivative modules—its anatomy. Figure 11.1 shows the package structure at the time of writing.

The lift-record JAR essentially provides you with an abstract base of traits and classes that act as building blocks for specific backend implementations. An application that implements it wouldn't typically include lift-record as a dependency directly; rather, it would be transitively resolved by the implementation you are using. For example, Lift Couch would be added to your project by including the following line, which negates the need to explicitly include the Record dependency:

```
val couch = "net.liftweb" %% "lift-couch" % liftVersion
```

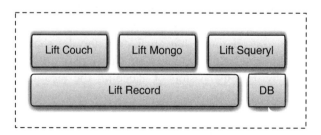

Figure 11.1 The package structure of Record and derivative projects

It's almost certain that you'll be working with a persistence store, but for the moment, let's assume that you don't have a persistence store composed into your implementation. Even with no storage mechanism, you can still make Records that model validation and other semantics, and ignore the fact that the data isn't actually going anywhere. For the sake of this exercise, add the following record dependency to your project configuration:

```
val record = "net.liftweb" %% "lift-record" % liftVersion
```

The following listing shows a simplistic usage of Record that has no way of saving data but that allows for validation of the Record instance, among other things.

Listing 11.1 Basic implementation of Record

```
import net.liftweb.record.{MetaRecord, Record}
import net.liftweb.record.field.{LongField,
  OptionalEmailField, StringField}

class Example extends Record[Example] {
  def meta = Example                                        Class and meta ❶

  val name = new StringField(this, ""){
    override def validations =                                              ❷ Field with
      valMinLen(5, "Must be more than 5 characters") _ ::                      validator
        super.validations
  }
  val funds = new LongField(this)                           Other field
  val email = new OptionalEmailField(this, 100)         ❸  types
}

object Example extends Example with MetaRecord[Example]
```

This is one of the most basic Record implementations. As you can see, it's composed of two parts ❶ in much the same way Mapper entities are, having both the class definition extending Record[T] and the meta or companion object that extends Meta-Record[T].

The record system comes complete with a whole set of field types that again are conceptually similar to the MappedField subtypes from Mapper, with the distinct addition of optional field types ❸. Fields in Record also allow for validation semantics, and some of those are included in the Field type ❷. You can also implement your own custom validation methods where applicable. Section 11.1.1 covers fields in more depth.

Irrespective of the persistence system that you ultimately elect to use with Record, the general concepts and idioms are typically the same. Nearly all records implement create, read, update, and delete semantics and provide contextually rich field types to add more meaning to a field over and above its persisted type.

Even with the example in listing 11.1, it's possible to implement validation and use all the display helpers Record supplies. Consider the following console session:

```
scala> import net.liftweb.common._; import sample.model._
import net.liftweb.common._
import sample.model._
```

```
scala>Example.createRecord.name("Tim").email(Empty)
res3: sample.model.Example = sample.model.Example@30dbd621

scala>Example.createRecord.name("tim").validate
res4: List[FieldError] =
List(Full(name_id) : Must be more than 5 characters)

scala>Example.createRecord.name("timothy").asJSON
res5: net.liftweb.http.js.JsExp =
  {"name": "timothy", "funds": 0, "email": null}
```

❶ Validate record

❷ Serialize to JSON

Notice that it's still possible to validate the record by calling the validate method ❶ and even serialize it to a JSON structure automatically by calling asJSON ❷. This is an important point, because it means that all records, regardless of any other implementation details, come with a whole set of baked-in functionality, including the ability to serialize to and from JSON, render the record instance as markup, and automatically construct a record instance directly from an incoming request. This means that any derivative implementations get a fairly comprehensive set of functionality without having to create their own plumbing. All you have to do is build on top of the provided defaults in a way that's specific to the backend data store.

11.1.1 *Common Record fields*

One of the main goals of Record is to apply higher-level contextual information to the data being operated on. For example, consider a java.util.Locale class; this is often persisted to the data store as a string and then converted back and forth in application code from locale to string and string to locale. In situations like these, it makes sense for the field to have this slightly richer interface, where the field or attribute knows how to present you with the strongly typed version of a value rather than just String or some other nondescript type.

One of the main differences in field design in Record, when compared to Lift's Mapper module, is that field types are composed rather than solely relying on inheritance. This generally promotes more code reuse, and you'll see signatures similar to the following:

```
class BinaryField[O <: Record[O]](rec: O)
  extends Field[Array[Byte], O]
  with MandatoryTypedField[Array[Byte]]
  with BinaryTypedField
```

Specifically note how the generic field functionality is composed with Mandatory-TypedField and the BinaryTypedField traits in order to deliver the correct product for the BinaryField class. This gives you a more flexible system if (or when) you want to make your own custom field types: there is far less reinvention of the wheel than is found in Mapper.

The base field types supplied in the generic lift-record package are fields for concrete implementations (which are actually usable) and also fields you can use to build other store-specific field types. For example, MongoDB uses BSON-documents as part of its persistence system, so the Mongo-Record integration has specialized fields that build on these abstract fields to represent the specific functionality required by Mongo. Table 11.1 shows the fields supplied with the generic Record package.

Table 11.1 Field-related traits contained in Record. Some fields also have an optional sister-field type that takes the form `OptionalXX`, such as `StringField` and `OptionalStringField`. If the field type has an optional variant, it's noted in the second column.

Field type	Optional?	Description and usage (if applicable)
BaseField	No	All field types must extend `BaseField`. This trait supplies general semantics to any field, irrespective of data store. For example, it determines whether or not the field is writable.
TypedField	No	Fields requiring a value should extend this trait in order to supply the methods for setting and getting the contained value.
OwnedField	No	Fields that belong to a specific record (which is practically all fields) should extend this trait in order to propagate type information about the containing Record class.
DisplayWithLabel	No	As fields know how to render themselves to XHTML markup, compose this trait with your field in order to prefix a `<label>` element to the output markup.
BinaryField	Yes	For generically representing `Array[Byte]` in your backend store, use this field. `object sample extends BinaryField(this)`
BooleanField	Yes	This is a container field for Booleans; supply a default in the second argument. `object sample extends BooleanField` `(this, true)`
CountryField	Yes	Much like the Mapper country field, this field uses a predetermined list of countries from the `Record.Countries` enumeration. `object sample extends CountryField(this)`
DateTimeField	Yes	Date fields take a `java.util.Calendar` instance as their second parameter. Implicit conversions exist in `util.Helpers` between various date formats. `object sample extends DateTimeField(this,` `    java.util.Calendar.getInstance)`
DecimalField	Yes	The decimal field has two possible apply constructors. The verbose one detailed here includes a `MathContext`, but this is optional and you can simply supply the `BigDecimal` if you prefer. `object sample extends DateTimeField(this,` `    MathContext.UNLIMITED,` `    new java.math.BigDecimal(10.5))`

Table 11.1　Field-related traits contained in Record. Some fields also have an optional sister-field type that takes the form `OptionalXX`, such as `StringField` and `OptionalStringField`. If the field type has an optional variant, it's noted in the second column. *(continued)*

Field type	Optional?	Description and usage (if applicable)
`DoubleField`	Yes	This is a container field for a `Double` value. `object sample extends DoubleField(this, 1D)`
`EmailField`	Yes	This rich string field includes validation of the content string as an email address. `object sample extends EmailField(this, 90)`

`EnumField`	Yes	This field persists the value part of an enumeration and will only accept value types of the specified enumeration as input values.
		
		`object Thing extends Enumeration {`
		`  val One, Two = Value`
		`}`
		`object sample extends EnumField(this, Thing)`

`IntField`	Yes	`IntField` is a container field for an `Int` value. `object sample extends IntField(this, 5)`

`LocaleField`	Yes	This is a rich field that contains a `java.util.Locale` but is persisted as a serialized string, such as en_GB. Use the `isAsLocale` method to get the field value as a `Locale` instance.
		
		`object sample extends LocaleField(this,`
		`    java.util.Locale.UK)`

`LongField`	Yes	This is a container field for a `Long` value. `object sample extends LongField(this, 1L)`
`PasswordField`	Yes	This higher-level abstraction upon `StringField` contains both a salt field and a value field. Backends commonly extend this trait to utilize their own specific encryption or storage choices. `object sample extends PasswordField(this,"")`

`PostalCodeField`	Yes	This container field for postal codes persists its value as a string but comes with some validation semantics baked in for certain countries, and all values must be bigger than three characters.
		
		`object sample extends PostalCodeField(this,`
		`yourCountryField)`

`StringField`	Yes	This is a container field for a `String` value. All other fields based upon strings typically extend this field type. `object sample extends StringField(this, "")`

Table 11.1 Field-related traits contained in Record. Some fields also have an optional sister-field type that takes the form `OptionalXX`, such as `StringField` and `OptionalStringField`. If the field type has an optional variant, it's noted in the second column. *(continued)*

Field type	Optional?	Description and usage (if applicable)
TextareaField	Yes	This field represents string-based content, but the `toForm` method produces a `<textarea>` element as opposed to an `<input>`. `object sample extends TextareaField` `(this, 200)`
TimeZoneField	Yes	You can persist a `java.util.TimeZone` value and access the field's `TimeZone` representation directly by calling `isAsTimeZone`. The value defaults to the `TimeZone` of the hosting JVM. `object sample extends TimeZoneField(this)`

All the fields listed in table 11.1 can be chained together by the caller, allowing you to have a usage API that looks like this:

```
MyThing.createRecord.fieldOne("whatever").someThing(1234).another(9)
```

This can be a fairly powerful idiom, and it's supplied at the common level in Record, so all subsequent implementations follow the same style.

Now that you've seen some of the common fields, the next section explains how these fields can be used to generate interfaces automatically using `LiftScreen`.

11.1.2 Integration with LiftScreen and Wizard

Back in chapter 6 (section 6.3.1), you saw part of Lift's form-handling support: `Lift-Screen`. In that section, you learned how to manually construct fields in a declarative fashion, define validation rules, and so on. In chapter 10 (section 10.2.5), you then saw how `LiftScreen` interoperates with Mapper automatically by determining the field types and presenting the correct presentation format for that particular field. The good news is that both Mapper and Record share this functionality, and Record can also be used in conjunction with `LiftScreen` and its bigger brother Wizard:

```
import net.liftweb.http.{LiftScreen,S}
import sample.model.mongo.Book

object ScreenSample extends LiftScreen {
  object book extends ScreenVar(Book.createRecord)
  addFields(() => book.is)
  def finish(){ S.redirectTo("/") }
}
```

As you can see, it only takes a few lines of code to produce an input for all the fields in the Record instance.

Record differs from Mapper because many of the backend storage implementations provide custom field types and mandatory *hidden* fields as part of their infrastructure. A good case in point is MongoDB, which *must* have its _id column in order to operate correctly at a database level, but you wouldn't particularly want to present it to the user, so it normally makes more sense to construct the screen and list the fields you want to display explicitly.

In the case that you're using a storage system that has custom field types such as MongoDB's nested document structures, you may want to consider overriding the toForm method of the field to provide your own implementation for that display logic. By default, Lift assumes that these custom field types won't be used directly in a user interface as there is no way of knowing how they should (or could) be presented.

The first type of Record implementation we'll look at provides support for working with RDBMS, but it has a very unique approach that is distinctly different from that of Lift's Mapper module.

11.2   *Record for relational databases*

Relational database systems still dominate persistence systems in web applications today. For the vast majority of developers, having a flexible and intuitive interface to that relational database is key to their development.

Record is all about providing a persistence interface that allows you to plug in the technologies you want to work with, and the wider Scala community has several very sophisticated abstractions on top of the popular Java JDBC interfaces. One of these projects that already has a Record integration is called Squeryl (http://squeryl.org/).

Squeryl was designed to be a type-safe abstraction that allows you to compose statements that are checked at compile time. This allows you to be 100 percent confident that the SQL statements you write to access your data won't fail because of a runtime syntax error. Squeryl provides a declarative DSL for query construction that's intuitive and that allows for a high degree of code reuse. As it stands, the Record abstraction doesn't interrupt the Squeryl DSL or any of the querying tools; it simply wraps the entity definition and provides the rich contextual fields where you need them for building your web applications.

In order to get started with the Squeryl-Record module, simply add the following dependency to your project configuration:

```
val squeryl = "net.liftweb" %% "lift-squeryl-record" % liftVersion
```

Once the dependency is added, don't forget to call reload and then update in the SBT console, so that the appropriate JARs are downloaded. The Squeryl classes will also be transitively resolved and downloaded in addition to the Lift module.

11.2.1   *Connecting and querying with Squeryl*

Squeryl uses JDBC to talk to the database, and at a base level it simply requires an active java.sql.Connection to function. Conveniently, Lift has a set of abstractions on these common database interactions, and Squeryl can make use of them without any glue code.

In order to connect to the database, you must specify connection settings in exactly the same way you would for Mapper. As this was discussed at some length in chapter 11 (section 11.1.1), the following only includes a brief recap and assumes that you have a connection string set up. Specifically, you'll need some code that looks similar to this in your Boot class to obtain a connection:

```
if (!DB.jndiJdbcConnAvailable_?){
  DB.defineConnectionManager(DefaultConnectionIdentifier, Database)
  LiftRules.unloadHooks.append(() =>Database.closeAllConnections_!())
}
```

NOTE If you want transactional semantics over the whole request cycle with Squeryl, you need to do the same thing as with Mapper: add the S.add-Around(DB.buildLoanWrapper) call into your application Boot class.

With the connection in place, there is one final thing your Boot class must feature in order to tell Squeryl what type of database you'd like to talk to:

```
import net.liftweb.squerylrecord.SquerylRecord
import org.squeryl.adapters.PostgreSqlAdapter

SquerylRecord.init(() => new PostgreSqlAdapter)
```

Simply pass the SquerylRecord.init method a function that yields the correct database adapter, and you should be good to go. Squeryl provides its own dialect drivers to convert its own statement syntax into the appropriate SQL. Table 11.2 lists the other possible driver options.

Table 11.2 Alternative Squeryl database dialect adapters

Database	Driver class
IBM DB2	SquerylRecord.init(() => new DB2Adapter)
H2	SquerylRecord.init(() => new H2Adapter)
Microsoft SQL Server	SquerylRecord.init(() => new MSSQLServer)
MySQL	SquerylRecord.init(() => new MySQLAdapter)
Oracle	SquerylRecord.init(() => new OracleAdapter)

One of the other significant differences between Squeryl and Mapper is that Squeryl advocates manual schema upgrades and alterations; its makers believe conducting automated migrations is too risky. With this in mind, however, Squeryl does provide an initial schema creation tool, and the ability to output the current data definition language (DDL) defined by the Squeryl entities. It's not really feasible to have Squeryl attempt to create the database every time your application loads, because it would throw exceptions about the tables that already exist, but if you want to use Squeryl to create your schema on a one-time basis, you can make this call:

```
import net.liftweb.mapper.{DB, DefaultConnectionIdentifier}
  DB.use(DefaultConnectionIdentifier){ connection => Bookstore.create }
```

Because it's not a good idea to have this happening upon every application boot-up, it can be nice to log the DDL that Squeryl will attempt to use so you can either make the necessary alterations or disregard it as appropriate. In order to do that, simply add the following to your `Boot` class:

```
if(Props.devMode)
  DB.use(DefaultConnectionIdentifier){ connection =>  Bookstore printDdl }
```

In both these commands, the `DB.use` block is required because it ensures that the Squeryl operation is conducted in the scope of the database connection.

Now that you have Squeryl-Record configured and ready, let's reconstruct the bookstore example from chapter 10, including the relationships and queries, to use Squeryl. This will demonstrate some of the powerful features Squeryl and Record bring to the party.

11.2.2 *A bookstore with Squeryl*

The model for the bookstore will remain exactly the same as in chapter 10, with the entity relationship being as it was defined in figure 10.1. This requires you to implement three Squeryl entities: `Publisher`, `Book`, and `Author`.

Unlike Mapper, Squeryl defines a central `Schema` subtype that defines the table-to-class mapping. The following listing defines an example.

Listing 11.2 Defining a Squeryl schema

```
import org.squeryl.Schema

object Bookstore extends Schema {
  val authors = table[Author]("authors")
  val books = table[Book]("books")
  val publishers = table[Publisher]("publishers")
}
```

This `Schema` subtype calls the `table` method and has a type parameter of the implementing class. It's this very method that connects the class to the table definition. The first parameter of the `table` method allows you to define a specific name for that table, which is useful if you're working with a legacy schema or are very particular about how your tables are named.

This won't compile yet because the specified entities don't yet exist. Let's start by creating the `Publisher` entity and consider how that differs from the Mapper version defined in listing 10.1. The next listing shows the Squeryl-Record implementation of the basic `Publisher` entity.

Listing 11.3   Squeryl-Record implementation of the `Publisher` entity

```
import net.liftweb.record.{MetaRecord, Record}
import net.liftweb.record.field.{LongField, LongTypedField, StringField}
import net.liftweb.squerylrecord.KeyedRecord
import net.liftweb.squerylrecord.RecordTypeMode._
import org.squeryl.Query
import org.squeryl.annotations.Column

class Publisher private ()
  extends Record[Publisher]
  with KeyedRecord[Long]{

  def meta = Publisher

  @Column(name="id")                          ❶ Fields for
  val idField = new LongField(this, 1)            record
  val name = new StringField(this, "")
}

object Publisher extends Publisher with MetaRecord[Publisher]
```

In this `Publisher` entity, you can first see that the constructor is made `private` and the class extends both `Record` and a special Squeryl-Record type called `KeyedRecord`. The class constructor is marked `private` so that new Records can't be constructed by way of the new `Publisher` method, which could interfere with the way in which Record introspects the field values. It's generally a good idea to mark the constructor `private`, which will then give you compile-time failures if you try to use the new keyword; Record instances should always be created using the `Publisher.createRecord` method to avoid these issues. In addition to the class definition, note that, like the Mapper implementation, Squeryl-Record has both an instance and a companion, or meta object.

Next, you can see two examples of implementing fields with Record ❶. Squeryl-Record has a slight nuance in that `KeyedRecord` already implements an `id` method, so you need to implement `idField` and provide the `@Column` annotation from the Squeryl distribution so that the `idField` correctly uses the ID column on the appropriate database table.

In order to complete the picture, let's define the remaining two entities and take a look at their relationships. The following listing shows the `Author` and `Book` entities.

Listing 11.4   Squeryl-Record implementation for the `Author` and `Book` entities

```
import net.liftweb.record.{MetaRecord, Record}
import net.liftweb.squerylrecord.KeyedRecord
import net.liftweb.squerylrecord.RecordTypeMode._
import net.liftweb.record.field._
import org.squeryl.annotations.Column

class Book private ()
    extends Record[Book]
    with KeyedRecord[Long] {
  def meta = Book
```

```
  @Column(name="id")
  val idField = new LongField(this, 100)
  val publisherId = new LongField(this, 0)
  val authorId = new LongField(this, 0)
  val title = new StringField(this, "")
  val publishedInYear = new IntField(this, 1990)
}

object Book extends Book with MetaRecord[Book]

class Author private ()
    extends Record[Author]
    with KeyedRecord[Long] {

  def meta = Author

  @Column(name="id")
  val idField = new LongField(this, 100)
  val name = new StringField(this, "")
  val age = new OptionalIntField(this)
  val birthday = new OptionalDateTimeField(this)
}

object Author extends Author with MetaRecord[Author]
```

❶ **Book record**

❷ **Author fields**

These two entities follow a very similar pattern to the Publisher entity by implementing the Record and KeyedRecord traits. Moreover, both records include some additional fields to contain the appropriate data attributes to model that particular entity ❶ and ❷.

SQUERYL CRUD STATEMENTS

With the entities defined, you can now start to play with the create, read, update, and delete syntax that Squeryl supplies. Remember that Record is a thin abstraction, so the statement syntax is used wholesale from the Squeryl library. The following sections explore some of this functionality, but Squeryl is an ORM in its own right and there is much functionality that can't be covered here. I strongly recommend you check out the Squeryl documentation (http://squeryl.org/introduction.html) for more specific information on what is possible.

The Publisher entity is quite straightforward, so let's start by inserting some data into it using the SBT console:

```
scala> import sample.model.squeryl._
import sample.model.squeryl._

scala> import net.liftweb.mapper.{DB,DefaultConnectionIdentifier}
import net.liftweb.mapper.{DB, DefaultConnectionIdentifier}

scala> import Bookstore._
import Bookstore._

scala> new bootstrap.liftweb.Boot().boot

scala>DB.use(DefaultConnectionIdentifier){ connection =>
     |    publishers.insert(
     |      Publisher.createRecord.name("Manning"))
     | }
res10: sample.model.squeryl.Publisher = sample.model.squeryl.Publisher@9
```

❶ **Insert to DB**

First, this code imports the types that are needed to interact with the Squeryl entities and, in addition, the Mapper database connection abstractions so the statements can connect to the backend database. But the real line of interest here is ❶. `publishers` refers to the value defined on the `Bookstore Schema`, so this line literally says "insert this passed object into the publishers table." The parameter in this case is an instance of `Publisher` that has been created with the `Publisher.createRecord` method to obtain a fresh (unsaved) instance to which a `name` has been applied.

With Squeryl, it's also possible to do batch insertions right from within your code, as shown:

```
publishers.insert(List(
  Publisher.createRecord.name("Manning"),
  Publisher.createRecord.name("Penguin"),
  Publisher.createRecord.name("Bloomsbury")
))
```

As it stands, this operation will throw an exception if the save operation fails, so remember to provide exception handling where appropriate.

At this point, we strongly recommend taking some time to play around with Squeryl by inserting various bits of data into the database from within the REPL. This will give you a good feel for how to construct records and for the interplay between Record and Squeryl types. In addition, you'll need to have some data in the tables to test out the querying syntax!

SQUERYL QUERYING STATEMENTS
Now that you have the entities set up and some data in your tables, let's take a quick tour around the querying syntax that Squeryl provides. The query DSL in Squeryl models itself on SQL. Unlike many ORM systems that attempt to ignore the fact that they're interacting with a relational database, Squeryl embraces this reality wholeheartedly.

The next listing shows several examples of query operations with the Squeryl-Record entities defined in the previous listings.

Listing 11.5 Various Squeryl query expressions

```
import org.squeryl.RecordTypeMode._

from(Bookstore.publishers)(p =>          ❶ Explicit
  where(p.id === 1) select(p)).single       query

import Bookstore._

publishers.where(_.id === 1).single      ❷ Import schema
                                            and query
publishers.toList

authors.where(_.age.is >= 20)            ❸ Operator
                                            examples
from(publishers, books)((p,b) =>
  where(b.title.is like "%in Action"     ❹ Type-safe joins
  and p.name.is === "Manning") select(b,p))
```

This listing shows you a small selection of Squeryl syntax. The first thing you must do in order to use the Squeryl query DSL is import the implicit conversions supplied by the library. The common import is shown at the top of the listing; without this import, you'll receive a whole set of errors from the compiler telling you that methods don't exist and so forth.

Next in the listing are several different examples of explicit queries using the Squeryl DSL. The first statement would be equivalent to this SQL:

```
SELECT * FROM publishers WHERE id = 1
```

The `from()` method takes tables that are defined in the `Schema` subtype; `Bookstore` in this instance from listing 11.2. This statement is a bit on the verbose side ❶, though, and it can thankfully be condensed somewhat.

Scala allows you to import object members into a particular scope, and as you're likely to execute these queries somewhere where you'd like access to that information, you can call `import Bookstore._` to save constantly having to prefix `Bookstore` to the table call. Here you can see the same query again, but without the `from()` component; it operates directly on the schema table. Also note the second example that has the `where()` clause removed ❷; this is, as you might expect, equivalent to running a `SELECT * FROM` table and converting it into a `List[Publisher]`. You should be able to see how the predicate you pass to `where()` is translated into the correct SQL under the hood by Squeryl

Another type of predicate is defined for greater than or equal to ❸. There are a whole set of optional predicates and combinations, so check the Squeryl documentation for more specific information (http://squeryl.org/selects.html).

Finally, listing 11.5 defines an ad hoc multi-table query ❹, much like you might do with SQL joins, but in this case you can see that the `like` method has been used to define a wildcard that looks for book titles ending with "in Action" and where the publisher name is "Manning."

As you can see, this is a very different approach to interacting with SQL data storage than is used by Mapper or other popular Java ORM systems, such as Hibernate. The real advantage of using Squeryl over something like Hibernate is that you can be sure that the query will execute if the code compiles: it has complete type-safety. The prospect of having a query engine that won't arbitrarily blow up on you at runtime is an attractive one, and with Record's rich field system you can also gain many of the conveniences you're used to from Mapper.

The next section moves away from traditional SQL data stores and takes a look at the emerging world of NoSQL and semi-structured data. These new systems are typically designed to be specialized storage systems for specific types of problems, but some of the products in the marketplace, such as MongoDB, are proving to be popular for solving more general problems because they fit more idiomatically with the way developers think of objects and data structures.

11.3 *Record for NoSQL stores*

Nearly every developer is familiar with SQL. It has been the reliable provider of data persistence for many years, both prior to mass adoption of the internet right up to the current day. The continued growth of the internet means that applications have to deal with more and more data in increasingly write-orientated architectures. Simply put, the massive amount of interaction that applications commonly require these days is progressively making SQL-based stores tricky to scale.

We can also all appreciate the elegant logic behind the normalization of database schema, but there's more often than not a mismatch between this structure and modern web programming paradigms. Developers often place ORM systems, such as Mapper, in between their application code and the underlying RDBMS in order to obtain a more OO feel to their data access.

Increasingly, particular organizations have started to wonder if there is perhaps a better, more natural way to work with their data that would better suit various specialized problem domains. Although these problem domains differ fairly widely, the various products are broadly united under the so-called NoSQL movement, because they all shun SQL in favor of a specialized interface. Examples include custom communication interfaces like Thrift, custom data formats like BSON, and custom query constructs like MapReduce. The Wikipedia article has more background about NoSQL (http://en.wikipedia.org/wiki/NoSQL).

> **NOTE** The NoSQL movement is still a relatively new development, and if you haven't had time to investigate it, you may be wondering what the purpose of all this specialized technology is. The majority of NoSQL solutions are designed to solve a *specific* use case, usually from the industry the vendor is from. Although many people are finding these technologies useful in a general sense, there's no need to worry about them if they don't fit your use case. Relational databases are still a really good fit for most applications.

There are many NoSQL stores currently available, and it's somewhat beyond the scope of this book to list them all and their various nuances, so the following section specifically covers Lift's integration with NoSQL stores and the Record abstractions the framework provides.

11.3.1 *NoSQL support in Lift*

NoSQL comes in many flavors, and each store provides different functionality. Lift's support for the different backends has grown rather organically as the NoSQL scene has expanded and evolved. At the time of writing, Lift provides out-of-the-box NoSQL support for CouchDB (http://couchdb.apache.org/) and MongoDB (http://www.mongodb.org/).

Both Couch and Mongo are what is known as document-oriented data stores. This essentially means that rather than using tables, as in relational database systems, schemaless JSON documents store information, where each document has properties and collections that can be accessed just like any other JSON document. You can retrieve a specific document by asking for a specific key. For example, imagine asking for a specific ISBN number to retrieve the book object you were interested in from among a collection of books. You can think of these keys as being analogous to the primary keys in RDBMS tables.

Record also provides certain idioms so that the different storage mechanisms have similar if not identical operational semantics. Typically, records can be created and persisted like so:

```
MyThing.createRecord.fieldOne("value").fieldTwo("tester").save
```

This is true for both the CouchDB and MongoDB implementations covered here, and it should generally be the case for most Record implementations.

Without further ado, let's walk through some of the basic functionality that each abstraction provides before going on to explore the MongoDB abstraction in greater depth.

COUCHDB

One of the first NoSQL stores to land in popular IT culture was CouchDB. Broadly speaking, Couch and Mongo appear to have many similarities, but they're mostly skin-deep. Couch typically excels in scenarios where you have master-master replication, typically found in applications that go offline or require the syncing of databases. A good example would be an email client syncing with the server—the local database would likely be out of date if the user was disconnected from the network for a period of time. In essence, if your problem requires eventual consistency over distributed storage nodes, or you require a MapReduce interface, CouchDB is a good candidate to evaluate.

Lift provides a Record abstraction to interoperate with CouchDB, and it allows you to interact with Couch in a manner that follows the Record idioms of having

Eventual consistency

With the rise of distributed systems, it quickly became apparent that building distributed systems (particularly data stores) that maintained the ACID properties (atomicity, consistency, isolation, durability) was going to be exceedingly difficult, and that such systems would be unlikely to scale to the needs of the humongous systems being constructed now and looking to the future.

Subsequently, the idea of a system that was eventually consistent was born. Given a multi-node database to which an update is sent and a sufficiently long period of time, you can assume that all updates are either applied to all nodes, or that the nodes that didn't take the updates retired from the service, so that the various distributed nodes of that system *eventually* become consistent. This is known as Basically Available, Soft-state, Eventual consistency (BASE), and it's a principle that nearly all distributed NoSQL stores adopt.

contextually rich fields. Before attempting to use the Couch module, make sure that you've included the dependency in your SBT project definition:

```
val couch = "net.liftweb" %% "lift-couchdb" % liftVersion
```

In order to start using the Lift integration with Couch, a small amount of setup is required for your `Boot` class:

```
import net.liftweb.couchdb.{CouchDB, Database}
import dispatch.{Http, StatusCode}

val database = new Database("bookstore")
database.createIfNotCreated(new Http())
CouchDB.defaultDatabase = database
```

The code in this example is pretty straightforward and should be fairly self-explanatory, with the possible exception of the `new Http()` statement. Lift's CouchDB client builds on top of the HTTP Dispatch project (http://dispatch.databinder.net/) in order to communicate back and forth with the Couch server. This statement essentially hands the CouchDB record a vehicle through which it can make HTTP calls. In this particular case, a database is defined and specified in the `CouchDB` configuration object so you don't have to pass the connection information later on, assuming you only want to communicate with a single Couch server.

With the database connection configured, you can start to interact with CouchDB by defining the specialized Record classes as detailed in the following listing.

Listing 11.6 Implementing a basic CouchDB record

```
import net.liftweb.record.field._
import net.liftweb.couchdb.{CouchRecord,CouchMetaRecord}

class Book private () extends CouchRecord[Book]{          ◁┐
  def meta = Book

  val title = new StringField(this, "")        ┃ Define field    Implement
  val publishedInYear = new IntField(this, 1990)  ┃ types          Couch types
}

object Book extends Book with CouchMetaRecord[Book]      ◁┘
```

The implementation here looks rather similar to the Squeryl variant detailed in listing 11.4. Specifically, note how the definitions of the fields are identical. The main difference between Squeryl and CouchDB here is the extension of the `CouchRecord` and `CouchMetaRecord` types. CouchDB requires a couple of different fields to be implemented in any given entity in order to control the versioning and revision systems, both of which are handled automatically for you by the `CouchRecord` supertype.

The `CouchMetaRecord` and `Database` types give you various convenience methods for interacting with the views provided by Couch for interacting with stored documents: both to create and query. CouchDB querying essentially utilizes these Map-Reduce views in order to obtain query-style data. The views themselves can be precreated and then used in your application at runtime.

To create a view using lift-couchdb, you can do something like this:

```
import net.liftweb.json.Implicits.{int2jvalue, string2jvalue}
import net.liftweb.json.JsonAST.{JObject}
import net.liftweb.json.JsonDSL.{jobject2assoc, pair2Assoc, pair2jvalue}

val design: JObject =
  ("language" -> "javascript") ~
  ("views"     -> ("oldest" ->
    (("map" -> "function(doc) {
if (doc.type == 'Book'){ emit(doc.title, doc.publishedInYear); }}") ~
    ("reduce" -> "function(keys, values) {
return Math.max.apply(null, values); }"))))

Http(database.design("design_name") put design)
```

❶ **Create new design**

If you're not too familiar with Couch, this may look somewhat odd. This is a specialized CouchDB MapReduce function that obtains the oldest book document. The key line sends the design with the assigned name "design_name" to the database ❶. Once it's in place, you can run a query via the `Book` meta record as shown:

```
val book = Book.queryView("design_name", "oldest")
```

This one line calls Couch and executes the predefined view to retrieve the oldest `Book` title held in the database.

CouchDB is a large subject in and of itself, but this should give you a sense, at a high level, of how the Lift implementation operates.

MONGODB

MongoDB, like CouchDB, is a document-oriented store, but rather than using prewritten views to obtain query data, Mongo is better suited to creating dynamic queries, similar to what you might construct using traditional SQL. Mongo uses a custom query syntax rather than using MapReduce, which although supported, is for data aggregation rather than general-purpose querying.

Mongo uses a custom binary protocol to communicate from your application to the data store, which generally yields a more flexible programming interface than is possible with HTTP. In addition, MongoDB positions itself as being a general-purpose NoSQL database that was designed from the ground up for use in internet applications.

Unlike the CouchDB implementation, the Mongo support in Lift comes in two parts: lift-mongo provides a thin Scala wrapper around the MongoDB driver for Java, and lift-mongo-record provides the integration for using Record with Mongo.

To get started, ensure you've added the dependency to your project and called `update` from the SBT shell:

```
val mongo = "net.liftweb" %% "lift-mongodb-record" % liftVersion
```

By default, Lift assumes that the MongoDB server is configured on the same machine (localhost), so for development and testing, it's likely you'll need no configuration in your `Boot` class. But if you need to specify where your Mongo installation is hosted, simply add the following lines:

```
import net.liftweb.mongodb.{MongoDB, DefaultMongoIdentifier,
  MongoAddress, MongoHost}
MongoDB.defineDb(
  DefaultMongoIdentifier,
  MongoAddress(MongoHost("localhost", 27017), "your_db"))
```

The call to `MongoDB.defineDb` essentially tells the MongoDB driver where to locate the MongoDB server. The following examples, however, assume that the MongoDB install is the default, local install.

Now that the connection is ready, the next thing is to define your Mongo Record. The next listing shows the most basic example.

Listing 11.7 Basic implementation of Mongo Record

```
import net.liftweb.record.field._
import net.liftweb.mongodb.record.{MongoRecord,MongoMetaRecord,MongoId}

object Book extends Book with MongoMetaRecord[Book]        ❶ Extend Mongo
                                                              classes
class Book private () extends MongoRecord[Book]
        with MongoId[Book]{
  def meta = Book

  object title extends StringField(this, "")
  object publishedInYear extends IntField(this, 1990)
}
```

This is nearly identical to the CouchDB and Squeryl examples previously listed, with the only change being the two supertypes, which are now `MongoRecord` and `Mongo-MetaRecord` ❶. `MongoRecord` supports the specialized querying for the backend store, just as `CouchRecord` does.

MongoDB deals with *collections*. These collections can be thought of as similar to tables, and each MongoDB Record entity you create generally represents a collection By default, the collection will use the pluralized name of the class—`Books` in this instance. Each *document* in the collection will be represented by a `Book` entity instance.

Let's assume you want to run a couple of queries:

```
import net.liftweb.json.JsonDSL._

Book.findAll("title" -> "Lift in Action")
Book.findAll("publishedInYear" -> ("$gte" -> 2005))
Book.findAll("$where" -> "function() {
  return this.publishedInYear == '2011'}")
```

There are three different queries here, but the first one should be fairly self-explanatory: Mongo will go looking for titles that match "Lift in Action". The second line defines a range query that will retrieve all documents where the `publishedInYear` is *greater than* 2005. Finally, the last line makes use of the special MongoDB query construct `$where` and passes a JavaScript function to confine the result set. Mongo has a whole set of these special identifiers, documented at http://www.mongodb.org/display/DOCS/Advanced+Queries, but by using the Lift abstraction, you can use whatever combinations you prefer.

That's the basics of using NoSQL with Record. Irrespective of these two different stores, you can see how Record brings a degree of uniformity that makes it smoother to change your backing store at a later date and also interoperate with other Lift infrastructure. Let's take the information from this section and re-implement the bookstore from earlier in the chapter with MongoDB.

11.3.2 *Bookstore with MongoDB*

NoSQL solutions have a rather different way of handling their data, and in many respects this significantly alters the way we as developers need to model our entities. Specifically with MongoDB, it's more idiomatic to store information using *embedded documents* that appear as collections on a given entity, if for the majority of time that data isn't changing. In practice, the data is just copied into each document. Sometimes having a reference is beneficial, but it depends on your use case.

With the Book, Publisher, and Author relationships, the Book entity will really be the main interaction point because once a Book has a Publisher, it's largely immutable—the same is true of Author. With this in mind, it isn't a problem to simply embed the appropriate Publisher and Author documents so that they appear as properties of the Book entity.

> **TIP** When using Mongo, a general rule of thumb is that you embed and copy data when it seems reasonable, and fall back to referencing separate entities when the use case demands it. Generally speaking, try to arrange your Mongo entities with the most commonly accessed aspect being the top level, and other aspects being either embedded documents or, in lesser cases, referenced entities. The classic scenario is a single blog post that has many comments; the comments are appended directly to the post entity document.

Let's add those two additional fields for Publisher and Author to the Book record, as shown in the next listing.

Listing 11.8 The full Book entity using `MongoRecord`

```
import net.liftweb.record.field._
import net.liftweb.mongodb.{JsonObject,JsonObjectMeta}
import net.liftweb.mongodb.record.{MongoRecord,MongoMetaRecord,MongoId}
import net.liftweb.mongodb.record.field._

class Book private () extends MongoRecord[Book]
    with MongoId[Book]{
  def meta = Book

  object title extends StringField(this, "")
  object publishedInYear extends IntField(this, 1990)

  object publisher
  extends JsonObjectField[Book, Publisher]
    ➥(this, Publisher) {                              ❶ Embedded
    def defaultValue = Publisher("", "")                publisher
  }
```

```
 object authors extends
   MongoJsonObjectListField[Book, Author](this, Author)
}

object Book extends Book with MongoMetaRecord[Book]

case class Publisher(name: String, description: String)
    extends JsonObject[Publisher] {
  def meta = Publisher
}

object Publisher extends JsonObjectMeta[Publisher]

case class Author(firstName: String,
    lastName: String)
    extends JsonObject[Author] {
  def meta = Author
}
object Author extends JsonObjectMeta[Author]
```

2 Embedded authors list

3 Publisher definition

4 Author definition

There's a fair amount going on here, over and above the initial implementation in listing 11.7. First, notice the publisher object at **1**. This inner object extends JsonObjectField, which essentially means it holds a nested Mongo document. In this particular case, the field is told that it should expect the Publisher type defined at **3**. The Publisher definition, itself, is a simple case class that extends JsonObject and has a companion object called JsonObjectMeta.

The same is true for the Author class defined at **4**, but because a single Book could feasibly have multiple authors, the entity property authors extends MongoJsonObjectListField **2**. As you might imagine, this contains a list of documents, as opposed to the single document required by publisher, so in practice you can think of this field as a simple list or array of documents.

Now that you have the MongoRecord for Book in place, you can start to play around with constructing and querying instances of Book:

```
scala> import sample.model.mongo._
import sample.model.mongo._

scala>Book.createRecord
.title("sample")
.authors(Authors(List(Author("tim","perrett"))))
.publisher(Publisher("Manning","")).save
res2: sample.model.mongo.Book = class sample.model.mongo.Book={...}

scala>Book.findAll
res3: List[sample.model.mongo.Book] = List(...)

scala>Book.find("title" -> "Lift in Action")
res21: net.liftweb.common.Box[sample.model.mongo.Book] = ...
```

You can see in this code snippet that it's easy to query Mongo for specific data in a simple case, such as finding a book by a title, but when you have larger, more complex queries, the syntax can become rather unwieldy. It's at this point that it would be great to add some more type-safety to the querying, as opposed to passing everything around as strings. This is where the type-safe Rogue DSL comes in.

Going Rogue: type-safe Mongo queries

One of the largest Lift users in the world is Foursquare, and at the beginning of 2011 they open-sourced part of their Record-based abstraction for working with MongoDB. This project was dubbed Rogue (https://github.com/foursquare/rogue).

Rouge provides a type-safe DSL for building complex queries right from within your application, and it eliminates the need to work with the Mongo identifiers directly, or to pass strings around. Using the DSL, you get fully type-safe interaction on all the various parts of Mongo query constructs.

If you'd like to use Rogue, be sure to add the dependency to your project definition and run `update` from the SBT shell:

```
val rogue = "com.foursquare" %% "rogue" % "1.0.2"
```

When Rogue is present in your project, you can create queries simply by adding the following import statement:

```
import com.foursquare.rogue.Rogue._
```

This then allows you to interact with Mongo using the DSL:

```
Book where (_.publishedInYeargte 1990) fetch()

Book where (_.title eqs "Lift in Action") limit(1) fetch()
```

This is the tip of the iceberg, and the abstraction can do a whole set of other things that are somewhat out of the scope of this section. If you'd like to know more about Rogue, check out the Foursquare engineering blog (http://engineering.foursquare.com/), and particularly the entry on Rogue and type safety (http://mng.bz/R58g), or the Foursquare repository on github.com: https://github.com/foursquare/rogue.

In this section, you've seen the NoSQL support that Lift provides out of the box through the Record abstraction. NoSQL through Record could feasibly take many forms, but this section has primarily focused on CouchDB and MongoDB, showing you how to leverage these exciting new technologies and still have the familiar Lift semantics and integration with infrastructure like `LiftScreen`.

11.4 Summary

Phew! There were a lot of different topics in this chapter and a bunch of different technologies. Broadly speaking, you've seen how Record can deliver an abstract facade for building persistence systems that talk to many different backend data stores, from relational databases right through to leading-edge NoSQL systems.

The first section covered the general concept of Record, including the anatomy of a generic Record instance. This exploration displayed the functionality that is baked into anything that builds upon Record, irrespective of the persistence system you wind up using. By default, each Record instance knows how to validate itself and render the value contents to JSON, and it provides a selection of helper methods for various operations. Each Record subtype you might make or work with implements subtypes of `Field`. These fields are contextually rich in that they represent a strongly typed value rather than simply working with the most basic type they can get away with. These fields can also be optional, by mixing in the `OptionalTypedField` trait. This then allows you to have a `Box[T]` value and eliminates the need to intrinsically check for `null` values and so on.

The next part of this chapter covered Record's interoperation with relational databases. Here Lift leverages a Scala library called Squeryl, which provides a type-safe DSL for making SQL calls. Squeryl embraces SQL idioms, so you end up with code that looks an awful lot like its raw SQL counterpart, but it's type-checked, and if the code compiles, the query will execute at runtime. Squeryl is a powerful and flexible library, and when it's coupled with Record you can use it from within your Lift applications in a seamless manner.

Finally, you learned about Lift's support for NoSQL data stores, specifically CouchDB and MongoDB. These systems offer a very different type of data storage operation than traditional RDBMS, yet the Record facade you work with in your Lift application is hardly different at all. In the case of CouchDB, you can run pretty complicated MapReduce functions right from within your Scala code. When using the MongoDB implementation, you can elect to use the standard Mongo query syntax or to layer on top the Foursquare Rogue abstraction to make interacting with Mongo type-safe and pretty.

The next chapter will take a break from persistence within Lift and focus on the increasingly important area of application internationalization. Lift has a range of features that makes implementing multicultural applications straightforward.

Localization 12

In this age of globalization and the apparent consolidation of many cultures, it may surprise you to know that there are still between 6,500 and 10,000 different languages spoken in the world today. The exact figure isn't known, but you can be sure that our world has a large amount of linguistic diversity. Traditionally, this has caused a large number of problems for software engineers because these different languages often have cultural differences that are specific to a certain locale.

Take something as simple as a greeting in two English-speaking countries, like Great Britain and Australia; the former would likely use *Good afternoon* and the latter would likely use *Good'ay*. Strictly speaking, both countries are English-speaking, but cultural differences lead to colloquialisms becoming commonplace and a subsequent divergence from the original dialect. As you might imagine, there's an infinite amount of variation in presentation styles and content, such as when comparing Latin-based text to Arabic or Hebrew, which are both written right-to-left, and not left-to-right. All these things and more combine to make writing software for the international market subtly difficult.

Fortunately both the Java platform and Lift provide some great features to help you make the best of this rather complex situation. The first section of this chapter looks at how you can implement Lift's localization helpers in your templates and application code. Then, the second section covers how you actually obtain localized content—where your code or template defines one of Lift's localization helpers, and where the content that ultimately replaces it comes from. There are three possible options and they're all illustrated with examples in section 12.2.

First, though, let's get into how you define localized content in your templates and code.

12.1 Implementing localization

The Java platform as a whole has good support for localization and for working with global systems that have large numbers of locale-specific, colloquial idioms. Because the JVM has had a localization strategy for a long time, the design of the system is largely oriented toward building desktop applications (such was the trend at the time). Lift provides a system that builds on top of JVM's robust localization infrastructure, specifically the `Locale` and `ResourceBundle` classes supplied with the standard Java distribution, but it also adds several very useful facilities that make localizing *web applications* much more flexible.

What is a locale?

If you're new to localization, the term *locale* is one you'll see thrown around a lot. There are two aspects to localization: languages and countries. These two words alone describe orthogonal parts of a culture, but locale defines the combination of the two. For example, French is spoken both in France and in North Africa, but the cultures aren't the same. French spoken in France is assigned a locale of fr_FR, whereas French spoken in Morocco is assigned a locale of fr_MA.

Strictly speaking, you can have a `java.util.Locale` instance that only represents the language, but generally a locale is a unification of both aspects. It's only useful to represent a language as a locale if you want to group together countries that speak the same language: such as American English, British English, and so on.

The language identifiers used by the Java locale infrastructure are the ISO 639-1 language codes, and the country codes are those in the ISO 3166-1 definitions. These are international standards and are widely used in many different systems.

Lift's localization strategy can be broken down into a couple of component parts: resources and templates.

Resources define locale-specific objects. These objects could be pretty much any type you like, but the most common use case is a string that needs to be presented in several languages. Lift will look at the resource bundles it has available, and load the appropriately localized string if it exists.

The second element of Lift's localization strategy is part of the template selection. Once you've got the localized content, there are often still issues with presenting that content. For example, German text is roughly 30 percent longer than English text for the same content, and this can have fairly serious impacts on the visual presentation of an application; ultimately, you need to find room for all this extra text. With this in mind, Lift allows you to be smart about templating. Consider a page called index.html; this would be fine for English, French, and Spanish, but perhaps you need to rearrange some of your markup to make space for the longer German text. In this case, you could simply have a secondary file called index_de_DE.html.

Before implementing the localizations, you need to instruct Lift on how it should determine which locale is the correct one to use for a request. This is done via the `localeCalculator` property of `LiftRules`.

12.1.1 *Implementing locale calculator*

Out of the box, Lift will grab the locale from the `Accept-Language` header of the incoming request. If a given request doesn't specify this particular header, Lift will assume the locale of the server to be the locale for this request. For example, if the JVM of the container you're running your application on has a locale of en_GB, and the request has not specified a preferred language with the `Accept-Language` header, the server will respond with the British English version.

> **NOTE** Most browsers in use today make web requests with what are known as accept headers. Their purpose is to indicate to the server application what responses would best fit the user's client. Accept headers exist for content types and even language. The latter is specifically helpful for determining what language the user speaks. For example, if the user has their browser language set to French (fr_FR), you can be fairly sure they would prefer reading content in French. You can read more about the Accept Language header in RFC 2616: http://www.w3.org/Protocols/rfc2616/rfc2616-sec14.html.

It's also highly likely that you'll want to provide users with some control over the locale, and you may want the application to remember the user's locale choice for the next time they visit. To illustrate this, let's assume you want to control the locale based on the query parameter hl. This would mean that if a request was sent to /foo?hl=en_GB or /bar?hl=fr-FR, the locale would be set to the value specified by the hl query parameter by parsing the string value and constructing a `java.util.Locale` instance.

All requests that hit your Lift application are routed through `Liftrules.locale-Calculator`, and this is where the parsing and construction of the locale will be done, based on the information contained in the request. This means you could use query parameters, cookies, and other factors to determine what the locale should be. In your `Boot` class, implement the locale calculator as shown in the following listing.

Listing 12.1 Example `localeCalculator` configuration

```
import java.util.Locale
import net.liftweb.http.LiftRules
import net.liftweb.common.Box
import net.liftweb.util.Helpers.tryo

LiftRules.localeCalculator = (request: Box[HTTPRequest]) => (for {
  r <- request
  p <- tryo(r.param("hl").head.split(Array('_','-')))
} yield p match {
  case Array(lang) => new Locale(lang)
  case Array(lang,country) => new Locale(lang,country)
}).openOr(Locale.getDefault))
```

`LiftRules.localeCalculator` takes a function from `Box[HTTPRequest]` => `Locale`, and in this sample a `for` comprehension is used to extract the boxed request value to the value r. Given that r is an `HTTPRequest`, you can call the `param` method to grab a value from the query string. Because this method could fail if the value isn't present, it's wrapped in the `tryo` control structure to capture the result as a `Box[String]`. Assuming the value of `hl` is of the format en_GB or en-GB, it's then split into its two component parts to instantiate a new `Locale`. Failing that, it will use the default locale for your JVM by calling the `Locale.getDefault` method.

You'd probably want to expand on this implementation to provide something a lot more robust that saves the value into the session, a cookie, or some other place. You'll generally want to keep track of the locale rather than calculating it on every request from scratch.

There's one important thing to be aware of with `localeCalculator` and the way in which Lift handles requests. As each page view is made up of a selection of requests, the function will, by default, execute for every request that makes up the page. If your `localeCalculator` is doing anything but the default, it's a good idea to memoize the function execution. By adding a request-scoped memoize, you can ensure that your locale calculation function is only executed once in the scope of a request; for every other call on that value, the cached result will be given rather than incurring the overhead of executing the function again.

NOTE You can find more information about memoization in the Wikipedia article: http://en.wikipedia.org/wiki/Memoization.

The following listing shows the implementation that makes use of memoization.

Listing 12.2 Implementing memoization with `localeCalculator`

```
import java.util.Locale
import net.liftweb.common.Box
import net.liftweb.util.Helpers.{tryo,randomString}
import net.liftweb.http.provider.HTTPRequest
import net.liftweb.http.{LiftRules,RequestMemoize}
```

```
object localeMemo extends RequestMemoize[Int, Locale] {        ❶  Memoization
  override protected def __nameSalt = randomString(20)              object
}

LiftRules.localeCalculator = (request: Box[HTTPRequest]) =>
  localeMemo(request.hashCode, (for {                           ◁┐  Call-by-name
    r <- request                                                ❷  function
    p <- tryo(r.param("hl").head.split(Array('_','-')))
  } yield p match {
    case Array(lang) => new Locale(lang)
    case Array(lang,country) => new Locale(lang,country)
  }).openOr(Locale.getDefault))
)
```

In order to apply the memoization, you need to import the `RequestMemoize` type and
set up a local object that extends it with two type parameters: a key type and a value
type ❶. The value type is `Locale`, and for simplicity sake it uses the instance `hashCode`
of the request as the key. This ensures that the locale is paired with the right request,
because each request will create a new `HTTPRequest` instance. Notice that in the actual
implementation of the locale calculator, the `localeMemo` object ❷ is applied with two
parameters: the `hashCode` of the incoming request and a block that's the same code
from listing 12.1. This second parameter is a call-by-name parameter, which means the
`localeMemo` object only executes it if it needs to.

> **TIP** You may be wondering if it's possible to access the calculated locale
> value from other places in your application code, such as a snippet. Fortu-
> nately, this is usually quite straightforward: if the location you'd like to obtain
> the value from is within session scope, you can just call `S.locale`.

Now that Lift can determine the correct locale for each request, let's do something
useful with this new information and load some localized content from both templates and your own code.

12.1.2 Localizing templates and code

Lift has a selection of ways to interact with localized content, depending upon where
and what you need to localize. Broadly speaking, these can be divided into two types:
localized templates and localized code.

LOCALIZED TEMPLATES

In the section introduction, we briefly touched upon the differences between languages and how, for example, English is a left-to-right text whereas Hebrew is written
right-to-left (RTL). These differences in language direction have an impact on how
the site looks and functions. Consider figure 12.1, which compares a page in Hebrew
and in English.

Try as you might, there will usually come a point when simply using resource bundles to swap content for given positions won't cut it. Verbose European languages may

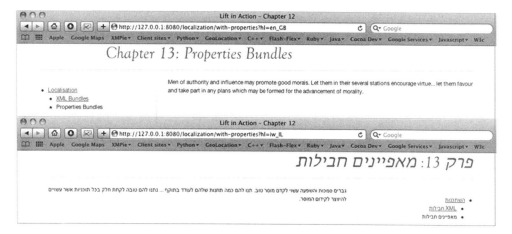

Figure 12.1 Comparing English and Hebrew localization

cause problems if you're tight on space, or implementing RTL languages may push things to the breaking point and then require some template alterations.

It's exactly these situations that Lift's template localization is designed for. The content itself is the same, but you want to change the way it's being presented. This may involve including a custom `<head>` or perhaps making some page-specific changes to accommodate content in a better manner.

When Lift receives a request and then goes looking for the template, it will also include a set of locale-specific templates in that search as well. Suppose you have index.html as your content file, but you want to make a special case for German. In order to implement this, you'd have both an index.html and an index_de.html file (or one that also specifies the country: index_de_DE.html).

This is great for per-page corner cases in different locales, but you may be wondering about what you'd do for something more global, such as a surround. Well, the same is true. Even if your content page has a call to `surround` that defines default, you can have a default_iw_HL.html (where iw_HL is the locale code for Israeli Hebrew), and that root surround would automatically be selected by Lift allowing you to use the same content for the page, but apply a RTL styling.

Finally, if you have content in a template that you want to localize, you have two possible ways to implement the Lift `Loc` snippet:

```
<lift:loc locid="greeting">Greeting goes here</lift:loc>
```

or

```
<p class="lift:loc?locid=greeting">Greeting goes here</p>
```

Both of these versions of template markup indicate to Lift that the content of that node should be replaced by resolving the `locid` as a key in the resource bundle system.

LOCALIZED CODE

In order to localize your own code, you need some way of telling Lift that it must grab this particular bit of content from the resource bundle rather than taking the literal from the code, much in the same way that the `Loc` snippet does in templates. For this, Lift provides a slightly odd-looking `S.?method`.

Consider these examples:

```
import net.liftweb.http.S.{?,??}

?("mything")
?("salutation", title, lastName)
??("ajax.error")
```

These are three examples of obtaining localized resources from the defined bundles. Notice that there are two methods in use here: `?` and `??`. The `?` method is used for obtaining your own resources, and then the `??` method is used to obtain resources that come bundled as part of Lift. For the most part, you'll usually implement the `?` method, but understanding the purpose of `??` is helpful if you see it in example code or you wish to override parts of Lift's functionality.

The first example in the preceding code shows the most common use case. Resource bundles that contain localized content always define a *key* to access the localized item, so imagine you have a literal string in a resource bundle that's accessible via the key "mything"—this method will just return the value as it's defined in that resource bundle.

The second example defines a formatted resource string where the value would be something like "Dcar %s%s", where the %s is a placeholder for the variable argument list passed to the second parameter. In this case, given `?("Dear %s %s", "Mr", "Perrett")` the result would be "Dear Mr Perrett". Such strategies can be used to localize the majority of your server-side text, such as the names of buttons or other generated content.

The other item of code that you'll likely want to localize is your sitemap location declarations. Fortunately, this is simple enough. You can just adjust the definition to use the `i` method on the `Menu` object:

```
Menu.i("Home") / "index"
```

With this definition, the sitemap builds upon the `S.?method` and uses the name of the page (`Home`, in this example) as the key to resolve the resource.

Because localization lookup is conducted using strings for keys, you may want to handle the case where an appropriate translation doesn't exist for a particular key. Lift supplies a hook for this, which allows you to execute any function you please in the event that a localization key isn't found in any of the available resource bundles. Add the following configuration to your application `Boot`:

```
LiftRules.localizationLookupFailureNotice = Full((key,locale) =>
  logger.warn("No %s text for %s".format(locale.getDisplayName, key)))
```

These two lines instruct Lift to log a warning when a translation key isn't present. In this instance, the function just logs an error, but it could just as easily execute any code you require.

You have now seen how to configure Lift with a dynamic locale, and you've also had an introduction to how you can implement localized resources from both templates and code. With this in mind, it's time to go through the various options available for loading localized content from resource bundles. The next three sections deal with these options and show you how to implement each option in turn. The first option you'll be looking at is Lift's XML-based resource bundles.

12.2 *Defining localized resources*

Web applications present a rather different localization problem compared to desktop applications. The traditional Java view on localization is that you have a single per-locale bundle that contains all your application resources, and for desktop builds this often makes sense. But with web applications, this can become a little unwieldy, as it's not uncommon for web applications to have a moderately complex structure with lots of nested folders and pages and even page fragments. Suddenly, the Java approach of using a single properties bundle can become rather restrictive.

Although Lift can still support the traditional Java resource bundles (covered in section 12.2.2), Lift avoids their shortcomings and provides a richer method of localization through UTF-8 XML resource files.

12.2.1 *Using XML resources*

XML resource bundles can be located in a variety of places, but they primarily allow you to split the localized content up into logical sections: different bundles for each page or a more traditional global bundle for all pages. For example, assuming that the page URL is /some/thing, Lift will attempt to look for resources based upon `3.locale` with the following search path in your WAR file:

1 webapp/some/_resources_thing
2 webapp/templates-hidden/some/_resources_thing
3 webapp/some/resources-hidden/_resources_thing
4 webapp/_resources
5 webapp/templates-hidden/_resources
6 webapp/resources-hidden/_resources

As you can see, there are quite a number of places Lift will search for resources. The great thing here is that the first three locations provide you with page-specific resource bundles, and the last three provide global locations for common elements.

Now that you know where resources can be placed, consider the following listing, which shows an example of the Lift resource XML.

Listing 12.3 Example of Lift's resource XML

```
<?xml version="1.0"?>
<resources>
  <res name="greeting"
    lang="en"
    country="GB"
    default="true">Welcome!</res>
  <res name="greeting" lang="en" country="US">Howdy!</res>
  <res name="greeting" lang="fr">Bienvenue!</res>
  <res name="greeting" lang="de">Willkommen!</res>
  <res name="greeting" lang="it">Benvenuti!</res>
</resources>
```

Each `res` node (short for resource) has several possible attributes. The first is the `name` attribute, which defines the key for the resource you want to localize. The important difference here is that unlike many other localization systems, you can have the same key in the same resource set multiple times, provided their `country` and `lang` attributes define a different locale. In this example, you can see that there are three generic language resources for the greeting key: French, German, and Italian. These resources would be applied for any country that applies those languages. Conversely, there are two English implementations: British English and American English. Notice that the British English version also includes the `default` attribute, which essentially tells Lift that in the event of only having the language part of the locale, it should assume the proper British English.

Using this resource XML is a very Lift-specific way of doing localization, and although it's more flexible than traditional Java localization techniques, it's important to understand how you can use Java properties files if you so wish. The next section walks you through using Java properties files for localized resources.

12.2.2 *Using Java properties resources*

Because Lift runs on the JVM, it's straightforward to utilize the existing infrastructure for localizing your applications. Unlike the Lift XML resources, traditional properties resource bundles can only contain content for a single locale. The result of this is that you'll most likely end up with a directory in src/main/resources/ that contains several files:

- lift_de.properties
- lift_en_GB.properties
- lift_en_US.properties
- lift_it.properties

The main drawback here is that all application resources for a given locale must exist in the same file, and that extended characters such as œ aren't properly encoded by default. This is due to Java properties bundles using ISO 8859-1 encoding and thus requiring conversion to escaped format, such as \u0153. Fortunately this process can be automated using tools like native2ascii but it's something else you need to think about. On the plus side, if you're migrating from an existing Java application, your localized files will still operate exactly as they did.

> **NOTE** Native2Ascii can be found at http://download.oracle.com/javase/ 1.4.2/docs/tooldocs/windows/native2ascii.html. There is also an SBT wrapper for native2ascii that autoconverts your raw text to escaped Unicode output. It can be found on GitHub: https://github.com/timperrett/ sbt-native2ascii-plugin.

By default, the resource base name that Lift uses to locate your resource bundles is actually the word *lift*, meaning it will look for lift_en.properties, for example. You can override this and provide the following configuration in your `Boot` class to customize the resource base name:

```
LiftRules.resourceNames = "content" :: LiftRules.resourceNames
```

With this configuration, Lift will attempt to resolve resource bundles first with the base name *content* and then secondly with *lift*.

If neither Lift resource XML nor traditional Java properties localization methods are to your liking, you can always implement your own resource bundle factory to, for example, pull localized content from a database or any other kind of text store.

12.2.3 Using custom resource factories

Depending upon the type of application you're building, there may come a point when having all the resources externalized in static files isn't quite enough, and you'd like to plug in your own custom bundle factory. A bundle factory is a facility whereby you can provide your own class implementation that extends `java.util.Resource-Bundle`, which essentially gives you the ability to pull the localized content from anywhere you can reach with that code; it's entirely up to you.

In order to implement a custom resource bundle factory, construct something similar to the following and yield your subtype of `ResourceBundle`:

```
LiftRules.resourceBundleFactories.append {
  case (key, locale) => // yield ResourceBundle
}
```

The partial function in this instance is passed a `Tuple2`, where the first element is the resource key and the second element is the specified locale instance. You can construct your own subtype of `ResourceBundle` in Scala and return it based upon this lookup. How you're actually storing the resource information will massively alter the lookup implementation, such as if you were storing the text in a NoSQL store versus using some kind of in-memory structure. The logic, however, would simply be to search the backing store (whatever that may be) looking for a key and locale that match the ones being passed to the partial function.

12.3 *Summary*

In this chapter, you've seen how to ready your application for the global market by leveraging Lift's sophisticated localization system to provide content to users in the manner to which they're accustomed. This included instructions on how to configure and optimize the locale calculator so your application can detect which locale it should apply for any given request. In addition, we also looked at how to bundle localized content and apply the content in both your template markup and application code.

The next chapter takes a look at a pair of subjects that are typically found in larger enterprise systems: concurrent programming models and integration with enterprise systems, making use of Lift's integration with JPA persistence. In addition, you'll be broadly introduced to the Akka distribution and concurrency toolkit to get a feel for how you could scale the backend of your Lift applications when building the next Twitter!

Distributed messaging and Java enterprise integration

This chapter covers

- Using Lift's AMQP support
- Building distributed systems using Akka
- Using Lift's integration with the Java Persistence API

The first part of this chapter is all about distributed and concurrent programming. You'll see how you can utilize Lift's baked-in AMQP module to build reliable message-based workflows atop a friendly actor-based abstraction. In addition, we'll look at Akka, the concurrency toolkit and scalability runtime.

This first section of the chapter will serve as an introduction to messaging. Messaging is a much broader topic than we can cover in this book, but you'll learn how to leverage Lift's support for AMQP and how to take advantage of the powerful actor abstractions Akka provides, such as supervised and remote actors. These technologies are becoming increasingly popular in the Scala ecosystem, so it's good to have a grounding in them and an appreciation of the flexibility and power that message-based systems provide.

Continuing with the theme of application development on a larger enterprise scale, section 13.2 is all about utilizing the Java Persistence API (JPA) persistence framework from Java Enterprise Edition (JEE). JPA is much more complicated than other persistence systems covered in this book, so this section focuses on the Lift wrappers around this technology rather than offering a guide to JPA in general.

JPA is popular in the enterprise space because it's a well-supported and proven ORM, and many developers, particularly those coming from the Java ecosystem, may want to continue to use an existing data access layer with Lift being only a part of a broader Java application. This section demonstrates the Lift wrappers that give JPA a more idiomatic Scala feel and that hide the typically mutable data structures found in JPA, all while remaining fully compatible with their Java counterparts. These abstractions are essentially a nice layer on top of the standard JPA infrastructure, and they aim to do two things: provide an API that will be far more familiar to Scala programmers, and provide integration with Lift's lifecycle for things such as activating and shutting down the JPA session for each request scope. More on this later.

First, we'll look at distributed programming and Lift's actor-based abstraction for AMQP.

13.1 *Distributed programming*

Today, applications have to deal with heavily write-orientated architectures and real-time user interfaces, coupled with the infrastructure challenges of automatically scaling in cloud-computing systems such as Amazon EC2. More and more demands are being placed upon these systems, so understanding how to distribute parts of your application and to design systems that are both resilient and lend themselves to easy distribution is increasingly important.

The Scala community is aware of this revolution. Its first step in making distributed and concurrent applications easier to build and maintain was to simplify concurrency patterns by implementing actor design patterns. The concept of actors and messaging has spread, and it turns out that many parts of the well-established Java infrastructure have a strong parity with actors. One of the strongest examples of this great fit is that of messaging technologies such as AMQP (http://www.amqp.org/): Lift provides a wrapper around messaging semantics atop the AMQ Protocol. This allows you to interact with the AMQP server and clients by using the bang (!) method to send messages to and from the AMQP broker.

In the Scala ecosystem, another project that has been flourishing in recent times is Akka (http://akka.io/). The Akka framework provides an extremely fast and lightweight implementation of actors, and it has several features that make it perfect for building fault-tolerant, highly scalable, and event-driven applications. Fortunately, Akka can play perfectly with Lift, so it's possible to build your applications with a robust, scalable backend while retaining all the rich interactivity provided by Lift.

The first thing we'll look at in this section is Lift's actor-based abstraction for interacting with AMQP. These wrappers allow you to send and receive messages from other pieces of AMQP-compatible infrastructure, all from within the actor implementation paradigm.

13.1.1 *Messaging with AMQP*

AMQP is an open standard for a robust messaging protocol that allows developers to build applications that communicate reliably via a binary message format. Protocols such as AMQP allow developers to split up independent parts of their application with minimal coupling between components. A new component can replace another simply by adhering to the AMQP protocol and knowing how to handle the same incoming messages.

AMQP and, in a more general sense, the paradigm of messaging, really become useful when your application starts to grow. A properly designed system that makes effective use of messaging can have highly decoupled components that are easier to replace, easier to maintain, and easier to scale. Ultimately the idea is that this is cheaper for the implementing business, and indeed this has been proven many times in the enterprise space.

There are, of course, complexities, and nothing is without problems: the choices you make in the design of your system are critical to the success of the system, and messaging is just one possible route. As always, you should analyze your use case and do a comparative study on different technologies to see which will best fit your needs for today, tomorrow, and next year; accepting additional complexity ahead of time will often save you money in the long run.

AMQP SUPPORT IN LIFT

Lift's AMQP support is provided by the client library of an AMQP implementation called RabbitMQ (http://www.rabbitmq.com/). RabbitMQ is one of the most popular implementations of AMQP available, and it's used by many large enterprises in exceedingly demanding scenarios.

Before we get into too many details, it's a good idea to have some familiarity with the terminology used by message queues in general and specifically RabbitMQ. Table 13.1 explains some common terms.

RabbitMQ itself is implemented with the Erlang programming language, so the *message broker* you'll use is external to your application and must be installed and configured before you can begin. The RabbitMQ brokers are usually available as an installer package for your operating system, and they then require some minimal configuration, but please refer to either the RabbitMQ installation instructions (http://www.rabbitmq.com/install.html) or Alvaro Videla and Jason Williams' *RabbitMQ in Action* book, also available from Manning.

Assuming you have a broker set up, you'll need to add the `lift-amqp` dependency to your project definition:

```
val amqp = "net.liftweb" %% "lift-amqp" % liftVersion
```

Once you have this in place, don't forget to run `reload` and `update` from the SBT shell.

Table 13.1 Common AMQP terms

Term	Description		
Virtual host	A virtual host represents a set of exchanges and all subordinate objects. Broadly speaking, virtual hosts are administrative functions that allow for access control and general organization of the broker setup.		
Exchange	The exchange is really the most fundamental part of an AMQP setup. It's the central point to which all messages are communicated and they're then distributed to its queues. More often than not, your virtual host will only have a handful of exchanges, and each exchange may have a selection of queues. Upon creating an exchange, you must first decide whether the exchange should be durable (whether it survives failure or reboot) and then select an algorithm to use for the distribution of the messages it receives. You have these options:		
	Direct	This is the default type of exchange. Strings are used as the routing key, so given a queue bound to an exchange with the key test, only messages that are posted with the key test will be routed to that queue.	
	Fanout	No routing keys are used; every message received by that exchange is routed out in a fanout fashion. What goes in, must go out!	
	Topic	Topic exchanges use the routing key as a pattern. Imagine you have three queues: animal.dog, animal.horse, and machine.car; any message that has a routing key of "animal.*" would route to the first two queues, but not to the machine.car queue.	
Queue	In an exchange are queues. Upon creating a queue, you bind it to an exchange. That is to say, any given queue is fed messages from a single exchange. Messages sent to the queue are processed in a first-in first-out (FIFO) manner if there's only a single consumer.		
Message	The message is the thing sent to an exchange, and it consists of both a header and a body; the latter is an opaque blob of binary data whereas the former is a lightweight envelope containing routing and message metadata. Messages will only be delivered to matching queues, and they will only be delivered once. Messages can also be made to be durable so that in the case of network failure or crash, you can be sure your messages will still get through after recovery occurs.		
Publisher	A publisher creates messages to send to the exchange.		
Consumer	A consumer subscribes or feeds on the messages supplied by the queues of any given exchange.		

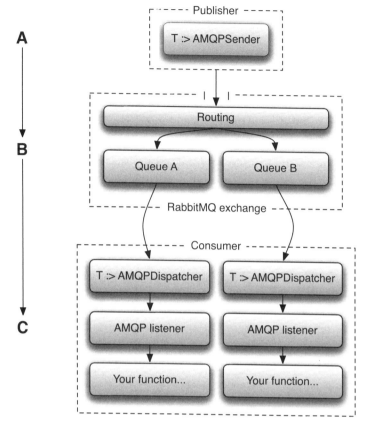

Figure 13.1 **Structure of the various sending and receiving classes in the AMQP abstraction**

There are a couple of key concepts in Lift's AMQP implementation, and architecturally these can be visualized as in figure 13.1.

In this figure, the first section at *A* represents the publishing application. Provided that this application implements a subtype of AMQPSender, it could be in another process or even on another server somewhere. After the message has been published to the exchange, RabbitMQ internally routes the message (*B*) to the correct queue based upon the routing key supplied in the message, and then it dispatches the message to the relevant consumer (*C*). The receiver can be implemented in a separate process in exactly the same way as the publisher.

AN AMQP EXAMPLE

In this section, you'll construct rudimentary client and server components that communicate via AMQP. This example has been tested with a RabbitMQ broker and it *should* work with any AMQP implementation on the broker side, but it may or may not work with other AMQP implementations.

In order to implement a publisher, you must implement a subtype of AMQPSender. It's important to do this so that the message you wish to send is properly serialized before it's sent over the wire.

> **TIP** When dealing with serialization in Scala, it's important to remember that not all things can be serialized effectively. For example, the FunctionN type series aren't good candidates for serialization; try to stick to more primitive values or even custom class types that you know how to properly serialize as a contained entity.

The following listing shows an example sender that publishes string messages and utilizes the StringAMQPSender that ships with Lift's AMQP library.

Listing 13.1 Implementing the publishing part of Lift's AMQP module

```
import com.rabbitmq.client.{ConnectionFactory,ConnectionParameters}
import net.liftweb.amqp.{AMQPSender,StringAMQPSender,AMQPMessage}

object BasicStringSender {
  val params = new ConnectionParameters
  params.setUsername("guest")                           ❶ Set RabbitMQ
  params.setPassword("guest")                              connection
  params.setVirtualHost("/")                               parameters
  params.setRequestedHeartbeat(0)

  val factory = new ConnectionFactory(params)           ❷ Connect to
  val amqp = new StringAMQPSender(factory,                 exchange
    "yourhost", 5672, "mult", "example.demo")             and queue

  def salute = amqp ! AMQPMessage("hey there!")    ⟵
}                                                     ❸ Send message
```

In this example implementation, you can see that there are several things going on. First the class defines the connection to the exchange and sets the relevant authentication credentials and some RabbitMQ-specific options ❶. Next, a connection is forged with the RabbitMQ server upon the object's creation ❷; a new instance of the StringAMQPSender actor is created, complete with parameters containing information about which virtual host and port this sender should connect to, what queue it should use, and what the routing key should be. Last, but certainly not least, is the salute method that sends an AMQPMessage to the exchange. Notice the use of the !method to send the message ❸, just like a regular actor. Lift has abstracted away most of the complexity so after the initial setup, the rest of your application code will only deal with sending messages of a predefined type.

Now that you have a method to produce and broadcast messages, you'll also want to implement something to consume those messages and do something useful. The final part of figure 13.1 outlines the consumer (C), and the following listing shows an implementation that can consume the string messages being sent by the producer constructed in listing 13.1.

Listing 13.2 Implementing the AMQP consumer

```
import com.rabbitmq.client.{ConnectionFactory,ConnectionParameters,Channel}
import net.liftweb.amqp.{AMQPDispatcher,AMQPAddListener,
                         AMQPMessage,SerializedConsumer}
import net.liftweb.actor.LiftActor

class ExampleAMQPDispatcher[T](                               ❶ Endpoint
  queueName: String,                                            dispatcher
  factory: ConnectionFactory,
  host: String, port: Int)
    extends AMQPDispatcher[T](factory, host, port){

  override def configure(channel: Channel) {
    channel.exchangeDeclare("mult", "fanout", true)
    channel.queueDeclare(queueName, true)
    channel.queueBind(queueName, "mult", "example.*")
    channel.basicConsume(queueName, false,
      new SerializedConsumer(channel, this))              ◁┐ Message
  }                                                        ❷ deserializer
}

class QueueListener(queueName: String){                   ◁┐ Queue
  val params = new ConnectionParameters                    ❸ listener
  params.setUsername("guest")
  params.setPassword("guest")
  params.setVirtualHost("/")
  params.setRequestedHeartbeat(0)

  val factory = new ConnectionFactory(params)
  val amqp = new ExampleAMQPDispatcher[String](
    queueName, factory, "yourhost", 5672)

  class StringListener extends LiftActor {
    override def messageHandler = {                        ❹ Receiving
      case msg@AMQPMessage(contents: String) =>              actor
        println("received: " + msg)
        msg
    }
  }
  amqp ! AMQPAddListener(new StringListener)              ◁┐ Listener registers
}                                                          ❺ with dispatcher
```

Implementing the consumer is a little bit more complicated than using the publisher. There are two distinct aspects to it: the dispatcher and the listener.

First, the dispatcher, which acts as the AMQP endpoint; like the publisher, it defines which exchange it will be working with ❶. Critically, inside the dispatcher defines how messages should be deserialized; it's highly likely you'll want to customize this implementation, but this example only deals with strings, so it's fine to use the defaults ❷.

QueueListener is the container class that creates the dispatcher for a given queue ❸. This dispatcher is then sent an instance of a basic LiftActor (defined at ❹) that knows how to handle AMQP messages of type string. Upon receiving such a message, the actor will print a notice to the standard output.

Finally, in order to let the dispatcher know which actor will be dealing with these incoming messages, you need to send the AMQPAddListener message to register this handler with the queue dispatcher ❺.

As mentioned in the introduction to this chapter, Lift isn't the only project in the Scala ecosystem to realize the power of actor semantics in general problem solving. Akka takes the actor paradigm and really goes to town, adding in lots of useful features such as fault-tolerance and remote actors. The next section shows you how to leverage some of Akka's toolchain and how to integrate that with your Lift application.

13.1.2   *Messaging with Akka*

The driving principle of Akka is to make concurrent programming easier by providing a lightweight, actor-based concurrency model. This simplifies concurrency and makes implementing parallelized execution much more maintainable. In addition, Akka provides a whole host of features for building fault-tolerant applications as well as add-on modules for a whole set of functionality, including systems integration, software transaction memory, and even dataflow concurrency!

In this section, we'll give you an overview of Akka and show you how to pass a message from an Akka backend into Lift, and then push that to the browser via Lift's CometActor. Akka actors implement something known as *remote actors*, which allow messages to come from other processes much like AMQP, but with a more idiomatic Scala feel. That's the part of Akka that we'll specifically explore in this section.

As an example, we'll set up a basic remote actor to illustrate sending a message from a remote Akka actor to an Akka actor in your Lift application. Before we start, though, you need to add the relevant dependencies and repositories to your project definition:

```
val actors = "se.scalablesolutions.akka" % "akka-actor" % "1.0"
val remote = "se.scalablesolutions.akka" % "akka-remote" % "1.0"

lazy val akkarepo = "akka.repo" at "http://akka.io/repository/"
```

Once this is in place, ensure that you reload and update from the SBT shell to download the required dependencies.

In this basic scenario, the first thing you need to do is set up a simplistic Akka actor as shown in the following listing.

Listing 13.3   Basic implementation using Akka actors

```
import akka.actor.Actor

class HelloWorldActor extends Actor {
  def receive = {
    case "Hello" => println("Message Received!")
  }
}
```

This implementation is probably the most straightforward actor you could create. Import the Actor type from the Akka package, and implement a new class that mixes in the Actor trait. Akka actors are different from both Lift actors and Scala actors in that they require you to implement the receive method to handle incoming messages. This particular example only handles the message "Hello", to which it will print a message to the standard output.

For the sake of this example, this HelloWorldActor will serve as the server component of the remote actor setup, so you need to initialize the actor when your application boots up.

> **NOTE** Akka actors differ from Lift actors in that they require explicit starting and stopping; all actor references have both a start()and stop() method. If you try to send a message to an Akka actor when it isn't running, you'll receive a runtime exception, so when using Akka in conjunction with Lift, it typically makes sense to start up your Akka actors within the Boot class.

Implement the following at the end of your Boot.boot method:

```
import akka.actor.Actor.{remote,actorOf}

remote.start("localhost", 2552)
remote.register("hello-service", actorOf[sample.actor.HelloWorldActor])
```

There are two things happening in this short snippet: first, a remote actor server is initialized on the localhost:2552 address, and then an actor service of a specific type is registered, which in this case is the actor defined a moment ago in listing 13.3. In short, this tells Akka that actors from a remote process will attempt to connect and interact with this particular actor using the service handle hello-service.

In order to call this particular actor remotely, you need to implement a client. To keep the code simple, let's define a static object that you can invoke from the console window in another instance of SBT.

The next listing shows the definition of this object.

Listing 13.4   Implementing a basic client for remote Akka actors

```
object HelloWorldRemoteCaller {
  import akka.actor.Actor.remote
  private val actor = remote.actorFor("hello-service", "localhost", 2552)
  def welcome = actor ! "Hello"
}
```

Given the definition of the server initialization, this caller should be fairly intuitive. The client essentially asks Akka to make a remote request to the hello-service on localhost:2552 by first obtaining a reference to the service actor and then sending the message "Hello". Note that Akka adopts the familiar actor syntax of using the ! method to communicate a message to an actor.

FAULT TOLERANCE THROUGH SUPERVISORS

When an actor is currently executing on a thread, it is more than likely running on a different call stack or thread than the message sender, so in the event of an exception occurring, the sender will not be aware that something went wrong. The only way of figuring out what actually went wrong is by looking at the stack-trace. Akka takes an approach to failure that originated in the telecoms industry, where extremely high levels of service are required and thus a huge level of fault-tolerance: embrace failure and let it crash. Initially, this may sound a touch strange, but consider that all applications at some point in time will go wrong. This is a fact of life; planning for that failure is what really matters. With this concept of embracing failure, you can build applications that can effectively recover from problems and self-heal.

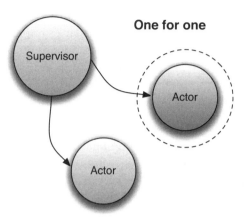

Figure 13.2   Visualization of the one-for-one restart strategy found in Akka supervisor hierarchies

From the technical standpoint, Akka achieves this by implementing supervisor hierarchies. The concept here is that in the event of a failure or problem with one of the child processes, the supervisor will adopt a predefined recovery strategy and deal with the issue at hand. Out of the box, there are two different strategies of recovery.

The first recovery strategy is known as *one for one* and can be visualized as in figure 13.2.

In the diagram, the actor with the dotted circle around it is being restarted after a problem occurred; the other actor that's also under supervision remains untouched because it's still operating within normal parameters.

The second strategy (as you might imagine) is *all for one*, as visualized in figure 13.3.

In an all for one scenario, if a particular actor under a particular supervisor has a problem, all the actors under that supervisor are restarted. This can be particularly useful when you're doing some processing, and in the event of an error you need to reset the state to a stable point across the board.

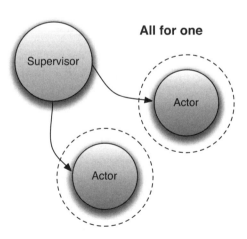

Figure 13.3   Visualization of the all-for-one restart strategy

> **NOTE** The actor paradigm can be applied to many parts of an application, in nearly every problem domain. Building applications entirely using actors can make them more scalable and more robust. This approach can often avoid CPU hot spots that are typically found in traditional application implementations.

Let's expand on the basic remote actor example from listing 13.4 to add supervision and a slightly more interesting message-processing step that could feasibly cause an error. In this case, the service will attempt to convert its incoming message to an `Int` via the `toInt` method. This could feasibly explode if the string isn't made up of numeric characters, and it would throw an exception. The following listing shows the modified caller and actor code.

Listing 13.5 Int transformer server alterations

```
import akka.actor.Actor

class IntTransformer extends Actor {
  def receive = {
    case (in: String) => println(in.toInt)          ❶ Dangerous
  }                                                       action
}

object IntTransformerRemoteCaller {
  import akka.actor.Actor.remote
  private val actor = remote.actorFor("sample.actor.IntTransformer",
    "localhost", 2552)
  def send(msg: String) = actor ! msg          ❷ Pass param
}                                                    as msg
```

There are two main alterations here. First, the message-handling function has been changed to something that could possibly explode ❶. In the event of receiving a regular string that isn't convertible to an integer, the result would be a `java.lang` `.NumberFormatException`. Second, the `send` method simply passes the string parameter as the message to the actor ❷.

None of these changes apply the supervision; that must be set in your `Boot` class with the code shown in the following listing.

Listing 13.6 Implementing Akka supervisor hierarchies

```
import akka.actor.Supervisor
import akka.config.Supervision.{SupervisorConfig,
  OneForOneStrategy, Supervise,Permanent}

Supervisor(
  SupervisorConfig(
    OneForOneStrategy(                                   ❶ Restart
      List(classOf[NumberFormatException]), 3, 1000),        strategy
    Supervise(
      actorOf[sample.actor.IntTransformer],
      Permanent, true                                    ❷ Actor lifecycle
    ) ::Nil))                                                and remote flag
```

This small block of code instructs Akka to implement a supervisor for the defined actors. In this case, it's only looking after a single actor, but the principle is the same. First, it defines the type of restart strategy to be used ❶, and you can also see that Number-FormatException has been specified as a valid exception case on which to restart the actor. This allows you to still have fall-through exceptions that won't cause a restart if there was, for example, some terminal error that really stopped the system from operating at all.

Next, the code selects the lifecycle of restarts for this actor ❷. Permanent specifies that this actor will always be restarted, no matter what. The other option is Temporary, which means that the actor will be gracefully shut down and will execute all the way through its lifecycle until it completes the postStop function.

The third and final argument of Supervise specifies whether the actor can be accessed as a remote actor service, so this must be set to true. Unlike before where you had to register the name of the remote actor service, using the supervisor causes Akka to automatically register the actor service as remote with the name of the fully qualified actor class name as its service name.

With this you have a fully functioning service that will recover after an unhandled exception occurs and will continue to operate normally. The next step is to have Akka pass messages back and forth with a Lift CometActor.

AKKA AND LIFT INTERACTION

So far, you've seen how you can essentially inject information into your application using Akka actors and its remoting protocol. But Akka supports a much richer feature set than this, and when you start to model your application entirely with actors, your frontend GUI can follow suit and also become fully event-driven. Back in chapter 9 we discussed Lift's awesome CometActor implementation that allows you to *push* data to the browser without needing additional requests from the client to pull that new data. This is an almost perfect fit with an event-driven application design, and you can use it to automatically push the result from an Akka backend right through to the client's browser.

In this section, you'll see how to leverage an actor concept called *futures*. As the name suggests, a Future is essentially a construct for saying, "In the future, you'll receive this value type as a message." The benefit of such a construct is that you can keep an asynchronous workflow without the need to explicitly pass caller references to the message target, which can quickly become somewhat cumbersome. One of the driving principals of actor designs is asynchronous messaging: having as little blocking code as you feasibly can get away with.

For this example, you'll construct two parts: an Akka actor to handle an arbitrary computation, and a Lift CometActor to collect input and display the asynchronous response from the Future. Figure 13.4 visualizes this relationship.

In the figure, you can see that the CometActor is presented to the user, who supplies some values, which are then sent to the Akka actor for processing at *A*. Upon sending this message, the CometActor understands that it will receive a response in the future (more on this in a moment), so it sends the message asynchronously. When the Akka actor has completed its processing, it responds to the CometActor, which in turn *pushes* the result to the user.

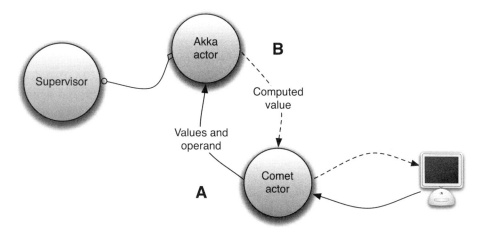

Figure 13.4   Interoperation between a Lift `CometActor` and a backend Akka actor, including a supervisor to handle failures

NOTE You could also implement the exact same type of workflow with `Lift-Actors` alone, because they too have the concept of futures, embodied by the `LAFuture` type. The purpose of using Akka here is to demonstrate how you can shunt information asynchronously through the different systems using message-passing semantics, because Akka has a lot of things that Lift doesn't when it comes to heavy-duty backend processing. Thus, the problems each project tackles are orthogonal, and understanding how you can interoperate between the different systems can be useful.

With these concepts in mind, let's explore some code. The example here will be a calculator: it collects input on the frontend, hands it off to Akka for arithmetic processing, and then receives the response.

The next listing shows the Akka backend actor.

Listing 13.7   Backend Akka implementation for calculator

```
import akka.actor.Actor

sealed case class Compute(                          ❶ Input
  thiz: Double, that: Double, by: String)             container

class Calculator extends Actor {
  def receive = {
    case Compute(a,b,by) => {
      val result = by match {
        case "*" => a * b
        case "+" => a + b                           ❷ Calculation
        case "/" => a / b
        case _ =>
          println("Unknown type of maths!")
          0D
      }
```

```
        self.reply(result)
    }
  }
}
```

⬅︎⤴ **③ Future reply**

As you can see, the implementation here is a simple calculator that takes two `Double` numbers from the incoming `Compute` message container ① and applies a user-selected operator ②. The result is then sent as a `Future[Double]` by calling `self.reply(result)` ③. There's a minimal amount of work going on here; in an actual implementation, the Akka backend would likely be distributing or processing work concurrently in order to play to its strengths.

> **TIP** If you're familiar with actor message passing and are wondering why I didn't wrap the operation signs in case objects, that was purely to avoid bloat in the example. In practice, it's a matter of style that makes no difference in operation, but I encourage the use of properly typed messages in place of arbitrary strings in your applications.

Irrespective of the actual work being conducted, the Akka backend will eventually complete the task and respond to the `CometActor`, which will push the result to the browser upon receiving the future response. The front-end `CometActor` is shown in the following listing.

Listing 13.8   Implementing the `CometActor` for calculator

```
import scala.xml.{NodeSeq,Text}
import net.liftweb.common.{Box,Full,Empty}
import net.liftweb.util.Helpers._
import net.liftweb.http.{CometActor,SHtml}
import net.liftweb.http.js.JsCmds.{SetHtml,Noop}
import akka.actor.Actor.registry
import akka.dispatch.Future

class CalculatorDisplay extends CometActor {
  private var one, two = 0D
  private var operation: Box[String] = Empty

  def doubleInput(f: Double => Any) =
    SHtml.text("0.0", v => f(asDouble(v).openOr(0D)))

  def render =
    "#value_one" #> doubleInput(one = _) &
    "#value_two" #> doubleInput(two = _) &
    "#operation" #> SHtml.select(Seq("+","/","*")
      .map(x => (x -> x)), operation,
      v => operation = Full(v)) &
    "type=submit" #> SHtml.ajaxSubmit("Submit", () => {
  val future: Future[Double] =
  registry.actorFor[Calculator].get !!!
    Compute(one,two,operation.openOr("+"))
      future.onComplete(f => this ! f.result)
```

① **Define internal variables**

② **Create input fields**

③ **Send user input to Akka actor**

```
      Noop
    }) andThen SHtml.makeFormsAjax

  override def lowPriority = {
    case Some(value: Double) =>
      partialUpdate(SetHtml(
        "result", Text(value.toString)))
  }
}
```

❹ **Push future response**

This `CometActor` houses a simple interface for entering values and choosing the type of mathematical operation you wish to carry out. The input values are held in private variables ❶ and are bound to the input elements ❷. This is all normal element binding, but the key difference here is that the Submit button actually takes the values, wraps them up in a `Compute` instance, and sends it to the Akka actor ❸. The message is sent by using the `!!!` method, which yields a `Future[T]`, which in this case is assigned to the value `future`.

The `Future` isn't the concrete value of the response you're looking for in its own right; rather, it's an indication that you'll eventually get the response you're expecting, and to that end you must specify what it needs to do when that response does arrive. This is configured through the `onComplete` method, and as you can see, this function simply forwards the resulting value to itself as a message, which is handled and pushed to the browser ❹.

LIFT INTERACTION WITHOUT USING FUTURES

Although the use of futures yields a working solution, it's not 100 percent ideal because it means the response is being handled by something other than the main `messageHandler`. When one Akka actor is communicating with another Akka actor, the recipient of a message can implicitly resolve the sender, even when the message was only sent with a single bang (`!`), by implicitly determining the `ActorRef`. But because `LiftActor` doesn't have anything to do with `ActorRef`, it's seemingly impossible to leverage Akka's reply semantics.

Fortunately, there's a solution, and it can make the `CalculatorDisplay` Comet-Actor much neater by removing the future and implicitly telling the calculator where it needs to respond. Consider the following listing.

> **Listing 13.9 Implicit `ActorRef` bridge between `CometActors` and Akka actors**

```
trait AkkaCometActor extends CometActor {
  implicit val akkaProxy: Option[ActorRef] =
    Some(Actor.actorOf(new Actor{
      protected def receive = {
        case a => AkkaCometActor.this ! a
      }
    }))
  override def localSetup {
    super.localSetup
    akkaProxy.foreach(_.start)
  }
```

❶ **Create implicit Akka proxy**

❷ **Start proxy on setup**

```
override def localShutdown {
  super.localShutdown
  akkaProxy.foreach(_.stop)
}
}
```

❸ Stop proxy on teardown

This trait essentially acts as an intermediary between the `CometActor` and the Akka actor. First, this trait defines an implicit proxy actor that forwards messages from the Akka actor to the `CometActor` ❶. When a message is sent to the Akka actor and Akka looks for an implicitly supplied reference for the sender, it will find the `akkaProxy` supplied here and use that as the place to respond to when the target calls `self.reply(...)`. When that proxy receives the reply for the Akka actor, it immediately forwards it to the `CometActor`, giving you the illusion of direct interaction between Lift's Comet infrastructure and the backend Akka setup. Finally, the `localSetup` and `localShutdown` methods hook into the `CometActor` lifecycle, so that the Akka proxy actor is shut down explicitly when the `CometActor` is shut down by Lift, which automatically happens when the user's session expires or the defined `CometActor`'s lifespan is exceeded ❷ and ❸.

With this implicit magic in place, the `CalculatorDisplay` needs some minor changes in order for the `CometActor` message handler to properly handle the message that the Akka actor replies with. The changes are shown in the following listing.

Listing 13.10   Alterations to `CalculatorDisplay` with implicit actor bridge

```
class CalculatorDisplay extends AkkaCometActor {
  ...
  def render =
    ...
    "type=submit" #> SHtml.ajaxSubmit("Submit", () => {
      registry.actorFor[Calculator].map {
        _ ! Compute(one,two,operation.openOr("+"))
      } Noop
    }) andThen SHtml.makeFormsAjax

  override def lowPriority = {
    case value: Double =>
      partialUpdate(SetHtml("result", Text(value.toString)))
  }
}
```

❶ Extend AkkaCometActor

❷ Remove future

❸ Remove Option[T]

The first change is to extend the new `AkkaCometActor` trait in place of the regular `CometActor` ❶. Secondly, but most importantly, you need to remove the future `!!!` call in place of a one-way `!` method ❷. The ramification of this is that Akka will then handle the response by way of its built-in reply semantics, letting you match on the value type directly rather than using an `Option[Double]` ❸.

The next section moves away from messaging to cover JEE persistence (JPA). If you're coming to Lift from other Java-based frameworks, or you have an existing investment in JEE technologies, worry not! These are fully interoperable with Lift, and in the case of JPA, Lift provides wrappers around the classic Java API to give these tools a more idiomatic Scala feel.

13.2 Integrating Lift into existing Java infrastructure

In previous chapters, you've seen several different persistence mechanisms that either ship with Lift (Mapper) or have neat integration layers through Record (Squeryl and others). With this in mind, you may be wondering what the purpose of discussing yet *another* database access system is. Well, if you're coming from the Java space and are familiar with JPA and the general Enterprise JavaBeans 3 (EJB3) setup, understanding how to work with Lift using this sort of system is important; particularly because many enterprise users already have existing investments in EJB-based systems.

Unlike the systems discussed in previous chapters, JPA makes fairly heavy use of annotations to drive various aspects of entity definition, and it takes a rather different approach to managing entity instances via its entity manager. We'll be exploring this in more detail later, but here are some top-level reasons why you may be interested in using JPA:

- JPA is fully interoperable with Java, so if you need Java code to call your entities, you can do so in a toll-free manner.
- JPA is generally very mature and it's a well-documented technology online. As such, advanced features such as second-level caching are well documented with examples.
- Given a larger database schema, JPA can often be a more robust choice, because you can generally make more intelligent choices about how joins are implemented and what the relationships are between different entities.

In addition to JPA, JEE also encompasses the Java Transaction API (JTA), which provides a general-purpose framework for constructing transactional semantics across multiple X/Open XA resources. There's a Lift module for working with JTA, but it's somewhat out of scope for this book.

13.2.1 JPA and Scala EntityManager

Lift's JPA module depends upon a project called Scala JPA. This project provides an abstraction upon the `EntityManager` class provided by JPA in order to provide an API that's much more comfortable for Scala programmers. Lift builds upon this work to provide some additional integration that's helpful when building web applications that include JPA.

JPA and general Java persistence is a large topic that could easily fill entire books (such as Debu Panda, Reza Rahman, and Derek Lane's *EJB 3 in Action*), so this section assumes you have a familiarity with the implementation of POJO entities. For readers who aren't directly familiar with JPA, see table 13.2 for a brief introduction to some common terms.

Table 13.2   Overview of common terms used in and around JPA

Term	Description
POJO	This stands for *plain old Java object* and is a common term in discussions relating to JPA. You'll be writing Scala, so the acronym doesn't hold true here, but you can read this term to mean a plain class that doesn't extend any specific class and that uses annotations to define field metadata.
EntityManager	The official definition is: "An `EntityManager` instance is associated with a persistence context. A persistence context is a set of entity instances in which for any persistent entity identity there is a unique entity instance. Within the persistence context, the entity instances and their lifecycle are managed. This interface defines the methods that are used to interact with the persistence context". This essentially means that if you want to do anything with JPA entities in your application, you'll require an `EntityManager` to interact with them.
Attached and detached objects	JPA entities have attached and detached modes. When an entity is attached, it's available in the live JPA session, and any model alterations are persisted appropriately. A detached object can be interacted with in the same way, but the changes aren't reflected in the database—you have to explicitly pull the entity back into the session via the `EntityManager`'s `merge` method.

In order to use JPA, you'll need to specify the following dependencies in your project class. In this case, the `EntityManager` implementation is coming from the Hibernate project:

```
val jpa = "net.liftweb" %% "lift-jpa" % liftVersion
val hibernate = "org.hibernate"
        ➥% "hibernate-entitymanager" % "3.6.0.Final"
val hibernatevali = "org.hibernate"
        ➥% "hibernate-validator-annotation-processor" % "4.1.0.Final"
```

These dependencies will allow you to define entity classes, complete with annotations, so that the JPA infrastructure can determine exactly what needs to happen, including validation. With your project now ready to use JPA, let's build a small application that adopts the bookshop-style example used in both chapters 10 and 11 to demonstrate some of the lift-jpa features.

The following listing shows the implementation for two sample entities: `Author` and `Book`.

Listing 13.11   Implementing the `Author` and `Book` JPA entities with Scala

```
import java.util.Date
import javax.persistence._
import javax.validation.constraints.Size

@Entity
class Book {
```

 ① Main entity annotation

```
  @Id
  @GeneratedValue(strategy = GenerationType.AUTO)
  var id : Long = _

  @Size(min = 3, max = 60)
  @Column(unique = true, nullable = false)
  var title : String = ""                              ◁─┐
                                                          │  ❷  JPA field
  @Temporal(TemporalType.DATE)                            │     annotations
  @Column(nullable = true)                                │
  var published : Date = new Date()                       │
                                                          │
  @ManyToOne(optional = false)                         ◁──┘
  var author : Author = _
}

@Entity
class Author {
  @Id
  @GeneratedValue(strategy = GenerationType.AUTO)
  var id : Long = _                                    ◁─┐
                                                          │  ❸  Field vars
  @Size(min = 3, max = 20)                                │
  @Column(unique = true, nullable = false)                │
  var name : String = ""                               ◁──┤
                                                          │
  @OneToMany(mappedBy = "author", targetEntity = classOf[Book])
  var books : java.util.Set[Book] =                       │
    new java.util.HashSet[Book]()                         │
}                                                      ───┘
```

This listing defines the two entities this example will use. Notice how they're regular
Scala classes that are accompanied by the JPA annotations. These annotations should
look pretty familiar if you've used JPA with Java before, but for the uninitiated, all entities must first be annotated with @Entity ❶, and then each field variable ❸ must be
annotated with one of the many JPA annotations ❷, depending upon how it maps to
the database.

Oh no, annotations!

Annotations have somewhat of a tarnished history with Scala, because many people really don't like them and avoid their use entirely. In fact, until Scala 2.8 annotations simply did not work properly within Scala.

Annotations are commonly used in Java because the language itself lacks more
sophisticated constructs that allow developers to write composable code. As
such, annotations are a convenient way to build generic functionality in Java.

With Scala being a much richer language, annotations aren't found in idiomatic
Scala code, and their usage is usually reserved for Java interoperation only, as is
the case with JPA. If you find yourself wanting to use annotations in your normal
Scala code, you can likely factor it out into a set of composable functions or traits.

Of particular interest in these annotations should be @Size. This is one of many validation annotations that Hibernate (or your EJB3 implementation of choice) provides. These validations will be automatically applied before persisting to the database, and specialized exceptions will be thrown if their conditions aren't properly satisfied.

Now that you have the entities in place, you need to ensure that you define a persistence.xml file in src/main/resources/META-INF so that the JPA library knows how to interact with your database. Your persistence.xml should look like the following listing.

Listing 13.12   Configuring JPA with persistence.xml

```xml
<?xml version="1.0"?>
<persistence>
  <persistence-unit name="chp13"                        ❶ Name of
    transaction-type="RESOURCE_LOCAL">                     persistence unit
    <properties>
      <property name="hibernate.connection.driver_class"
        value="org.h2.Driver"/>
      <property name="hibernate.connection.url"
        value="jdbc:h2:database/chp_13;FILE_LOCK=NO"/>          ❷ Database
      <property name="hibernate.dialect"                          connection
        value="org.hibernate.dialect.H2Dialect"/>                 settings
      <property name="hibernate.connection.username" value="sa"/>
      <property name="hibernate.connection.password" value=""/>
      <property name="hibernate.max_fetch_depth" value="3"/>
      <property name="hibernate.show_sql" value="true"/>
      <property name="hibernate.hbm2ddl.auto" value="update"/>
    </properties>
  </persistence-unit>
</persistence>
```

This file defines the connection parameters and gives JPA the information it needs to effectively determine how to construct queries using the right type of SQL dialect for your database. The first configuration point of interest is the name attribute on the <persistence-unit> element ❶. This is the name you'll refer to from your code, so use something meaningful.

Next the XML file defines the type of database and connection string JPA will use to establish that connection. This example is using the H2 database, so it specifies a path to the database file on disk and defines the SQL dialect that it should use when generating SQL queries. If your database requires security credentials, ensure these are populated in the hibernate.connection.username and hibernate.connection .password settings respectively ❷.

The second part of configuring JPA is to define an orm.xml file. Developers often argue that elements of entity definitions should not exist as inline code, but rather should be externally configured. This is essentially the role of orm.xml, and you can use it to define queries that each entity can execute and also to augment the definition that exists in the entity. This file must be created alongside persistence.xml in META-INF, and it should look like the following listing.

Listing 13.13 Augmenting entities with orm.xml

```
<?xml version="1.0" encoding="UTF-8" ?>
<entity-mappings version="1.0"
  xmlns="http://java.sun.com/xml/ns/persistence/orm"
  xmlns:xsi="http://www.w3.org/2001/XMLSchema-instance"
  xsi:schemaLocation="http://java.sun.com/xml/ns/persistence/orm
                      http://java.sun.com/xml/ns/persistence/orm_1_0.xsd">

  <package>sample.model</package>              ❶  Entity package
  <entity class="Book">
    <named-query name="findBooksByAuthor">
      <query><![CDATA[
        from Book b                            ❷  Book entity
        where b.author.id = :id                   and query
        order by b.title
      ]]></query>
    </named-query>
  </entity>
  <entity class="Author">
    <named-query name="findAllAuthors">
      <query><![CDATA[from Author a order by a.name]]></query>
    </named-query>
  </entity>
</entity-mappings>
```

You can see that this file is a descriptor of the entities in your application. You can define entities ❶ and also the queries your application will make ❷. The JPA query syntax is quite extensive, so we encourage you to check the online reference: http://download.oracle.com/javaee/5/tutorial/doc/bnbtl.html. Also understand that these queries are what are known as *named queries*—in the calling code you'll look up the query by its identifying name, such as findBooksByAuthor.

As mentioned previously, it's also possible to augment the entity information defined in the entity. For example, let's imagine you wanted to specify a name for a given column. You could do something like this:

```
<entity name="Book">
  ...
  <attribute-override name="title">
    <column name="book_title" >
  </attribute-override>
</entity>
```

This would then change the name of the column in the database to be "book_title" as opposed to "name", which was defined in the entity code.

With this setup done, your application should now be able to talk to the database. But note that the implementation is lazy, in that it will only attempt to connect upon the first call to the entity manager.

OBJECTS AND THE ENTITY MANAGER

Now that you have your entities and queries defined, you'd like to start interacting with them. For this you'll require an entity manager, and Lift provides some neat abstractions for this atop of the default Java infrastructure so that the concept feels more native to Scala.

In order to create an entity manager, define an object that extends the `lift-jpa` type `LocalEMF` and extends `RequestVarEM`:

```
import org.scala_libs.jpa.LocalEMF
import net.liftweb.jpa.RequestVarEM

object Model extends LocalEMF("chp13") with RequestVarEM
```

Scala objects are lazily created, so again this will only connect to the database when you touch it for the first time. Note that the `LocalEMF` class creates a connection from your application to the database, but if you'd prefer to look up a data source via JNDI, you can swap this class out for `JndiEMF` instead. Finally, the composed `RequestVarEM` is important because it allows you to define this singleton for accessing the underlying entity manager and keeps the JPA session live for each request, so you don't have to do any additional plumbing. As the name implies, the `RequstVarEM` is underpinned by Lift's `RequestVar` functionality, which keeps the entity manager request-scoped.

The entity manager typically has two modes for interacting with JPA entities: attached and detached. The entity manager monitors attached entity instances until it's instructed to `flush` these entities, when it will modify the underlying database with the appropriate changes. The practical advantage of object detachment in Lift is that you can obtain a reference to an entity object in the initial request cycle and make changes, and then easily reattach it to the live JPA session in the next request, complete with any changes you made. Objects can be explicitly attached to the JPA session via entity manager methods like `merge` and `persist`, or they can be implicitly attached using methods like `find` and `getReference`.

Now that you have everything in place to start making queries, let's make a simple listing and add an interface for adding `Author` entities to the database. The first thing you need to add is a new class called `Authors`. This class will contain two snippet methods that take care of the listing and adding of authors. The following listing shows the implementation.

> Listing 13.14 Implementing the `Author` snippet

```
import scala.xml.{NodeSeq,Text}
import scala.collection.JavaConversions._
import javax.validation.ConstraintViolationException
import net.liftweb.common.{Failure,Empty,Full}
import net.liftweb.util.Helpers._
import net.liftweb.http.{RequestVar,SHtml,S}
import sample.model.{Book,Author,Model}

object Authors {
  object authorVar extends RequestVar(new Author)    ❶ Define author RequestVar
}
```

```
class Authors {
  import Authors._
  def author = authorVar.is

  def list =
    "tr" #> Model.createNamedQuery[Author](            ❷ Get all
      ➡"findAllAuthors").getResultList.map { a =>          authors
      ".name" #> a.name &
      ".books" #> SHtml.link("/jee/books/add",
          () => authorVar(a),
          Text("%s books (Add more)".format(          ❸ Bind links
          ➡.books.size))) &
      ".edit" #> SHtml.link("add", () =>
        authorVar(a), Text("Edit"))
    }

  def add = {
    val current = author
    "type=hidden" #> SHtml.hidden(
      () => authorVar(current)) &
    "type=text" #> SHtml.text(author.name, author.name = _) &
    "type=submit" #> SHtml.onSubmitUnit(() =>
      tryo(Model.mergeAndFlush(author)) match {
        case Failure(msg,
        ➡ Full(err: ConstraintViolationException),_) =>    ❹ Persist new
            S.error(err.getConstraintViolations               instance
             .toList.flatMap(c =>
            <p>{c.getMessage}</p>))
        case _ => S.redirectTo("index")
      })
  }
}
```

The Authors class contains two snippets, list and add, and it contains a RequestVar that's shared for the class instance ❶. This RequestVar contains a new Author entity instance, so that even if the Add page is loaded, it will always have a reference to an Author that can subsequently be saved.

Looking first at the list snippet, you can see that it details using the Model entity manager to execute the predefined (named) query ❷ from the orm.xml file created earlier in this section. It retrieves a list of all the authors in the database by using the Model.createNamedQuery method. Note the type parameter here, which tells the entity manager what the return type of this method will be; JPA is largely constructed of runtime operations, so it needs additional information about the types involved. After returning a list, the list snippet iterates through each item in the list, binding both a link to add books for this author and a link to edit this author's previously saved information ❸. In both cases, note that the function bound to the link sets the current author value into the class RequestVar, authorVar. This way, when the page reloads with the Edit screen, for example, the author's information is already prepopulated and the entity instance is attached to the live JPA session, ready for editing.

The add snippet should look like a fairly regular snippet method by now, but the main thing to make note of is how the `submit` function calls `Model.mergeAnd-Flush(author)` ❹. This is essentially telling the entity manager to take the changes already made to the model and update them in the database; this could result in either an update or insert operation in the underlying store.

This section has shown you how you can make use of Lift's integration with the popular JPA libraries and infrastructure. Specifically, you've seen how to configure and get up and running with JPA while making use of Lift's wrappers around the rather verbose JPA. This removes the Java-esque feel of its API and reduces what would typically be a set of method calls and `try/catch` statements into simple one-line calls.

13.3 Summary

In this chapter, you've seen how to leverage Lift's integration of commonplace Java enterprise technologies—specifically the Java Persistence API. You saw how Lift provides some idiomatic abstractions upon JPA, specifically related to its entity manager and resolving the JPA sessions in the scope of any given request. Lift's integration is designed to provide Scala-like interfaces for well-known Java technology, so for the most part JPA is left as is, in terms of querying and persistence semantics.

Finally, this chapter covered distribution and messaging. Lift comes with an integration module for AMQP, which is based upon the actor-programming model. This allows you to both publish and receive messages from the AMQP broker using the familiar actor abstraction. Additionally, we touched upon the Akka service framework and how you can make use of its robust distributed and concurrent programming abstractions to push dynamic, event-driven data into your application and right through to the browser.

The next chapter covers testing, which includes leveraging Lift's testing helpers to mock requests and Lift's stateful components, so that you can write test suites or specifications for your snippets. Additionally, TestKit also provides a mechanism for testing your RESTful services with a live, sandboxed Jetty server.

Application testing
14

This chapter covers

- Using Scala testing frameworks
- Writing testable code
- Using Lift's TestKit

Testing is an important part of the modern application development lifecycle, and testing web applications comes with its own unique problems. This chapter deals with testing as an independent entity, away from the main development of an application. Broadly speaking, you should really write tests iteratively, while you're developing an application, to ensure that all the great new features you're adding don't break any of the existing functionality. With that being said, testing is covered here in one homogeneous block, so be sure to take what you learn in this chapter and apply it within each iteration of your development cycle.

With Scala being based on the JVM and sharing a great deal of common ground with Java, you have a plethora of testing tools available to choose from. Popular Java testing tools like JUnit (http://www.junit.org/) will still work with your Scala code, but the first section of this chapter focuses on the testing tools that have come from the Scala ecosystem and gives you an introduction to three popular testing tools:

- *ScalaTest*—http://www.scalatest.org/
- *Specs*—http://code.google.com/p/specs/
- *ScalaCheck*—http://code.google.com/p/scalacheck/

In addition, the first section concludes with an introduction to generating code-coverage reports from your SBT project to give you an indication as to what level of untested code your application currently has.

The next section deals with how to write nicely decoupled code by using proven Scala programming practices, such as the Cake pattern, and it also covers some of Lift's utility constructs for creating scoped values.

Finally, after you have a grounding in the various tools available to help facilitate the testing process, and you have an appreciation for how to effectively write decoupled application code, you'll see how to leverage the Lift TestKit, which allows you to mock HTTP requests and conduct full integration tests on your RESTful services. As an additional part of these integration tests, you'll see how you can implement the web application–testing tool Selenium (http://seleniumhq.org/).

Before getting into these later topics, though, let's first look at some of the Scala testing frameworks available today.

14.1   *Scala testing frameworks*

There is a whole range of testing frameworks available to Scala developers today, from well-known Java frameworks like JUnit and TestNG right through to new Scala tools such as Specs. These tools are largely interoperable because Scala ultimately boils down to Java bytecode. So much so, in fact, that you can even test your Java code with a Scala testing tool like Specs!

Each tool takes a slightly different approach, and in some aspects the problems they tackle are orthogonal. For example, ScalaTest and Specs are unit-testing tools that allow you to work in a test-driven development (TDD) style or even a behavior-driven development (BDD) style, whereas ScalaCheck primarily focuses on property-driven development (PDD) by allowing the developer to specify a property that defines behavior and ScalaCheck will generate arbitrary input in an attempt to falsify that property assertion.

You might be familiar with TDD and BDD testing approaches, so to begin with let's take a look at ScalaTest and then the Specs framework.

14.1.1 *ScalaTest*

ScalaTest is one of the older projects in the Scala ecosystem, and it's a popular choice for testing applications for several reasons:

- It's well maintained.
- It has a comprehensive feature set that includes the ability organize tests into suites.
- It tests both Scala and Java code.

- It facilitates several different styles of testing.
- It has a convenient API.

To get started with ScalaTest, add the following to your SBT project definition:

```
val scalatest = "org.scalatest" % "scalatest" % "1.3" % "test"
```

Notice the `%` `"test"` appended to the end of the dependency declaration. This is important because it ensures that SBT doesn't package ScalaTest in your output JAR or WAR file; essentially it's a test-phase only dependency. As always, be sure to call `reload` and `update` after adding the dependency.

Now that you have ScalaTest available, let's take a look at a fairly straightforward test that utilizes a type known as `FunSuite`. The *fun* part of the name refers to *function*, and a *suite* is what ScalaTest calls a group of tests. The most basic of test cases is shown in the following listing. It simply checks that calling the `tail` method on a `List[String]` returns all but the first element.

Listing 14.1 Basic example of using ScalaTest's `FunSuite`

```
import org.scalatest.FunSuite

class BasicSuite extends FunSuite {
  val shared = List("a","b","c")
  test("that tail yields 'b' and 'c'"){
    assert(shared.tail === List("b","c"))
  }
}
```

This exceedingly basic test demonstrates some of the ScalaTest features. First, it defines a `shared` fixture that all tests in this suite can access, which is simply a list of letters.

> **NOTE** The word *fixture* can have different connotations. In the context of this chapter, a fixture is something that's necessary for the test to complete its work. That could be anything from a static value, to a file containing sample data, right through to a database connection.

The suite itself has only a single test (as defined by the `test(..)` method) that checks to see if the result of calling `tail` on the shared `List[String]` will result in `List("b","c")`. The result is determined by using the `assert` method from Scala-Test's `FunSuite` to define the expected result.

If you have any experience with a modern test framework (in any language), this should be a familiar paradigm.

14.1.2 *Scala Specs*

Specs was originally inspired by the Ruby testing framework RSpec (http://rspec.info/), and it differs from ScalaTest in that it primarily promotes a behavior-driven development (BDD) style of testing that revolves around defining *specifications* that are readable by programmers and business folk alike.

In order to add Specs to your project, you must add the following test dependency:

```
val specs = "org.scala-tools.testing" %% "specs" % "1.6.7.2" % "test"
```

Be sure to run `reload` and `update` from the SBT console before continuing.

After SBT has downloaded the Specs dependencies, you can set to work creating your first specification, as defined in the following listing. This specification defines a simple pair of tests that run some trivial operations on a string to validate its behavior.

Listing 14.2 Implementing hello world with Specs

```
import org.specs._

class SpecsExample extends Specification {
  "hello world" should {
    "have 11 characters" in {
      "hello world".size must_== 11
    }
    "match 'h.* w.*'" in {
      "hello world" must be matching("h.* w.*")
    }
  }
}
```

The class extends `Specification`, which is the Specs trait that provides the value matchers and syntactic sugar, such as the `should` keyword. All your Specs tests must extend `Specification`.

This particular specification defines a list of features that the string "hello world" should exhibit. In a more realistic example, you would likely define features relevant to your model or a specific unit of functionality rather than for a simple string. But even though you're only testing a string, note that there are two separate tests that check first if the string has a size of 11 characters, and second whether the string "hello world" matches the pattern h.* w.*. Take particular note of how this is applied:

```
"hello world" must be matching("h.* w.*")
```

It's almost like regular English prose, and that's the point. Even if you don't know much about the Specs library, you could still look at this line of code and make sense of what it's doing.

These language constructs (`must`, `must_==`, `be`, `matching`, and so on) are known as *matchers*. A matcher is a construct that compares two values to verify a particular condition, and Specs supports many different matchers. For the most part, these matchers are composable, so you can combine them together however you see fit. Check out the Specs documentation for the full list of default matchers and more specific information on making your own: http://code.google.com/p/specs/wiki/Matchers Guide#Be/Have_matchers.

Now that you have a basic understanding of Specs and how to compose matchers, consider the more useful example in the next listing. It checks that passing `null` to the `Option` apply method properly returns `None`. Additionally, this test runs operations before and after the specification by utilizing Specs' `beforeSpec` and `afterSpec` functions.

Listing 14.3 Wrapping the specification with before and after actions

```scala
trait SetupAndTearDown {
  def construcEnvironment() =
    println("Construcing the environment!")
  def tearDownEnvironment() =
    println("Tearing down the environment!")
}

class AnotherExample extends Specification with SetupAndTearDown {
  construcEnvironment().beforeSpec
  "An Option" should {
    "Be None if supplied a null value" in {
      Option(null) must_== None
    }
  }
  tearDownEnvironment().afterSpec
}
```

❶ Trait definition

❷ Before action

❸ After action

In this example, Specs provides some useful hooks for executing actions before any after specifications ❷ and ❸, and additionally before and after each test. These hooks are particularly useful when you need to run tests against an external system, such as a database. The functions allow you to run arbitrary functions that, in this example, only print messages to the console ❶, but later in section 14.3.2 you'll see how you can run tests against the database and create a freshly sandboxed in-memory database before each test or specification.

In addition to the features supplied by both Specs and ScalaTest, they both also integrate nicely with another testing library called ScalaCheck. ScalaCheck provides facilities for automatic test case generation.

14.1.3 *ScalaCheck*

In standard testing systems, you define the problem you want to test for, and then you implement the test method itself. With ScalaCheck, this scenario is essentially reversed: you define a property or behavior you wish to test and provide outer bounds for that behavior. For example, you define a function that takes two parameters, and ScalaCheck will randomly generate values for those parameters to ensure that the property or behavior you defined in that function still holds true.

Although ScalaCheck is a standalone project and can be used independently from any other testing framework, it's commonly used in conjunction with either ScalaTest or Specs. The following listing shows an example of using Specs with its ScalaCheck integration.

```
                 Listing 14.4   Implementing ScalaCheck with Specs
import org.specs._
import org.scalacheck.Prop._

class ScalaCheckExample extends Specification with ScalaCheck {
  "Strings" should {
    "Start with" in {
      forAll {                                                ❶  ScalaCheck
        (a: String, b: String) => (a + b).startsWith(a)          function
      } must pass
    }
  }
}
```

This listing shows a specification that mixes in the ScalaCheck integration trait, which is part of the Specs package. Notice that the test declaration uses the forAll keyword imported from the ScalaCheck Prop object. The forAll method ❶ essentially takes a function that ScalaCheck will then execute with randomly generated parameters. You can even set the number of tests that ScalaCheck will generate by using the set method as shown:

```
forAll {
  (a: String, b: String) => (a + b).startsWith(a)
} must pass(set(minTestsOk -> 1000))
```

The addition of the minTestsOk tuple ensures that ScalaCheck generates 1,000 tests before the test itself is satisfied. You can alter the parameters passed to the pass method with a range of conditions to vary what ScalaCheck will actually pass to the method.

Now that you know the basics of the testing frameworks, let's look at how code-coverage reports can provide an indication of just how much of your code base is covered by test cases.

14.1.4 Code coverage reports

After you've spent some time writing tests, it can be helpful to have your build tool generate a report on the so-called *coverage* that your tests have achieved in your project. If you have five classes, but your tests only cover three of them, you *potentially* have a large hole in the completeness of your test suite. As your codebase grows, this problem can also grow fairly quickly, so having an automated way to determine the amount of test coverage your code has can be rather useful.

There are many code-coverage tools in the Java ecosystem, such as Cobertura (http://cobertura.sourceforge.net/), that were created specifically for Java. These tools have a limited level of effectiveness with Scala, because during the compilation phase, the Scala compiler creates a lot of anonymous classes if you're using closures, traits, and many of the other great language features. These anonymous classes make it difficult for the Java-oriented tools to give you a true representation of the coverage because they simply have no concept of what all these classes are for or how they interoperate.

At the end of 2010, however, a project called Scala Code Coverage Tool (SCCT, http://mtkopone.github.com/scct/) was launched to create a Scala-specific coverage tool. It was designed to be aware of these special classes and handle them properly, giving you a much more accurate representation of code coverage.

> **NOTE** It's important to recognize that nearly all code-coverage tools can be tricked. You should think of SCCT and other such tools as indicators of coverage; they only show you which lines of your codebase have been touched by tests. The bottom line is that you're only as good as the tests you write, and if your tests cover all the code, but they're bad tests, you still may well have a broken application—you just won't be aware of it until the client calls!

In order to use SCCT in your project, you must first add the SCCT plugin to your SBT project. If you aren't familiar with SBT plugins, ensure that you have a file called Plugins.scala that resides in ${root}/project/plugins/Plugins.scala. This file should then contain something like this:

```
import sbt._
class Plugins(info: ProjectInfo) extends PluginDefinition(info) {
  ...
  lazy val scctPlugin = "reaktor" % "sbt-scct-for-2.8" % "0.1-SNAPSHOT"
  val scctRepo = "scct" at "http://mtkopone.github.com/scct/maven-repo/"
}
```

The final thing you need to do is add the ScctProject trait to your project. This trait delivers the actions that let you generate the coverage reports. Your project definition should then look something like this:

```
import sbt._
import reaktor.scct.ScctProject
class ChapterFourteen(info: ProjectInfo)
  extends DefaultWebProject(info)
  with ScctProject
```

After adding these two things, restart SBT and you'll notice that several JARs are downloaded. These are the SCCT JARs and their dependencies, and you should now have two additional actions available on your project:

```
test-coverage
test-coverage-compile
```

These actions are provided by SCCT, and they allow you to generate code-coverage reports that look similar to figure 14.1. The progress bars and percentages indicate the level of coverage each class, object, or trait has in the project. Although code-coverage reports aren't foolproof, it will usually give you a pretty reasonable indication as to the level of testing your project has.

In order to increase your chances of having strong coverage, the next section covers several things you can do when structuring your application to make it as testable as possible.

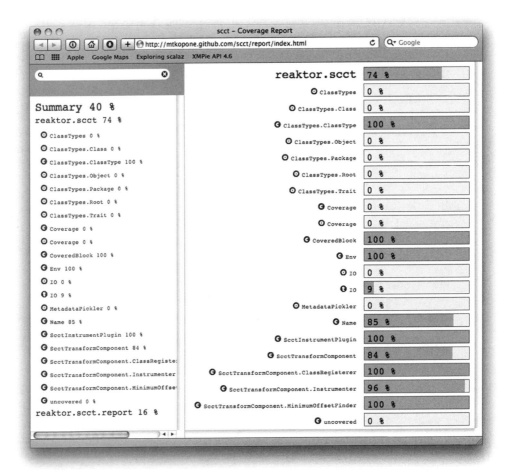

Figure 14.1   Example of a SCCT coverage report. It details all the packages and their classes on the left and provides a more detailed report on the right.

14.2   *Writing testable code*

In the previous chapters, you saw how Lift's sophisticated state handling can simplify some of the most complex things developers have to contend. But although Lift makes many common tasks easier and more secure, certain things become slightly more difficult to unit test. This section covers some methodologies that will make testing your code easier; it also takes an honest look at some aspects of Lift that are more complex to unit test as a result of Lift's stateful nature.

> **NOTE** The purpose of illustrating these current testing difficulties is to give you a full and frank picture of Lift. As time goes by, this situation will likely improve, but at the time of writing there were several complexities with unit testing code that's tightly coupled to Lift's state handling. More on this in section 14.2.1.

When writing application code, there are many things you can do in the Scala language itself that can greatly improve the testability and separation of your code. This separation can be exceedingly helpful because it allows you to both reuse chunks of code and split different parts out into more manageable elements. Traits, implicit conversions, and higher-order functions are just some of the powerful tools that can make this division possible and relatively pain-free to implement.

Many developers today will be familiar with dependency injection (DI) frameworks such as Google Guice (http://code.google.com/p/google-guice/). Although these types of tools are exceedingly popular in the wider Java community, they have, for the most part, found less traction in the Scala community. In idiomatic Scala code, the preference has been to use a couple of different patterns of implementation to achieve the dependency wiring, as opposed to using runtime injection.

Before getting into dependency injection, though, let's start by looking at Lift's design and at what things can make writing particular unit tests more involved.

14.2.1 *Complexities of testing state*

When it comes to testing your Lift application, it's important to understand how the stateful components of Lift can play a critical role in determining how testable a particular unit of your application is. At the time of writing, in order to unit-test application code that accesses Lift's stateful components, it is necessary to mock the incoming request so that the state mechanism is operational.

For example, consider a snippet that directly calls S.param or any of the other S methods that access session- or request-specific thread-local data. These methods require a properly initialized LiftSession to exist before they can be used. In order to set up S properly, you need to mock the incoming request and engage some related standard configuration by instantiating the application environment. Strictly speaking, this is probably a bit too much infrastructure to be classified as a strict unit test. This kind of global setup is more commonly associated with integration testing rather than unit testing, but because its normally only a case of using a single mock request, we'll overlook this and refer to it as unit testing.

The problem with requiring a properly initialized session is that you can't just write a standard unit test using Specs or one of the other testing tools covered in the first section. Rather, you need to leverage one of the tools from Lift's TestKit module that will properly initialize the system prior to executing a test. Consider the following listing, which defines a basic class that would be rather typical of an implementation that's tightly coupled with Lift's state mechanism.

Listing 14.5 Example of a class that's tightly coupled to Lift state

```
import scala.xml.{NodeSeq,Text}
import net.liftweb.http.S

class CookieList {
  def render(xhtml: NodeSeq): NodeSeq =
```

```
    S.receivedCookies.flatMap(c => Text(c.name) ++ <br />)
}
```

With a class such as this, it's important to be aware that without a fully initialized session context, `S.receivedCookies` will always be an empty `List`, meaning you'll never have anything to actually test for. As mentioned a moment ago, Lift's TestKit can help here by providing a testing construct known as `WebSpec` that initializes the `S` context and allows you to execute operations that require sessions, request scope, and more. By utilizing `WebSpec`, you can mock an incoming request that includes some cookies and that then allows you to execute the page template and evaluate the response using Scala's built-in XML handling. It's this XML handling that can sometimes be a little verbose in your test implementation and add some accidental complexity to the test. You can find examples of how to use `WebSpec` later in section 14.3.1.

The takeaway from this example is that at the points where you couple your application code tightly with Lift's stateful components, like `S` and `SHtml`, you're (at the time of writing) not able to write standalone unit tests for those tightly coupled components. Instead, you need to fall back on higher-level integration testing with `WebSpec`. This is a key point to understand, because it can impact the way your code is designed. Depending upon your use case for a specific snippet or a set of snippets, you may want to break standalone or reusable functionality out into common traits that can be mixed into many classes, or you might want to delegate out to separate objects for specific functionality.

The purpose of splitting a snippet class might be to decouple the work of actually validating user input and rendering the user input. This should give you more-testable units of functionality and help reduce the amount of coupling between snippets, models, and Lift itself. Consider figure 14.2.

This diagram illustrates a snippet that typically makes heavy use of Lift's stateful components. The right side of the figure indicates the state-bound components that can only have integration tests, and the left side illustrates some delegate objects that can be both unit tested and integration tested.

The next section covers a topic that many developers coming from Java will be familiar with: dependency injection (DI). DI is often used to build loosely coupled

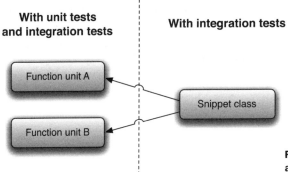

**With unit tests
and integration tests**

With integration tests

Function unit A

Snippet class

Function unit B

**Figure 14.2 Delegating functionality
away from state-bound classes**

components of application logic, which are typically more testable than tightly coupled, procedural code.

14.2.2 *Dependency injection*

Dependency injection (DI) is popular among Java frameworks to provide so-called inversion of control in dependent components. If you aren't familiar with DI, just think of it as a programming idiom that allows you to delay the coupling of components until the last moment. This way, if you want to replace or simply maintain those components at a later date, the code will be loosely coupled, so you can replace that component without affecting the dependent components.

In the Java ecosystem, implementing DI typically involves using an injection framework such as Google Guice or a Spring IoC container. From a Lift perspective, there's nothing stopping you from using these kinds of frameworks, but typically you'll see users implementing patterns of Scala coding that service the need for dependency injection by leveraging powerful language features. Two patterns that have become fairly popular are the so-called *Cake pattern*, which takes an object-oriented approach to DI, and the more functional style of DI: *function currying*. The aim with both patters is to defer committing to an implementation of a component until the latest possible point at compile time.

In addition to these two general patterns, Lift has two types designed to assist with DI called `Injector` and `Factory`. These types again take a different approach from DI in that you can give them a function to perform a particular action, and then *inject* different functions at different scopes in your application, or replace the function entirely for testing purposes.

Before we cover these approaches in detail, it's important to note the power that can be delivered with relative simplicity by structuring your code into traits and organizing things so Lift can make intelligent decisions about what it actually needs to load.

Consider a system in which you have a snippet, and the snippet calls into a legacy service that's really, really slow. It would kill development time to constantly wait for this process, so you decide that it's best to provide a stub class instead, while you get the rest of the application working. Structuring a few traits and providing manual wiring for the snippet creation can easily achieve what is shown in the following listing.

Listing 14.6 Organizing code to assist with DI

```
import scala.xml.{NodeSeq,Text}
import net.liftweb.http.{S,DispatchSnippet}

class Service extends DispatchSnippet {
  def dispatch = {
    case _ => render _
  }
  def render(xhtml: NodeSeq): NodeSeq = {
    fetch
    Text("Done!")
  }
```

❶ Snippet action

```
  protected def fetch { Thread.sleep(5000) }
}
class StubService extends Service {
  override def fetch = { }
}

trait Environment {
  def serviceSnippet: Service
}
object Development extends Environment {
  def serviceSnippet = new StubService
}
object Production extends Environment {
  def serviceSnippet = new Service
}
```

❷ Fake service call

❸ Service stub

❹ Environment definition

❺ Specialized environments

This example defines a simple snippet called `Service` with a snippet method ❶ that has a deliberately slow `render` method ❷. Next, there's a `StubService` without the delay that renders the fixed outcome to speed up development in this fictional scenario ❸. The important step here is defined at ❹, which details a trait called `Environment`. This trait acts as an interface that defines the snippets (and feasibly other application components), which then have two separate implementations: `Production` and `Development` ❺. Each implementation carries the appropriate instance of the snippet.

This allows you to dynamically select the correct snippet by deploying something similar to the following listing in your application `Boot`.

Listing 14.7   Controlling snippet instantiation

```
class Boot {
  def boot {
    ...
    val environment: Environment = Props.mode match {
      case Props.RunModes.Production => Production
      case _ => Development
    }
    LiftRules.snippetDispatch.append {
      case "service" => environment.serviceSnippet
    }
  }
}
```

❶ Control implementation

❷ Wire up snippet

Here it's just a case of instantiating the `Environment` value with the correct implementation, as determined by pattern matching on `Props.mode` ❶. `Props.mode` is the accessor supplied by the Lift `util` package, and it has its value determined by the supplied `run.mode` JVM property. In this case, if `run.mode=production`, the `Production` snippet instance will be served at ❷ rather than the temporary stub. Although this is a very simple pattern, it can quite effectively assist you in providing different implementations based upon the run mode.

More broadly speaking, one of the important things to note about this example is the ability to control snippet instantiation. In this way, you can effectively use whatever DI system or idiom you'd prefer. You can also provide data to the constructor of the snippet, which should give you sufficient control to do whatever you'd like in terms of DI for snippets.

You've now seen a simple strategy for externalizing configurable items in your `Boot` class. But although this can be simple and effective, there are some more sophisticated patterns in the wider Scala ecosystem that can be applied to your code to achieve a DI-style setup. The next three sections cover these differing techniques, starting with the object-orientated Cake pattern, followed by the more functional style of function currying, and concluding with a mechanism in Lift called injectors.

CAKE PATTERN

One of the most popular DI patterns within Scala is known as the Cake pattern, and it first surfaced in a paper written by Martin Odersky, the creator of Scala. Since that paper was written, the language itself has evolved and the idioms developers use have progressed, but the general Cake pattern is very applicable and can greatly assist in decoupling aspects of your implementation.

> **NOTE** Martin Odersky and Matthias Zenger's paper on the Cake pattern, "Scalable Component Abstractions," can be found at http://lamp.epfl.ch/~odersky/papers/ScalableComponent.pdf. In addition, Jonas Bonér wrote a rather excellent "Dependency Injection (DI)" blog post on the Cake pattern as part of his Real-World Scala series: http://jonasboner.com/2008/10/06/real-world-scala-dependency-injection-di.html.

To illustrate the use of the Cake pattern, we'll build a simple book-management service for a library. It will be able to request book details by ISBN number and also add new books to the system.

> **NOTE** This example loosely follows the Repository pattern of implementation. If you're not familiar with this pattern, you can read more about it here: http://martinfowler.com/eaaCatalog/repository.html

The first thing to do is define the interfaces for the service and the repository that make up the service, as shown in the following listing.

Listing 14.8 Interface definitions for the book services

```
trait BookRepository {
  def lookup(isbn: String): Option[Book]     ❶ Data
  def add(book: Book): Unit                      repository
}

trait BookService {
  def lookupBook(isbn: String): Option[Book]  ❷ Service
  def addBook(book: Book): Unit                   interface
}
```

These two traits form the basis of the Cake pattern; they outline the contract for data access through the repository ❶ and the contract for the domain service ❷. If you aren't familiar with these terms, think of the repository as a mediator between the objects and the data storage abstraction.

> **TIP**   In these listings, the *add* functionally returns `Unit`. Although having referentially transparent functions is typically preferable, defining a method or function as explicitly side-effecting is generally OK, provided you declare it as side-effecting with the `Unit` return type. It is, however, frowned upon to execute side effects from your functions when the types state they're referentially transparent, so be sure to use the `Unit` return type if your functions cause side-effects.

Consider the following listing, which defines the implementing *components* of these interfaces and provides default implementations for the service and repository.

Listing 14.9   Implementation of repository and service components

```
trait BookRepositoryComponent {
  def repository: BookRepository

  class DefaultBookRepository extends BookRepository {      ❶ Define
    def lookup(isbn: String): Option[Book] =                  repository
      Library.books.find(_.isbn == isbn)
    def add(book: Book): Unit = {}
  }
}
                                                           ❷ Define
trait BookServiceComponent { _: BookRepositoryComponent =>   dependant type
  def service: BookService
                                                           ❸ Define
  class DefaultBookService extends BookService {              service
    def lookupBook(isbn: String) = repository.lookup(isbn)
    def addBook(book: Book) = repository.add(book)
  }
}
```

These two components wrap up access to their particular interfaces in such a way that they mark an abstract method for repository ❶ and service ❸ and then define default implementations of both.

The critical thing here is the self-type annotation ❷, which defines what's known as a self-type annotation. In practice, this self-type marks the dependency between `BookServiceComponent` and `BookRepositoryComponent`. In addition, notice that each component carries a default implementation, but neither has actually been instantiated. The instantiation is saved until the latest possible moment and done at the actual assembly site:

```
object BookServiceAssembly
    extends BookRepositoryComponent
    with BookServiceComponent {
  val repository = new DefaultBookRepository
```

```
    val service = new DefaultBookService
}
```

Only when the `BookServiceAssembly` is created does the dependency become concrete. In this way, your components are loosely coupled, and you could easily mix in another type of service component when constructing the assembly, provided it conformed to the `BookService` interface definition. You could easily supply a different implementation or perhaps mock objects for testing purposes.

The Cake pattern is an object-orientated methodology for dependency injection that uses the Scala type system to define dependencies. As Scala is a multi-paradigm language, the same DI concept can also be implemented with a more functional approach: function currying.

FUNCTION CURRYING

Scala provides a rich, expressive language to program in, and there are often many ways to do the same thing. One of the really interesting things is the way you can mix functional idioms right into your object-oriented code and benefit from both language approaches.

Let's build on the trait definitions of the repository from listing 14.8 in the previous section and implement the service contract with functions. The following listing shows the implementation.

Listing 14.10 Implementing the `BookService` using functions

```
trait BookService {
  val lookupBook: BookRepository => String => Option[Book] =
    repository => isbn => repository.lookup(isbn)
  val addBook: BookRepository => Book => Unit =
    repository => book => repository.add(book)
}
```

This service definition is quite different from the one defined in the Cake pattern because it makes use of Scala functions. These functions can be *partially* applied so that different implementations of the repository can be substituted without the remainder of the function being aware. To illustrate this, consider the following:

```
object ExampleBookService extends BookService {
  val lookup = lookupBook(new DefaultBookRepository)
  val add = addBook(new DefaultBookRepository)
}
```

This `ExampleBookService` object partially applies the functions that are implemented in the service interface, which then results in the two values being assigned their own functions. The `lookup` value now has the type `String => Option[Book]` because the first parameter has been *curried*. The result here is that the calling code is unaware of the actual implementation of the repository; it just calls the straight function.

Consider this example usage:

```
import ExampleBookService._
val book = lookup("1234")
```

The caller only has to supply the required parameter to service a response. If the repository is replaced or altered at a later date, none of the calling code has to change.

The last type of dependency injection this section covers utilizes Lift's `Injector` and `Factory` types. They take a different route than the other two approaches you've seen here.

FACTORY AND INJECTOR

In addition to the previous Scala idioms, Lift has two specific utility types to assist with dependency injection: `Injector` and `Factory`. As `Factory` extends one of the `Injector` subtypes, we'll look first at the `Injector` definition.

`Injector` only defines an `inject` method that takes a single implicit parameter:

```
trait Injector {
  implicit def inject[T](implicit man: Manifest[T]): Box[T]
}
```

This trait allows you to define a type that supplies a boxed value for a given (or inferred) type, which is determined by the Scala manifest.

> **TIP** Manifests are a Scala feature that helps work around some of the problems with type erasure on the JVM. An introduction to manifests can be found here: http://www.scala-blogs.org/2008/10/manifests-reified-types.html.

The result is boxed in case the `Injector` doesn't know how to produce a value for that type, in which case you'd receive `Empty`. In short, if the `Injector` knows how to produce type `T`, it will do so by using the appropriate function definition.

The base `Injector` trait is missing quite a lot of functionality, so Lift provides `SimpleInjector` (also from the `util` package), which gives you a practical implementation to work with from the start. Consider the usage of `SimpleInjector` shown in the following listing.

Listing 14.11   Example usage of `SimpleInjector`

```
import net.liftweb.util._
import net.liftweb.common._

class Service
object ServiceInjector extends SimpleInjector

ServiceInjector.registerInjection(() => new Service)
```

The last line in listing 14.11 defines the injector. In this case, it's a simple extension of the base type into a singleton object that then has `registerInjection` invoked with a function instance being passed. The passed function is used to build the output value, and can be called like this:

```
scala> ServiceInjector.inject[Service]
res3: Box[Service] = Full(Service@65fd1116)
```

Calling the `inject` method and specifying the type returns the correctly boxed value. The compiler should also be able to infer that type if you specify the return type for a value or method.

It's also possible to refactor `ServiceInjector` somewhat so that it returns the naked `Service` instance, as opposed to the `Box[Service]`. The following example shows the changes:

```
object ServiceInjector extends SimpleInjector {
val service = new Inject(() => new Service){}
}
```

The distinct difference here is the assignment of the service value in the `MyInjector` definition. This allows you to the call the injector as shown:

```
scala> AnInjector.service.vend
res4: Service = Service@60eb407d
```

The final thing that injectors provide is the ability to override the value in a given scope. The concept here is that you can supply a different implementation, such as a mock for testing purposes. Here's an example:

```
trait ServiceMock extends Service

ServiceInjector.service.doWith(new Service with ServiceMock {}){
  ServiceInjector.service.vend
}
```

Here the `doWith` method takes a parameter that's of the same type as the value type of the `service`, but the passed value is a `Service` that has `ServiceMock` mixed into the instance. This allows you to arbitrarily redefine the value of `service` within the subordinate block. The other injection utility, `Factory`, extends `SimpleInjector`, but with some additional qualities. Unlike `Injector`, `Factory` resides in the Lift WebKit package and has access to the state of a request and session.

The syntax for defining a `Factory` is rather similar to that of an `Injector`:

```
object ServiceInjector extends Factory {
  val service = new FactoryMaker(() -> new Service){}
}
```

The primary difference is that the object extends `Factory` and uses `FactoryMaker` rather than `Injector` as the inner class. Specifically, the difference comes when you want to call the `service` `FactoryMaker`. In the same way that you can call `doWith` on the injector (as in the previous example), each implementation of `Factory-Maker` allows you to set a value scoped to the request, to the session, or globally. Here's an example:

```
ServiceInjector.service.request.set(
  (r: Req) => new Service with Extensions with MobileExtensions {})

ServiceInjector.service.session.set(
  (r: Req) => new Service with Extensions {})
```

These invocations set the function value into the factory for the specified scope. This can be particularly helpful when setting configuration options. For example, consider being able to change the values used for a specific session if the request was coming from an iPhone.

The next section covers how to conduct integration testing with Lift, including how to make use of Lift's TestKit and the specific helpers it provides for mocking Lift's stateful components.

14.3   *Testing strategies*

At the start of this chapter, you saw some unit tests for general Scala code that utilized several different Scala testing frameworks. Then, in section 14.2.1, you learned how Lift's stateful nature, while it solves many problems, introduces some complexity when it comes to writing tests. These tests are really looked upon as functional, or integration, tests because they generally require the initialization of several pieces of Lift infrastructure.

With this in mind, the next few sections cover how to test different parts of your Lift application and leverage Lift's TestKit module to assist in this process.

14.3.1   *Testing snippets*

You've seen that tightly coupling your snippet code to Lift's state mechanism can add additional complexity when trying to test those units of functionality. In order to alleviate this problem, you can utilize some helpers from Lift's TestKit. TestKit is a module from the Lift Modules repository (https://github.com/lift/modules), and its primary goal is assisting application tests that are accessing Lift's state system. Additionally, it provides a wrapper for some of the common operations users have to contend with when writing tests for web applications. Specifically, this includes mocking of the request and response cycle, and executing tests in the context of initialized stateful components, like S and SHtml.

Earlier, in listing 14.5, you saw a typical snippet definition that's tied to Lift's state mechanism. In order to test such a snippet, you'd typically use a helper from TestKit known as WebSpec in conjunction with Scala's XML support. Consider listing 14.12, which demonstrates a possible test implementation for the CookieList snippet test. This test example uses a couple of things that are different from previous listings: the CookieListSpec object extends both the Lift-specific WebSpec trait and a utility trait called SetupAndTearDown, which looks like this:

```
trait SetupAndTearDown { _: WebSpec =>
  setup().beforeSpec
  def setup() =
    new bootstrap.liftweb.Boot().boot
  def destroy() =
    LiftRules.unloadHooks.toList.foreach(_())
  destroy().afterSpec
}
```

The purpose of this setup and teardown process is to initialize the Lift application environment. Note that you only need to initialize the boot process once per test phase, so in this case it's simply attached to the spec.

Listing 14.12 Example of using `WebSpec` to test `CookieList` snippet

```
import scala.xml.NodeSeq
import javax.servlet.http.Cookie
import net.liftweb.http.S
import net.liftweb.mockweb.WebSpec
import net.liftweb.mocks.MockHttpServletRequest

object CookieListSpec extends WebSpec with SetupAndTearDown {

  "CookieList Snippet" should {
    val cookieName = "thing"
    val r = new MockHttpServletRequest("/")         ❶ Mock request
    r.cookies = List(new Cookie(cookieName, "value"))     with cookie

    "List all cookies, separated by a break line"   ❷ Use withSFor
    ➥withSFor(r) in {
      val xml = S.runTemplate(List("testkit","cookies"))   ❸ Execute
                openOr NodeSeq.Empty                           template

      xml must \\(<div id="output">thing<br></br></div>)
    }
  }

}
```

Within the `should` test block, the code first defines a mock incoming request using the `MockHttpServletRequest` ❶. The purpose of this is to define some context that can be passed to the `withSFor(request)` block ❷. The `withSFor` method comes from `WebSpec`, and it's a special Lift helper that when passed a mock request will initialize Lift's stateful components in the context of the block, allowing you to test snippets, request parameters, and even session variables.

Because there's no actual request here, just a mock one, you need to execute the snippet somehow. In this example, `S.runTemplate` is used to programmatically execute the whole template and associated snippets ❸, and then match on the output. Be aware that this will execute all the snippets used by that template, just as if you requested the page using that template in browser and looked at the generated HTML source code: you would see markup that was the result of snippet execution. In the context of this test case, the resulting markup from executing the template is then assigned to the `xml` value. As XML in Scala is a `NodeSeq` type, it's possible to use Specs' built-in matchers for XML such as the `\\` matcher ❸. Table 14.1 lists some of the commonly used XML matchers in Specs.

Table 14.1 Commonly used XML matchers from the Specs framework

Matcher	Description and usage

`==/`	Checks to see if two sequences of nodes are equal. It's interchangeable with the `equalIgnoreSpace` matcher.
	
	`<div><span id="value">Thing</span></div> must ==/(`
	`<div><span id="value">Thing</span></div>)`

Table 14.1 Commonly used XML matchers from the Specs framework *(continued)*

Matcher	Description and usage
\	Finds immediate child nodes that match (XPath semantics). `<div> </div> must \("br")` or `<div> </div> must \( )`

\\	Finds matching nodes in a deep sequence of nodes (XPath semantics).
	
	`<div><p><a>Link</a></p></div> must \\("a")`
	
	or
	
	`<div><p><a>Link</a></p></div> must \\(<a>Link</a>)`

These XML matchers can be extremely useful for testing several parts of Lift, and you'll be using them again in the next section to test a REST service.

14.3.2 *Testing web services*

Many applications today have large and comprehensive web-based APIs that are exposed via HTTP. As you saw in chapter 8, Lift makes the creation of these services pretty straightforward. Helpfully, Lift TestKit also provides some good integration-testing tools for working with these types of services.

Consider the following definition of some simple services.

Listing 14.13 Definition of a basic HTTP service using `RestHelper`

```
import net.liftweb.http.{ForbiddenResponse,OkResponse,SessionVar}
import net.liftweb.http.rest.RestHelper

object Authenticated extends SessionVar(false)

object Example extends RestHelper {
  val days = List("Monday","Tuesday","Wednesday","Thursday","Friday")
  serve {
    case "t" :: "services" :: "days" :: Nil Get _ =>
      <days>{days.flatMap(d => <day>{d}</day>)}</days>          ❶ Days and
    case "t" :: "services" :: "login" :: Nil Post _ =>             login service
      Authenticated(true); OkResponse()
    case "t" :: "services" :: "secret" :: Nil Get _ =>          ❷ "Secure"
      if(Authenticated.is) OkResponse()                           service
      else ForbiddenResponse("Its secret!")
  }
}
```

This listing defines a few simple services. First, there's a straightforward XML service that lists the days of the week, the next provides a pseudo-login service that sets a session variable to affirm that the user is logged in ❶, and the third serves up some top-secret content if you've previously authenticated ❷. This means that in order to access the third service, it will be necessary to first post to the second and then make a GET request to the third.

In order to do this, we'll use the `TestKit` trait from Lift TestKit. This trait essentially delivers a set of functionality around making requests, parsing responses, and effectively handling errors. The first thing you need to do is define a Jetty server that you can interact with programmatically from your tests. The following listing shows one possible implementation that boots up Jetty and sets its path to the `src` directory in the project tree.

Listing 14.14 Implementing Jetty for testing purposes

```
import org.mortbay.jetty.{Server,Connector}
import org.mortbay.jetty.servlet.ServletHolder
import org.mortbay.jetty.webapp.WebAppContext
import org.mortbay.jetty.nio.SelectChannelConnector

object JettyTestServer {
  private val server: Server = {
    val svr = new Server
    val connector = new SelectChannelConnector
    connector.setMaxIdleTime(30000);

    val context = new WebAppContext
    context.setServer(svr)
    context.setContextPath("/")
    context.setWar("chapter-14/src/main/webapp")

    svr.setConnectors(Array(connector));
    svr.addHandler(context)
    svr
  }

  lazy val port = server.getConnectors.head.getLocalPort
  lazy val url = "http://localhost:" + port

  def baseUrl = url

  lazy val = server.start()                              ❶ Startup

  def stop(){
    server.stop()                                        ❷ Shutdown
    server.join()
  }
}
```

The listing literally does the bare minimum and only provides a mechanism to start the server ❶ and then stop it ❷.

At the time of writing, this utility was not built into Lift's TestKit, but it *may* be included in future versions of Lift. In the interim, simply define a trait that can be mixed in to start and stop the Jetty server:

```
trait JettySetupAndTearDown {
  def setup() = JettyTestServer.start
  def destroy() = JettyTestServer.stop()
}
```

This simple trait lets you avoid putting the boilerplate start and stop code in every test group you write.

Now that you have the testing tools set up, let's consider an actual test that uses this Jetty instance to service requests back and forth with the TestKit helpers. The next listing shows a basic test implementation for the list of days web service, created in listing 14.13 and accessible at the URL /t/services/days.

Listing 14.15   Example usage of TestKit

```
import org.specs.Specification
import net.liftweb.http.testing.{TestKit,ReportFailure,HttpResponse}

class WebServiceSpec extends Specification                          ❶ Extend
with JettySetupAndTearDown with TestKit {                              TestKit

  implicit val reportError = new ReportFailure {                    ❷ Provide
    def fail(msg: String): Nothing =                                  ReportFailure
      WebServiceSpec.this.fail(msg)                                   implicit
  }

  lazy val baseUrl = JettyTestServer.baseUrl

  "Example web service" should {
    "List the days of the week in order" in {
      for {
        days <- get("/t/services/days")                            ❸ Send
                  !@ "Unable to get day list"                        requests
        xml <- days.xml
      } {
        xml must ==/(<days>
          <day>Monday</day><day>Tuesday</day>                      ❹ Match
          <day>Wednesday</day><day>Thursday</day>                    result
          <day>Friday</day>
        </days>)
      }
    }
  }
}
```

This example constructs a specification that implements Lift's TestKit trait ❶, which imports the functions for making web requests and handling the responses. The reportError value defines an implicit value that creates a ReportFailure instance ❷, the purpose of which is to capture specific error messages from chained web requests (more on this in a moment). You may notice that the definition returns the Scala type Nothing; you'll hardly ever see this because Nothing never returns control to the caller, but in the context of testing, this is useful because it will fail the test immediately with the specified message.

The main thrust of the listing is the for comprehension that makes use of the get method from TestKit ❸. As you might imagine, this method makes a GET request to the specified URL. TestKit supports the standard set of HTTP verbs (GET, PUT, POST, and DELETE) via the same word in lowercase. These requests return a subtype of

Response, which is a TestKit type. This type has a selection of methods that allow you to assert the desired response; in this usage, the !@ means "receive a HTTP 200 response or report failure" (table 14.2 lists all of the available operators). Once you have a response, it's possible to extract the XML body as the second step of the for comprehension. With the result in hand, you can once again use the Specs XML matchers to assert the result ❹.

Table 14.2 Response matchers available in TestKit

Matcher	Description and usage
!@	Checks the response for an HTTP 200 status, and if not it uses the error report function to send the specified failure message. `get("/foo/bar") !@ "Unable to get day list"`

!	Tests that the server responded, where any response is valid. It's also overloaded with a second method signature that allows you to specify a given status code.
	
	`get("/foo/bar") ! "The server responded"`
	or
	`get("/foo/bar") ! (403,`
	`   "Access should fail with unauthorized status")`

\\
and the reverse
!\\
	Checks the response for an exact sequence of XML nodes anywhere in the response.
	
	`get("/foo/bar") \\ (<span id="special">thing</span>,`
	`                   "Missing XML nodes")`

\
and the reverse
!\
	Checks the response for a specific node sequence from the root node.
	
	`get("/foo/bar") \ (<span id="special">thing</span>,`
	`                  "Missing XML nodes")`

These matchers form the basis of testing in TestKit, so let's look at a more robust example. Consider a scenario whereby you need to chain requests in the same session, perhaps to log in to a web service before making requests. This can also be achieved with TestKit, as shown in the next listing.

Listing 14.16 Making multiple HTTP calls in the same session

```
"Gain access to secret stuff if they are logged in" in {
  for {
    auth <- post("/testkit/services/login") !@ "Unable to login!"
    resp <- auth.get("/testkit/services/secret") !@ "Not authenticated"
  }{
    resp must haveClass[HttpResponse]
  }
}
```

To keep this example concise, the listing is an extract from a broader specification group that extends `TestKit`, but consider specifically the `auth` and `resp` generators within the `for` comprehension. The initial request is made and assigned to the `auth` value, which is then used to launch a second request by way of the `auth.get` call. The key point here is that it's possible to launch secondary requests from the result of an initial request, which ensures that both requests are executed in the context of the same session. In terms of the actual test result, simply checking the response to see if it's the correct type is fine because if either of the `TestKit` matchers fails, the test will throw an exception and report a failed test to the user.

`TestKit` provides a fairly robust abstraction for testing web services that would otherwise be rather difficult to test. The next section covers testing with Mapper, including configuring tests to run against a disposable, in-memory database and autoloading testing fixtures into your tables.

14.3.3 *Testing with Mapper*

During your application build, there will often be times when you need to test components that actually interact with the database, to ensure things operate as expected. During testing, you may want to run your application tests against a sandbox database, so in this section we'll look at how to configure Lift to use an in-memory H2 database purely for testing purposes. Moreover, because this database is in memory, you'll need to load up predefined fixture data in order to populate the table with something meaningful.

Lift automatically detects when it's being run as part of the testing classloader and enables its test mode by default. This allows you to automatically load different configurations or supply different components based upon that mode. This is particularly useful when setting up the database, because you can dynamically supply different connection information. Back in chapter 10 (section 10.1.1) you may remember configuring the database using an external properties file. Well, Lift is clever enough to load different properties files based upon different run modes, so simply by having test.default.props and default.props, you can define a sandbox in-memory database that should be used just for the test suites.

This leaves you with two different files:

- src/main/resources/default.props
  ```
  db.class=org.h2.Driver
  db.url=jdbc:h2:database/chapter_14;FILE_LOCK=NO
  ```
- src/main/resources/test.default.props
  ```
  db.class=org.h2.Driver
  db.url=jdbc:h2:mem:sandbox;DB_CLOSE_DELAY=-1
  ```

Specifically note the different connection URLs. No code changes are required to the database connection loading or `Schemifier` code in your `Boot` class.

Now that Lift will forge different connections to different databases for testing and development (or for any other mode, for that matter), you'll want some mechanism for loading a sample set of data into the database; these are known as fixtures. Consider the following listing, which details an example of overriding the callback function available in Mapper to automatically populate a table with data.

Listing 14.17 Implementing the table-creation hooks in Mapper to load fixtures

```
import net.liftweb.mapper._
import net.liftweb.common.Full

class Book extends LongKeyedMapper[Book] with IdPK {
  def getSingleton = Book
  object title extends MappedString(this, 255)
}
object Book extends Book with LongKeyedMetaMapper[Book]{
  override def dbTableName = "books"
  override def dbAddTable = Full(populate _)
  private def populate {
    val titles =
      "Lift in Action" ::
      "Scala in Depth" ::
      "Scala in Action" ::
      "Hadoop in Action" :: Nil

    for(title <- titles)
      Book.create.title(title).save
  }
}
```

❶ Fixture hook

❷ Fixture loading

This listing defines a simple Mapper entity for storing books in a database. The important thing to note here is the overridden method definition for dbAddTable ❶. This method is invoked when Schemifier attempts to create a table for this entity, and you can execute an arbitrary () => Unit function. Typically, this function is used for loading fixture data into the table at hand, prior to any tests being executed ❷.

> **NOTE** At the time of writing, there was no specific serialization format that automatically loaded fixtures, but implementing your own file-based loading is a fairly trivial exercise due to Scala's native XML support.

The final piece of the testing puzzle that we haven't yet addressed is working with Comet and AJAX. The next section addresses these topics and demonstrates some strategies for testing these rich interfaces.

14.3.4 Testing Comet and AJAX

Comet and AJAX are typically rather tricky aspects of any application to test because these kinds of GUIs are heavily event-based. AJAX responds asynchronously to user input, and Comet responds to server-based events. Either way, this can be a tricky thing to get in the middle of and test. Plus, as mentioned earlier, Lift's stateful nature adds some complexity. For example, when generating forms or other user interactions like AJAX, Lift will by default create elements that look like this:

```
<input class="text" name="F1268385771525JRDB3L" type="text" value="" />
```

In chapter 6, you may remember learning how Lift randomly generates these function-mapped opaque GUIDs for state-bound components on each and every request, to combat hacking strategies like cross-site request forgery (CSRF). Although this is critically important in production mode, it can be a bit of a nightmare when testing your application—during testing, you don't need the security aspects, but you do require stability in the naming of components.

Fortunately, when test mode is enabled, Lift will generate stable identifiers for each and every state-bound component that the page needs to render. This transforms the preceding element so it looks like this:

```
<input type="text" value=""
name="f00000000010000000_f6cbf1d075cb60f72e00095e5552f15c52edb785" />
```

This identifier then becomes fixed and persists over Jetty and JVM restarts so you can essentially hardcode these values in your tests and be sure that they will remain constant. This can be rather useful when conducting functional testing with Selenium. Selenium (http://seleniumhq.org/) is a popular tool for automated function testing, and it allows your application to interact with a programmatically controlled browser, from which you can slurp feedback into your test's specification.

Tools such as Selenium can be exceedingly handy for programmatically testing asynchronous or highly dynamic parts of your application, which would otherwise be difficult to test. Broadly speaking, AJAX and Comet fall into this category, because both have highly asynchronous workflows. For AJAX, it's usually possible to break out the function definition and unit test that in isolation to ensure the right response is being generated, but this is only appropriate in some cases. For example, this wouldn't be appropriate if your function was causing some side effect elsewhere that subsequently updated the page while returning `Noop` itself.

In the case of Comet, testing the `CometActor` itself in an isolated unit test can be very difficult because you will, at some point, update the browser directly or trade JavaScript with the client. Simply put, determining whether the JavaScript code sent to the client asynchronously is operating as expected, without having a sandbox environment in which to run that code, is very difficult. Thus, for these components, functional testing with Selenium can be a good fit.

In order to set up functional testing with Selenium, it's necessary to provide some testing utilities that build on the `JettyTestServer` you set up earlier in this chapter. The first thing you need to do is add Selenium to your project definition, as shown:

```
val sl = "org.seleniumhq.selenium" % "selenium" % "2.0b1" % "test"
val slsvr = "org.seleniumhq.selenium" %
  ➥ "selenium-server" % "2.0b1" % "test"
```

Don't forget to `reload` and `update` from the SBT shell.

One the dependencies are in place, set up an object to contain the Selenium server, as shown in the following listing.

Listing 14.18 Selenium server utility

```
import org.openqa.selenium.server.RemoteControlConfiguration
import org.openqa.selenium.server.SeleniumServer

object SeleniumTestServer {
  private val rc = new RemoteControlConfiguration        ❶ Create
  rc.setPort(port)                                          remote client

  private val seleniumserver = new SeleniumServer(rc)     ◁─ Create
  lazy val port = System.getProperty(                    ❷   server
    "selenium.server.port", "4444").toInt

  def start(){
    seleniumserver.boot()
    seleniumserver.start()
    seleniumserver.getPort()                             ❸ Boot and
  }                                                         shutdown
  def stop(){
    seleniumserver.stop()
  }
}
```

Broadly speaking this is a convenience wrapper around the boot and shutdown process of Selenium server ❸. This server is booted up after the Jetty server and is used to handle results communicated from the remote client ❶ to the Selenium server ❷.

To make integration with the Specification straightforward, you can construct a utility trait, as defined in the next listing, that will handle both boot up and shutdown of the Selenium server and client.

Listing 14.19 Convenience trait for working with Selenium

```
import com.thoughtworks.selenium.DefaultSelenium

trait SeleniumSetupAndTearDown extends JettySetupAndTearDown {
    _: Specification =>

  override def setup(){
    super.setup()
    SeleniumTestServer.start()
    Thread.sleep(1000)
    SeleniumTestClient.start()                          ❶ Server startup
  }                                                        and shutdown
  override def destroy(){
    SeleniumTestClient.stop()
    Thread.sleep(1000)
    SeleniumTestServer.stop()
    super.destroy()
  }
```

```
object SeleniumTestClient {
  lazy val browser = new DefaultSelenium("localhost",
    SeleniumTestServer.port, "*firefox",
    ➥ JettyTestServer.url+"/")

  def start(){
    browser.start()
  }
  def stop(){
    browser.stop()
  }
}
}
```

❷ Browser client

This trait first specifies the actual startup and shutdown process of the Selenium server and client **❶**. The client is implemented **❷**, and it uses Firefox as its slave browser. These methods are to be called surrounding the start and finish of the Specification implementation; notice how the trait extends JettyStartupAnd-TearDown so that it will also start the Jetty server that runs the application.

Second, the nested object SeleniumTestClient is designed to be imported into the Specification scope to provide the caller with a convenient way to send instructions to the browser. With this in mind, consider the following listing, which implements this utility trait and makes calls to the browser to verify that a Lift AJAX button replaces an element dynamically.

Listing 14.20 Implementing the Selenium test client

```
class SeleniumExampleSpec extends Specification
                    with SeleniumSetupAndTearDown {
  "/testkit/ajax" should {
    import SeleniumTestClient._
    "replace the button with text when clicked" in {
      browser.open("/testkit/ajax")
      browser.click("clickme")

      browser.waitForCondition("""
        selenium.browserbot
        .getCurrentWindow().document
        .getElementById('ajax_button')
        .innerHTML == 'Clicked'""",
        "1000")
      browser.isTextPresent("Clicked") mustBe true
    }
  }
}
```

❶ Open URL and click button

❷ Wait for async update

In this test implementation, note how the inner object SeleniumTestClient is imported, which places the browser value in scope for the whole specification. Next, it's just a case of instructing the browser client what to do. In this specific example, you want the browser to first open the appropriate URL and then click the button with an ID of clickme. These steps are conducted by calling browser.open and `browser.click` respectively **❶**. This is the corresponding markup that you would be interacting with via Selenium:

```
<span id="ajax_button">
  <button onclick="liftAjax.lift_ajaxHandler(
  &quot;F7600141090484VJ0VU=true&quot;, null, null, null); return false;"
  id="clickme">Hello</button>
</span>
```

Because clicking this link causes an AJAX request to be sent from the browser to the server, a varying amount of time could pass before the server responds. The Selenium solution here is to provide a snippet of JavaScript that can execute in the context of the current browser test. This JavaScript is executed every second until the predetermined timeout has passed or the condition has been satisfied **❷**. In this case, the snippet is simple and just returns a string with minimal processing, so the response is fairly instant. Finally, a Specs matcher is used to verify the result of executing the Selenium tests; simply checking that the text was properly replaced by calling `browser.isTextPresent` and setting that this must be `true` is sufficient to satisfy the test case.

The same testing approach is generically applicable to Comet applications because the asynchronous updating of pages is the same in principle, and it also typically happens in response to a user action. The only other point of consideration for Comet would be the need to communicate messages to a given `CometActor` before running the Selenium test.

14.4 Summary

This chapter has covered the basics of testing Lift applications and, more broadly, Scala code in general. First, you heard about how the Scala ecosystem has fostered several different testing frameworks that take different but complementary approaches to testing. Starting with ScalaTest, you saw how to construct basic test (function) suites, and that was followed by an exploration of the Specs BDD testing framework. Specs and ScalaTest are equally popular, but the majority of this chapter leveraged the Specs framework purely because it's our personal preference. Specs also has rather nice integration with the property-driven development framework ScalaCheck. Specifically, ScalaCheck can randomly generate function input to provide testing with arbitrary random values. We also took a look at code-coverage reports.

The second section explored some of the realistic complexities in testing highly stateful applications and presented some possible routes for more effective, isolated testing. You also saw several techniques for dependency injection in Scala. But this discussion was by no means 100 percent complete, and we highly recommend reading *Scala in Action* by Nilanjan Raychaudhuri or *Scala in Depth* by Joshua D. Suereth for more information on idiomatic dependency-injection patterns in Scala.

The third section of the chapter covered techniques for implementing full-stack integration and functional testing of your application. This included leveraging some of Lift's testing infrastructure from the supplementary Lift TestKit module. These tests included creating mock requests and utilizing the WebSpec testing trait. Additionally, you saw how to use the TestKit trait to test dispatch-based web services with a real, live Jetty instance. This Jetty instance was then coupled with the popular Selenium testing tool to cover the need to test asynchronous browser-based workflows for Comet and AJAX.

The next chapter covers deployment and scaling, touching on topics such as servlet containers, handling state during failover, Lift tools that can help your application when it goes into the wild, and some recipes for implementing application monitoring using the Ostrich toolkit from Twitter.

Deployment and scaling

In this book, you've seen a lot of different aspects of Lift and how they can affect your development cycle. Hopefully you've learned enough to build an application that you'd actually like to publish in the real world and expose to end users. For the most part, Lift applications can be deployed in much the same way regular Java web applications can. By default, this means packaging your application as a WAR file, which can be done by pretty much any of the build tools commonly used in the Scala and Java ecosystems. Moreover, with Scala and Lift being based on the JVM, you can benefit from the many years of research, tuning, and overall improvement in the platform, not to mention great security, protection from things like buffer overflow attacks, and blistering performance even at very high load.

Although there are many great servlet containers available, you can benefit from having a better understanding of how to leverage particular servlet containers. To that end, the first thing covered in this chapter is how to choose a container. This chapter presents some broad options, but we'll focus on one main route of implementation that a lot of people use. Note that it's by no means the *only* route available to you with regard to choosing a system configuration.

With a container in place, we'll then explore Lift's state-handling mechanism and learn why stateful systems are ultimately more secure and more performant than their stateless counterparts that use the so-called *share nothing* architecture. There are many myths about the costs of deploying stateful applications, and we'll show you how you can build an extremely performant system based entirely upon an open source software stack.

Lift is an application framework that was built for use in the real world, and as such there are a lot of pragmatic choices that have been distilled into common use components. A selection of these can be particularly useful when taking your application into production. You'll see some of the techniques and tools that you should use when deploying your applications to get the best out of Lift and the environment you have available for hosting.

Finally, we'll look at the experiences of two of the largest Lift applications in the world: the vibrant location-based social network Foursquare.com and the enterprise social collaboration service Novell Vibe. These users are running Lift in very large installations and have had firsthand experience in developing and deploying Lift applications.

But the first thing you'll need when taking your application to deployment is a servlet container, so without further ado, let's look at some of the things you should consider before choosing a container.

15.1 *Choosing a servlet container*

Selecting a servlet container these days is often difficult because the difference between products is small. There are many commercial and open source options; both variants provide extremely professional software that's good for development and production environments alike. With such a competitive field, choosing a container has become a somewhat religious affair (much like for build tools), and the vast majority of functionality is inconsequentially different.

From an application standpoint, Lift will run nearly identically in any container, be it Tomcat (http://tomcat.apache.org/), Resin (http://www.caucho.com/products/resin/), or another. So where's the point of differentiation, you may be wondering? Well, throughout the course of this book, we've talked a lot about real-time applications and using Comet-based page components. One of the things we haven't talked a great deal about is how Comet actually works under the hood, and what that means for the container.

Let's assume that you're running a Lift application complete with Comet in a popular container such as Tomcat 6. For each Comet operation, Lift would essentially be consuming a thread for that request. Both from a developer and user experience perspective, this is transparent. But consuming threads like this doesn't scale, because you'd eventually run out of threads. Fortunately, there's a solution that some

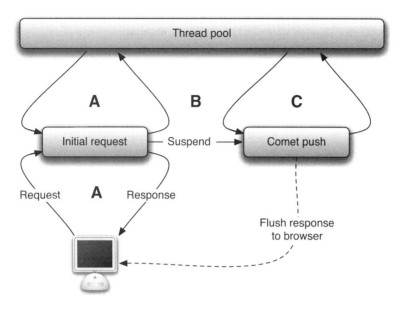

Figure 15.1   Visualization of request suspension (or continuations) in the Jetty container. The initial request is serviced, the request is suspended, and a thread is pulled to service any subsequent response (push) operations on that request. The thread doesn't block indefinitely.

containers implement; this can be thought of as *request suspension* and it's also sometimes referred to as *continuations*. Figure 15.1 illustrates the request-suspension process.

In this process there's usually a thread pool that's used to service requests, and as soon as the response is returned to the browser (*A* in the figure), and assuming the web page has one or more Comet components, the request is suspended (at *B*) and the thread that was servicing that request is returned to the pool. If that request requires more data to be pushed to the browser, the request is resumed; again a thread is taken from the pool to complete the servicing and it's returned to the pool when the servicing is complete. This is a far more efficient approach and scales inordinately better than consuming a thread for the entire duration of the Comet request.

At the time of writing, Jetty 6 (and later) features such a request-suspension API, and the servlet 3.0 specification goes a step further to standardize asynchronous response handling. Going forward, all the major containers will almost certainly support the servlet 3.0 specification, which will mean your Lift applications can ultimately take advantage of effectively scaling Comet in any container.

NOTE   You can read more about the servlet 3.0 specification at http:// jcp.org/aboutJava/communityprocess/final/jsr315/index.html.

In practice, this means that if you're building a Comet-enabled application, you have to think a little more carefully about exactly which container you'd like to use, because there are positives and negatives for each. If your application leverages Lift's awesome

Comet support, this will likely have a large bearing on the container you choose to deploy with. At the time of writing, Lift's Comet mechanism supports three different Comet implementations:

- Servlet 3.0–compatible containers
- Jetty 6 continuations
- Jetty 7 continuations

Lift will automatically detect whether it's running in a compatible container, and if not, it will fall back to a thread-consuming strategy, as mentioned earlier in this chapter. If your application isn't sporting any Comet components, any servlet container should work.

Table 15.1 provides a very broad comparison of three servlet containers: Jetty (http://jetty.codehaus.org/jetty/), Tomcat (http://tomcat.apache.org/), and Winstone (http://winstone.sourceforge.net/). This table provides a rough guide for readers who may not be familiar with the ecosystem. There are many factors to consider, and here I focused on these:

- *Static file performance*—This is important for web applications with a lot of imagery or JavaScript. Here Jetty has a slight edge over Tomcat in that it uses a specialized form of nonblocking I/O to instruct the host system to send the file at maximum direct memory access speed without entering user or JVM memory space.
- *Memory footprint*—Although RAM may be cheap, having a lightweight application is still a consideration for many environments. Here, Winstone gives you a super lightweight implementation because it only provides bare-bones servlet support. With that being said, both Jetty and Tomcat can be stripped down to be more lightweight than their defaults. If you need lightweight embedding, either Winstone or Jetty are great choices.
- *Comet support*—Jetty currently has the best support for Comet in Lift because of its dedicated continuation API, so it will give you the best out-of-the-box experience with Comet. Moreover, at the time of writing, Jetty appears to be the most popular container in the Lift community. Tomcat 7 provides a servlet 3.0 implementation and should provide good Comet support going forward. At the time of writing, Tomcat 7 was in the final stages of beta, so more people might adopt Tomcat with Lift applications as time passes.
- *Scalability*—Both Jetty and Tomcat are proven in the enterprise space, and there isn't a huge amount to choose between them. Either would be a fine choice for a production environment.

In addition to the containers listed in this table, there are also some online services that take care of the whole deployment for you, meaning that you don't have to worry about server setup at all. Examples of such services are CloudBees (http://www.cloudbees .com/), Amazon's Elastic Beanstalk (http://aws.amazon.com/elasticbeanstalk/), and Google App Engine (http://code.google.com/appengine/).

Table 15.1   Some points on the merits of different servlet containers. These ratings are based partially on product features and experience in the field. They should provide a loose direction in making a choice for your environment.

	Jetty 6+	Tomcat 7	Winstone
Static file performance	★★★★★	★★★★☆	★★★☆☆
Memory footprint	★★★★☆	★★★☆☆	★★★★★
Comet support	★★★★★	★★★★★	★☆☆☆☆
Scalability	★★★★★	★★★★★	★★★☆☆

Now that you have a broad understanding of what your application can be deployed into, let's take a look at some of the specific problems common in web application deployment, and subsequent solutions that both Lift and the Java platform provide.

15.2   Handling state

Effective state handling is one of the biggest problems in web application development. The most common (but not only) state-related problem comes in the form of session management. In many frameworks, including Ruby on Rails and Java Struts, serializing the state into a persistent object and then referencing that persistent object using a secure session token in the incoming request is how they manage session state. This secure token might be encoded in the URL or in a cookie passed with each request, but the object that stores that state is typically external to the application—it could be a cookie, a hidden form field, Memcached (http://memcached.org/), or anything else, even a database.

The benefit of such an approach is that the server isn't responsible for handling the state between requests, so any backend server in a cluster can deal with any given request and still have access to its state, because the application grabs it from an external source. But although this approach sounds reasonable, it's often abused, and the sheer amount of serialized state that's being handed around in any moderately complex application becomes very unwieldy. It actually slows the whole process down, because there's so much deserialization, processing, mutation, and reserialization of the same state. Moreover, when the state is global and any request to any web application process in the cluster can mutate the session in any way, you're presented with an interesting concurrency problem. Imagine interacting with an application using multiple browser tabs, and the request in one tab is handled by server *A* while the second tab is handled by server *B*; if they're both operating on the same state at the same time, which process is the right one to use? There's an obvious race condition and concurrency issue here, and a strategy such as this can be extremely hard to maintain and very hard to debug when it becomes operationally problematic if the developers did not provide for such scenarios.

These different approaches to state handling are flawed for the reasons outlined, and the all-too-often side effect is unwanted security holes in your application. That's why Lift chose a different route of implementation: it keeps all its state in process. This is generally why Lift is referred to as a stateful framework. Throughout the course of this book, you've interacted with Lift's stateful functions and seen how Lift leverages this stateful behavior to yield a superior feature set. A good example of such behavior is Lift's secure session-specific opaque GUIDs that all Lift form elements are assigned dynamically. Strategies such as this make it impossible to attack the application with cross-site request forgery (CSRF), for example. This is but one example, and we touched on many of the other benefits in previous chapters.

So where's the catch? Well, being stateful essentially means that when the very first request reaches the server from a new client, a session is created for them on that *specific* server. Any subsequent requests must also reach that very same server in order to access the session information. This scenario is cheerily referred to as *sticky sessions*, because each request is *stuck* to a particular server in order to access its session state.

15.2.1 *Sticky session strategies*

With the understanding that each request must reach the same server in order to be consistently handled, you may be wondering how this is implemented in practice and what it means operationally. There are typically two ways to handle this: a software solution that may or may not be on multiple pieces of hardware, and a pure-hardware solution that operates at the layer 4 network level via what are usually very expensive pieces of equipment. The majority of deployments will use the software route, due to cost or organizational restrictions, so this is what we'll now explore.

Broadly speaking, there are two solutions that are largely prevalent in the open source software load-balancing space for web applications: HAProxy (http://haproxy .1wt.eu/) and NGINX (http://wiki.nginx.org/Main), pronounced *engine x*. These two products are both open source and completely free, they offer very sophisticated configurations, and they're implemented in lots of high-profile sites including Foursquare.com, WordPress.com, and Github.com. It's also worth noting that if you opt for cloud-based hosting, your service provider may have built-in support for stick session load balancing, such as can be found with Amazon's Elastic Load Balancing (http:// aws.amazon.com/elasticloadbalancing/).

HAPROXY

HAProxy is primarily a TCP and HTTP load balancer. It has proven to be very, very fast and highly reliable even under extreme load. HAProxy has even been benchmarked and reaches saturation around half a million requests *per second*. As you can no doubt appreciate, this is far more than most applications would see in an entire day, let alone per second. So it's fast, scalable, and can be configured to have complete redundancy: all the characteristics of a great production platform.

With regard to sticky sessions, HAProxy comes equipped for this kind of workflow, and it's even possible to configure your system to perform seamless application updates without the need for the ubiquitous "down for maintenance" page.

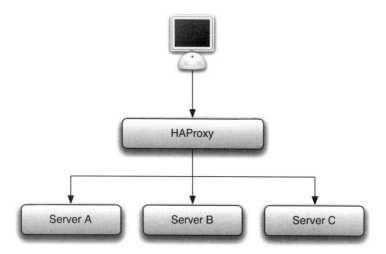

Figure 15.2 A typical HAProxy deployment. Web traffic connects to HAProxy, which in turn load-balances traffic to application servers inside the LAN.

Figure 15.2 shows a typical HAProxy deployment setup. The configuration detailed here is a fairly typical proxying setup.

Let's take a look at the configuration needed to implement such a setup. HAProxy takes all of its configuration options from a file called haproxy.cfg, which is typically located in /etc/haproxy/, but this is system-specific and not an absolute rule. You can achieve a simple setup as shown in the following listing.

Listing 15.1 HAProxy configuration

```
global
  daemon
  maxconn 10000
  log 127.0.0.1 local4

defaults
  log global
  clitimeout 60000
  srvtimeout 30000
  contimeout 4000
  retries 3
  option redispatch
  option http-server-close
  option abortonclose
  option httplog

listen yourdomain_cluster 1.2.3.4:80
  mode http
  balance roundrobin
  capture cookie JSESSIONID len 34
  appsession JSESSIONID len 34 timeout 3h request-learn
  option forwardfor except 1.2.3.4
```

❶ Implement sticky sessions

```
    server server1 10.1.1.2:80 cookie s1
    ➥ weight 1 maxconn 2000 check
    server server2 10.1.1.3:80 cookie s2
    ➥ weight 1 maxconn 2000 check
    server server3 10.1.1.4:80 cookie s3
    ➥ weight 1 maxconn 2000 check
listen  lb1_stats [load balancer's public ip]:80
  mode http
  stats uri /
  stats auth username:password
  stats refresh 10s
```

❷ The backend
containers

This configuration essentially tells HAProxy that it will be dispatching requests to three backend servers with the defined IP addresses ❷ and that it should use the JSESSIONID as an identifier to do the dispatching in a sticky manner ❶. The configuration also instructs HAProxy to conduct a round-robin style of load balancing to determine which server it should dispatch a new request to. There are a range of options here, and detailing them is beyond the scope of this chapter, so I heartily recommend checking the HAProxy documentation for more information on this and other parameters you can use to tune the setup for your particular requirements.

So far, so good. There are, however, a couple of catches with HAProxy (aren't there always). At the time of writing, there was no support for SSL out of the box, so if this is a hard requirement for your application or you wish to protect your users from session hijacking and other security vulnerabilities, there are currently a couple of options:

- Use Stunnel (http://www.stunnel.org/) to decode the incoming SSL and apply an optional (but official) patch to HAProxy in order to support SSL handling in a single software solution. (The patch can be found at http://haproxy.1wt.eu/download/patches/stunnel-4.34-exceliance-aloha-unix-sockets.diff.)
- Place another software component in front of HAProxy to handle the SSL decoding, and hand off the request to HAProxy for load balancing and distribution to the backend.

These are only catches if you require SSL. Either way, HAProxy is a great tool, and there is a whole raft of things that you can do with it that we won't even begin to touch on here.

HAProxy is a great product, but everyone likes to shop around and check out the other options. Or perhaps you'd like to have a frontend for things like URI rewriting or serving static files, so you need something more like a web server than a proxy. The second project we'll look at here is NGINX, a popular open source web server.

NGINX

Unlike HAProxy, NGINX is a web server, which means it does things other than just proxying. There are a whole host of web servers available today, but NGINX is a fine choice because it's fast, reliable, and has a good selection of features. Out of the box, it also supports sticky sessions, reverse proxying, and all the normal serving features that one would expect to find in a web server, such as SSL decoding, rewriting, and file serving. This only scratches the surface, however. A lot of plugins have been written by the community that extend its feature set to a magnitude larger than could possibly be covered here.

You may be wondering why you shouldn't just run NGINX as your primary proxy, instead of complicating matters with HAProxy. Well, many people do run NGINX as their frontend to the backend containers without any problems at all. We'll be covering how to make these kinds of choices in section 15.3, and we'll illustrate when it's sensible to opt for different routes.

Getting back to NGINX, though, it's very simple to configure, and it only requires a few lines in /etc/nginx/nginx.conf to configure sticky sessions and reverse proxying. The proxying and session affinity functionality is part of a module called NGINX HTTP Upstream (http://wiki.nginx.org/NginxHttpUpstreamModule), so ensure that your build of NGINX includes this module, or you'll get errors upon trying to start the service. The next listing shows an example entry in nginx.conf.

Listing 15.2   Configuring NGINX with proxying and session affinity

```
upstream backend  {
  ip_hash;
  server 10.0.0.1:8080 weight=3;                              ❶ Define backend
  server 10.0.0.2:8080 max_fails=3   fail_timeout=30s;            cluster
  server 10.0.0.3:8080;
}

server {
  listen 80;

  server_name yourdomain.com;
  access_log  /some/path/yourdomain.access.log main;

  location / {
    proxy_pass http://backend;
    proxy_set_header  X-Real-IP  $remote_addr;
    proxy_read_timeout 700;                                    ❷ Proxy incoming
    proxy_set_header Host $http_host;                             requests
    proxy_set_header X-Forwarded-For
    ➥$proxy_add_x_forwarded_for;
  }
}
```

This is a bare-bones configuration and it's the declaration for a single application that has multiple backend servers. The first thing you'll notice is that you define the cluster of application servers that you'd like to delegate to ❶, ensuring that you enable ip_hash. The ip_hash directive essentially creates a hash of the C-class IP address of the incoming client and uses that to continually route their request to the same backend server, if it's still active and fully available. It's even possible to apply weighting semantics and a selection of other parameters to fine-tune the behavior of delegation to the backend servers if need be. Do check the NGINX documentation for more information on that if it's of interest to your deployment.

The next section defines the application location ❷, but because NGINX is handling everything off to be processed, you can simply specify the root URI (/). If you want to do any other rewriting or request handling, you could either do it in this block or define another location if applicable. Finally, within this block, NGINX proxies incoming requests to the predefined backend cluster by way of the `proxy_pass http://backend` directive. We've also defined some proxy flags here, but these are just for example. In production, you'd likely want a more comprehensive set than what is implemented here.

Here you've seen two different open source projects that offer robust, performant solutions for proxying requests to your Lift applications, complete with session affinity. But despite your best efforts, many things can go wrong in production, and it's important to understand what the options are for managing your application state when operational issues occur.

15.2.2 *Distributing critical state*

Earlier in this section, I outlined some of the problems with the state-handling strategies implemented by other popular frameworks available today, one of which was session distribution. When using session affinity, there is always the concern that the server your session is located on may have some hardware failure, or become unavailable for some other reason. There are also situations where you may want a user to remain logged in over a period of time, rather than having to log in on every single visit to the site, irrespective of operational issues that may arise.

Consider a fairly basic application with some simple state. Let's assume that this application requires a login, and during the lifetime of this session, the code refers to this individual user by user ID. Imagine that the user conducts the login on server 1 of this two-server cluster, but, unexpectedly, server 1 dies and the user's subsequent requests are routed through to server 2. But wait, the user's session isn't present here, so what happens to the active login? By default, the user would have to log in once more to become active in the scope of this new session. This is, of course, a less than ideal situation—the user experience is suffering because of operational issues. There are solutions for such a problem.

EXTENDED SESSIONS

The first strategy you'll often see is called *extended sessions*, and it fits simple use cases such as this. In essence, extended sessions provide you with a simplistic mechanism for allowing the user to remain logged in irrespective of server restarts or other issues that may arise. It manages this by saving a user identifier into a cookie and keeping a database table of that state, which is persisted to the cookie.

If you're using Lift's Mapper, there is a prototypical trait that you can use to speed the process of implementing an extended session. We'll look at an example that assumes you're using the `ProtoUser` traits covered earlier in chapter 3. This isn't to say you can't use extended sessions with your own custom code, but this gives us a concise example that uses plumbing code you're already familiar with.

> ## Be aware of sidejacking
>
> It seems appropriate at this point to illustrate the inherent dangers with saving data to cookies that reside on the user's machine and that are subsequently transmitted with each request to the server. Unless this information is being communicated with transport-level security, HTTPS (SSL) in this case, the cookies' contents are essentially open to packet sniffing and thus the so-called sidejacking or session hijacking attack. During such an attack, the villain simply steals the cookie's contents and passes that in their request to the server. In this situation, the server thinks that the attacker is the real user's valid session.
>
> In short, if you're going to place anything in cookies related to users or sessions, it's best to do it over HTTPS if possible.

To get started with extended sessions, the first thing you'll need to do is ensure that you have lift-mapper on your project classpath. Second, we'll assume that you have a subtype of `ProtoUser` called `User` in order to model each person in this system. The following listing shows the code required to implement the proto-trait for extended sessions.

Listing 15.3 Extended sessions example

```
import net.liftweb.common.Box
import net.liftweb.mapper.{MetaProtoExtendedSession,ProtoExtendedSession}

object ExtendedSession
    extends ExtendedSession
    with MetaProtoExtendedSession[ExtendedSession]{
  override def dbTableName = "extended_sessions"
  def logUserIdIn(uid: String): Unit =          ❶ Log the
    User.logUserIdIn(uid)                            user in
  def recoverUserId: Box[String] = User.currentUserId
  type UserType = User                          ❷ Get the
}                                                  current user

class ExtendedSession extends ProtoExtendedSession[ExtendedSession]{
  def getSingleton = ExtendedSession
}
```

The listing here shows a sample implementation of using the extended sessions by implementing the Mapper traits `MetaProtoExtendedSession` and `ProtoExtended-Session` respectively. This definition creates a table in the database called extended_sessions, and it contains several different columns that relate to expiration timing of the cookie and the ID of the user the particular cookie relates to.

There are two methods you need to implement here: The first defines the function that will be executed to log this particular user in ❶. As this sample assumes the `User` type is an extension of `ProtoUser`, you can simply call `logUserIdIn`, which is supplied by the proto trait, but there is nothing stopping you having any code you need here that suits your setup. The second method is `recoverUserId` ❷, and it does pretty much what you might imagine; it grabs the currently logged-in user identifier (from the session, in this case). The `recoverUserId` function is ultimately wired into the mechanism that executes functions early in the request lifecycle to automatically log the user in.

Add this to your Boot class to enable the extended session functionality:

```
LiftRules.earlyInStateful.append(
  ExtendedSession.testCookieEarlyInStateful)
```

In brief, this line tells Lift to test for the presence of an extended session cookie during an early stage of the stateful request processing. If the cookie is found, the user is automatically logged in.

TERRACOTTA

At the very beginning of this section, I did somewhat bash the notion of distributing state, and it may seem that what I'm going to show you here contradicts that somewhat. The thing to remember here is that this strategy doesn't distribute all application state, only specific members that are defined by you for the purpose of failover, application resilience, or consistent user experience in the event of unforeseen operational problems.

By default, Lift has its own internal session map and doesn't use the `HTTPSession` that's part of the regular `javax.servlet` setup. The upside of this is that Lift is, for the most part, free of nondescript `Object` or `Any` types, and even items in the session can be complex closures or other things that typically wouldn't be acceptable items for placing into the session. But the benefit of using the `javax.servlet.HTTPSession` infrastructure is that it has been around for a long time, and many useful components for building applications are layered on top of this infrastructure.

One of the areas that has had a good level of investment and subsequent work over the past years has been distributing the serializable contents of the `HTTPSession`, so that state can be transparently utilized by several servers in a cluster. If, for example, one of the servers dealing with a particular user's session fails, the user is then completely unaware that their session is being serviced by another machine.

Considering both of these useful qualities, Lift has a halfway house of compromise called `ContainerVar`. In essence, this type gives you a strongly typed abstraction for access to the generally untyped (or at least, `Object` typed) world of `HTTPSession`. Moreover, because you're leveraging `HTTPSession`, you can use any Java infrastructure that could normally be applied to container sessions.

There is, however, a trade-off. With the ultimate store being based upon `HTTP-Session`, all the items you place into it that you wish to distribute must implement `java.io.Serializable` or feature the `@Serializable` annotation. The upshot of this is that you can't store Scala functions or other complex types in `ContainerVar` implementations as they are simply not `Serializable`.

With these points in mind, you may be wondering what the purpose of `Container-Var` is when you already have `SessionVar`, `RequestVar`, and even `TransientRequestVar`. You can think of `ContainerVar` as being at the same level or lifecycle as `SessionVar`. A

`ContainerVar` spans multiple requests in exactly the same way that a `SessionVar` does, with the ultimate difference being that `SessionVar` can be populated with any type and is stored with Lift's internal session map (`LiftSession`), whereas `ContainerVar` can only take serializable values and is stored in the container's `HTTPSession`, and thus can be distributed if the need arises.

> ## ContainerVar or SessionVar?
>
> Before using a `ContainerVar` over a `SessionVar`, it's a good idea to examine your use case. When you need to store something in the session, your first port of call should always be to use a `SessionVar` up to the point when your use case demands otherwise.
>
> Lift uses `SessionVar` and `RequestVar` internally, so don't assume that you can cluster the whole of `LiftSession`; you can't.`ContainerVar` just gives you the flexibility to choose what you want, when you need it, as opposed to being mandated a particular route of session storage by Lift.
>
> The closest feature Lift has to clustering the entire session is what is known as *migrated session mode*. This mode is essentially a cut-down version of Lift session, but it will stop you using the state-bound aspects of Lift, such as SHtml and S. It's availability versus functionality in this instance as Lift's function binding uses `LiftSession`-based state to store closures in memory, so it wouldn't be physically possible to cluster the whole session yourself.

We'll now look at an example of distributing systems using an open source product called Terracotta Web Sessions (http://terracotta.org/downloads/open-source/catalog). Terracotta is a Java clustering solution, and this particular component is (as the name suggest) a specialized HTTP session distribution system. It's worth noting that there are a plethora of clustering solutions out there; I'm demonstrating Terracotta here because it's one of the most popular solutions, but other perfectly good options would be Hazelcast (http://www.hazelcast.com/), JGroups (http://www.jgroups.org/), and Oracle Coherence (http://www.oracle.com/technetwork/middleware/coherence/overview/index.html). It really is a matter of understanding your use case and using a solution that works for you—open source or commercial.

Before you continue, download the Terracotta open source version and make sure you have two JAR files from the distribution named terracotta-session and terracotta-toolkit-1.1-runtime placed in your lib directory at the top level of your SBT project. At the time of writing, the Maven repository for Terracotta was (and had been) down for some time, so if service has been resumed you can simply add these add dependencies in your SBT project and have SBT download them for you. Either way, the result is exactly the same: the Terracotta classes will be present on your application classpath.

The first change you need to make to your application is to add the Terracotta configuration to your web.xml file. Ensure that your application uses javax.servlet 2.4 or greater as that's what Terracotta requires; be aware that the default Lift templates are targeted toward javax.servlet 2.3. The change is minimal but necessary. The following listing demonstrates the required changes to the web.xml file.

Listing 15.4 Web.xml configuration

```
<?xml version="1.0" encoding="UTF-8"?>
<web-app
  xmlns="http://java.sun.com/xml/ns/javaee"
  xmlns:xsi="http://www.w3.org/2001/XMLSchema-instance"
  version="2.5"
  xsi:schemaLocation="http://java.sun.com/xml/ns/javaee
  http://java.sun.com/xml/ns/javaee/web-app_2_5.xsd">

  <filter>
    <filter-name>terracotta-filter</filter-name>
    <filter-class>
      org.terracotta.session                          ❶ Container-specific
      ➥.TerracottaJetty61xSessionFilter                 session filter
    </filter-class>
    <init-param>
      <param-name>tcConfigUrl</param-name>            ❷ Terracotta
      <param-value>localhost:9510</param-value>          server
    </init-param>
  </filter>
  <filter>
    <filter-name>LiftFilter</filter-name>
    <display-name>Lift Filter</display-name>
    <description>The Filter that intercepts lift calls</description>
    <filter-class>net.liftweb.http.LiftFilter</filter-class>
  </filter>

  <filter-mapping>
    <filter-name>terracotta-filter</filter-name>
    <url-pattern>/*</url-pattern>
    <dispatcher>ERROR</dispatcher>                    ❸ Terracotta
    <dispatcher>INCLUDE</dispatcher>                     filter config
    <dispatcher>FORWARD</dispatcher>
    <dispatcher>REQUEST</dispatcher>
  </filter-mapping>
  <filter-mapping>
    <filter-name>LiftFilter</filter-name>
    <url-pattern>/*</url-pattern>
  </filter-mapping>

</web-app>
```

Here you have what is a very stock Terracotta configuration alongside the default Lift filter setup that you're likely familiar with by now. First, this web.xml defines a container-specific clustering implementation, which in this case will use Jetty ❶. Terracotta supports a whole host of options by default, so check the manual if you're using a container other than Jetty. Next, the configuration defines the location of the Terracotta server that will handle the session state ❷. It's possible to configure this in a fault-tolerant setup, but here you'll likely just have the server included with the Terracotta package download running locally, so it only points to a single, local Terracotta server. During the application boot-up phase, it will look for this server and continue to do so until it finds it, so ensure that your Terracotta server is running before starting the Jetty instance. Finally, the configuration details the stock filter mapping required to run Terracotta ❸; again, for more information on this, check out the Terracotta manual.

With the web.xml configuration in place, you can get around to using `Container-Var`. Because it also extends the `AnyVar` trait, it has a near-identical API to `RequestVar` and `SessionVar`, both of which you've already seen. Here's an example:

```
class MySnippet extends DispatchSnippet {
  object WordHolder extends ContainerVar[String]("n/a")
  ...
}
```

Here you simply create an object that extends `ContainerVar`. The caveat is that the parameterized type (`String` in this instance) must be serializable.

What you don't see in the preceding example is the full signature of `ContainerVar` which looks like this:

```
abstract class ContainerVar[T](dflt: => T)(
  implicit containerSerializer: ContainerSerializer[T])
  extends AnyVar[T, ContainerVar[T]](dflt) with LazyLoggable { ... }
```

The important thing to note here is that the second parameter group is defined as an implicit parameter of type `ContainerSerializer`. This serializer holds a set of implicit conversions to effectively serialize and deserialize the specified type to an `Array[Byte]`, and the compiler selects the correct implicit to use at compile time. There are no magic beans here; you're essentially using `ContainerVar` as a Lift abstraction to distribute particular parts of application state. This adds additional levels of robustness to your application via proven Java web infrastructure.

There are a lot of options in the wider Java ecosystem, both with regard to servlet containers and clustering solutions. The question is: how do you choose which to use? There are many factors that contribute to an answer to that question; some are tangible, but others are more a matter of taste or preference. In the next section, we'll look at some of the things you should consider, and I'll supply suggestions and justifications for two different implementations that would work well.

15.3 *Choosing a configuration*

In the previous two sections, you've seen some discussion of Java servlet containers, software load balancing, and sophisticated state-handling techniques that ensure your application is resilient and provides a robust, seamless user experience even in the face of server failure. But there are many choices in this field, and it can often be difficult to determine which configuration is right for you and your operation.

We'll outline two different scales of deployment configuration as a basic guide in assisting you in choosing your own deployment setup. The two ends of the spectrum we'll discuss are first small, with a single server setup, and then a second, much larger multiple server setup that handles redundancy and has more moving parts, but would handle far more load. By no means is either of these the de facto way to deploy Lift applications. There are many, many ways to handle deployment, and it's a fiercely debated subject in many organizations. To that end, bear in mind that these are just guidelines and not the panacea of deployment setup.

15.3.1 Single server

If your project is a small to medium-sized application, you'll likely be surprised at just how far you can take a single machine. The JVM is 64-bit compatible and can run with large quantities of RAM assigned to it, giving lots of space to store the in-process information needed for things like SessionVar and SHtml bind functions. With the large-capacity cloud computing offered by the likes of Amazon EC2 (http://aws.amazon.com/ec2/), it's relatively cheap to acquire machines with 17, 34, or even 68 GB of memory. Such an installation could feasibly support a fairly steady volume of traffic daily.

Given a single server setup and the use of a managed cloud, such as EC2, it would make most sense to run a simple configuration using NGINX and Jetty. Figure 15.3 details this simple setup.

In this configuration, you can simply configure your virtual hosts in NGINX on the frontend, and host the Lift application in Jetty and proxy to it from NGINX using a direct proxy. In practice, this means that the configuration would be the same as in listing 15.2, except that rather than having a proxy rule of proxy_pass http://backend; it would be something like proxy_pass http://127.0.0.1:9090/ to simply relay the traffic to the alternate localhost port.

Why choose NGINX in this configuration? Well, it's a full web server unlike HAProxy, and it can give you some flexibility that you may want. For example, the ability to host other sites or technologies alongside Lift is a complementary feature, as is

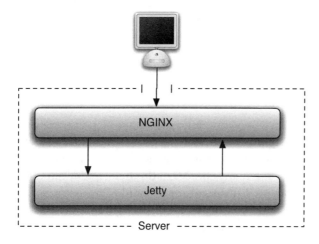

Figure 15.3   A simple single-server setup with NGINX fronting a Jetty instance

rewriting or static file serving. When you only have a single server to play with, it can be preferable to trade a degree of extreme performance that you likely won't miss for more flexibility.

15.3.2 Multiple servers

Moving to the other end of the spectrum, let's imagine we're running a large operation that requires three instances of Lift, load-balancing, and seamless upgrades. Obviously, this is a very different scenario, and the demands on the technology would be different. The configuration detailed in figure 15.4 shows one possible solution.

This setup is obviously far more complex and has many more moving parts than the single-server setup, but it could service a magnitude more traffic and be resilient in the case of failure. In the figure, the two frontend servers *A* and *B* include NGINX for HTTP decoding (SSL) and any facilities you may require, and HAProxy for load-balancing. These servers could feasibly be located in separate availability zones

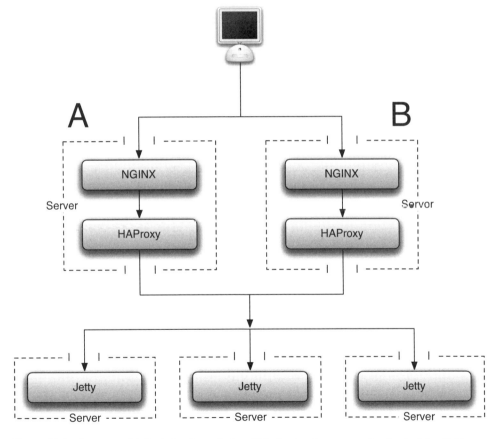

Figure 15.4 A more-sophisticated setup using multiple backend servers and redundant frontend request handling and load-balancing

around the world, such as server *A* in west coast USA and server B in east coast USA.[1] Both frontend servers could dispatch to the bevy of backend servers, which, once again, could feasibly be distributed around the world. This would give you a scenario whereby you'd have near-zero downtime in the event of a failure, either at the ISP level or at the application server level. In the event of a Jetty server going down, HAProxy would simply route your request to one of the other available nodes, and in the event of a systemic failure at hosting location *A*, site *B* would continue service with limited capacity.

The two examples shown here represent different ends of the deployment spectrum and service rather different application types. It should go without saying that there are many, many different ways to set up your environment; the point of illustrating these two configurations is to understand that Lift can scale in any number of ways, right up to servicing massively redundant applications that require high availability. Moreover, Lift also comes with a selection of facilities that can help when preparing your codebase for production. The Scala ecosystem similarly has some great tools to assist you. The next section looks at these tools and techniques.

15.4   *Deployment tools and techniques*

Going into production is likely one of the biggest steps your application will ever undertake, and it can be a daunting process. There are often many unexpected challenges that appear from out of the blue, and there are also problems that plague all applications and that still need solving. Yes, deployment can be a troubling and stressful time.

To minimize the stress of taking your Lift applications into production, this section looks at both tools and techniques that can hopefully assist in your deployment and save you some angst. This includes monitoring and dealing with your application once it has successfully been deployed. As you may or may not know, Twitter is a large user of Scala, and they released a lot of their code under open source projects. One of these projects is called Ostrich, and it's used for monitoring and collecting statistics on your application. You'll see how you can implement Ostrich in your own application and leverage its statistical reporting interface.

Before that, though, we'll explore some of the built-in Lift components and items of functionality that can be useful when nearing production. This includes built-in snippets and coding techniques that can save you CPU cycles.

15.4.1 *Built-in assistance*

Lift, unfortunately, can't help you a great deal with things that were not dealt with effectively during the development cycle, but it can help ease the pain of preparing for deployment and help with solving commonly occurring problems. In this section, you'll see how Lift can help you prepare and provide infrastructure to alter

---

[1] In order to actually achieve this, you'd also need to employ the services of dynamic DNS or Amazon's Elastic Load Balancing. This is a regular network issue, though, so it's somewhat beyond the scope of this book.

behavior between environments, and provide assistance in solving common problems faced by applications in the wild. The first component we'll be looking at is environment run modes.

PROPERTIES AND RUN MODES

Traditionally, one of the things that can be tricky with deploying applications is the configuration difference between development, testing, staging, and production systems. You often see people either hacking together custom scripts or following deployment procedures by hand to ensure they change all the configuration values relevant to that particular environment.

Lift has a solution for this problem. Part of the lift-util package is an object called `Props`. This object has a few functions, and one of those is to determine Lift's *run mode*. What's a run mode you might ask? Well, Lift uses these different modes to provide different implementations and functionality for different parts of the development cycle. For example, if you were using convention-based snippets that are resolved via reflection, and Lift was unable to determine the class you wanted, Lift would display, when you're running in development mode, a rather helpful box on the page where the snippet should be located, and it would inform you that the snippet you wanted was unable to be found. In production mode, however, no such message would be displayed to the user.

You can access the run mode in your application code simply by calling

```
import net.liftweb.util.Props
val m = Props.mode
```

In this example, `m` is assigned a value type of the `Props.RunModes` enumeration. There are a bevy of convenience methods defined on `Props` to access the run mode, so check out the documentation for more specific information.

The run mode itself must be set early in the application boot phase, so much so that it's generally supplied as a system property via the `-Drun.mode=production` style parameter to the JVM of the container. If you were running your application in an environment where you didn't have access to the system-level properties, you'd need to ensure that you have a filter in front of the `LiftFilter` to set the run mode explicitly using `System.setProperty`. This is somewhat crude, though, so it's typically preferable to set the run mode as a JVM startup argument where possible.

TEMPLATE CACHING

When running in production mode, Lift makes a whole set of optimizations and alterations to the way it operates. One of these is the caching of page templates.

During development, each template is loaded, parsed, and processed for each request. This allows you to make running changes to the application and see immediate feedback, but obviously you don't want to change your code in production, so this is needless overhead. To that end, Lift implements a template cache so that the HTML templates themselves are only loaded on the first request, and then each subsequent request pulls the template markup from a predefined cache that can hold up to 500 templates inside an in-memory LRU cache.

If you wish to override the default template-caching behavior, simply do the following:

```
LiftRules.templateCache = Full(InMemoryCache(100))
```

Any caching implementation you wish to use must extend `net.liftweb.util.Template-Cache`. The rest is up to you!

CLIENT CONTENT EXPIRY

When rolling out different versions of your web application, it can sometimes be a struggle ensuring that the client browser has the latest version of all your static content, like CSS and JavaScript. This can often cause problems in that when you make visual changes, the user's browser may be using a cached version from when they previously browsed the site. To them, at least, the user experience may be damaged.

This problem can be neatly sidestepped by making use of the `with-resource-id` snippet that's built into Lift and that you can use in your templates. Any time you want to reference static files, simply surround them as shown:

```
<lift:with-resource-id>
  <script type="text/javascript" src="/path/to/file.js"></script>
</lift:with-resource-id>
```

The result here is that file.js would have a GUID appended to the end of its URI. This GUID is calculated once per application boot, so every time you roll out a new version of your application, you can be sure that the end user always sees the latest version. In addition, if you are deploying your application into a clustered environment, you'll want to alter the logic that generates these identifiers so that it's consistent across that version or deployment, perhaps using the build number or hash. The logic for the resource ID generation can be customized via the `LiftRules.attach-ResourceId` hook.

EXCEPTION HANDLERS

In production, you'll likely want to give some kind of "oops, something went wrong" message in the very unlikely event that your application throws an exception. Fortunately, Lift provides a hook for this—all exceptions that occur bubble up through `LiftRules.exceptionHandler`. This allows you to intercept the error and handle it specifically, logging particular parts of the request if it was a certain exception type, for example.

Implementing your own exception handler is simple:

```
LiftRules.exceptionHandler.prepend {
  case (Props.RunModes.Production, _, exception) =>
    RedirectResponse("/error")
}
```

In this example, the code simply returns a `RedirectResponse`, but as you can return any `LiftResponse` subtype, you could flush a template to the browser, or pretty much do anything you like.

15.4.2 *Monitoring*

Once your application is in production, it can often be tricky to keep track of specific operations or to get live metrics from the system about how well it's performing or what operations are being used a lot. For example, perhaps you want to know how many people are logged in at any one time, or perhaps you'd like to take a particular measurement about how long requests are taking to process. These types of metrics can be really helpful as an application grows and there are more moving parts.

Twitter runs quite a number of large-scale Scala systems to handle the fire hose of 140 million+ tweets per day; monitoring has become an important function for them. Helpfully, Twitter has released a lot of their in-house projects as open source efforts, so that others can also benefit from them.

Ostrich is one such project (https://github.com/twitter/ostrich). Ostrich provides additional reporting facilities over and above what is offered by normal Java Management Extensions (JMX) that allow you to conduct three types of operations, as detailed in table 15.2.

Table 15.2 The different Ostrich metric types

Metric type	Description
Counters	A counter is something that never decreases its numeric value; it's a forever-increasing amount. Things that a counter could be applied to would be, for example, births. Every time a baby is born, the value will increase; it's not possible for someone to be unborn, so the value could never go down.
Gauges	Imagine yourself checking the oil in a car. You'd use a dipstick to get an indication of the oil level at that precise moment. If you checked it again the following day, the reading would likely be different. This is a gauge: a one-off reading of a specific thing at a specific time.
Metrics	These typically measure the time it takes for *n* operation to occur. In the case of a web application, you may want to measure the duration of a particular resource request whose speed you were concerned about.
Labels	A key/value pair that's normally used to indicate the state of a specific system. For example, webservice=offline.

Now that you know what's possible with Ostrich, let's put this into practice and look at how to implement Ostrich in your application to start collecting stats. The first thing you need to do is add the twitter repository and dependency to your project definition, as shown:

```
val ostrich = "com.twitter" % "ostrich" % "4.1.0" % "compile"
val twitterRepo = "twitter-repo" at "http://maven.twttr.com/"
```

Don't forget to call `reload` and `update` if you're already running the SBT shell so that SBT recompiles the project and downloads Ostrich.

The next thing you need to do is alter your application `Boot` class so that during the application startup, the Ostrich server is also started and registered. Likewise, when your application shuts down, you need to close the Ostrich server gracefully. The next listing shows the alteration to `Boot`.

Listing 15.5   Ostrich initialization code in the `Boot` class

```
class Boot {
  import com.twitter.ostrich._,

    admin.{RuntimeEnvironment},
    admin.config.{StatsConfig,AdminServiceConfig,TimeSeriesCollectorConfig}

  object OstrichWebAdmin extends AdminServiceConfig {
    httpPort = 9990
    statsNodes = new StatsConfig {                          ❶  Configure
      reporters = new TimeSeriesCollectorConfig :: Nil         Ostrich
    } :: Nil
    lazy val service =
      super.apply()(new RuntimeEnvironment(this))
  }

  def boot {
    ...                                                    ❷  Start
    OstrichWebAdmin.service                                   Ostrich

    LiftRules.unloadHooks.append(                          ❸  Close Ostrich
      () => OstrichWebAdmin.service.foreach(_.shutdown))      on shutdown
    ...
  }
}
```

First you need to define an Ostrich configuration object that specifies the settings Ostrich needs to run ❶. There is a whole range of possible options here, but in this example, the configuration defines the port number on which Ostrich's HTTP interface will run. This will allow you to get text, JSON, and graph representations of the collected data. Next, the `Boot` class calls the lazy value defined in the configuration object, which causes the Ostrich service to load ❷. This same service value is used again to shut down the service when the Lift application closes ❸, ensuring a graceful shutdown of Ostrich.

Now that you have Ostrich set up and running in your Lift application, you'll probably want to start collecting some statistical data. The most common type of metric you're likely to use is a counter. Let's assume you have a situation in which you want to record the number of times that an event takes place. This is a fit with the *counter* style of metric outlined in table 15.2. All you need to do is define an identifier for this event and do the following:

```
import com.twitter.ostrich.stats.Stats
Stats.incr("nameOfThisCounter")
```

This becomes exceedingly useful when you want to monitor specific aspects of your system, because you can just load up the monitoring graphs to check out what's going

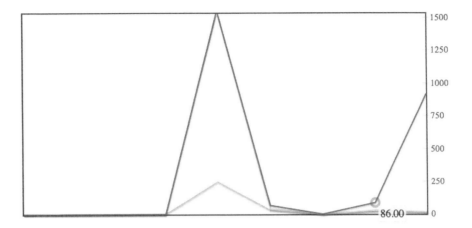

Figure 15.5 Example of an Ostrich graph

on and get the high-level overview of what those metrics look like. In fact, all of the Ostrich metrics can be accessed via the HTTP port you defined in the configuration object, and you can get that information as either a range of graphs or as raw data. Figure 15.5 shows an example of the graph detailing request duration, which you can see for yourself at http://127.0.0.1:9990/graph/?g=metric:request_duration.

In addition to these nice graphs, Ostrich also exposes all its data in JSON format, so if you have a cluster of machines, you could feasibly have a cluster monitor that consumes individual node data from each Ostrich instance, and then aggregates that with a tool such as Ganglia (http://ganglia.sourceforge.net/). Ostrich essentially gives you a standardized interface from which to collate analytical information from your applications.

The following subsections detail the specific types of Ostrich metrics and show how to implement them in your Lift applications, complete with working examples.

USING GAUGES

It's often useful to gain a snapshot of part of your application, monitoring specific parts of your app to take a one-time specific reading of an aspect. For example, you might like to know at any given time how many active sessions an instance is dealing with.

Lift has an object called `SessionMaster` that deals with the session setup and teardown, and it provides a hook called `sessionWatchers`. This hook allows you to supply your own actor object that will be notified every 10 seconds with an updated list of sessions. You can supply a listener actor here to pipe that information to Ostrich as a gauge. The following listing defines a basic listener.

Listing 15.6 Example `SessionMonitor` implementation

```
import net.liftweb.actor.LiftActor
import net.liftweb.http.SessionWatcherInfo
```

```
object SessionMonitor extends LiftActor {

  private var sessionSize = 0
  protected def messageHandler = {
    case SessionWatcherInfo(sessions) =>
      sessionSize = sessions.size
  }
  def count = sessionSize
}
```

❶ Update session count

Here we simply create a singleton object that implements `LiftActor`. This is a Lift-specific implementation of the actor paradigm and requires no start call to be sent, like the actors in the Scala standard library do; simply reference the object, and the actor will do the right thing.

Because this object is extending `LiftActor`, you need to implement the `message-Handler` method to define the function that should execute upon receiving the `SessionWatcherInfo` instance from the `SessionMaster` hook. The first parameter being extracted within the `messageHandler` (called `sessions`) is a map of live sessions. In this example, you simply want to get the size of that map and save it to an internal variable called `sessionSize`, so you ask the session map for its size ❶ so that whenever the gauge is asked for the number of sessions, there will always be an answer, even if it's a few seconds out of date.

Now that you have this implementation for the listener, you need to wire it up to the `SessionMaster` so that it receives notifications from Lift about the number of sessions and also implements the Ostrich gauge to collect the results. You simply need to do the following in your `Boot` class:

```
SessionMaster.sessionWatchers =
  SessionMonitor :: SessionMaster.sessionWatchers

Stats.makeGauge("current_session_count"){
  SessionMonitor.count.toDouble
}
```

The first definition prepends the `SessionMonitor` actor to the list of actors that the `SessionMaster` will notify with the list of sessions, whereas the latter definition configures the gauge measurement. Whenever the gauge is requested from the monitoring application, Ostrich will ask `SessionMonitor` to return the `count`.

METRICS

The last type of metric Ostrich supports is what is known as a metric. Metrics are collected as aggregates, and they include the number of operations performed, sum, maximum, and minimum, all of which are useful for determining the standard deviation of a particular activity's results.

In a web application, you may want to record the duration of a particular resource request. Like the session hook, there are also facilities to hook into request timing. The following listing shows a simple request timer.

Listing 15.7 Calculating request duration

```
import com.twitter.ostrich._, stats.Stats, admin.Service

object RequestTimer extends Service {
  object startTime extends RequestVar(0L)

  def beginServicing(session: LiftSession, req: Req){
    startTime(Helpers.millis)
  }

  def endServicing(session: LiftSession, req: Req,
      response: Box[LiftResponse]){
    val delta = Helpers.millis - startTime.is
    Stats.addMetric("request_duration", delta.toInt)
  }
  override def start(){}
  override def shutdown(){}
  override def quiesce(){}
}
```

This listing defines a simple object that has two methods: `beginServicing` and `end-Servicing`. These methods will be wired into the `LiftSession.onBeginServicing` and `LiftSession.onEndServicing` hooks respectively. The implementation here is rather simple: you assign a timer value into a `RequestVar` when the request starts processing, and then, in the `endServicing` method, the value held in the `startTime` variable is subtracted from the new time, which yields the duration delta. This data is then piped to Ostrich via the `Stats.addMetric` method.

The only thing remaining is to once again wire this into your application `Boot` as shown:

```
LiftSession.onBeginServicing = RequestTimer.beginServicing _ ::
  LiftSession.onBeginServicing

LiftSession.onEndServicing = RequestTimer.endServicing _ ::
  LiftSession.onEndServicing
```

This is nearly identical to the `SessionMaster` example in that `LiftSession` hooks define a list of executable functions that are called at the appropriate lifecycle stages of a request.

This concludes the section on tooling. You've seen many different things that you can use to both ease your deployment and gain critical application information when you actually get into the wild. With this in mind, you'll now learn about some of the real-life Lift users who run large-scale deployments in commercial environments.

15.5 *Case studies*

When evaluating new technology, it's common for people to look for others who have also adopted before them, to learn from their experiences and gain a better handle on whether or not a particular tool or system is going to be the right fit for them or their business. To that end, you'll now see two separate case studies: one from Foursquare.com and the other from Novell Vibe. Both of these are high-profile Lift users that operate in distinctly different spaces yet have found Lift to be a robust, reliable platform that boosted their overall productivity.

If you're either an existing Lift user, or are just getting to know Lift and are thinking about taking it into production for the first time, the following two subsections will give you a small glimpse into what others are doing in production and the levels of traffic they're handling with relative ease.

15.5.1 *Foursquare*

Foursquare is a new mobile application that makes cities easier to discover and more interesting to explore. Think of it as a social city guide and a game that challenges its users to experience new things, and rewards them for doing so. In order to tell friends when you're at a particular location, Foursquare lets users check in to a place and track the history of where they've been and who they've been there with.

More recently, Foursquare has done deals with large brands like GAP and Safeway to offer customized offers based upon both your loyalty card history and your check-in behavior. For example, if you had achieved the Gym Rat badge in the Foursquare game, Safeway might offer you a bonus on energy drinks, and deliver a set a coupons specifically for you to use at the Safeway checkout.

At the time of writing, Foursquare has a user base of approximately 12 million, and is growing that figure rapidly. In that user base, there are roughly 3 million check-ins daily, and from the second quarter of 2010 to the second quarter of 2011, there were just short of half a billion check-ins overall. By the time you read this, it's likely that these figures will have grown considerably, but understand that Foursquare serves all this traffic on approximately 30 frontend Lift servers and somewhere in the region of 50 MongoDB instances. Of the 30 Lift instances, 10 of those support the main website, Foursquare.com, and 20 service the Foursquare API, which all the mobile clients interact with and where the majority of the request load is located. Foursquare is a highly stateful application, but there have been no material issues in actually operating this in a heavily loaded site over time.

Infrastructure-wise, Foursquare is running with a pair of redundant NGINX servers up front for SSL decoding, and HAProxy as a middle tier that proxies requests to the backend Lift application servers that are all based upon Jetty. This entire operation exists in the Amazon EC2 cloud, so adding servers is a really trivial exercise and can be done at the flick of a switch.

15.5.2 *Novell Vibe*

During the second half of 2010, Novel launched a collaborative authoring environment called Vibe (http://www.novell.com/products/vibe-cloud/). Vibe can be both a cloud-based product delivered as a service, or an on-premises installation; either way, the goal is to transform engaging with your business's customers, sales channels, and partners into one slick and unified process. Vibe combines social messaging, real-time collaboration, and content sharing to deliver a one-stop shop that allows you to break free of departmental restrictions and form virtual cross-function teams that are ultimately more effective.

Vibe itself is split between its frontend Lift application servers and a backend that handles state and persistence. Each Lift application server is completely self-contained, and no state sharing is done at all. Novell has a bevy of backend servers that communicate back and forth with the Lift instances via Advanced Message Queuing Protocol (AMQP) messages. When the frontend requires the backend to do something, it sends an asynchronous message, and after the change has been made, the backend broadcasts asynchronous messages back to *all* frontend Lift servers to ensure consistency across all nodes, even if they suffer a machine failure.

The architecture of Vibe is heavily based around message-passing concurrency and actor design patterns. As such, Novell reports that it hasn't seen any CPU hotspots during the deployment and scaling of their system; it has essentially scaled linearly over all the CPU cores in the hardware. Novell also runs their own cloud infrastructure to host the Vibe service, and unlike Foursquare use all hardware load-balancing rather than a software solution. Overall, Lift has made it easy for the Vibe team to create very sophisticated user interfaces that are backed by a robust, durable enterprise-grade solution. At the time of writing, Novell was serving several thousand users with minimal impact on their cluster.

15.6 Summary

This chapter provided a broad introduction to the world of servlet containers, and it explored how to choose a platform that will give you the best out-of-the-box experience when using all of Lift's advanced features. Right now, Jetty is the servlet container of choice, and we would certainly recommend it for getting started with your first Lift production environment. You also saw how you could successfully support sticky sessions using two different software proxy platforms: HAProxy and NGINX. HAProxy is an extremely high-performance TCP/HTTP proxy. It only supports proxying, unlike NGINX, which is a full-featured high-performance web-server that includes proxy and load-balancing modules. These tools both have their pros and cons, so it's a case of choosing the right tool or software stack for the job.

You've also seen how Lift supports large-scale applications and provides a robust abstraction for distributing critical application state by both serializing data into cookies and using proven Java infrastructure to cluster the underlying servlet session. It's important to understand the limitations of the servlet session, however, and use Java clustering for key pieces of state while using the type-safety and flexibility of the Lift session for your regular session-scoped values. With the `ContainerVar` abstraction, you're free to use any clustering technology you want, but in this chapter you saw how easy it was to apply the Terracotta configuration to the existing web.xml, and everything else was seamlessly wired up. Next, we discussed how to navigate through the vast array of deployment choices, depending upon the size and scalability required in your application. Right from a simple, single-server setup through to a clustered multiple-server configuration, Lift is easy to deploy and leverages proven Java infrastructure throughout.

This chapter also showed you that Lift provides some helpful tools to make your application respond differently based upon its system run mode. When the application is running in production mode, Lift internally makes a set of optimizations both for performance and end-user experience. In production mode, Lift won't display missing snippet errors or stack traces to the end user, and you can simply append an exception handler to customize the user experience. The other tool you saw here was the Ostrich monitoring system from Twitter. Monitoring can be an extremely powerful tool for collecting statistical and operational information from your applications at runtime. Using Ostrich, you've seen how you can accumulate metrics over time using counters, obtain snapshot dipsticks using gauges, and build service timers to collect and aggregate metrics about the duration of function execution.

Deployment is difficult. This is an unfortunate fact and the real takeaway from this chapter is that there is no single way to deploy Lift into production. There are lots of factors, many of which will influence your choices in choosing a software stack. The best thing you can do is use the advice here as part of your information-gathering process, and make your own informed choices. Some of the patterns outlined here are in use in production sites and they're known to be reliable, but ultimately every environment and application is different. Be pragmatic, write lots of unit and functional tests to make sure your code is as good as it can be, and ensure you do effective monitoring from the start of production deployment. Employ these techniques on top of some of the guides outlined here, and you won't go far wrong.

Finally, thanks for sticking with me throughout this book! It's been a long journey, and I hope that you've found it both interesting and informative. You've built several small applications throughout the course, covering everything from basic snippets right through to awesome interactive features like Comet and AJAX. Lift is an amazingly powerful toolkit, and it will take time for you to master it fully, but stick with it and you'll be rewarded with stable, secure applications that are hugely interactive and that your users love.

appendix A
Introduction to Scala

Scala is a powerful combination of both object oriented and functional programming approaches, and its language constructs can often seem somewhat terse to newcomers. This appendix aims to give you a rough guide to Scala and serve as enough background for you to make full use of this book. Understand that this is only a top-level view of Scala features and it can't cover anywhere near all of Scala's capabilities. For a more detailed introduction to the broader language, I suggest picking up a copy of Nilanjan Raychaudhuri's *Scala in Action*, also from Manning.

As a language, Scala only has a few core features. The vast majority of features are implemented as libraries, which results in a language that has a very tight core. The following sections cover this core of features that are then used to build the rest of the standard library.

A.1 Variables, values, and immutability

Scala uses a range of mechanisms to allocate objects in memory, and if you've programmed in nearly any other language, you'll be familiar with the concept of a variable. It's an item that you typically assign something (like a string) to, and then reference (and possibly mutate) at a later stage in your program.

To create variables in Scala you can do the following:

```
var thing = "sdfdsf"
var another: Int = 1234
```

This provides a means to create a variable, which can be mutated later in your application code.

Additionally, notice that the `thing` variable does not have an explicit type annotation: Scala is clever enough to *infer* the type based upon the assigned content. In this case, it can determine that it must use a `String` type. Scala can infer the types of values in nearly all situations, but there are times when explicit annotation can either assist the compiler by removing type ambiguity or simply act as documentation for other programmers reading your code, if it's not immediately clear what a particular line does.

Assigning content to variables is not a commonly used idiom within Scala programs, except for purely internal state. By using variables that are anything other than internal state, you are prone to threading and locking issues when you introduce any level of concurrency. Don't worry too much at the moment about the specifics of this reasoning; just understand that when making assignments within your code, it is usually preferable to use the val keyword and create an immutable value. Consider the following:

```
scala> val abc = 1234
abc: Int = 1234

scala> abc = 6789
<console>:6: error: reassignment to val
       abc = 6789
```

Any attempt to reassign the value results in a compile-time error stating that you can't reassign immutable values. Broadly speaking, you should always try to use the val keyword and only fall back to using var when there is absolutely no other choice.

This idea of immutability runs deep within Scala and functional programming languages in general. This is the most basic example of its usage within assignment, but in the next section you'll see how to construct immutable classes and how you can leverage the language support for such structures.

A.2   *Classes, methods, traits, and functions*

Like many languages, Scala exhibits fairly typical constructs such as *classes* and *methods*. These classes and methods operate nearly identically to those found in Java, for example, but with some additional sugar to make their use slightly nicer. Although having sugar for regular constructs is convenient, Scala also exhibits *traits* and *functions*. These are language features that really allow you to build highly reusable pieces of code and they're not found in many programming languages. The following sections cover these four Scala constructs and show you some basic usage principles, starting with the likely familiar class paradigm.

A.2.1   *Classes*

As Scala exhibits both object oriented and functional qualities, you can happily construct classes and B extends A semantics. These classes can have instance variables, methods, and everything else that is common in object-oriented code.

Consider the following class definition:

```
class Foo(bar: Int){
  def whatever =
    if(bar > 3) "Awesome" else "Amazing"
}
```

This simple class `Foo` has a single constructor argument that takes an integer "value." The constructor argument, `bar`, is accessible for all the methods or properties of that class but it isn't accessible for external callers: it is essentially not `public`.

If you wanted to make the `bar` property publicly available, the definition would need to add the `val` keyword before the constructor argument:

```
class Foo(val bar: Int){ ... }
```

This modification then allows the following interaction:

```
scala> class Foo(val bar: Int)
defined class Foo

scala> new Foo(123).bar
res0: Int = 123
```

By creating an instance of the class, an external caller can reference the `bar` property by name to obtain its value. Being defined as `val`, this property is immutable.

In addition to allowing you to define normal classes, Scala also supports singletons as language constructs. These are created by way of the `object` keyword. Consider the following:

```
object Thing {
  def now = new java.util.Date().toString
}
```

The `object` keyword defines a lazy singleton object that won't be instantiated until it's *touched* by calling code. Because the `Thing` object is a singleton that Scala is managing for you, when you call the object, you can invoke it like a static member with something like this:

```
scala> Thing.now
res1: java.lang.String = Sat Mar 26 15:23:49 GMT 2011
```

Objects can also be used to encapsulate other components of functionality, but that's beyond the scope of this quick overview.

> **NOTE** It is typically idiomatic within Scala to give methods that have zero arguments no trailing parenthesis if the function is referentially transparent. For example `Thing.foo` is fine given a referentially transparent method, but if the method has side effects it would be idiomatic to write `Thing.foo()`.

For more information on advanced Scala topics, you may find Joshua D. Suereth's *Scala in Depth* useful.

Finally, both objects and classes can have the `case` modifier applied to their definition to create what are known as *case classes*. Consider this example:

```
case class Foo(bar: Int, whiz: String)
```

By applying this keyword to the class definition, the Scala compiler will add certain conveniences to that class, such as providing a factory function that negates the need to create instances with the new keyword. Additionally all the constructor arguments are automatically made available as immutable properties of that instance:

```
scala> val x = Foo(123,"Sample")
x: Foo = Foo(123,Sample)

scala> x.bar
res4: Int = 123

scala> x.whiz
res5: String = Sample
```

On top of these helpful conveniences, case classes also provide you with friendly and predictable implementations of the toString, equals, and hashCode methods. This means you can do handy comparisons of case class instances and receive sensible representations of instances when calling toString.

A.2.2   *Traits*

In addition to defining a single line of class inheritance, Scala also supports polymorphism or multiple-inheritance via a construct known as *traits*. These traits allow you to break up your logic into defined blocks of functionality that can be *composed* together.

Consider the following example that models the components of sporting events:

```
trait Discipline { ... }
trait Run extends Discipline { ... }
trait Cycle extends Discipline { ... }
trait Swim extends Discipline { ... }

trait Competition { ... }

case class Triathalon(name: String) extends Competition
  with Run                                                  Compose traits
  with Cycle                                                together
  with Swim
```

With a model of traits configured such as this, it's possible to create instances that compose together the desired functionality. If some change was required for all running events, you would only need to make a single change to events that included the Run trait, and the change would be immediately propagated.

In addition, you can define the required composition for each trait without explicitly extending the trait itself. It's essentially like telling the compiler "when this trait gets used, it must also be composed with trait ABC." This is done via a self-type notation:

```
trait ABC { self: XYZ =>
  ...
}
```

In this example, the trait ABC can only ever be composed into another class when the XYZ type is also present in the mix. This is a powerful idiom within Scala that you don't need to fully understand now, but as your system grows it can become exceedingly helpful.

A.2.3 *Methods*

Methods are defined upon classes by using the `def` keyword, and in this case the resulting type is again *inferred* by the compiler to be a string. Class methods in Scala don't need to be explicitly wrapped in curly braces unless the method requires some kind of internal assignment, because all control structures within Scala return a concrete type. Consider the following two method definitions:

```
def whatever =
  if(bar > 3) "Awesome" else "Amazing"

def another {
  if(bar > 3) "Awesome" else "Amazing"
}
```

These two method implementations look exceedingly similar, and the unfamiliar eye might assume that they do the same thing. In fact, `whatever` returns a `String` whereas `another` returns a special Scala type called `Unit`. The reason for this is that the definition of `another` lacks the equals sign (`=`) after the method name and immediately wraps the whole method in curly braces; this makes Scala assume that the method is side-effecting and thus returns nothing directly useful. If you're coming from other statically typed languages, you can think of the `Unit` type as being analogous to the `void` construct.

Methods can also take arguments in exactly the same way that Java methods can, but within Scala it's also possible have multiple *argument groups*. This can be useful, because it allows you to make flexible APIs that can have both arguments and pseudo-blocks. Here's an example of the definition:

```
scala> def whatever(n: Int)(s: String) = "%s %s".format(n.toString, s)
whatever: (n: Int)(s: String)String
```

And here's an example of its usage:

```
scala> whatever(123){
     | "asda"
     | }
res10: String = 123 asda
```

These argument groups are separate, but both are available in the definition of the method body, so when you call the method you can pass arguments as either a single normal argument or as a block. You can even mix styles together to create whatever API suits your requirements.

The final thing to note about methods is that your operators can be called anything you want, even using Unicode operators. These operators can be called either directly or with what is known as *infix notation*. For example, calling the + operator with two integers and infix notation would give the familiar: 2 + 2. But in Scala, the same method call can be written as 2.+(2). For the most part, you'll use the dot notation to invoke methods, but often within Lift you'll see infix notation when using List types. For example, `List(1,2,3)` is the exact same thing as 1 :: 2 :: 3 :: Nil, where the :: (cons) operator builds a list of the integer values.

A.2.4   *Functions*

With the blend of object oriented and functional styles, Scala sports the concept of general functions. That is to say, a specific instance of a function can be passed around and is in and of itself a specific type. Functions are first-class values in Scala, which essentially means that you can create generic functions that take A and return B. Such a relationship is typically expressed as A => B and is referred to as a lambda function.

Consider the following example:

```
scala> val f = (s: String) => s.toLowerCase
f: (String) => java.lang.String = <function1>

scala> f("SOMeThInG")
res8: java.lang.String = something
```

Here, a function that takes a String and returns a String is assigned as the value f and has the type Function1. With this function defined, it's possible to pass a single argument to f and treat the value function like you would any other method; the only difference being that the function is itself an instance rather than being contained within a class.

In essence, this is the basis of all functional programming within Scala: functions can be any type to any type, and functions can even take other functions as arguments, resulting in what are known as *higher-order functions*. Functions themselves can have zero or more arguments and will have their appropriate type automatically applied by the compiler. For example, String => String would be equivalent to saying Function1[String,String].

The benefit of all this function madness is that you can conveniently encapsulate a piece of logic and only care about the type-level interfaces, essentially allowing parts of your system to replace whole bits of functionality simply by passing another function that returns the same type but gets to the output via a different means.

This description really only scratches the surface of what is possible with function-based programming in Scala, but functions are heavily used within Lift for all manner of purposes, so it's helpful to have a reasonable understanding of the concept.

A.3   *Collections*

By default, Scala provides a whole set of immutable data structures for modeling collections, and of those List[T] is a commonly used type within Lift. These collections all support a variety of common operations, irrespective of the implementing type. Consider table A.1, which lists commonly used collection functions.

Scala collections have a wide range of operations, and the methods listed here are just a few that will help you get up to speed with the examples in this book. For more detailed information on particular use cases or other possible methods, see the online Scala API documentation: http://www.scala-lang.org/api/.

Table A.1 Common collection functions

Operation	Description

map	Many collections implement the map function, which takes a function of type A => B. The following example maps a list of integers and multiplies each integer by 2, resulting in a new List[Int] that has values exactly double that of the starting list.
	
	`List(1,2,3,4).map(_ * 2)`
	
	Results in
	
	`List[Int] = List(2, 4, 6, 8)`

flatMap	Like map, flatMap applies the given function to every element within the collection, but rather than returning type B, the function must return a subtype of scala.collection.Traversable. In lay terms, this means that given a List[List[T]], for example, flatMap flattens the lists into a single list.
	
	`List(List(1,2,3), List(4,5,6))`
	`  .flatMap(identity)`
	
	Results in
	
	`List[Int] = List(1, 2, 3, 4, 5, 6)`
	
	In this example, identity just provides a function of A => A. It does not modify the value it's passed, so in this case utilizing identity with flatMap just passes the value through into the resulting List[Int].

filter	As the name implies, this method filters the collection based upon the *predicate function* passed to it. In the following example, the function checks to see if the element is less than 2, meaning that the result only includes elements for which the predicate evaluates to true.
	
	`List(1,2,3,4).filter(_ <= 2)`
	
	Results in
	
	`List[Int] = List(1, 2)`

foldLeft, foldRight and reduceLeft, reduceRight	It's common to want to reduce (or fold) the contents of a collection. Scala has several methods for this: foldLeft collapses the collection left to right, and foldRight does the opposite. The difference between folding and reduction is that fold methods require a seed element or value from which to start the execution.
	
	`List(1,2,3,4).reduceLeft(_ + _)`
	
	Results in
	
	`Int = 10`
	
	`List(1,2,3,4).foldLeft(0)(_ + _)`
	
	Results in
	
	`Int = 10`

A.4   *Pattern matching*

Scala has a general pattern-matching facility that allows you to match on general data types and execute particular functions based on the result of the match. Consider the following example:

```
def matcher(x: Any): Any = x match {
  case 1 => "one"
  case "two" => 2
  case x: Int => "scala.Int"
}
```

This example defines a method that accepts a general input value and then uses the match keyword to start the sequence of matching cases defined by the case keyword. The first two cases are examples of matching on concrete values, whereas the third case matches on the *type* of the input value.

A.5   *Implicits*

Another powerful feature of Scala is known as *implicits*. Let's first look at the notion of something being implicit and consider what this actually means. The dictionary definition of implicit is *implied though not plainly expressed*, and this pretty much matches the Scala meaning: you are not explicitly applying something in your code; rather, the compiler is applying it for you. The invocation or conversion is not explicit; rather, it is *implicit*.

Implicits come in two primary forms: *implicit conversions* and *implicit parameters*. Let's look at implicit conversions first.

Consider a method that returns type A, but your code only yields type B. By default, this would be a compile-time error that would need manual resolution to make sure that your code properly returns type A. But let's assume that the following implicit conversion was within scope:

```
implicit def convertBtoA(in: B): A = in.someConversionMethod
```

By having the special implicit keyword before the method definition, you are telling the compiler that if it expects an A, but only has a B, it can automatically use this method to convert between the two types. While this may not seem that useful, such techniques can allow you to automatically convert between types without any additional noise in the code itself.

Consider this more concrete example:

```
scala> val regex = "/foo".r
regex: scala.util.matching.Regex = /foo
```

Here the .r method does not exist on java.lang.String, so an implicit conversion that's available as part of scala.Predef and that's in scope by default within all Scala code, converts the regular java.lang.String to a scala.collection.immutable.StringLike that has the predefined r method, which in turn creates the regular expression instance.

These kinds of practices can be extremely useful when creating DSLs and other utilities to remove clutter from your API.

The second type of implicit functionality within Scala is *implicit parameters*. Earlier in section A.2.3, you saw how to define methods with multiple argument groups, and it's possible to define one of these groups as implicit so that the value is automatically applied as an argument by the compiler. Consider the following example:

```
scala> implicit val sneeky: Int = 1234
sneeky: Int = 1234

scala> def thing(implicit numbers: Int) = "Sneeky: "+numbers.toString
thing: (implicit numbers: Int)String

scala> thing
res9: String = Sneeky: 1234
```

The first line in this example defines an implicit value of 1234. The fact that it's marked implicit at this point doesn't really do anything; you can still directly reference the value and use it however you would normally. The second this example details is the definition of a method that has an *implicit parameter group* of type Int. It's important to note that, in this example, the parameter group only has one value, but it could just as easily have multiple values and still only require the single implicit keyword. In exactly the same way as the value can be interacted with directly, this method could also interact with it, despite the implicit declaration. Finally, the thing method is invoked with zero parameters and the compiler automatically chooses the implicit value sneeky, thus satisfying the need for the argument.

The implicit functionality within Scala is exceedingly powerful and can be used to build some flexible and clutter-free APIs. On the other hand, implicit conversions can also make an API too confusing or seemingly work like magic. Learning to wield implicits effectively can take some time, but the effort of learning the correct balance within your own application domain will be well worth it.

appendix B
Configuring an IDE

Throughout this book, the code and explanations have assumed you're using the base level of tooling required to actually work with Lift. Specifically, this means a build tool and a text editor. While this can be a very effective environment for power users or those who prefer a no-frills development workflow, many people prefer to use an integrated development environment (IDE) to centralize their working.

At the time of writing, there was a range of IDEs available for Scala coding, and this appendix will show you how to take a base SBT project and set it up to work with two of the most popular IDEs: JetBrains IntelliJ and Eclipse.

The following two sections assume that you have set up a fresh SBT project by creating a new directory, running SBT, and answering the initial startup questions. Because tooling support is typically provided by external companies, the details of these (and other) tools may have changed or improved significantly by the time you read this. Nevertheless, this appendix should provide you with a working base from which you can get up and running.

B.1   IntelliJ

JetBrains IntelliJ (http://www.jetbrains.com/idea/) is a popular IDE with support for many different languages, including Scala. Since the 2.7.x Scala releases, IntelliJ has had the best Scala support of any editor, and it continues to have great language support and be popular among the Scala community. To get started, you just need to install the Scala plugin, which is available via the IntelliJ plugin installation menu, as displayed in figure B.1.

The IntelliJ Scala plugin provides the relevant language support, such as color coding and code completion, so it's important to make sure you set this up before continuing.

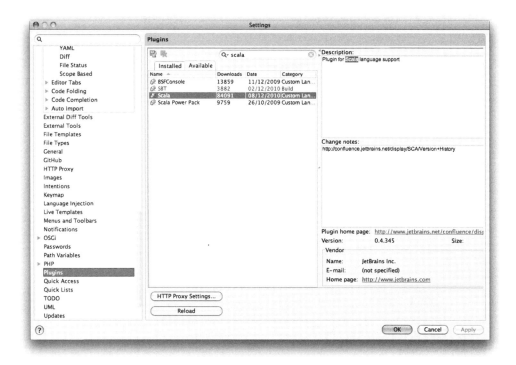

Figure B.1   Install the IntelliJ Scala plugin

TIP   In addition to the Scala language plugin for IntelliJ, there's also a plugin to support the SBT build tool directly within the IntelliJ interface. Using it isn't mandatory by any means, but if you'd prefer not to keep switching between a terminal window and the IDE, this can be a nice addition.

Given the popularity of IntelliJ, the community has created an SBT plugin to automatically generate the right IntelliJ project configurations for you (https://github.com/mpeltonen/sbt-idea/tree/sbt-0.7). Load up the SBT shell in a terminal window and issue the following commands:

```
> *sbtIdeaRepo at http://mpeltonen.github.com/maven/
> *idea is com.github.mpeltonen sbt-idea-processor 0.4.0
... run other commands
> update
> idea
```

This command generates project .iml files that are correctly configured with the right dependencies and so on. Any time you need to add or alter dependencies in the SBT project file, you can just invoke the `idea` command again from the SBT shell.

After opening the project directory within IntelliJ, the IDE will take a few moments to generate the appropriate metadata it needs for the dependencies and classpath,

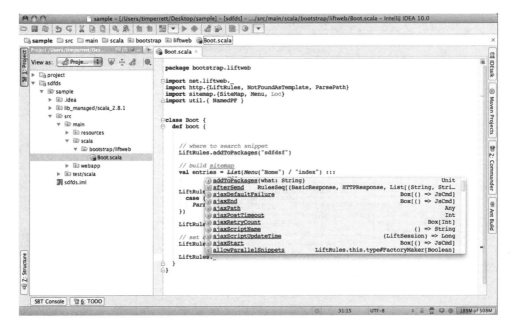

Figure B.2   A new SBT project, complete with code completion

but when that finishes, you'll have access to all the project code with full IDE support, as shown in figure B.2.

B.2   Eclipse

Another very popular IDE is Eclipse (http://www.eclipse.org/), and many users who are familiar with Eclipse from the Java space may want to continue using it when they transition into the Scala world. Broadly speaking, the Scala support within Eclipse is fairly good, but unlike IntelliJ, the support is completely provided by the community through the Scala IDE project: http://www.scala-ide.org/. The project site has all the relevant instructions on how to install the Scala language support into Eclipse; check the site directly for the most up-to-date information.

With the language support in place, you'll need to import your SBT project into Eclipse. Helpfully, the community has provided an automated way to do this via an SBT plugin (https://github.com/musk/SbtEclipsify/tree/0.8.0), which requires just a bit of configuration to use. First, add the plugin definition to a file called project/plugins/Plugins.scala:

```
import sbt._

class Plugins(info: ProjectInfo) extends PluginDefinition(info) {
  lazy val eclipse = "de.element34" % "sbt-eclipsify" % "0.7.0"
  ...
}
```

With this in place, you now need to add the plugin trait to your project definition so that the `eclipse` action is available to you within the SBT shell:

```
import sbt._

class LiftProject(info: ProjectInfo)
  extends DefaultWebProject(info)
  with de.element34.sbteclipsify.Eclipsify {
  ...
}
```

If you already have the SBT shell running, call the `reload` command so that SBT fetches the appropriate dependencies. After a short moment, the JARs will be downloaded and you can invoke the `eclipse` command from the SBT shell. You can then do a File > Import within the Eclipse IDE and add the project to your workspace. The result should be as displayed in figure B.3.

Upon adding the project to Eclipse, there will be a brief moment while the metadata is generated, and that's it.

There are a range of options available to tweak how the Eclipse project files are generated by the SBT plugin, and I advise checking the documentation if the default behavior is not what you were expecting.

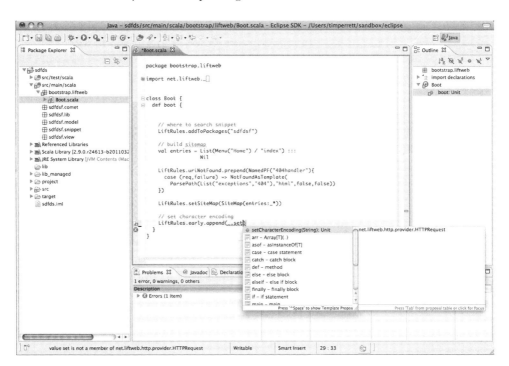

Figure B.3 Successfully imported SBT project into Eclipse IDE.

appendix C
Options and boxes

If you have any experience with any other programming language, you'll no doubt have seen code that does some guard-style operation, like this:

```
if (thing != null)
{
    thing.whatever();
}
```

The purpose is to prevent one from calling the whatever() method on someobject when it is null; otherwise the method would explode with a NullPointerException at runtime because null is not a proper object instance. This style of programming can add a lot of noise to your code, and Scala has a solution for this: the Option type.

Scala abstracts the whole idea of a value being *something* or *nothing*, so rather than having to continually create guards within your code, you wrap your type with an Option and then, when you want to do something with that value, you pass the Option instance a function that's only executed if the value is *something*.

Let's illustrate that with an example:

```
scala> Option[String]("Tim").map(_.toLowerCase)
res1: Option[java.lang.String] = Some(tim)
```

Option is a generic type constructor, so you either need to specify the contained type or let Scala infer it. In this case, the content is of type String. The preceding example defines a new Option[String] instance with an explicit value of "Tim", and it defines a function to be executed in the event that it contains a value. As "Tim" is being explicitly passed to the apply method of the Option type, the result is Some("tim"). Some is a subtype of Option, and it's used to represent options that have a value, which means it is *something*.

Suppose the value "Tim" was not hardcoded, but was passed from somewhere else in the system and could feasibly be a null value. You still want to execute the function if the value exists, so let's simulate this by explicitly passing `null` to the `Option` type's `apply` method:

```
scala> Option[String](null).map(_.toLowerCase)
res2: Option[java.lang.String] = None
```

Notice that the definition is exactly the same as before, but the value is explicitly `null`. The function definition is the same, but it doesn't explode with a `NullPointer-Exception` because the function is never executed. `Option` is clever enough to realize that the value is `null`, so it returns the strongly typed representation of a non-value: `None`.

These two examples are explicit, but trivial. Consider something more likely to crop up within your application. Perhaps you query the database for a value, but the value you're looking for may not exist. In that case, it would be a lot better to receive a properly represented result in the form of `None` than it would be to simply receive `null`.

Appendix A (section A.2) describes some of the actions typically associated with collections and data structures within Scala, covering the `map` and `flatMap` functions found in most Scala collections. `Option` also sports these methods, and by virtue of `map` and `flatMap` it's possible to use what is known as a *for-comprehension* as some nice syntactic sugar for interacting with collection types. Because `Option` is also a collection type, using for-comprehensions allows you to chain options together, so that they only fall through to the next function if the value is *something*. Consider the following:

```
scala> for {
    a <- Some(10)
    b <- Some(5)
  } yield a * b
res: Option[Int] = Some(50)
```

Here, two integers wrapped with options are multiplied together, and the resulting value is also encased within a `Some` instance. This is fairly logical behavior, but what happens if one of the values is `None`? Here's an example:

```
scala> val one = Some(10)
one: Some[Int] = Some(10)

scala> val two: Option[Int] = None
two: Option[Int] = None

scala> for {
     | a <- one
     | b <- two
     | } yield a * b
res3: Option[Int] = None
```

In this case, because one of the values is `None`, the result of the comprehension is itself `None`. This turns out to be pretty useful when building applications, because it means you can safely provide a sensible default value if one is applicable.

The `Option` type includes a method called `getOrElse`, which you can use to provide a default, like so:

```
scala> res3 getOrElse 0
res8: Int = 0
```

This is just one convenience provided by `Option` types. Thus far, the examples in this appendix have only covered the `scala.Option` type, which is by no means exclusive to Lift.

Lift has a very similar type called `Box`, where the equivalent to `None` is `Empty`, and the equivalent to `Some` is `Full`; `Box` also has the concept of `Failure`. The purpose of this structure is to capture both the fact that the `Box` is `Empty` and provide information about why that `Box` is `Empty`.

> **NOTE** If you have previous experience with Scala, you may be wondering what the purpose of this is, considering the similarities this has to `Either[Option[A], Exception]`. This is a point of debate, but broadly speaking the concepts can be thought of as similar in the sense that you have a data structure that could hold a value or an error.

Let's look at a few examples of how Lift uses `Box` and how you can utilize the `Failure` aspect in your code. Consider this example that loads a product from a Mapper model:

```
import net.liftweb._, http.S, common.{Box,Full,Empty,Failure}

for {
  id <- S.param("pid") ?~ "Product ID not present in request"
  product <- Product.find(id) ?~ "Product does not exist"
} yield product
```

In order to use the `Box` functionality, be sure to import the appropriate types as in the first line of this code. The goal here is to use information from the incoming request to load a model record from the database. As these things may not exist at runtime, it makes sense to give them the optional functionality supplied by `Box`. Otherwise, if the request didn't contain the appropriate request parameter, there would be no way to know which record should be loaded from the database.

The for-comprehension is a neat construct for this kind of problem, and the example demonstrates that you can obtain the request parameter as a `Box[String]` by using the `S.param` method. As you saw earlier with the `Option` type within for-comprehensions, when the values are `None` or `Empty`, the `Empty` result just falls through to the `yield` value. The ramification of this is that if the request parameter doesn't exist, the whole expression gracefully falls through and returns `Empty`.

Presently the small preceding example above could have mostly been achieved by using the `Option` type, but the real `Box`-only feature here is the `?~` method. This strange looking symbol essentially tells `Box` to generate a `Failure` instance that contains the supplied friendly error message in the event that the value is `Empty`. Here's an explicit example of this in action:

```
scala> val x: Box[String] = Empty
x: net.liftweb.common.Box[String] = Empty
```

```
scala> x ?~ "Oops, your value is empty"
res12: Box[String] = Failure(Oops, your value is empty,Empty,Empty)
```

Here the `Empty` is automatically converted to `Failure` and it provides the appropriate error message. This idiom is heavily prevalent within Lift, and it's something you'll see a lot in both application code and the internal Lift code.

The astute reader will notice that the `Failure` instance has two additional parameters, both of which are defined as `Empty`. The `Failure` class takes two additional parameters:

- A `Throwable` instance if the boxed value is `Empty` due to an exception being thrown at runtime.
- A chain of nested failures. In the case that this failure is part of a stack of possible failing scenarios, you might want to nest (or aggregate) those failures for later processing.

Depending upon your particular use case, you may use these properties or you may just happily ignore them. Also note that it isn't common to create your own instances of `Failure`; more likely you would be pattern-match against a value that could possibly be a `Failure`, and you might want to extract the error information.

It can take time to really understand how to properly leverage the `Option` and `Box` structures, but the investment in time will make your applications more robust, more predictable, and free of all those noisy guards.

index

values, Scala language 375–376
VARCHAR type 256
variables, Scala language
    375–376
Vibe environment,
    Novell 372–373
View First 6, 8
view-affecting parameter 148
viewDispatch 127
views 125–128
virtual host 296

W

WAR (Web Application
    Archives) 27
WAR file 289, 319, 347
Web Application Archives. *See*
    WAR

web services
    HTTP dispatching and
      174–185
      DSL 176–179
      REST service 179–185
    testing 336–340
web.xml file 27
webapp directory 164
webapp/templates-hidden
    directory 133
WEB-INF directory 27
WebKit, Lift. *See* Lift WebKit
WebSpec 326, 334–335, 346
where() method 272
wide.html 44
widgets 137–139
    AutoComplete 137–138
    Gravatar 138–139
wiki 158
wiki.html template 157

WikiEntry class 153–156
wildcard syntax 142
wiring 203–207
WiringUI object 204–206
with-resource-id 111, 366
withSFor method 335
Wizard system, LiftScreen
    mechanism and 135–136,
    265–266

X

XHTML templates 43
XML (Extensible Markup
    Language) 289–290
XmlGet type 178, 180–181,
    185
XmlResponse type 177